Noble Power during the French

The Guise Affinity and the Catholic Cause in Normandy

Noble affinities were the essence of power in sixteenth-century France. This is the first book to analyse the development of a noble following during the whole course of the Wars of Religion and the first substantial study of the Guise – the most powerful family of the period – to appear this century.

The Guise, champions of the catholic cause, were the largest landowners in Normandy and used the province – the wealthiest in France – as a base for their support of catholicism in the British Isles. The family exploited religious dissension to build a formidable ultra-catholic party in Normandy which ultimately challenged the monarchy. This study breaks new ground by illuminating the relationship between high politics and popular confessional solidarities, especially the rise of radical catholicism. It exploits new archival sources to consider all groups in political society, reinterpreting court politics and discussing groups usually excluded from the traditional political narrative, such as the peasantry.

STUART CARROLL is Lecturer in History, University of York

CAMBRIDGE STUDIES IN EARLY MODERN HISTORY

The idea of an 'early modern' period of European history from the fifteenth to the late eighteenth century is now widely accepted among historians. The purpose of Cambridge Studies in Early Modern History is to publish monographs and studies which illuminate the character of the period as a whole, and in particular focus attention on a dominant theme within it, the interplay of continuity and change as they are presented by the continuity of medieval ideas, political and social organization, and by the impact of new ideas, new methods and new demands on the traditional structure.

For a list of titles published in the series, please see end of book

Noble Power during the French Wars of Religion

The Guise Affinity and the Catholic Cause in Normandy

STUART CARROLL

CAMBRIDGE
UNIVERSITY PRESS

CAMBRIDGE UNIVERSITY PRESS
Cambridge, New York, Melbourne, Madrid, Cape Town, Singapore, São Paulo

Cambridge University Press
The Edinburgh Building, Cambridge CB2 2RU, UK

Published in the United States of America by Cambridge University Press, New York

www.cambridge.org
Information on this title: www.cambridge.org/9780521624046

First published 1998
This digitally printed first paperback version 2005

A catalogue record for this publication is available from the British Library

Library of Congress Cataloguing in Publication data

Carroll, Stuart, 1965–
Noble Power during the French Wars of Religion: the Guise Affinity and
the Catholic Cause in Normandy/Stuart Carroll.
p. cm. – (Cambridge Studies in Early Modern History)
Includes bibliographical references and indexes.
ISBN 0 521 62404 5
1. Normandy (France) – History – Religious aspects. 2. France –
– History – Wars of the Huguenots, 1562–1598. 3. Guise, House of.
4. Nobility – France – Normandy – Political activity. 5. Catholic
Church – France – Normandy – History – 16th century. I. title.
II. Series.
DC611.N894C37 1998
944'.2–dc21 97–38680 CIP

ISBN-13 978-0-521-62404-6 hardback
ISBN-10 0-521-62404-5 hardback

ISBN-13 978-0-521-02387-0 paperback
ISBN-10 0-521-02387-4 paperback

To Deborah

Contents

Illustrations

PLATES

FIGURES

MAPS

Illustrations

TABLES

Abbreviations

ACR	Archives Communales de Rouen
ADC	Archives Départementales de Calvados, Caen
ADE	Archives Départementales de l'Eure, Evreux
ADSM	Archives Départementales de la Seine-Maritime, Rouen
AMC	Archives de la Musée Condé, Chantilly
AN	Archives Nationales, Paris
AP	Archives Privées
MC	Minutier Central
Anselme	Le P. Anselme, *Histoire généalogique et chronologique de la maison royale de France, des pairs, grands officiers de la couronne & de la maison du roy* (9 vols., Paris, 1726–33)
BM	Bibliothèque Municipale de Rouen
BN	Bibliothèque Nationale, Paris
MS Fr	Manuscrits Français
NA Fr	Nouvelles Acquisitions Françaises
Bouillé	R. de Bouillé du Chariol. *Histoire des ducs de Guise* (4 vols., Paris, 1849–50)
Brantôme	Pierre de Bourdeille, sieur de Brantôme. *Oeuvres*, L. Lalanne, ed. (11 vols., Paris, 1864–82)
Chenaye-Desbois	F. de La Chenaye-Desbois and Badier. *Dictionnaire de la noblesse* (19 vols., Paris, 1863–76)
Cimber and Danjou	L. Cimber and F. Danjou, eds. *Archives curieuses de l'histoire de France*, 1st ser. (15 vols., Paris, 1834–7)
CSPF	*Calendar of State Papers, foreign series, of the reign of Elizabeth*. J. Stevenson et al., eds. (London, 1863–1950)
DBF	*Dictionnaire de biographie française*
Floquet	A. Floquet, *Histoire du parlement de Normandie* (7 vols., Rouen, 1840–2)
Frondeville *Conseillers*	H. de Frondeville, *Les conseillers du parlement de Nor-*

	mandie au seizième siècle, 1499–1594 (Paris and Rouen, 1960)
Présidents	H. de Frondeville, *Les présidents du parlement de Normandie, 1499–1790* (Paris and Rouen, 1953)
Michaud and Poujoulat	J.-F. Michaud and J.-J.-F. Poujoulat, eds., *Nouvelle collection des mémoires sur l'histoire de France* (series 1, 13 vols.; series 2, 10 vols.; Paris, 1836–54)
de Thou	J.-A. de Thou, *Histoire universelle de 1543 jusqu'en 1607* (16 vols., London, 1734)
Vindry	F. Vindry, *Dictionnaire de l'état major au seizième siècle*, pt 1: *La gendarmerie* (Paris, 1901)

A note on usage

Dates are in the old style until the calendar reform of 1583, except that the year is presumed to have begun on 1 January. French words have been italicised except for titles and commonly used words, such as parlement. I have retained the original orthography in order to convey the flavour of the language, adding accents and punctuation where necessary.

The capital value of *rentes* in Rouen was ten times the purchase value and paid 10 per cent interest per annum. In Paris capital value was twelve times the purchase value and yielded 8.33 per cent per annum. The *écu* fluctuated in value. For accounting purposes in the later sixteenth century it was worth 3 *livres tournois* (*l*).

Acknowledgements

The research foundations were laid with the help of a British Academy Postgraduate Scholarship, an Institute of Historical Research Fellowship and a bursary from the Society for the Study of French History. Two generous British Academy awards enabled me to visit the Paris archives in 1993 and 1994 and a bursary from the Twenty-Seven Foundation facilitated research in Rouen in 1995.

This book would not have been completed without the support of many friends and colleagues. Gayle Brunelle first showed me the richness of the Rouennais notarial archives and has been unfailingly generous with her own research material ever since. In Rouen, Philippe Cailleux's hospitality and humour maintained my sanity. The Department of History at the University of York, as well as providing two sabbatical terms, has been a congenial and stimulating environment. John Bossy shared his knowledge of English catholic exiles and forced me to rethink my ideas, and Alan Forrest has been a friendly guide and mentor. The small band of *seizièmistes* in the UK has given advice and help along the way. In particular, Joe Bergin first urged me to explore the Minutier Central in Paris; once there Robert Descimon advised me on its riches.

Philip Catchpole, Roger Mettam, Gareth Prosser, David Potter and Jonathan Powis kindly agreed to read and comment on the script, enabling me to correct the more egregious errors. David Potter has not only given valuable advice from the early days, but his knowledge of the Picard nobility has been fundamentally important to my understanding of the morphology of power networks. Roger Mettam has given encouragement and support when others doubted and his sensitivity to noble mores and values is unsurpassed. Gareth Prosser, in whose company many an evening has been spent in search of the Norman nobility, deserves special thanks. He drew most of the maps and his knowledge of fifteenth-century France has been a constant source of information and inspiration.

Introduction

Political society during the Wars of Religion

> L'historiographie contemporaine . . . a été contrainte, préjudiciellement, de tuer pour vivre: elle a condamné à une quasi-mort, voici quelques décennies, l'histoire événementielle et la biographie atomistique.[1]
>
> Contemporary historiography . . . has been forced, regrettably, to kill in order to live: in recent decades it has condemned to death narrative history and atomised biography.

Emmanuel Le Roy Ladurie's frank admission exemplifies the *Annaliste* attitude to the study of political society at the height of its hegemony.[2] The *Annalistes* associated the study of politics and institutions with the nineteenth-century epistemological tradition they so despised. While their attack on narrow positivist 'event' history was long overdue, it failed to lead to a revaluation of what constituted the political in pre-modern society. Their interest in sociology and later anthropology was never systematically applied to political society and its institutions and, consequently, their conception of the political remained largely undeveloped. For decades the academic elite in France viewed early modern politics in conventional terms, and political history had pejorative connotations and was not considered a field for serious study. In the 1960s and 1970s the pre-eminence of *Annales* and its obsession with quantitative history, structures and conjunctures reinforced the orthodox view of the causes of the Wars of Religion as essentially the product of socio-economic trends. The rise of Calvinism and the religious conflict of the sixteenth century, for both Marxists and non-Marxists, were regarded largely as the manifestation of deeper socio-economic forces or class conflicts.[3] During the 1970s a number of works began to challenge the functionalist orthodoxy. Influenced by Durkheim and his successors, this new generation of historians examined the social function of religious ritual and the cultural values of early modern belief.[4]

[1] E. Le Roy Ladurie, *Le territoire de l'historien* (Paris, 1973), p. 169.

[2] For a brilliant critique of *Annaliste* discourse and methodology: P. Carrard, *Poetics of the new history: French historical discourse from Braudel to Chartier* (Baltimore, 1992).

[3] As Peter Burke has pointed out in *The French historical revolution* (Oxford, 1990), p. 63, Le Roy Ladurie was unique among his colleagues in discussing religious and cultural trends in his thesis *Les paysans de Languedoc* (2 vols., Paris, 1966). However, he was conventional in arguing that religious change and conflict were contingent on wider economic and demographic conjunctures.

[4] N. Z. Davis, *Society and culture in early modern France* (Stanford, 1975); J. Bossy, 'The counter-reformation and the people of catholic Europe', *Past and Present*, 46 (1970), 51–70; 'Some elementary forms of Durkheim', *Past and Present*, 95 (1982), 3–18.

Noble power during the French Wars of Religion

Few historians would now challenge the central and autonomous role played by religion as a motivating force during the Wars of Religion. Popular violence and deep confessional cleavages shaped the character of French society in the second half of the sixteenth century. The study of religious mentalities has led to the emergence of a new orthodoxy. The scholarly consensus now accords primacy to the role of popular religious mentalities in shaping the Wars of Religion. The best of these studies recognise the interaction between political and religious factors, but a number of influential works have rejected both the role of high politics and wider socio-economic forces in shaping the events of the later sixteenth-century in France.[5] Denis Crouzet's monumental thesis on the psychology of religious violence represents the culmination of the new orthodoxy. His phenomenological approach rejects both socio-economic and political factors as a means to explain the Wars of Religion and dismisses the claims of empirical archival research.[6]

During the past twenty-five years the study of *ancien régime* society has been profoundly influenced by the methodological innovations of social and cultural history. The debate among historians of eighteenth-century France concerning the nature and development of political culture has been particularly productive.[7] In contrast, the political history of the Wars of Religion is a poor relation, marginal and unfashionable. Only in studies of the high nobility has our knowledge advanced substantially in recent years. Admirable as many of these studies are, the focus on the upper strata of the nobility as the sole constituent of the political class has reflected the traditional view of politics as the preserve of a narrow group of elite families.[8] Historians of the French Wars of Religion often portray a society in which politics, by which they mean court faction, had little impact on and little relationship to popular confessional conflict. Factional high politics, in which aristocrats often displayed an opportunistic attitude to religion, is contrasted to a populace motivated by anxieties about salvation to fight in defence of the sacred. Although it is correct to highlight the crucial role played by popular forces, it is also necessary to reconsider some of the most cherished notions of the new orthodoxy.

[5] P. Benedict, *Rouen during the Wars of Religion* (Cambridge, 1980), p. xii explicitly sets out to integrate the social history of religion and the political narrative. The study of political events in their contemporary socio-economic context has been most evident in recent work on Paris: R. Descimon, 'La Ligue à Paris: une révision', *Annales ESC*, 37 (1982), 72–128; B. Diefendorf, *Beneath the cross: Catholics and Huguenots in sixteenth-century Paris* (Oxford, 1991). The new orthodoxy is judiciously summarised by M. Holt, 'Putting religion back into the Wars of Religion', *French Historical Studies*, 18 (1993), 524–51. See also H. Heller, 'A reply to Mack P. Holt' and Holt's rejoinder, in *French Historical Studies*, 19 (1996), 853–73.

[6] D. Crouzet, *Les guerriers de Dieu: la violence au temps des troubles de religion vers 1525 – vers 1610* (2 vols., Paris, 1990).

[7] For an overview of the debates and a discussion of the elements of *ancien régime* politics: P. R. Campbell, *Power and politics in old regime France, 1720–1745* (London, 1996), introduction.

[8] Some examples are: R. Harding, *Anatomy of a power elite: the provincial governors of early modern France* (New Haven and London. 1978); A. Jouanna, *Le devoir de révolte: la noblesse française et la gestation de l'Etat moderne, 1559–1661* (Paris, 1989); L. Bourquin, *Noblesse seconde et pouvoir en Champagne aux XVIe et XVIIe siècles* (Paris, 1994).

The current understanding of the parameters of political society is too narrow and the distinction between 'elite' politics and 'popular' confessional conflict more ambiguous than generally recognised.

It is still common to perceive politics in Renaissance France as the preserve of a small elite of courtiers, aristocrats and royal officers. It is undeniable that the aristocracy played a preponderant role in political life, but Russell Major has shown how the power of the French monarchy in the sixteenth century in practice depended largely on the goodwill of representative institutions and the provincial elites. Power was diffuse and the towns and provinces remained largely autonomous of royal control. That the king should govern with the consent of and in consultation with his people had gained wide acceptance by the beginning of the Wars of Religion. The doctrine of popular sovereignty was developed by the protestant monarchomachs in the 1560s and 1570s and its principles were put into practice by the Catholic League in 1589.[9] The religious divisions of the sixteenth century permeated all levels of society and introduced an ideological element to politics. During the civil wars religion and politics, both at court and in the localities, became intertwined. During the 1560s and 1570s the essential instability of the polity was revealed by the breakdown of the traditional patronage structure of the Renaissance monarchy. The dynastic weakness of the Valois monarchy not only contributed to the transformation of the political climate but its critics taunted its failures in the language of religious morality. Stability was guaranteed if the king ruled in the interests of the majority of the various factions and corporate interest groups and produced a male heir. Government and administration involved the judicious distribution of patronage and the manipulation of networks of personal influence. Historians of the seventeenth century have been particularly adept at portraying the reasons for and the consequences of the collapse of monarchical authority. Stability was threatened in the first half of the century by the dynastic weakness of the Bourbons and by the fiscal innovations of Richelieu and Mazarin. Fissures within elite society exacerbated and fostered popular rebellion. Louis XIV's early disdain for administrative innovation and his desire to bolster hierarchy and authority earned him the admiration of the elites. His return to the traditional norms of government was aided by the 'contagion of loyalty' among the provincial elites, terrified by the disorder of the Frondes.[10]

In early modern France the boundaries of political activity are commonly defined by struggles among individuals and among corporate bodies. Nobles competed with each other for social status and over claims to honour, and institutions defended rights, privileges and prerogatives against rival claims. The chaotic

[9] Major's ideas are synthesised in *From renaissance monarchy to absolute monarchy* (Baltimore, 1994). On popular sovereignty, see R. Giesey, 'The monarchomach triumvirs: Hotman, Beza and Mornay, *Bibliothèque d'Humanisme et Renaissance*, 32 (1970), 41–56; R. Jackson, 'Elective kingship and *consensus populi* in sixteenth-century France', *Journal of Modern History*, 44 (1972), 155–71.

[10] W. Beik, *Absolutism and society in seventeenth-century France: state power and provincial aristocracy in Languedoc* (Cambridge, 1985); R. Mettam, *Power and faction in Louis XIV's France* (Oxford, 1988).

nature of the Wars of Religion is best grasped if it is understood that politics was conducted in the context of a culture of feud. Anthropologists have argued for the complexities of feuding and recognised it as an organised institution. Feud did not always entail violence and could be pursued in a number of ways, usually through the law courts or by publicly dishonouring a rival.[11] The feud with the Montmorency dominated Guise family strategy and exacerbated the breakdown of order in the 1560s, but it is only the most notorious example of a more widespread phenomenon.

Political action cannot simply be confined to an aristocratic elite, since magnate affinities were not only composed of sword nobles. Aristocratic influence was extensive among urban oligarchies before the Wars of Religion, and during the civil wars magnates attempted to expand their urban power bases. Politics consisted partly of the struggle between magnate affinities or shifting factions based around confessional solidarity. However, there is plenty of evidence to suggest the vitality of the public sphere in the sixteenth century. Political ideology was articulated in terms of religious morality, the defence of traditional rights and Aristotelean ideas of the 'bien publique', but new ideas were also developed to justify the political objectives of the Calvinists and later the Catholic League. Propaganda in the form of pamphlets, tracts and *affiches* had an unprecedented circulation and reached a wide audience in urban areas. During the Wars of Religion the provincial estates, assemblies of notables and the Estates-General were arenas for public debate which on a number of occasions resulted in open criticism of the king. At a lower level of society fraternities and youth groups were aware of the tremendous religious and political upheavals and used more traditional methods to comment on political events. In 1536 the Abbaye de Conards, a Rouennais confraternity, proclaimed that any man under the age of 101 could take two wives – a clear reference to François I's recent alliance with the Turk. Critiques often went beyond harmless mockery, and the Abbaye was banned during the hegemony of the Catholic League for its scandalous attacks on the Guise.[12]

The boundary between elite and popular culture is less distinct than it seemed to historians twenty years ago. Even during the upsurge of penitential piety in the 1580s the reformation of popular manners and belief was still only the aspiration of a godly minority. An unconventionally devout man like Henri III who, according to

[11] The classic anthropological approach is J. Black-Michaud, *Cohesive force: feud in the Mediterranean and the Middle East* (Oxford, 1975). I am in the process of beginning a project on noble feud in early modern France. For some preliminary considerations, see M. Greenshields, *An economy of violence in early modern France: crime and justice in the Haute Auvergne, 1587–1664* (Philadelphia, 1995); F. Billaçois, *Le duel dans la société française des XVIe–XVIIe siècles: essai de psychosociologie historique* (Paris, 1986). For sixteenth-century comparisons: K. Brown, *Bloodfeud in Scotland, 1573–1625: violence, justice and politics in early modern society* (Edinburgh, 1986); E. Muir, *Mad blood stirring: vendetta and factions in Friuli during the Renaissance* (Baltimore, 1993).

[12] A. Corvisier, 'Une société ludique au XVIe siècle: l'Abbaye de Conards de Rouen', *Annales de Normandie*, 22 (1977), p. 183, 191. See also E. Le Roy Ladurie, *Carnaval de Romans* (Paris, 1979).

L'Estoile 'vivait plus en capucin qu'en roi', revelled in the disorderly and profane activities of carnival in Paris.[13] Similarly, it is erroneous to make a clear distinction between noble and popular motivation during the Wars of Religion. Many of the worst perpetrators of religious violence were nobles and many of those non-nobles engaged in urban religious conflict were much wealthier, better educated and of higher social status than the rural gentry. It has long been recognised that religious riots and rites of violent purification, far from being spontaneous and undirected outbursts of popular anger, were highly organised and structured. In 'Rites of violence' Natalie Davis seeks to explain 'popular' religious violence, but many of her examples involve the leadership and organisational abilities of noblemen and elements of the city elites.[14] In Toulouse in May 1562 the confessional conflict resembled a bitter local civil war in which all social orders were involved. As Mark Greengrass has pointed out, this conflict was more about *rights* than *rites*. The Huguenot uprising in Toulouse was a defensive response to the imminent suppression of their right to worship, which had been guaranteed by law. The catholic elite crushed the revolt brutally when its authority was challenged.[15] During the catholic religious revival of the 1580s the interplay between aristocratic factional politics and popular confessional anxiety is even clearer. The huge penitential processions of 1583 and 1584 in the north-east took place in the dioceses of reforming bishops sympathetic to the Catholic League. At Reims the cardinal de Guise exploited the devotional upsurge by printing and distributing small books to the faithful, containing prayers which sought the intercession of the Almighty for the birth of a catholic heir to the throne.[16]

Urban historians of sixteenth-century France are beginning to study the competing networks of influence which struggled for power in towns and cities in much the same way as neighbourhood, kinship and clientage loyalties mapped the boundaries of factional support in Italian cities during the Renaissance.[17] City militias were a significant factor in urban politics and in the perpetration of violence. The axes of solidarity in militia companies were formed by both horizontal and vertical ties. In the two largest cities in northern France, Rouen and Paris, militia units increasingly fell under the influence of catholic zealots, men drawn

[13] Pierre de L'Estoile, *Journal du règne de Henri III*, L.-R. Lefèvre, ed. (Paris, 1943), pp. 350, 446.

[14] *Society and culture in early modern France*, pp. 185. Drawing a distinction between spontaneous and organised violence is problematic as the current debate on the origins of the Saint Bartholomew's Day massacre shows.

[15] M. Greengrass, 'The anatomy of a religious riot in Toulouse in May 1562', *Journal of Ecclesiastical History*, 34 (1983), 367–91.

[16] A. Ramsey 'Piety in Paris during the League, 1585–90: an urban community in transition', unpub. Ph.D. thesis (University of Columbia, 1991), p. 133.

[17] W. Kaiser, *Marseille im Bürgerkrieg, Sozialgefüge, Religionskonflikt und Faktionskämpfe* (Göttingen, 1991); K. Robbins, 'The social mechanisms of urban rebellion: a case study of leadership of the 1614 revolt at La Rochelle', *French Historical Studies*, 19 (1995), 559–90. On Florence: D. Kent and F. W. Kent, *Neighbours and neighbourhood in Renaissance Florence: the district of the Red Lion in the fifteenth century* (New York, 1982).

from high-status trades and professions. In urban areas, high literacy rates ensured wide participation in political and theological discourse. In Paris and Rouen the large legal community, the *basoche*, was at the core of catholic militancy in the 1580s. To what extent were the *basochien* a 'popular' force? Most of the *gens de loi* attached to the sovereign courts, though not part of the ruling oligarchy, were both intellectually and aspirationally part of the elite, possessing networks of influence among the lesser ranks of ushers and clerks.[18] The categories traditionally employed by historians to analyse the political and religious upheavals of the civil wars are imprecise and need modification. This study reconsiders the parameters of politics by analysing the composition and growth of an aristocratic following during the Wars of Religion.

Many facets of sixteenth-century political society remain poorly researched. At the apex much has still to be written about court politics and in the localities we remain ignorant of the attitudes of the lesser nobility. The succeeding chapters shed new light on the relationship between politics at the court and the localities. In contrast, the subject of clientage and patron–client relations has produced a plethora of publications. The literature is vast and it is not intended to exhume the familiar debates. Traditionally the patron–client relationship was regarded as a static and exclusive bond. It was a mutual relationship in which the lord could call on the unconditional support of clients who were rewarded by patronage. The patron–client model of structuring political society was supported by the theories of functional sociologists. As Kristen Neuschel has shown, the traditional patron–client model does not reflect the realities of sixteenth-century lordship and service. Clients usually had a number of patrons and followed independent strategies conditioned largely by the honour code. Neuschel's critique of the existing literature is welcome, but her methodology is flawed since she concentrates largely on the correspondence of the elite of Picard society who were the social equals of the prince de Condé, being allies rather than clients. Analysis of the formulaic nature of contemporary correspondence elucidates only partially the nature of noble relations, and her polemic against the patron–client model blinds her to the factors which fostered group solidarity.[19] Neuschel has provided a valuable corrective to the existing literature but the originality of her conclusions is open to doubt. A study of sixteenth-century 'warrior culture' needs to be placed in the context of medieval chivalric mores.

Historians of late-medieval England have long recognised the fluctuating ties and diverse bonds which comprised a noble following. Research has increasingly focused on the strategies and the mentalities of the gentry. In the expression of

[18] A. Fabre, *Etudes historiques sur les clercs de la basoche* (Paris, 1875). For evidence of *basochien* piety: Ramsey, 'Piety in Paris during the League', pp. 13, 402–513.

[19] K. Neuschel, *Word of Honor: interpreting noble culture in sixteenth-century France* (Ithaca, N.Y., 1989). The literature is summarised in S. Kettering, 'Patronage in early modern France', *French Historical Studies*, 17 (1992), 872–81.

Colin Richmond, the lesser nobility were not 'Pavlovian dogs'.[20] Movement and change are inherent in all social relations. The relationships among individuals in a following were multiplex. An affinity was not a monolithic entity but the ties of affinity were potential communication channels. Individuals were not free agents unconstrained by socio-economic or cultural factors. The network of personal bonds that constituted an affinity was 'a social environment' which exerted influence to pressure behaviour. Bonds of kinship, sociability and amity – as important to affinal solidarity as the vertical ties of patronage and clientage – placed obligations on the individual and constrained his or her behaviour. The strength of relations in the network depended on a number of variables and varied over time and according to circumstance. The structure of an affinity is best explained as a motif of concentric circles, which denote differing types of bond and strengths of relationship. At the core of an affinity – the household and council – were to be found the intimates and kin in whom a great deal of emotional and material resources were invested. Lords clearly had less dialogue with clients on the periphery of their following, they invested fewer resources in maintaining the channel of communications and could expect less obligation.[21]

This study elucidates patterns of noble affiliation and networks of urban support during the Wars of Religion. Its purpose is not to reclaim a place for the vanished epistemological tradition which lauded the deeds of 'great men' and accepted unquestionably the primacy of high politics. Rather, it reinterprets the political narrative by paying careful attention both to the contemporary social context and to the structure of factions and followings. This is imperative because the contours of political and religious conflict cannot be followed without a clear understanding of the dynamics, morphology and atrophy of power networks. As political and religious cleavages tore apart the body politic, social groups usually considered outside political society were summoned to enter the political arena. As early as May 1562 the catholic authorities of Toulouse called on the support of the religiously conservative peasantry in their suppression of the Huguenot uprising. The role played by peasants and petty nobles in the defence of orthodoxy was echoed in Normandy, where religious anxieties and anti-tax sentiment combined to facilitate the mobilisation of large areas of the province in support of the catholic princes in the 1580s.[22] The term 'affinity' has been adopted because it best expresses the range of ties in noble followings, of which the patron–client relationship was but one aspect. While recognising that the bonds in political society were multifarious, non-exclusive and fluctuated over time, I have concentrated on the factors which reinforced the solidarity of a following.

[20] C. Richmond, 'After Macfarlane', *History*, 68 (1983), p. 57. Current research on late-medieval and early modern England, which has gone much further in its consideration of the power and autonomy of the lesser nobility, is summarised in M. Hicks, *Bastard feudalism* (London, 1995).

[21] J. Boissevain, *Friends of friends: networks, manipulators and coalitions* (Oxford, 1974).

[22] See below pp. 222–32.

THE GUISE IN HISTORY: PROBLEMS AND SOURCES

Le feu roy devina ce point
Que ceux de la maison de Guyse
Mettroyent ses enfants en pourpoint
Et son pauvre peuple en chemise.[23]

The debate in the 1980s about the origins of the Catholic League and the recent vituperative exchanges over the causes and course of the massacre of Saint Bartholomew testify to the revival of interest in human agency in explaining the causation of events, as well as the contemporary representation of historical events. Several *Annalistes*, who had once proclaimed the death of 'event' history have, in recent years, disinterred its corpse and committed themselves to traditional biography and textbooks on political history.[24] This revival has yet to engender a return to the archival sources for high politics and many old prejudices and stale orthodoxies remain. A comprehensive modern study of the political history of the Wars of Religion does not exist and the works of Romier and Mariéjol, written earlier this century, remain unsurpassed.

An examination of the relationship between the Guise, the most powerful magnate lineage in sixteenth-century France, and their followers in the localities is long overdue. Despite its enormous influence on political life during the Wars of Religion, the family has attracted little serious scholarship this century, and our knowledge of the Guise affinity and its relation to popular support for ultra-catholicism is limited.[25] Analysis of the Guise affinity also elucidates the relationship between court faction and conflict in the provinces.

Mastering the sources for political society at the level of both local society and the court is a major undertaking, compounded by the gaps in our knowledge and the obsolescence of much of the existing secondary literature. The range of Guise interests was vast and the longevity and complexity of the Wars of Religion defy attempts to write comprehensive accounts of events at both centre and periphery. Striking a balance between maintaining a lucid narrative and analysing the structures of patronage is demanding.[26] It has been necessary to schematise the political narrative and concentrate on events which illuminate the strategy of the Guise and the activities of their clients, recognising that future detailed studies may modify conclusions derived largely from a study of a single magnate family.

This study concentrates on the expansion of the Guise power base in Normandy. Anyone familiar with the history of the Wars of Religion might question the merits

[23] Attributed to François I by protestant propagandist Regnier de La Planche.

[24] See, for example, E. Le Roy Ladurie, *L'état royal, 1460–1610* (Paris, 1987), and my review of the English translation in *French History*, 8 (1994), 474–5.

[25] The most recent work by J.-M. Constant, *Les Guises* (Paris, 1984), is a conventional biography based largely on the printed sources.

[26] Appendix G provides a summary of clients' careers.

of such an undertaking. The Guise are commonly seen as an eastern lineage whose lands and power were largely concentrated in Champagne. The seat of the family at Joinville reflects its historic identification with eastern France, but in most other respects the common assumptions concerning the Guise power base are misguided. This study originated as a Ph.D. thesis on Norman political society in the sixteenth century. As the research progressed it soon became apparent that the landed power and influence of the Guise in Normandy had been overlooked. This oversight contributed not only to the misinterpretation of Norman society during the Wars of Religion, but it seemed emblematic of the general neglect both of the study of political society and of the role played by aristocratic lineages in local confessional conflict. The neglect of the Guise has been partly due to the dispersal of the family archives following the extinction of the senior line in the late seventeenth century, in contrast to the abundant sources surviving for the Montmorency, the Bourbon and the Nevers. The best work, and unlikely to be surpassed for narrative detail, is Bouillé du Chariol's *Histoire des ducs de Guise*. A fine example of nineteenth-century positivist history, Bouillé leans heavily on seventeenth-century manuscript histories written decades after the events they purport to describe.[27]

The research for this book included the traditional sources of political history, such as letters, memoirs and the official records left by institutions. But these sources alone are insufficient to reveal the operation of informal power networks, since the surviving corpus of documents pertains largely to the activities of the aristocratic elite. A large number of Guise letters survive from the 1540s and 1550s, but the correspondence which survives for the period of the Wars of Religion is modest. Correspondence alone is inadequate for reconstructing the profile of an affinity and its functioning. During the turmoil of the civil wars it was safer to communicate orally and the stylised nature of letters reveals more about exchanges of honour than patterns of allegiance. The justificatory memoirs left by protaganists of the civil wars should be treated with circumspection, particularly those which correlate closely with Bourbon hagiography. This study is founded on a range of contemporary manuscript sources in Paris, Chantilly and Normandy unexploited either by Bouillé or by more recent scholars. It supplements the traditional sources of political history by mining the rich notarial archives in Rouen, Paris and elsewhere to reconstruct the mundane activities of clients and servants acting on behalf of their lords. Notarial archives also reveal patterns of sociability, kinship and, when read in conjunction with other sources, political activity. Notaries served all social ranks and the archives they left furnish information about groups normally excluded from the traditional narrative. The research for this project owes much to the labours of the often maligned nineteenth-century antiquarians and local genealogists; they understood the context of local power and this study attempts to rescue the lesser nobility and gentry from neglect. The nineteenth-century tradition

[27] According to the Bibliothèque Nationale catalogue, Oudin's manuscript is dated 1647.

Brussels
Amiens
PICARDY
Rouen
NORMANDY
ILE-DE
FRANCE
Paris
Reims
CHAMPAGNE
Verdun
Metz
Bar
Toul
Nancy
Troyes
BRETAGNE
Rennes
MAINE
Le Mans
Orléans
ORLÉANAIS
Angers
ANJOU
Nantes
Tours
TOUR-
AINE
Bourges
BERRY
NIVERNAIS
Nevers
Dijon
AUNIS
Poitiers

Map 1 The provinces of France in the sixteenth century

which Bouillé typifies had confidence in the achievement of heroic individuals. His study was largely interested in the role of the most prominent members of the family, notably the cardinal de Lorraine and Henri and François de Guise, in shaping the major events of the Wars of Religion. It is intended to re-examine the traditional interpretation of events by paying close attention to the *structures* of politics. To understand family strategy it is necessary to explore the relationship between all members of the family, male and female, including the neglected cadets, and to illustrate the role of clients and counsellors in formulating and executing family strategy. Finally, it is intended to explore the role of an affinity as a convector of aristocratic influence in local society and among the lower orders.

A study which concentrates on Normandy has a number of advantages over other provinces where the Guise enjoyed influence. Normandy was a *pays d'états* and the provincial Estates proved an important source for reconstructing magnate influence. Rouen was both the seat of a parlement and a major centre of trade and commerce. It is possible to reconstruct the Guisard faction in the parlement and to identify those city merchants who managed the family estates and provided credit. Normandy, which paid one-quarter of the total *taille*, was the most important provincial pillar of Valois finances, and as the crown lost control of regions during the Wars of Religion so its political and economic significance increased.[28] Unlike Champagne, it was one of the chief strongholds of French protestantism.

The subdivision of chapters has been partly dictated by the awareness that readers are interested in distinct aspects of the history of the Guise family. Chapter 1 shows how patterns of land ownership shaped the regional character of a following and induced an element of inertia in recruitment. Men in the localities tended to follow their 'natural lord' if he displayed the attributes of good lordship, conforming to the conventions of noble virtue and honour. Chapter 2 emphasises the role played by counsel, patronage, service and kinship in fostering a sense of group solidarity and identity. The succeeding chapters follow chronologically the development of the Guise affinity during the Wars of Religion and examine the interface between factional politics and the confessional conflict, revealing the centrality of the affinity to the ultra-catholic cause. Chapters 4 and 5 demonstrate how the Guise affinity expanded in the face of the protestant threat and elucidate the contribution of Guise clients to the combat against heresy. Chapters 6 and 7 show that the success of the Catholic League depended on the leadership of Guise clients supported by 'popular' elements in Rouen. But this is far from being a purely local study. Guise influence was especially strong in the upper Norman marches which had close geographic and socio-economic ties to Picardy and the Ile de France. The landed interest in the Norman marches was complemented by estates held in Picardy and the Vexin Français.

Normandy's geographic proximity and historic ties to the British Isles provide

[28] P. Hamon, *L'argent du roi: les finances sous François Ier* (Paris, 1994), p. 75.

an opportunity to understand the function of a provincial power base in the wider dynastic ambitions of a princely family. The growing interest of the family in English and Scottish affairs, in particular the support of Mary Stuart's cause, entailed the establishment of an operational base in Normandy and the mobilisation of local contacts. The commencement of the building of a magnificent new family seat at Eu in the 1580s illustrates the reorientation of the Guise family from the marches of eastern France to the Channel coast, from where dynastic policy could be efficiently administered. Following the execution of Mary Stuart and the composition of the Wars of Religion, Normandy lost its significance for the Guise, a fact exemplified by the dilatory attitude to the construction of the château of Eu. During the seventeenth century the senior line once again turned its attention to its primal dynastic ambitions in Italy.

I

The rise of the house of Lorraine in Normandy

Landholding was the essence of status and authority in sixteenth-century France, and its study is fundamental to understanding contemporary political society. Land was not merely an economic commodity. It defined a lineage as a social and political entity and engendered emotional and historic identification with particular regions. The existing historiography has given the impression that the landed power base of the Guise was largely confined to eastern France. This misguided notion not only underestimates the spatial distribution of the family estates, but has ensured that the strategy of the Guise during the Wars of Religion has been misunderstood. It is imperative to correct misconceptions by outlining the parameters of the landed interest and by locating the Norman seigneuries within the wider pattern of land inheritance, acquisition and sale. As well as permitting a detailed analysis of aggregate income, a consideration of the landed power base will illustrate that family strategy encompassed a much wider range of concerns beyond its traditional interest in eastern France.

THE DEVELOPMENT OF THE NORMAN LANDED INTEREST OF THE HOUSE OF LORRAINE

The Guise descended from the most ancient surviving house of the Franco-Imperial borderlands. The lineage was the product of the dynastic convolutions of the houses of Lorraine and Anjou in the fifteenth century. The extinction of the elder ducal patrilineage of Lorraine in 1428 triggered a conflict into which the great powers of Valois, Lancaster and Burgundy were drawn: the duchy was recurrently the focus of Franco-Burgundian power politics right down to 1477. The succession war was a classic confrontation between the heir in the female line, René d'Anjou, and the heir in the junior male line, Antoine de Lorraine comte de Vaudémont. Despite the crushing Angevin defeat of Bulgnéville in 1431, Vaudémont could not unseat duke René d'Anjou. Nonetheless, the very favourable terms which he secured for ending his challenge were the roots of the close association which developed between the two lineages. Particularly important was the marriage of Jean de Lorraine's eldest son Ferry and René's daughter Yolande d'Anjou: it was in

Yolande's right that her son René claimed the duchy on the death of Nicolas d'Anjou in 1473.[1]

It was only in January 1477, after the great triumph of the Lorraine and their Swiss allies at Nancy over Charles Le Teméraire and his Burgundians, that René II secured undisturbed possession of the duchy. Unable or unwilling to obstruct the ambitions of his allies Louis XI, Charles VIII and Louis XII, he failed to secure recognition as proper heir of the house of Anjou on its extinction in 1481. René passed Lorraine and Bar to Antoine his eldest son, but Angevin claims in Provence, Naples and elsewhere were never forgotten. The inheritance in the kingdom of France was passed to the second son, Claude duc de Guise.

This inheritance was a substantial one in its own right. It was enhanced by the generosity with which Louis XII in particular was prepared to treat the Lorraine cadets, three of whom arrived at his court in 1501. François de Lorraine, upon whom the Provençal lands had devolved, was slain in French service at the disaster of Pavia in 1525. The third son, Jean de Lorraine, was the founder of the Guise ecclesiastical dynasty, becoming archbishop of Reims and a cardinal. Claude himself was raised at the French court and naturalised French in 1506. His stature grew in tandem with the intensification of the Valois–Habsburg conflict. He made a good marriage in 1513 to Antoinette de Bourbon, eldest daughter of François de Bourbon comte de Vendôme and Marie de Luxembourg comtesse de Saint-Pol. Although he was not an intimate of François I he was favoured by the queen-mother Louise de Savoie, under whose auspices he entered the regency council following the king's capture at Pavia. He was rewarded with the office of *grand veneur*, and with the elevation of the comté of Guise to a *duché-pairie* in 1527 credit at court peaked around 1540: he had married his eldest daughter Marie to James V king of Scots in 1538.[2]

With his patrimony scattered all over northern France, Claude had established his seat at Joinville within easy reach of Nancy and Paris. In this he was not solely guided by his Lorraine filiation: he was particularly engaged in royal service on the sensitive eastern frontier, as governor of Champagne from 1524 to 1543, then Burgundy to 1550. The geographical emphasis of his service did not fully reflect his territorial power: of a landed income in 1542 amounting to 39,917*l*, almost 40 per cent derived from Normandy. But Norman income was a much smaller proportion of total income – 65,352*l* – and the figures may be distorted by the depression of revenues from war-ravaged Picardy.[3] Claude made little effort to employ Normans:

[1] For this and following: A. Lecoy de La Marche, *Le roi René* (2 vols., Paris, 1875); R.-L. Moulierac-Lamoureux, *Le roi René, ou les hasards du destin, 1409–1480* (Avignon, 1980); B. Schnerb, *Bulgnéville: l'état bourguignon prend pied en Lorraine* (Paris, 1994); G. Prosser, 'After the reduction: restructuring Norman political society and the *Bien Public*, 1450–65', unpub. Ph.D. thesis (University of London, 1996).

[2] Bouillé, i, p. 46; Constant, *Les Guises*, p. 21–2.

[3] BN MS Fr 8182 fos. 323–45; Bouillé, i, pp. 536–45. The aggregate figures given in the document are marginally inaccurate and do not include the lands in Provence which were farmed in 1543 for 900*l*:

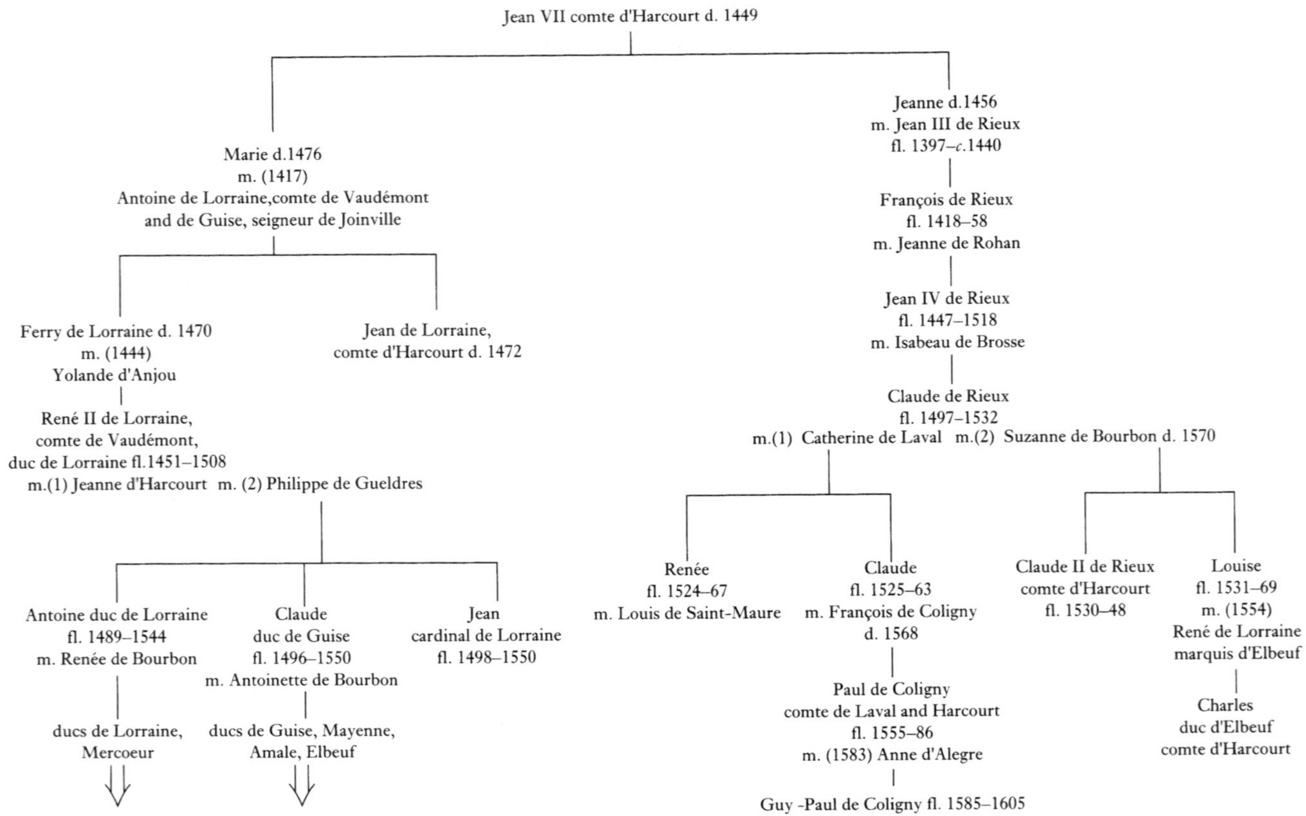

Figure 1.1 The Harcourt and Rieux inheritances

the composition of his household reflected his paternal ancestry, with easterners such as the des Boves and the Lenoncourt dominating household office, and strong representation of Picards like the Aumale and the des Essars.[4] Nonetheless, the large Norman component of Claude's landed interest meant that from the beginning Normandy was a latent presence in Guise designs. In the first half of the sixteenth century Norman affairs were delegated to the Le Roux, an important Rouennais *robin* lineage which had begun its ascent in the service of the comtes d'Harcourt in the previous century.[5]

The Guise position in Normandy was founded on the 1417 marriage of Marie d'Harcourt to Antoine comte de Vaudémont. The succession of her brother Jean VI d'Harcourt (d. 1452), the last male representative of the greatest Norman comital house, was considerable: he was comte d'Harcourt and d'Aumale in Normandy, baron de Mayenne in the Maine and vicomte de Châtellerault in Touraine. On his death Marie and her second son Jean de Lorraine took effective control of his lands through legal and political dexterity. Jean de Lorraine took part in Charles VII's reconquest of Normandy in 1449–50, gave homage for the comté of Harcourt, became a significant player in the politics of Normandy, Brittany and Anjou, and even challenged for control of the ephemeral Norman apanage of Charles de France during the *Bien Public* revolt against Louis XI in 1465. The attempt was abortive, and thereafter his provincial importance diminished somewhat. Nonetheless, mother and son managed to restrict for a generation the share of the Harcourt succession which fell to the co-heirs, the Breton house of Rieux-Rochefort. When Jean died in 1472 he became the first member of the house of Lorraine to be buried in Normandy, at La Saussaye.[6]

After 1454 the Rieux enjoyed the comté of Aumale, while the Harcourt-Vaudémont continued to enjoy Harcourt and its appurtenances of Lillebonne, Gravençon, Brionne, Elbeuf, La Saussaye and Routout. In 1476 the young René de Lorraine succeeded his grandmother in the lands. His first marriage, to the great

AMC GE 20 liasse 3, 6 June 1543. A breakdown of income by province followed by figures in brackets reflecting landed income demonstrates the importance of Normandy: Picardy 4 per cent (7 per cent), Normandy 24 per cent (39 per cent), Champagne 9 per cent (14 per cent), Barrois and Lorraine 10 per cent (16 per cent), Provence 1 per cent (2 per cent), the Maine 13 per cent (22 per cent).

4 BN MS Fr 8181 fos. 269–73; 8182 fo. 353.

5 Claude Le Roux, seigneur de Tilly, *conseiller* in the parlement of Rouen from 1521 until his death in 1536, besides being a magistrate for the Guise in the comté of Aumale, handled affairs in the parlement of Rouen. The Le Roux were well rewarded for their endeavours. Claude's grandfather had been *intendant* and secretary to Marie d'Harcourt and vicomte d'Elbeuf in the mid-fifteenth century; and his father, Guillaume, was both vicomte d'Elbeuf and *procureur* of René II de Lorraine in the *échiquier* of Rouen in 1499: G.-A. de La Roque, *Histoire généalogique de la maison d'Harcourt* (4 vols., n.p., 1664), i, pp. 458–9, 479; Frondeville, *Présidents*, p. 294; BN MS Fr 20649 fos. 166–9. The Le Roux were provided with the abbey of Aumale throughout the first half of the sixteenth century: E. Semichon, *Histoire de la ville d'Aumale* (2 vols., Paris, 1862), ii, pp. 53–4.

6 La Roque, *Histoire généalogique de la maison d'Harcourt*, i, p. 461; H.-M. Saint-Denis, *Notices historiques sur les communes des environs d'Elbeuf* (8 vols., Elbeuf, 1885–90), ii, p. 33; Prosser, 'After the reduction', pp. 211–16.

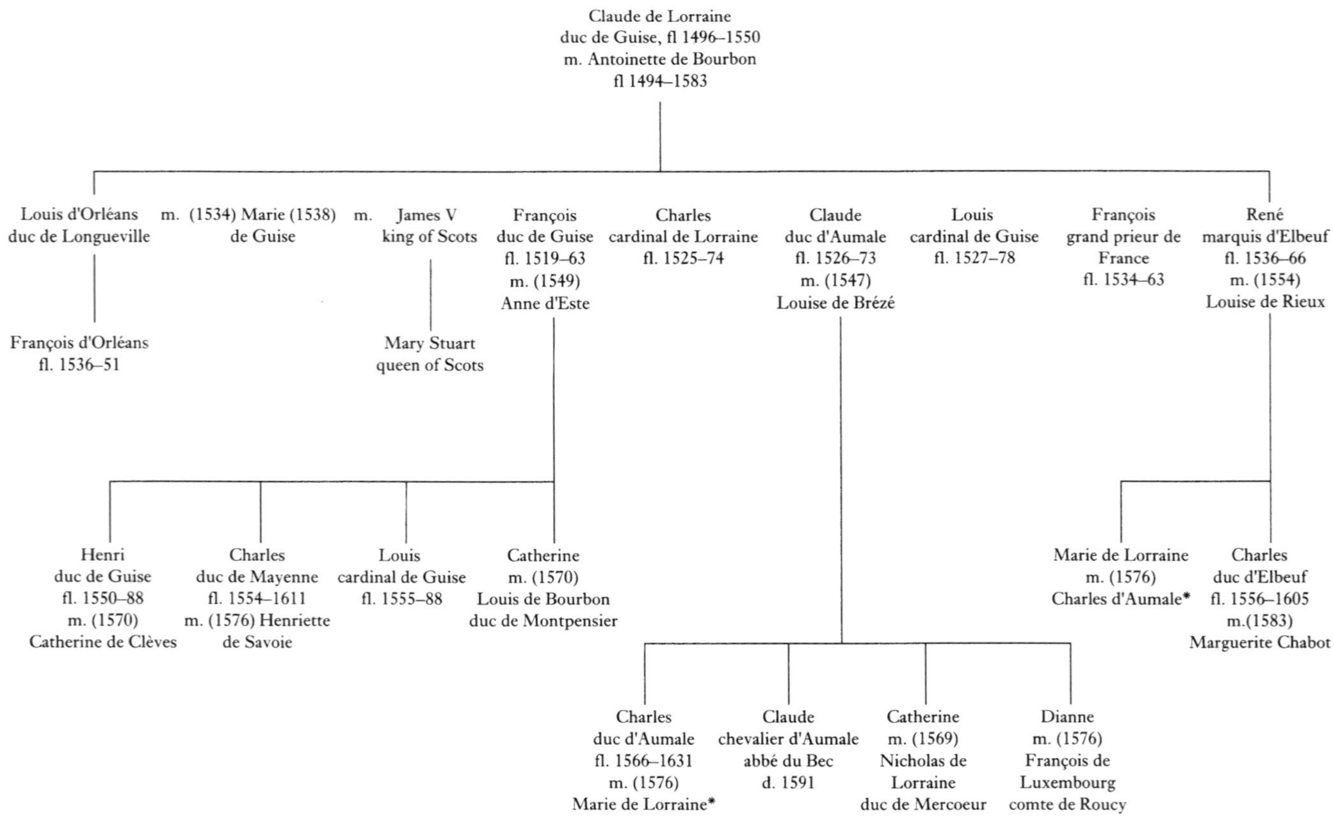

Figure 1.2 The house of Guise in the sixteenth century: abbreviated genealogy

upper Norman heiress Jeanne comtesse de Tancarville, had the potential to consolidate effective domination of the lower Seine valley. This outcome did not materialise: René's attention was drawn to his eastern dukedoms; his marriage was dissolved because of Jeanne's sterility, her vast Cauchois patrimony falling eventually to the house of Orléans–Longueville; and in 1493–96 the Rieux finally succeeded in modifying the forty-year-old partition of the Harcourt succession. René emerged with the comté of Aumale and the baronies of Elbeuf and Brionne.

The Harcourt succession as finalised in 1496 was the basis for the great expansion of the Guise landed interest in Normandy under Claude de Guise's children. The expansion was achieved through marriage and purchase facilitated by ecclesiastical empire-building. On his death in 1550 Claude I de Guise left ten children to be provided for. A successful *partage* was fundamental if internal bitterness was to be avoided and the competing claims of the siblings satisfied. The surviving children and the widow, Antoinette de Bourbon, had to be provided for while at the same time ensuring the integrity of the inheritance. The partition of 1550 was dealt with in exemplary fashion. The favoured position enjoyed by the Guise in the French church was exploited to the full in order to prevent the fragmentation of the patrimony. Two sons and two daughters had been designated for the church from an early age. The second son, Charles, inherited the benefices of his uncle and the fourth son, Louis, had been bishop of Troyes since 1545 when he was only eighteen.[7] In 1549 the king made the fifth son, François, *grand prieur* of France, ensuring that the inheritance would be divided only among three male heirs. François obtained special dispensation from the pope permitting him to hold the office without taking holy orders. In addition, he enjoyed the revenues of four *commanderies*; these provided an income of approximately 12,000*l*.[8]

The lands were divided strictly according to province.[9] The eldest son, François, received all those lands outside Normandy, namely in Picardy, Champagne, Provence, Lorraine and the Maine. The Norman possessions were divided up between two younger sons. The fourth son, Claude II, took the title and duchy of Aumale while René, the sixth son, received the barony of Elbeuf in addition to a number of smaller seigneuries in the Roumois. The partition of 1550 created two largely Norman lords.[10] The accounts of 1542 show that, in terms of revenue, Claude and René divided up these Norman possessions equally.

As he aged, Claude I's military capacities and hence court influence waned. His sons moved closer to the dauphin as François I turned to new advisers. Hence, the Guise were well provided for in the palace revolution which marked the accession of Henri II. François de Guise saw his comté of Aumale raised to a *duché-pairie*, was

7 *DBF*, xvii, p. 331; Anselme, iii, p. 486.

8 E. Mannier, *Les commanderies du grand-prieuré de France d'après les documents inédits conservés aux Archives Nationales* (Paris, 1872). The *commanderies* were Saint Jean-en-l'Ile-lez-Corbeil, Troyes, Maison-Neuve-lez-Coulommiers and Vaumion-Louvières in the Vexin Français.

9 The testament is printed by Bouillé, i, p. 219.

10 Claude duc d'Aumale also received the barony of Boves in Picardy.

made governor of Dauphiné and admitted to the *conseil des affaires*, along with his younger brother Charles.[11] The collective influence of the brothers surpassed that of their father, now rarely present at court. Yet they did not achieve the intimacy which marked the relationship between Henri II and Anne de Montmorency, the newly recalled constable. The king's mistress, Diane de Poitiers duchesse de Valentinois (d. 1566), sought to counterbalance her lover's dependency on Montmorency by patronising the Guise.[12]

The relationship with Diane was to transform the Guise position in Normandy. She was herself a major political presence in the province as the widow of the late governor and *grand sénéchal* Louis de Brézé (d. 1531). Diane remained in control of the large affinity and landholding interest which had made Louis an important provincial nobleman, last head of a lineage important in Normandy since the Valois reconquest. The marriages of their two daughters were used to extend her authority. The elder, Françoise de Brézé, married Robert IV de La Marck (d. 1556), duc de Bouillon, in 1539. In 1547 the younger, Louise, married Claude II de Lorraine marquis de Mayenne and duc d'Aumale from his father's death in 1550. The patronage of his mother-in-law elevated his status at court and assisted him to establish his own line.

Louise de Brézé was dowered with the barony of Mauny on the Seine below Rouen, which Claude frequented in the 1550s – the first member of his house to reside in the province since Jean de Lorraine a century earlier.[13] Claude maintained his eastern connections notwithstanding his Norman landed interest. His residences at Mauny and later Anet were subsidiaries of the family seat at Joinville, where his children were raised by their grandmother Antoinette de Bourbon, and where Louise herself resided.[14] Aumale was a great courtly figure who was busy outside Normandy: he was governor of Burgundy and commanded forces in the campaigns against the Habsburgs.[15] In the 1560s he began to make a conscious effort to strengthen his ties in the province. Between 1561 and 1566 the rest of the inheritance was partitioned between the Aumale and their La Marck in-laws. Claude and Louise gave up Mauny in order to secure the prize of Anet with its magnificent Renaissance château, together with the baronies of Ivry and Garennes and the seigneuries of Breval and Montchauvet which lie on the Eure borders of Normandy and the Ile de

[11] François became duc de Guise on the death of his father in 1550. The third son Claude II, formerly marquis de Mayenne, received the duchy of Aumale.

[12] F. Baumgartner, *Henry II king of France, 1547–1559* (Durham and London, 1988), pp. 43–8.

[13] BN MS NA Fr 21165 fo. 70. Homage of Alain Bellebarbe to 'haut puissant prince Claude duc d'Aumale, baron de Mauny à cause de sa femme Louise de Brézé', 1553. For instances of Aumale's residence at Mauny: BN MS Fr 3121 fo. 42, duc d'Aumale to duc de Nemours, Mauny, 25 Mar 1555; 4638 fo. 42, Aumale to Saulx-Tavannes, Mauny, 26 Nov 1558; 4640 fo. 39, Claude to Saulx-Tavannes, Mauny, 4 Jan 1559.

[14] G. de Pimodan, *La mère des Guises: Antoinette de Bourbon, 1494–1583* (Paris, 1889), pp.159, 182, 373.

[15] H. Drouot, *Mayenne et la Bourgogne: étude sur la Ligue, 1587–1596* (2 vols., Paris, 1937), i,p. 76. Gaspard de Saulx-Tavannes, *Mémoires*, Michaud and Poujoulat, 1st ser., viii, p. 205, states that 'le gouvernement avoit esté donnée par la faveur de madame de Valentinois à M.d'Aumalle'.

1. Diane de Poitiers, duchesse de Valentinois and *grande sénéchale* of Normandy. The most powerful woman in the kingdom in the 1550s.

France.[16] The financial difficulties of their nephew Henri-Robert de La Marck, duc de Bouillon, permitted the couple to expand their share of the Brézé inheritance. In 1562 they purchased the comté of Maulévrier and the barony of Bec Crespin, both in the Caux. Further land acquisitions were made in 1565 and 1567.[17] By the late 1560s Claude was one of the greatest upper Norman landowners.

Claude's younger brother René remained in the wardship of their mother Antoinette de Bourbon for most of the 1550s. It was she who administered the estates

[16] F.-J. Maudit, *Histoire d'Ivry-la-Bataille et de l'abbaye de Notre Dame d'Ivry* (Evreux, 1899), p. 230. In 1574 these lands were worth 12,210*l* per annum: AN MC VIII 379 fo. 214, 23 Feb 1574.

[17] A. Lechevalier, *Notice historique sur les barons et la baronnie du Bec* (Paris, 1898), p. 12; ADSM J 138, 'Documents concernant le comté de Maulévrier, 1468–1779'. The title of comte de Maulévrier was still used by the Bouillon after the sale. Four fiefs were purchased between 1565 and 1567 at a cost of 41,000*l*: ADSM 2E1 329, 19 Feb 1565; AN 300 AP I 223, 17 Sep 1567.

Eu
Harcourt
Mauny
Mayenne
Rennes
Le Mans
Orléans
Angers
Ancenis
Nantes
Ussé
Tours
Poitiers

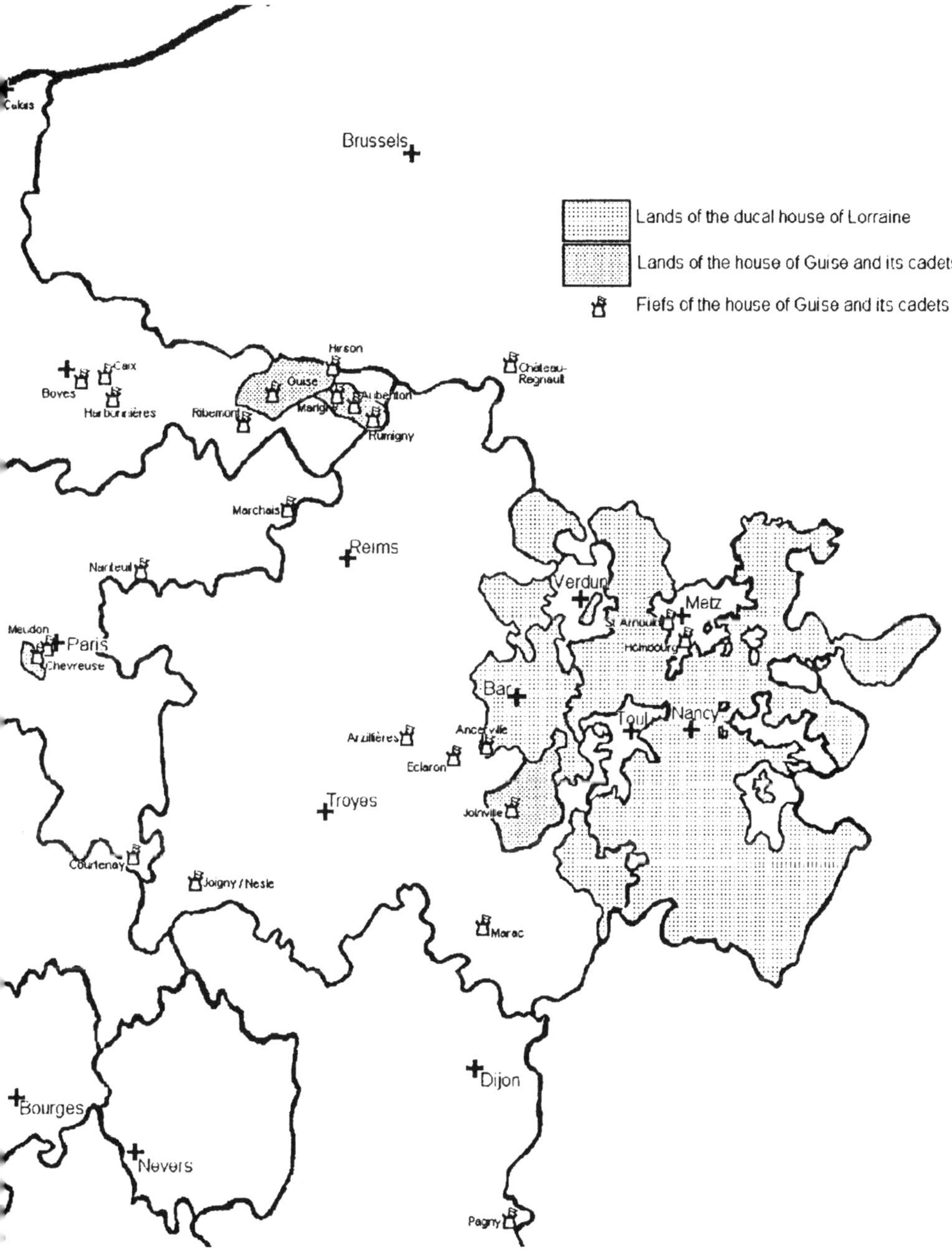

Map 2 Principal lands of the house of Guise-Lorraine in northern France

and oversaw the five-year struggle with the parlement of Paris over the elevation of his barony of Elbeuf to a marquisate.[18] She relied heavily on a small group of trusted Guise *domestiques* who went on to figure strongly in the Elbeuf affinity over the next generation. Particularly important was Charles des Boves, a young Champenois of a family with a history of Guise associations and lands in the French Vexin. As Elbeuf's tutor he governed his charge 'très bien et sagement', and several of his reports from Rouen to Joinville regarding the details of marriage negotiations and the elevation process are extant.[19] Continuity and reciprocal loyalty were fostered by the service of the des Boves across three generations.[20] Nobles from traditional areas of Guise support in eastern France predominated in Elbeuf's household and *ordonnance* company. These features of the affinity illuminate the renowned family solidarity that the Guise exhibited in the sixteenth century. Antoinette used the patronage of her children to reward clients and servants from longstanding areas of Guise power, showing little inclination to augment the affinity in Normandy.[21] Nonetheless, the Elbeuf landed interest in the province was expanding.

Elbeuf, like Aumale, built his Norman fortunes on a good marriage, to the daughter and co-heiress of Claude de Rieux and Suzanne de Bourbon in 1550.[22] The dowry of the much-pursued Louise de Rieux consisted of the large Loire barony of Ancenis, but from the death of her brother in 1548 she also anticipated a share with her two sisters of the vast Rieux inheritance in Brittany, Anjou and Normandy. Absence of legal records hampers the reconstruction of the course of the Rieux succession, which is complicated by the various forfeitures of Huguenot property during the religious wars. In addition, the underage heirs fell into wardship as the three Rieux daughters died relatively young. The eldest, Renée, died childless in 1567; the second, Claude, in 1563 leaving a son Paul de Coligny; and the third, Louise, in 1569, leaving her son by René de Lorraine, Charles duc d'Elbeuf. The latter fell into the guardianship of his maternal grandmother Suzanne de Bourbon and the cardinal de Lorraine, while Huguenot leader admiral de Coligny held the wardship of his nephew Paul.[23] Despite the obvious coincidence of family and

[18] BN MS Fr 20468 fo. 83, Antoinette to Elbeuf, Joinville, 2 Mar 1551; 20649 fo. 144, Antoinette to Hauteville, her *trésorier-général*, Joinville, 15 Jun 1552; P. Maille, *Recherches sur Elbeuf: esquisses ou silhouettes de ses seigneurs de la maison de Lorraine* (3 vols., Elbeuf, 1859–63), ii, p. 71.

[19] Brantôme, iv, p. 280; BN MS Fr 20532 fo. 11, des Boves to Antoinette, 21 May 1549; 20517fo. 79, des Boves to Guise, 5 Jan 1554; Pimodan, *La mère des Guises*, p. 385.

[20] BN MS Fr 8182 fo. 353; 22429 fos. 130, 136, 143, 150, 155, 161. François des Boves was *maître d'hôtel* and *conseiller* of the duc de Guise between 1542 and 1562. Antoine des Boves was also in the household in 1542. Charles's son was an officer in the Elbeuf *ordonnance* company in the 1580s.

[21] The Champenois Martin de Romencourt was *maître de logis* of the Elbeuf company of the*ordonnance* from 1559 until 1569, having been a *maître d'hôtel* of Antoinette de Bourbon:Vindry, p. 304.

[22] The actual marriage took place in 1554: E. Maillard, *Histoire d'Ancenis et de ses barons*(Nantes, 1860), p. 81.

[23] For the letters establishing the wardship of the marquis d'Elbeuf in 1567: BN MS Clairambault 1204 fo. 96. Suzanne de Bourbon may have been sympathetic to Calvinism. When she held Lillebonne as her dower, a Calvinist chapel flourished: C.-M. Bost, *Les seigneurs de Lillebonne* (Luneray, 1987), p. 111.

religious divides, there is no evidence that political and religious antipathies hindered the joint administration of the inheritance.[24] As Elbeuf reached majority in the late 1570s he was able to obtain provision to other parts of the comté of Harcourt, but his share diminished on the full *partage* of 1584, when Harcourt proper fell to the Coligny, while Brionne and Lillebonne remained in the hands of Elbeuf.[25] But on Paul de Coligny's death in 1586 Elbeuf obtained the wardship of his son Guy, effectively reuniting control of the entire Rieux succession. On Guy's death in 1605 the inheritance fell definitively to the Elbeuf.[26] Through a combination of wardship, dynastic accident and the politics of the civil wars, Elbeuf relentlessly acquired the comté of Harcourt: by the 1580s he had ascended into the first ranks of Norman magnates.

LANDHOLDING AND WEALTH IN THE SECOND HALF OF THE SIXTEENTH CENTURY

In order to appreciate fully the importance of Normandy to the Guise it is necessary to investigate the income from all their possessions. No corpus of documents survives which permits a comprehensive analysis of income and expenditure.[27] Even the most detailed document, dating from 1542, is far from complete. The reconstruction of family landholding patterns and the estimation of landed income entails the painstaking collection of data from disparate archives. Information regarding non-landed revenue, such as *rentes*, pensions and offices, though far from comprehensive, will also be considered in order to give an approximation of aggregate wealth. It is notoriously difficult to calculate accurately noble income but some evidence has been collated in recent years, as table 1.1 demonstrates.

The landed income of the duc de Guise in the mid-1570s as set out in table 1.2 can be conservatively estimated at 130,000*l* a figure comparable to the income of his peers. This represents the ducal landed fortune at its height following Henri duc de Guise's marriage and his inheritance of the cardinal de Lorraine's temporal property, but before the alienations of the later 1570s. Although impressive it is a notional figure which takes into account income neither from *rentes* nor from royal land held in usufruct. In addition, assignations for dower and interest payments are omitted.[28] A detailed document of 1571 provides a much clearer picture of income

[24] Coligny and Elbeuf collected their revenues and protected their rights together 'chacun en leur partie comtes d'Harcourt': ADC E 239, 5 Mar 1577 and 5 Jun 1582; ADSM 2E1 904, 16 and 17 Jun 1574.

[25] ADSM 1E 482, 1584.

[26] B. de Broussillon, *La maison de Laval, 1020–1605. Etude historique accompagné du cartulaire de Laval et de Vitré* (5 vols., 1895–1903), iv, pp. 229–324.

[27] Richer sources permit a more detailed examination: S. Eurich, *The economics of power: the private finances of the House of Foix-Navarre-Albret during the Religious Wars* (Ann Arbor, 1994).

[28] In 1550 François received the royal lands of the *vicomté* of Loyaux (Nantes) and Saint-Dizier for life, and his wife was granted Argilly, Rouvres and Pontailler-sur-Saône: *Catalogue des actes de Henri II*, M.-N. Baudoin-Matuszek and A. Merlin-Chazelas, eds. (Paris, 1979–), 1550, pp. 87, 117, 238. In 1570 the dowry provided by the duke for his sister Catherine included 5,000*l* of *rentes* on the hôtel de

Table 1.1 *Examples of aristocratic landed income in the sixteenth century*

Family	Date	Amount (livres)
Bourbon	1549	71,154 (Picardy only)
Foix-Navarre-Albret	1557–8	151,247
	1564	191,520
Nevers-Clèves	1551	115,000
Montmorency	1564	125–148,600

Neuschel, *Word of Honor*, p. 138; Major, *From renaissance monarchy to absolute monarchy*, p. 77; M. Greengrass, 'Property and politics in sixteenth-century France: the landed fortune of the Constable Anne de Montmorency', *French History*, 2 (1988), pp. 376–7; Harding, *Anatomy of a power elite*, p. 144.

and expenditure. During this year income from all sources totalled 235,507*l* while total expenses reached 221,229*l*.[29] This document must be used with caution. The huge figure for income represents the total wealth of the elder line before the partition between the ducs de Guise and de Mayenne, but it is safe to conclude that the income of the duc de Guise in the 1560s and early 1570s was greater than any other lay magnate, though the level of his indebtedness may have been correspondingly higher.[30] In nearly thirty years both the landed income and the total income of the duke had more than tripled, while expenditure had risen less rapidly. This reflects the ascent of the family in the 1550s and early 1560s and accounts for the surplus in 1571, in comparison to the deficit recorded in 1542.[31]

As Denis Crouzet has pointed out, wealth and thus power cannot be measured purely in terms of income; it has also to be evaluated in terms of expenditure, since this indicates the potential amount of dispensable patronage. In 1571 the regular wage bill of the Guise household alone amounted to 10,610*l* and a further 24,438*l* was disbursed to 'plusieurs personnes pour nos affaires', accounting for 16 per cent of expenditure.[32] This was surpassed by the 33 per cent of total expenditure

ville. In 1566 the dower of Anne d'Este, which included the royal lands of Dourdan, Provins and Saumur, had a capital value of 156,000*l*, and was originally held in usufruct by the duke: AN MC VIII 374 fo. 434; 372 fo. 361.

29 AMC A 14 liasse 7, 'Estat de la Re[te] et despences . . . pour l'année commançant le premier jour de janvier 1571'. Income includes 25,000*l* for his marriage gift from the king.

30 The account roll of 1571 shows that 18,190*l* was spent on the payment of *rentes* at a capital value of 218,280*l*, or less than one year's income. Henri de Guise inherited an income from his father of 200,000*l* per annum and debts estimated at 200,000 *écus*: D. Potter, *A history of France, 1460–1560* (London, 1995), p. 182; Brantôme, iv, p. 270. The 1571 roll may conceal the true extend of the duke's indebtedness; equally it may be that his advantageous marriage and royal largesse compensated for the burdens of raising troops in the civil war.

31 Bouillé, i, pp. 536–45. In the account of 1542 *rentes* on the duchy of Bar were recorded as landed income. For the sake of clarity they have been placed under non-landed income.

32 AMC A 14, liasse 7, 'Estat de . . . 1571'; D. Crouzet, 'Recherches sur la crise de l'aristocratie en France: les dettes de la maison de Nevers', *Histoire, Economie et Société*, 1 (1982), 7–50.

allocated for the ordinary expenses of the duchesse de Guise, an indication of her influential status and her importance as a patron. The income of a great lord could be remarkably elastic. In order to amass specie quickly valuable timber could be cut, *rentes* sold and, in the most desperate situations, land alienated. Land imparted status and its steady returns also allowed the lord to secure credit. The mortgaging of property was a common feature of noble finance during the Wars of Religion, since cash had to be raised rapidly in order to recruit and pay for troops.

It is not intended to provide an in-depth study of the fortunes of the elder line, but rather to place Normandy in the wider context of the Guise landed interest. All branches profited greatly from the ascendancy at court in the 1550s. The process is best seen in the elder line when both François de Guise and the cardinal de Lorraine invested the profits from high office in the acquisition of land. During the 1550s purchases were in the Ile de France and dictated by the need of the family to have residences closer to the court. Rivalry with the Montmorency was reflected in the competition between the families for land in the vicinity of Paris.[33] Splendid new residences were also acquired. The hôtel de Guise in Paris was constructed by buying and amalgamating a number of adjacent properties. The cardinal de Lorraine bought the château of Marchais in the Laonnais in 1553 and began to build another residence on the recently purchased estate at Meudon south of Paris.[34] During the 1550s the cardinal and his elder brother spent in excess of 500,000*l* buying property and estates in Paris and the Ile de France, profiting from the misfortune of the disgraced former royal mistress Anne de Pisseleu.[35] Some of these lands were heavily mortgaged in order to facilitate their purchase and they were sold in the 1570s when debts became pressing.

Henri de Guise, like his father and grandfather, employed few Normans in his household. The majority of his men-at-arms came from Champagne.[36] The family attachment to Champagne and its power base in the province was founded on historical precedent and, after 1562, on its tenure of the governorship. The main family seat was at Joinville where Antoinette de Bourbon, a dominating matriarch, resided for most of her life. As Laurent Bourquin has pointed out, the Guise were only one of a number of princely houses competing for power in the province.[37] Moreover their lands in Champagne, though important, constituted only a fraction of total income. In 1570 Henri married Catherine de Clèves, comtesse d'Eu,

[33] Greengrass, 'Property and politics in sixteenth-century France: the landed fortune of the Constable Anne de Montmorency', *French History*, 2 (1988), pp. 391–2.

[34] P. Biver, *Histoire du château de Meudon* (Paris, 1923); L.-H. Labande, *Le château et la baronnie de Marchais* (Paris, 1927).

[35] For details of these transactions: A. Moutié, *Chevreuse. Recherches historiques, archéologiques et généalogiques* (2 vols., Rambouillet, 1874–6); AMC GE 114 E1 fo. 41, 16 Feb 1552; GE 32 (tour) fo. 1; A 14 liasse 4, 30 Oct 1562; CB 2 liasse 8, 11 Nov 1555.

[36] BN MS NA Fr 8625 fo. 13, muster roll of sixty men-at-arms and forty archers, Chaumont-en-Bassigny, 31 Aug 1564; BN MS Fr 25808 fo. 167, muster roll of sixty men-at-arms and eighty archers, Ezry, 25 Aug 1575.

[37] Bourquin, *Noblesse seconde et pouvoir en Champagne.*

thereby confirming his family as the most important non-royal landowners in Normandy. Eu was, after the royal duchy of Alençon, the most valuable and prestigious lordship in Normandy; its elevation to the *pairie* dates back to 1458.[38] It was the most important territory in his possession, accounting for one-quarter of all landed income. The duke had an affection for Eu and after his visit in 1578 he decided to build a magnificent new residence.

Table 1.2 demonstrates the diversity of the Guise landed interest; it does not include those lands in the Maine which were inherited by Charles de Mayenne the younger brother of Henri. In 1571 these lands were worth around 25,000*l*.[39] Mayenne's inheritance was soon enhanced by the acquisition of the governorship of Burgundy on the death of his uncle, Claude d'Aumale, and by his dazzling marriage to the daughter of the comte de Tende in 1576, which brought him the comté of Montpezat among other lands in Guyenne.[40]

The fortunes of the branch of the ducs d'Aumale were founded on the Brézé inheritance in Normandy (see table 1.4). At the height of his territorial power in 1570 the duke received a landed income of approximately 50,000*l*, 60 per cent of which came from his Norman lands. Estimates of aggregate wealth are difficult, since it is impossible to assess the precise value of the offices of governor of Burgundy and of *grand veneur* beyond their regular stipend. His total gross income in the early 1570s was probably in the region of 100,000*l*. The loss of the governorship of Burgundy to the duc de Mayenne on the death of Claude in 1573 reduced this figure, but was compensated by the dowry of 100,000*l* paid by the duc de Guise to Charles duc d'Aumale when he married his cousin, Marie de Lorraine, in 1576. The desire to secure a governorship befitting his rank was to dominate his political career.

In the 1560s Claude d'Aumale attempted to capitalise on his position in Normandy by acquiring other territories such as the comté of Maulévrier and the barony of Bec Crespin, as well as some minor seigneuries. Financial difficulties in the 1570s eventually forced a change in this policy and Bec Crespin was sold. The most important concentrations of ducal territory were on the Norman borders. Aumale itself lies on the Norman–Picard border and is closer to Abbeville than to Rouen. The duke's influence was strong in the pays de Vimeu in Picardy but he also had some smaller lands near Amiens. The ducal retinue always had a strong Picard element, which expanded as the Wars of Religion progressed. Anet and Ivry were situated on the Eure – the border between Normandy and the *gouvernement* of the Ile de France. Aumale was a marcher lord whose influence transcended the provincial boundaries, demonstrating that territorial power did not necessarily conform to the regions formed by royal political and administrative jurisdictions.

[38] Anselme, iii, p. 325.

[39] This figure is an estimate based on the account of 1571 in which the figures are artificially high due to the extraordinary sales of timber for La Ferté Bernard: AMC A 14 liasse 7, 1571.

[40] Bouillé, iii, p. 37.

Table 1.2 *Landed income of the branch of Guise*

Seigneury and date of acquisition and sale	Date	Amount in livres p.a.
Champagne:		
Joinville	1603	9,168 (*domaine affermé*)
Arzillières (1556)	1571	6,591
	1580	5,000
Eclaron	1568	4,600
	1571	16,400 (artificially high due to sales of timber)
Joigny/Nesle (1553–71)	1553	1,600 (estimate)
	1571	4,400 (estimate)
Ile de France:		
Chevreuse (1552)	1583	14,000
	1586	13,000
	1591	12,000
Marchais (1553)	1553	1,000
Meudon (1552)	1587	1,350
Nanteuil-le-Hardouin (1555–78)	1559	8,000
	1571–2	16,865 (2 years' revenue)
	1576	11,000
Courtenay (1582)	1582	2,000 + (estimate)
Normandy:		
Eu (1570)	1571	32,258
	1600	26,700
Cuverville (1559)	1600	2,100
Picardy:		
Guise	1568	11,000
	1575	12,000
Rumigny, Aubenton, Marigny	1568	10,000
Hirson	1568	1,500
Ribemont-s-Oise	1569	700
Lands around Calais (1558–72)	1572	2,000 ?
Provence:		
Lambesc, Orgon, Esgaillières	1563	3,680
Barrois and Lorraine:		
Montier-sur-Saulx	1542	527
Ancerville (sold 1588)	1568	4,000 + timber at 1,200
Saint-Avold, Hombourg (1572–81)	1581	11,000
Other non-French possessions:		
Château-Regnault (1570)	1571	4,182 (Catherine de Clèves's dowry from her first marriage)
	1579	5,000

The temporal lands of the cardinal de Lorraine passed to the ducal line on his death in 1574. The figures for landed income are compiled from the following sources: AMC A 14 liasse 7, 'Estat de . . . 1571'; CB 2 liasse 8, 30 Jan 1559; D 3, 12 Jan 1575; GE 20 liasse 3, 31 Mar 1562; AN MC VIII 372 fos. 361–4, 26 Jun 1568; 380 fo. 987, Nov 1575; 393 fo. 547, May 1584; 392 fo. 117, 1 Jul 1583; 398 fo. 241, 6 Aug 1586; 399 fo. 463, Mar 1587; 406 fo. 65, Feb 1591; 373 fo. 306, 29 Apr 1569; 381 fo. 126, 16 Feb 1576; 386, 20 Nov 1579; 408 fo. 137, 19 Jul 1593; AP 300 I 102 liasse 2, 10 May 1600; 300 II 224, 1603.

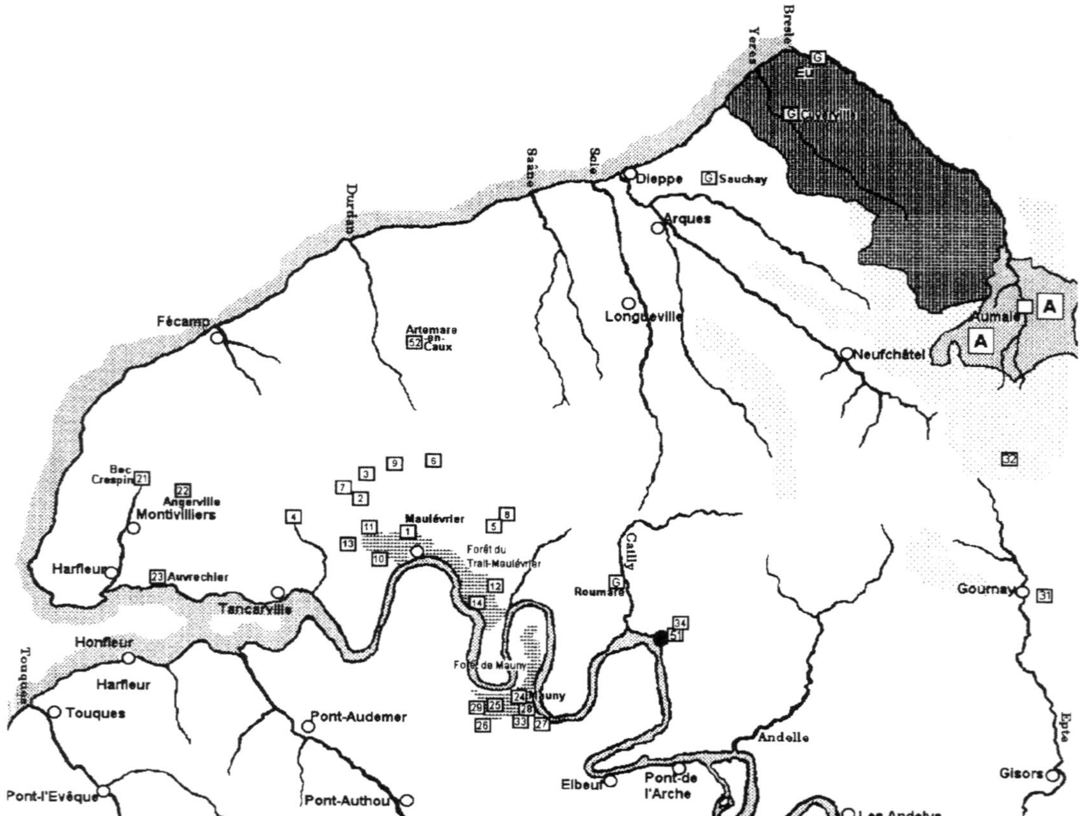
Bresle
Yeres
Eu
Saâne
Scie
Dieppe
Sauchay
Durdan
Arques
Fécamp
Longueville
Artemare-en-Caux
Aumale
Neufchâtel
Bec Crespin
Angerville
Montivilliers
Maulévrier
Forêt du Trait-Maulévrier
Harfleur
Auvrechier
Tancarville
Cailly
Roumare
Gournay
Honfleur
Forêt de Mauny
Touques
Mauny
Pont-Audemer
Andelle
Epte
Gisors
Elbeuf
Pont-de l'Arche
Pont-l'Evêque
Pont-Authou
Les Andelys

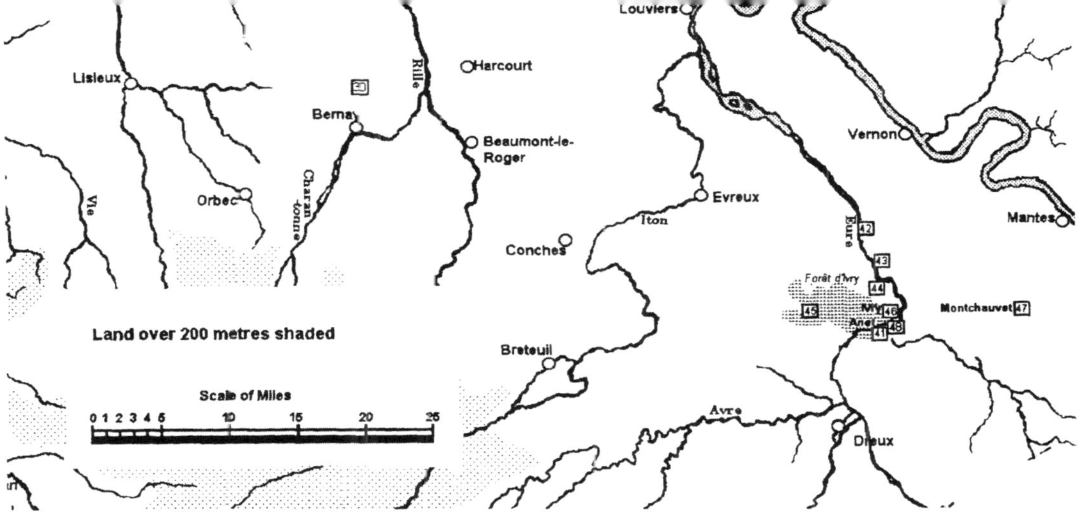

A. The duchy of Aumale

B. The parishes of the high justice of the comté of Maulévrier. The comté's seat was in the *Prétoire de Maulévrier* in the *faubourgs* of Caudebec.
1. Maulévrier 2. Alvimare 3. Bermonville 4. Bolbec 5. Carville
6. Etoutteville 7. Fourcart 8. Fréville 9. Roquefort 10. Saint-Arnoult
11. Saint-Gilles-de-Crétot 12. Sainte-Marguerite 13. Saint-Sylvestre
14. Trait

C. The baronies of Bec Crespin and Mauny (including Thouberville, Plasnes and Vivier).
21. Bec Crespin 22. Angerville 23. Auvrechier (mod. Orcher)
24. Mauny 25. Barneville 26. Bosgouet 27. La Bouille 28. Caumont
29. Guenouville 30. Plasnes 31. Ferrières 32. Grumesni
33. Thouberville 34. Vivier

D. Lands on the Norman-Chartrain borders: Anet, Ivry, Garennes, Montchauvet.

41. Anet 42. Breuilpont 43. Bueil 44. La Futelaye 45. Garennes
46. Ivry 47. Montchauvet 48. Dollaines

E. Other lands
51. Longpaon 52. Artemare-en-Caux

G. Appurtenanceis of the comté of Eu

Map 3 The Norman lands of the branches of Guise and Aumale in the second half of the sixteenth century

Table 1.3 *Non-landed income of the branch of Guise*

	Date	Amount (livres)
Captain of 100 lances		2,800
Royal pension	1571	16,000
	1579	16,000
Pension from cardinal de Lorraine	1571	6,000
Pension from cardinal de Guise	1584	4,000
Grand maître	1571	12,000
Colonel *chevaux-légers*	1571	10,800
Governor of Champagne		16,000 (estimate)
Rentes on Château Porcien (1570)	1575	677
Rentes on Bar-s-Aube	1568	250
Rentes on *aides* of Bar-s-Aube	1575	1,000
Rentes on Bar-le-Duc	1568	4,000
'Don du roi pour les noces'	1570	100,000
Dons du roi	1571	21,764
Assignation on *recette-général* of Champagne	1575	21,000 (perhaps for royal pensions, etc.)
Succession of Louis de Adhémar	1575	30,000 (capital)
Succession of Antoine de Croy	1578	30,000 (capital)
	1582	17,000
Dons du roi:	1581	200,000 ?
(offices in chancellery of Dijon)	1586	4,500 each
	1586	11,000
	1588	10,500

Information on non-landed income is fragmentary and this table is designed merely as a guide. Details are to be found in: AMC A 14, liasse 7, 'Estat de . . . 1571', 'Parties et sommes extraordinaires fournies . . . durant le mois de juillet 1581', 12 Jan 1584; AN MC VIII 372 fos. 3614, 28 Oct 1568; 380 fo. 708, 25 Aug 1575 fos. 9891, Nov 1575; 393 fo. 500, May 1584; 389 fo. 94, 19 Feb 1582; 390 fo. 245, 19 Sep 1582; 383 fo. 396, 4 May 1578; 397 fo. 134, 11 Feb 1586; 398 fo. 251, 7 Aug 1586; 401 fo. 275, 11 Mar 1588; BN MS Fr 26170 fo. 37, 1580.

Marriage between cousins was a common way of maintaining family inheritances, and Charles duc d'Aumale received a number of seigneuries in the Loire valley belonging to his bride, the daughter of René marquis d'Elbeuf.[41] These were peripheral to the ducal landed interest and were sold to quit debts in the 1580s. More significant was the inheritance of Diane de Poitiers' lands in Dauphiné, mainly consisting of the comté of Saint-Vallier and accounting for 25 per cent of landed income.

[41] AN AP 300 I 215, 28 Dec 1582; MC VIII 398 fo. 696, 18 Nov 1586.

Although the Elbeuf were the junior branch of the house of Guise their landed income grew steadily, reaching a peak of 50,000*l* at the end of the sixteenth century.[42] This was sufficient to maintain princely status and the betrothal of Charles duc d'Elbeuf in 1583 to Marguerite Chabot, dame de Pagny, was sealed with a dowry large enough to rival other princely matches.[43] Total income was somewhat below the level enjoyed by the other branches, since the Elbeuf did not hold significant royal office until the seventeenth century.[44] The marquises, later ducs, d'Elbeuf were the most characteristically Norman of the Guise; their lands were situated in the heartland of Normandy, dominating the rich pays de Roumois. The importance of Normandy in the wider landholding pattern is clear. The branches of Elbeuf and Aumale were predominantly Norman landowners and in 1571 the comté of Eu represented one-quarter of the duc de Guise's landed wealth, a fraction which would increase in the next ten years as peripheral lands were sold. Normandy was the most valuable province of the Valois monarchy and its prosperity is reflected in the size of seigneurial income.

No picture of Guise wealth would be complete without a discussion of their ecclesiastical benefices. Although some of the princely families matched them in temporal wealth, none possessed as much income from the church. Control of ecclesiastical patronage was at the heart of Guise power throughout the sixteenth century. It was under Jean cardinal de Lorraine that the foundations of a formidable ecclesiastical empire were laid, which flourished under his nephew Charles de Lorraine (1525–74), second son of Claude duc de Guise. In 1550 Jean was in possession of six abbeys and six dioceses.[45] The most prestigious benefice in France was the archbishopric of Reims, which conferred the title *premier pair de France* and to which Jean ascended in 1533.[46] The family enjoyed the fruits of the two richest abbeys in Normandy. Jean was made abbot of Fécamp in 1523 and on his death it passed into the possession of Charles. Louis (d. 1578), the fourth son of Claude and Antoinette de Bourbon, was cardinal de Guise and abbot of Bec in Normandy from 1558 until 1572.[47] It was during the reign of Henri II that the empire was extended and consolidated. After his accession, Charles de Lorraine was raised to the cardinalate, became an important member of the *conseil du roi* and was made chancellor of the order of Saint-Michel. Charles's status on the highest royal council, the privy council, was second only to that of Anne de

[42] Details on landed income are to be found in AN T 199/24, 31 Dec 1595; ADC E 3, 10 Oct 1540; ADSM 1er Meubles, 24 Feb 1586; Maillard, *Histoire d'Ancenis*, p. 589.

[43] BN Cabinet d'Hozier 216 fo. 101.

[44] On non-landed income: BN MS Fr 3942 fo. 35, 12 Aug 1560 fo. 279, 23 Oct 1565; 26170 fo. 135, 1584; Pièces Originales 1749–50; AN K 92B fo. 29, 30 Oct 1564.

[45] J. Bergin, 'The decline and fall of the House of the Guise as an ecclesiastical dynasty', *Historical Journal*, 25 (1982), pp. 782–803. For a fuller treatment of Guise ecclesiastical power: J. Baker, 'The House of Guise and the church *c.* 1550–1588', unpub. D.Phil. thesis (University of Oxford, 1995).

[46] Anselme, ii, p. 70.

[47] A. A. Porée, *Histoire de l'abbaye de Bec* (2 vols., Evreux, 1901), ii, p. 338.

Table 1.4 *Income of the branch of Aumale*

Seigneury and date of acquisition and sale	Date	Amount in livres p.a.
Normandy:		
Aumale	1574	9,500 + sale of timber at 6,400
	1583	9,800
Mauny (1556–66)	late 16th c	4–5,000 (estimate)[1]
Bec Crespin (1562–79)	1574	2,250 (including seigneury of Bretheville)
Anet (1566–1614)	1574	3,000 + sale of timber at 914+2,000 *minutz d'avoine*
	1578	3,200
Dollaines	1574	300
Ivry and Garennes (1566–1614)	1574	7,000 + sale of timber at 6,323
Park of Ivry and Garennes	1574	500 (Garennes only)
	1591	1,000
Ballineau and Grandeville	1574	40
Breuilpont (1566–1614)	1574	570 + sale of timber at 990
Montchauvet (1566–1614)	1574	300
Longpaon, du Vivier, Geole (1564)	1565	900
Maulévrier (1562)	1568	1,000
Artemare-en-Caux (1565)	1565	500 (estimate)
Picardy:		
Boves, Caix, Harbonnières (1550)	1574	5,000
	1581	5,100
Dauphiné:		
Comté of Saint-Vallier, etc. (1566)	1574	13,000
Lands in the Loire valley (inheritance of Suzanne de Bourbon received as dowry in 1576):		
Ussé (1576)	1589	3,000
Barony of Briolay (1576–86)	1586	3,000 (estimate)
Ecclesiastical benefices (inherited/acquired by the chevalier d'Aumale):		
Abbey of Bec Hellouin (1572–91)	1559	19,500
Abbey of Bourg-en-Deols (1574–91)	1574	7,000
Priory of Choisy (1574–?)	1574	1,300
Priory of Saint Nicholas (Senlis) (1574–?)	1574	4,500
Abbey of Saint-Pierre en Vallée (1574–91)	1587	8,200
Abbey of Troisfontaines (1574–91)	unknown	
Abbey of Auchy-les-Aumale	unknown	
Non-landed income:		
100 lances	1572	2,800
50 lances	1573	2,200
Captain *of chevaux-légers*	1551	3,600
Royal pension	1564	16,000
	1574	12,000
	1580s	12,000
Grand veneur de France	1563	4,400
	1581	3,750
	1583	4,800

Table 1.4 *Continued*

Seigneury and date of acquisition and sale	Date	Amount in livres p.a.
Bailli of Caen (1557–9)	1559	21,780 (capital value)
Governorship of Champagne (15638)	1564	6,000
Governorship of Burgundy (1550–73)		16,000 (estimate)
Rente on Château-Porcien	1575	677
Rentes – inheritance of Suzanne de Bourbon	1579	5,000
Usufruct of Ile de Rhuys, Brittany	(1550s)	1,560 ?
Herring farm of Amiens (1566–7)	1567 (sale)	10,300 (capital value)
Don of duc de Guise on marriage of duc d'Aumale	1576	100,000
Don of Catholic League	1589	30,000

[1] Extrapolated from the figure given for the 1670s in G. A Prevost, ed., *Notes du premier président Pellot sur la Normandie, 1670–83* (Rouen and Paris, 1915), p. 160.

On the duke's landed income: AN MC VIII 379 fo. 214, 21 Feb 1574; AN AP 300 I 223, 3 Dec 1581; 219, 28 May 1577; ADSM 1B 703, 1 Feb 1591; J 138, 29 Apr 1567; BN Pièces Originales 1750 fo. 235, 24 Mar 1583. On non-landed income: AN KK 145 fo. 11, 1584; MC VIII 379 fo. 215, 25 Feb 1574; 369 fos. 378–80, 21 Oct 1566; 370 fo. 303, 14 May 1567; 388 fo. 1216, Nov 1581; AN AP 300 I 223, 16 May 1579; ADSM 1B 700, 30 Sep 1589; 1ER 1764, 8 May 1560; BN MS Fr 3942 fo. 265, Jun 1564; Pièces Originales 1749–50.

Montmorency.[48] In the 1550s Bec was valued at 19,500*l* of revenue per annum and Fécamp at 40,000*l*.[49] On the eve of the Wars of Religion the annual revenue of these two benefices was comparable to the gross income of the duc de Guise in 1542 – a vast sum which demonstrates the power of ecclesiastical princes.

The Guise domination of ecclesiastical patronage, established during the reign of Henri II, was maintained by the resignation of benefices to other family members or to faithful clients. This ensured continuity of patronage and enhanced the loyalty of clients. The abundance of ecclesiastical benefices enabled provision to be made for younger sons, in order to maintain the integrity of the patrimony. For example, Claude de Lorraine, chevalier d'Aumale, second son of Claude duc d'Aumale, held a number of abbeys *in commendam*, most of which were bequeathed by his guardian, the cardinal de Guise. These benefices provided the young chevalier de Saint-Jean an annual income in excess of 40,000*l*.[50] Fécamp, like Bec, remained firmly in the grip of the Guise throughout the sixteenth century. It was resigned by the cardinal de Lorraine on his death to his nephew Louis II cardinal de Guise. The monopoly of these lucrative abbeys only ended with the murder of Louis II at Blois in 1588 and the death of the chevalier d'Aumale in battle in 1591.[51] The patronage available

[48] Baumgartner, *Henry II*, pp. 50–2.

[49] Porée, *Histoire de l'abbaye de Bec*, ii, pp. 345, 354; L. Romier, *Les origines politiques des guerres de religion* (2 vols., Paris, 1913). The income of Bec rose to 22,000*l* in 1568 and to 24,000*l* in 1576.

[50] AN MC VIII 379 fo. 215, 23 Feb 1574; 400 fo. 139, 8 Aug 1587; *Lettres de Henri III*, M. François, ed. (4 vols. to date, Paris, 1959–), iii, p. 499, iv, p. 70.

[51] Bergin, 'The decline and fall of the House of Guise', pp. 786–9.

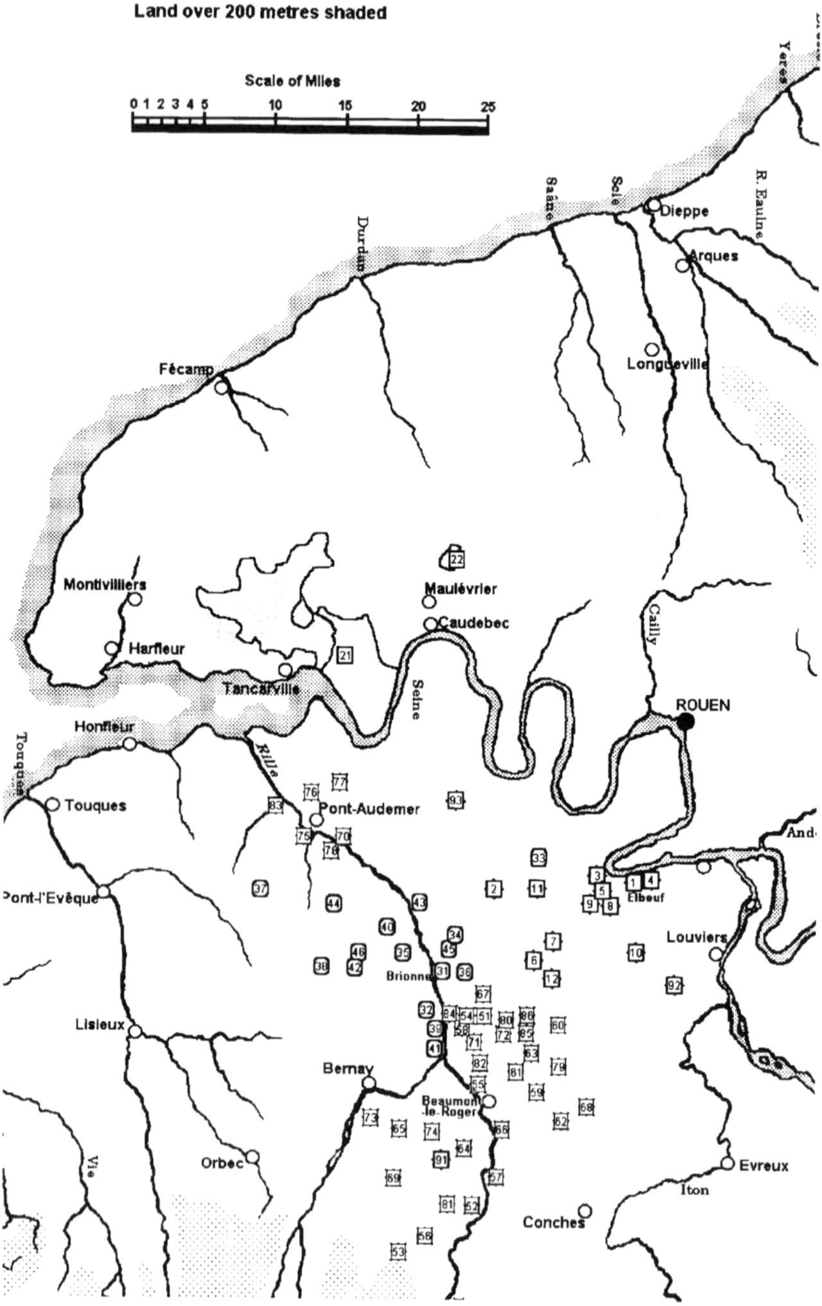
Land over 200 metres shaded
Scale of Miles
0 1 2 3 4 5 10 15 20 25
Dieppe
Arques
Longueville
Fécamp
Montivilliers
Harfleur
Tancarville
Honfleur
Maulévrier
Caudebec
ROUEN
Touques
Pont-Audemer
Pont-l'Evêque
Elbeuf
Louviers
Brionne
Lisieux
Bernay
Beaumont -le-Roger
Orbec
Conches
Evreux
Iton
Seine
Rille
Cailly
Durdan
Saâne
Scie
R. Eauline
Yeres
Touques
Vie

A, *Prévôtes* of the high justice of Elbeuf
1. Elbeuf
2. Boissey-le-Châtel
3. Le Buquet
4. Caudebec-lés-Elbeuf
5. Les Escameaux
6. Le Gros-Theil
7. La Haye-du-Theil
8. Le Thuit-Angers
9. Le Thuit-Signol
10. Mandeville
11. Marcouville
12. Saint-Nicolas-du-Bosc

B, Parishes of the high justice of the comté of Lillebonne
21. Lillebonne
22. Saint-Clair-des-Monts

C, The comté of Brionne
31. Brionne
32. Aclou
33. Angouville
34. Bosrobert
35. Bretigny
36. Calleville
37. Epaignes
38. Epreville-en-Lieuvin
39. Fontaine-la-Sorat
40. Livet-sur-Authou
41. Nassandres
42. Notre-Dame-d'Epine
43. Pont-Authou
44. Saint-Etienne-l'Allier
45. Saint-Martin-du-Parc
46. Saint-Victor-d'Epine

D, The comté of Harcourt
51. Harcourt
52. Ajou
53. La Barre-en-Ouche
54. Beauficiel
55. Beaumont-la-Ville
56. Bosc-Renoult-en-Ouche
57. Le Chatelier
58. Chretienville
59. Combon
60. Crosville-la-Vielle
61. Ecardenville-la-Campagne
62. Emanville
63. Epreville
65. Gouttières
66. Grandchain
67. Grosley
68. La Haye
69. Lambert
70. Landepereuse
71. Manneville-sur-Risle
73. Perriers-la-Campagne
74. Rouge-Perriers
75. Saint-Aubin-le-Guichard
76. Saint-Aubin-le-Vertueux
77. Saint-Germain-Village
78. Saint-Mards-de-Blacarville
79. Saint-Ouen-des-Champs
80. Saint-Paul-sur-Risle
81. Sainte-Colombe-la-Cammanderie
82. Sainte-Opportune
83. Thevray
84. Le Tilleul
85. Le Tilleul-Odon
86. Toutainville
87. Valieville
88. Villez-sous-le Neubourg
89. Vitotel

E, Lands added to form the duchy of Elbeuf in 1583
91. Beaumesnil
92. Quatremare
93. Routout

Map 4 The Norman lands of the Elbeuf in the second half of the sixteenth century

Table 1.5 *Income of the branch of Elbeuf*

Seigneury and date of acquisition	Date	Amount in livres p.a.
Normandy:		
Elbeuf	1595	13,000
Lillebonne (1570)	1540	3,339
	1570	7,300
Brionne (1567)	1540	2,884
	1570	6,000 (estimate)
Harcourt (1567)	1540	4,218
	1584	8,600 [1] (estimate)
Brittany:		
Ancenis (1554–99)	1599	20,000 (estimate)
Champagne:		
Marac	unknown	
Burgundy:		
Pagny (1583)	unknown	
Non-landed income:		
Capitaine-général des galères	1564	5,540
Captain 50 lances	1573	2,200
Captain 60 lances	1579	2,800
Royal pension	1584	6,000
Pension from cardinal de Lorraine	1561	2,000
Rentes on Château-Porcien	1575	677
Dowry from marriage in *rentes*	1583	8,000
Governor of the Bourbonnais (1586–8)	unknown	
Governor of Poitiers (1593–1605)	unknown	
Don du roi	1560	4,000
Don du roi	1565	20,000
Lump sum payments from marriage	1583	12,000

[1] As part of the partition of 1584 Elbeuf received 2,000*l* from the revenues of Harcourt. Within two years his co-heritor was dead and Elbeuf administered Harcourt as guardian of Guy-Paul de Coligny.

to the abbot of Fécamp alone was formidable. The abbey possessed the right to appoint to the captaincy of the town and its jurisdiction extended over twelve priories and twenty-nine churches of the diocese of Rouen; in addition it was patron of forty-three churches in the diocese. The temporal property of the abbey consisted of nine baronies, all with high justice appealing directly to the parlement of Rouen. Until the mid-seventeenth century most monks came from aristocratic families, thus 'les familles nobles du Pays de Caux, empêchées de partager leur bien par le coutume de Caux, trouvent là pour leurs cadets un débouché commode'.[52] The abbot was one of the most significant figures in local political society.

It is clear from these figures that individual members of the Guise family were immensely wealthy and on a par with other great princely families. If the income of the lay members is added to the lucrative ecclesiastical benefices the aggregate wealth of the family calculated by contemporaries at 600,000*l* in the 1560s is a valuable estimate. The cardinal de Lorraine accounted for half the total.[53] At the height of their power in the late 1550s and early 1560s the Guise were the wealthiest family in the kingdom. This partly explains why, during this period, the cardinal de Lorraine was such an influential figure on the royal finance council. His personal wealth and contacts in the world of banking were invaluable to the impoverished monarchy. Few would have been capable of finding the resources to maintain the French army in front of Calais as he did in the winter of 1557–8, and he continued to play an important role in financing the royalist war effort in the 1560s.[54]

The power of the house of Guise was derived not from the prominent individuals of the senior ducal branch at its apex, but from the collective strength and wealth of its united branches. The remarkable solidarity of the Guise was partly due to the carefully planned and sensible partitions of their legacy. Cadets were well provided for without damaging the integrity of the inheritance; this was facilitated by the abundance of ecclesiastical benefices controlled by the family. The duc d'Aumale and the marquis d'Elbeuf were able to maintain their status as princes and the rancour that could have ensued from a disputed partition was avoided. Kinship solidarity was maintained by the equitable treatment of all family members which fostered stronger feelings of fidelity among servants and clients, since they were often patronised by more than one branch. Loyalty and affection to the house of Guise as a whole was thus cultivated.

THE GUISE AND THE NORMAN ELITE

Existing associations with the Norman landed elite facilitated the growth of Guise influence in the region as the family's landed interest and affinity expanded in the second half of the century. Central to this process were alliances with the masters of the old Brézé affinity, with Charles de Bourbon-Vendôme cardinal-archbishop of Rouen, with the Orléans-Longueville, the Este and the La Marck.

52 G. Lemarchand, 'Le temporel et les revenus de l'abbaye de Fécamp pendant le XVIIe et le XVIIIe siècle', *Annales de Normandie*, 15 (1965), p. 525; A. Hellot, *Fécamp au temps de la Ligue. La légende de Boisrozé* (Yvetot, 1897), p. 5.

53 Bouillé, i, p. 223. The figure of 300,000*l* for Lorraine's income is not improbable, since the bishopric of Metz alone was valued at 80,000–100,000*l* per annum and the abbey of Saint-Denis at 49,170*l* in the 1580s: Baker, 'The House of Guise and the church', p. 55; F. Ayzac, *Histoire de Saint-Denis en France* (2 vols., Paris, 1861), ii, p. 515.

54 D. Potter, 'The duc de Guise and the fall of Calais', *English Historical Review*, 118 (1983), 481–512. The cardinal purchased *rentes* on the hôtel de ville in order to resell them and aid the war effort: AN MC VIII 373 fos. 443–524.

Map 5 Benefices of the house of Guise in Normandy in the second half of the sixteenth century

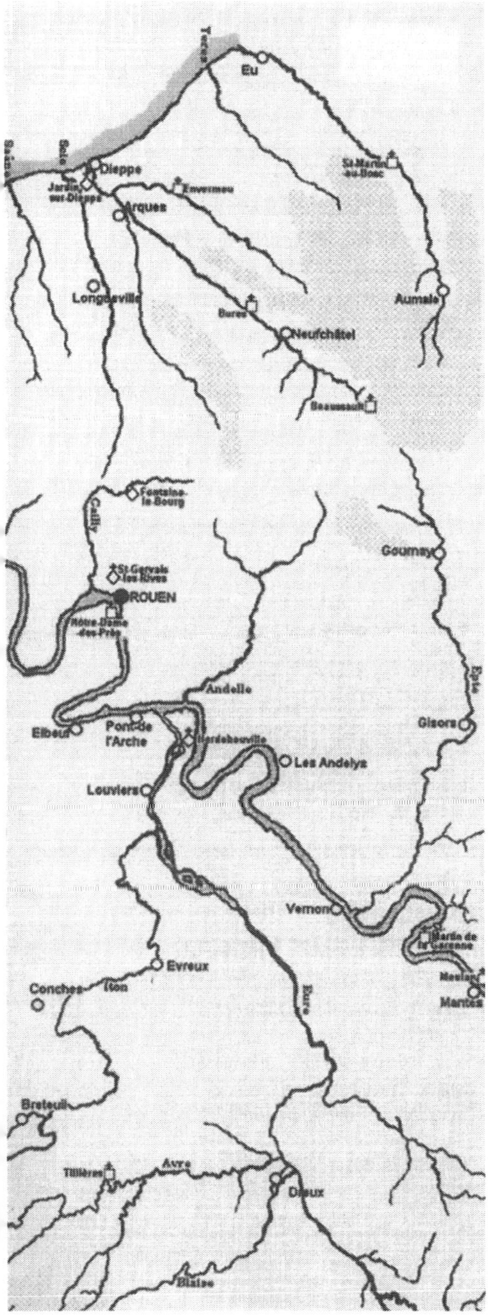

Eu
Dieppe
Envermeu
Arques
Aumale
Longueville
Bures
Neufchâtel
Beaussault
Fontaine-le-Bourg
Cailly
Gournay
ROUEN
Andelle
Epte
Gisors
Elbeuf
Pont-de l'Arche
Les Andelys
Louviers
Vernon
Mantes
Evreux
Conches
Iton
Eure
Breteuil
Tillières
Avre
Dreux
Blaise

As *de facto* heads of the French church the Guise were the object of both supplications for patronage and offers of service from all over France and beyond. Before establishing a core of servants in Normandy, they were able to forge close links with the existing Norman ecclesiastical hierarchy. For example, the Le Veneur were an established ecclesiastical family well before the Guise reached their ascendant position in the church. Jean Le Veneur became a cardinal in 1533, having been bishop of Lisieux and abbot of Bec and Mont Saint-Michel. His family was close to the Brézé and in 1531 he was appointed guardian of Louis de Brézé's children, in conjunction with Diane de Poitiers.[55] Gabriel Le Veneur inherited many of the benefices of his great-uncles, Ambrose and Jean. Bishop of Evreux from 1531, he cultivated an intimate relationship with Charles, cardinal de Lorraine. His early association with the Guise is attested by the funeral oration he gave at the funeral of Claude de Guise in 1550, and ten years later he became chancellor of the order of Saint-Michel on Lorraine's resignation.[56] At the funeral of Henri II Gabriel assisted the cardinal in the capacity of *sous diacre* and in 1562 he accompanied his patron to the Council of Trent. At his death in 1574 he was the most important prelate in Normandy, being bishop of Evreux and abbot of Jumièges, Notre Dame de Lyre, Saint-Evroult and Saint-Taurin.[57] The fact that Gabriel's elder brother was 'fort aimé du duc de Guise' was also a reason for the continued prosperity of the Le Veneur during the Wars of Religion.[58]

On Louis de Brézé's death much of his influence in the province passed to the lieutenant of his *ordonnance* company, Claude d'Annebaut.[59] The story of Annebaut's rise from the ranks of the Norman *noblesse seconde* to pre-eminence at the court of the ailing François I in the 1540s is tangential to the growth of the Guise affinity. However, it is noteworthy that, although he was banished from court on the accession of Henri II in 1547 as an enemy of the Montmorency, he was promoted to the governorship of Normandy. His appointment may have been brokered by Diane because, as an enemy of the Montmorency and a former servant of her family, he was a useful ally. Annebaut therefore returned to the position of alliance with the Brézé and was part of a faction which included the Guise. His son, Jean, fought under the Guise in Italy in the 1550s and with the duc d'Aumale in 1562.[60] More significantly, there is a strong correlation between the families which

55 Ambrose Le Veneur, bishop of Evreux from 1511 until 1531, the last bishop to be elected by the chapter, delivered Louis de Brézé's funeral oration: Bonnenfant, *Histoire générale du diocèse d'Evreux* (2 vols., Paris, 1933), i, p. 131; *DBF*, ii, p. 1358; E. Lefèvre, *Recherches historiques sur la principauté d'Anet* (Chartres, 1862), p. 22.

56 BM Collection Leber 5176 fo. 4; D. de Sainte-Marthe, *Gallia Christiana* (13 vols., Paris, 1715), xi, p. 611.

57 It may have been through the good offices of the Guise that Gabriel received the abbey of Jumièges in 1549, since the man who resigned was the cardinal of Ferrara, brother-in-law of François de Lorraine, duc de Guise: L. Jouen, *Jumièges* (Rouen, 1925), pp. 62–3; G. Bonnenfant, *Histoire générale du diocèse d'Evreux*, i, p. 133.

58 BN Dossiers Bleus 661 fo. 1.

59 Annebaut took over the captaincy of the Brézé company: Vindry, p. 23.

60 *DBF*, pp. 1356–9.

formed the core of the Brézé–Annebaut affinity in the first half of the sixteenth century and those families which formed the backbone of the Guise following in Normandy during the Wars of Religion. The Brézé inheritance required the employment of legal and financial officials to administer the lands and give counsel; consequently many former servants of the Brézé now entered Guise service.[61] It is no coincidence that the Clères, the Vieuxpont and the Le Veneur became integral parts of the ultra-catholic faction in Normandy in the 1560s.[62] Kinship ties bound the fortunes of the Le Veneur and the Annebaut. Jacques d'Annebaut became bishop of Lisieux on the resignation of his uncle, cardinal Jean Le Veneur, in 1539. When Le Veneur died in 1543 Jacques was raised to the cardinalate within a year, taking his uncle's title of Sainte-Susanne. As the fortunes of the Annebaut waned in the 1550s, the Le Veneur attached themselves to their natural successors, the Guise.

The cardinal de Bourbon was primate of Normandy from 1550 until his death in 1590.[63] Charles de Bourbon-Vendôme was a prince of the blood, the younger brother of Antoine, king of Navarre, and some years older than Louis, prince de Condé. The alliance that was forged between the Guise and the cardinal was the product of years of cooperation and friendship, which later became the pivotal axis of the ultra-catholic faction. Usually dismissed as a nonentity by historians, the role played by the cardinal in this faction cannot be overstated, chiefly because of his status. He was later hailed by the Catholic League as Charles X, king of France. In addition to being archbishop of Rouen, the cardinal possessed a number of other benefices in Normandy he was abbot both of Jumièges (on the death of Gabriel Le Veneur) and Saint-Ouen de Rouen. In 1588 his income was 63,000*l*, 58 per cent of which came from his Norman benefices.[64] The choicest abbeys in Normandy were reserved exclusively for himself and the Guise. Through this alliance the Guise extended their contacts with Normans and augmented their influence in the province. The cardinal de Bourbon had amicable relations with the cardinal de Lorraine. In their youth they had attended the Collège de Navarre together, and it was through the good offices of Lorraine that Bourbon received his cardinal's hat. Unlike his brothers the cardinal never wavered in his faith. As the Wars of Religion dragged on, he moved further into open alliance with the Guise and by 1574 had severed contacts with his nephews Condé and Navarre. Relations between Bourbon and the Guise were fostered by the interaction of their respective servants in

[61] The Brevedent, a *noblesse de robe* family associated with the Brézé, 'grew wealthy from the protection of Diane de Poitiers, duchesse de Valentinois, and in their house . . . the arms of the Brézé are to be seen in several places': J. Dewald, *The formation of a provincial nobility: the magistrates of the parlement of Rouen, 1499–1610* (Princeton, 1980), p. 88. Jacques de Brevedent, *conseiller* at the parlement (1537–60) and lieutenant-general of the *bailliage* of Rouen (1547–67), was in the confidence of the Guise and was a trusted financial agent of the duc d'Aumale in the 1550s. The family were intimately associated with the ultra-catholic faction in Rouen in the 1560s.

[62] These families will be dealt with in detail in succeeding chapters.

[63] E. Saulnier, *Le rôle politique du cardinal de Bourbon (Charles X), 1523–1590* (Paris, 1912).

[64] AN MC VIII 401 fo. 339, 7 Apr 1588.

KEY TO FIEFS:

1. La Vaupalière
2. Lindboeuf
3. Bacqueville
4. Anserville
5. La Londe
6. Ancourt
7. Cuverville
8. Bréauté and Neville
9. Merey
10. Auzebosc
11. Clères
12. Etelan
13. Maigneux and Lignieres
14. Flavacourt
15. Cuverville and Colombelles
16. Nonant and Le Merlerault
17. Tillières
18. Carrouges
19. Renneville
20. Saint-Just
21. Fumechon
22. Montgomméry
23. Ducey
24. Brécey
25. La Mésangère
26. La Mellieraye
27. Pierrecourt
28. Ry
29. Bellencombre
30. Riberpré
31. Richebourg
32. Saint-Contest
33. Saint-Cyr
34. Le Thuit
35. Auvers
36. Pretot
37. Saint-Martin
38. Pont Saint-Pierre
39. Maineville
40. Baizieux
41. Ernes and Saint-Sylvain
42. La Roche-Guyon
43. Connelles, Bupain and Daubeuf
44. Chailloué
45. Auzouville
46. Vieuxpont
47. Becthomas

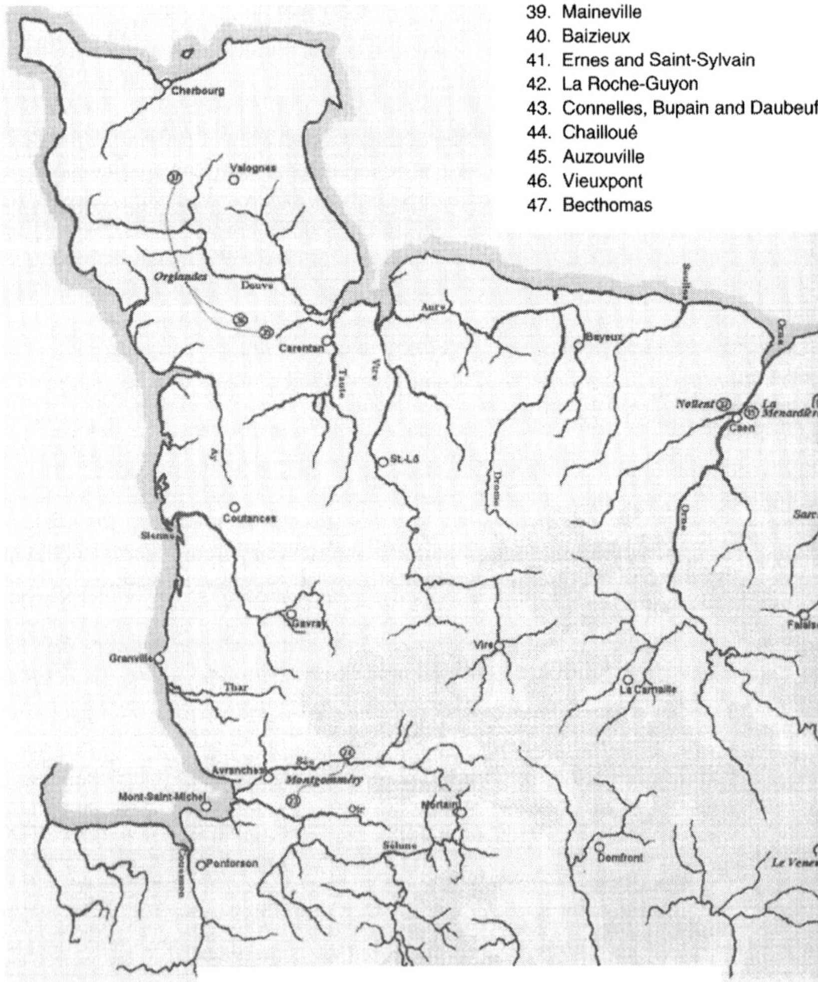

Map 6 Normandy and some Norman lineages in the sixteenth century

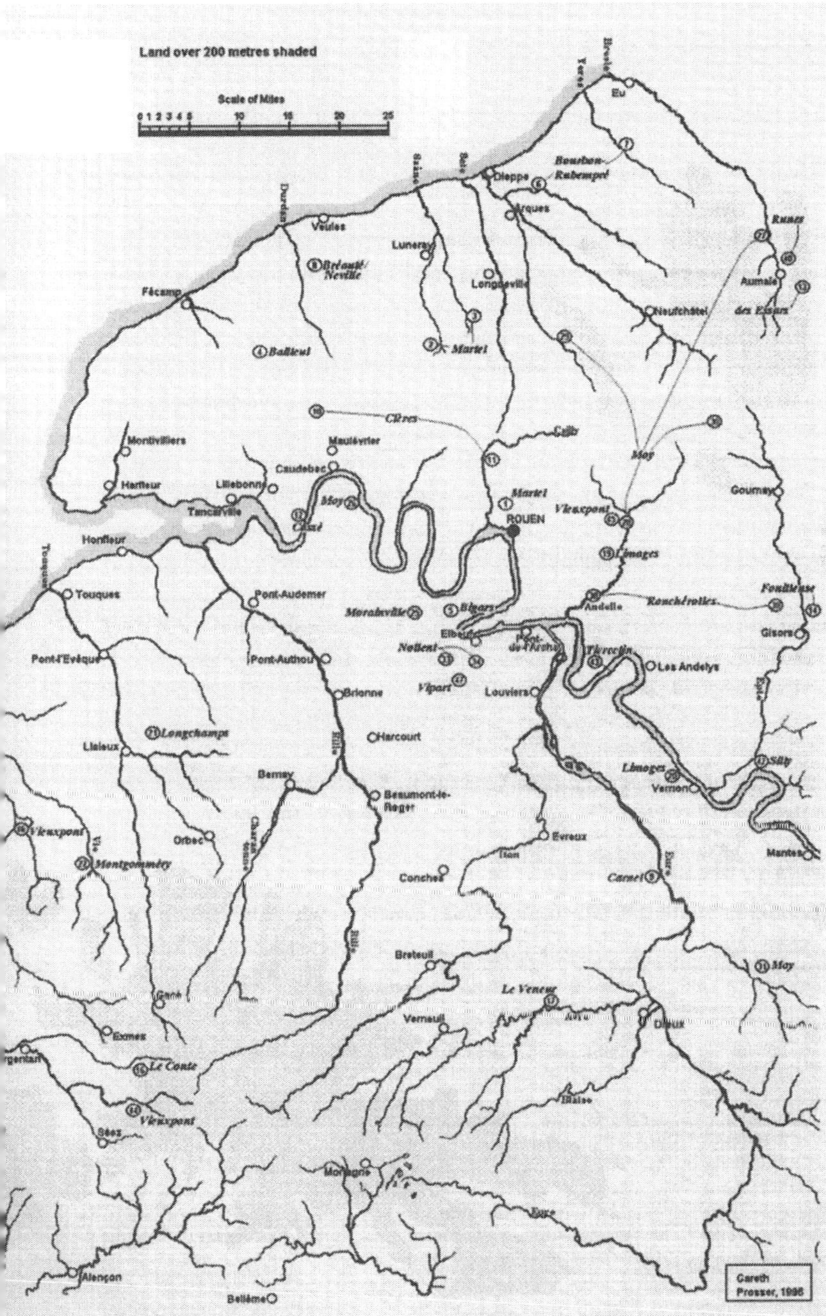
Land over 200 metres shaded
Scale of Miles
0 1 2 3 4 5 10 15 20 25
Eu
Bourbon-Rubempré
Dieppe
Arques
Runes
Veules
Luneray
Bréauté/Neville
Longueville
Aumale
Fécamp
Neufchâtel
des Essarts
Martel
Bailleul
Clères
Montivilliers
Maulévrier
Caudebec
Moy
Harfleur
Lillebonne
Tancarville
Martel
ROUEN
Vieuxpont
Gournay
Moy
Cailly
Honfleur
Limoges
Touques
Pont-Audemer
Andelle
Ronchérolles
Fouilleuse
Moraineville
Bigars
Elbeuf
Gisors
Noilent
Pont-de-l'Arche
Tirecelin
Les Andelys
Pont-l'Evêque
Pont-Authou
Vipart
Louviers
Brionne
Longchamps
Harcourt
Lisieux
Silly
Limoges
Vernon
Bernay
Beaumont-le-Roger
Vieuxpont
Orbec
Evreux
Mantes
Montgommery
Conches
Carnel
Breteuil
Moy
Le Veneur
Gacé
Verneuil
Dreux
Exmes
Argentan
Le Conte
Vieuxpont
Sées
Mortagne
Alençon
Bellême
Gareth Prosser, 1996

Normandy. Benefices were administered by a group of men linked by ties of kinship and sociability.[65]

Undoubtedly the largest landholders in upper Normandy at the accession of Henri II were the Orléans-Longueville, a bastard offshoot of the Valois-Orléans who would figure so prominently in the province in the seventeenth century.[66] Their lands were situated principally in the Loire valley and the Beauce, where they possessed the comté of Dunois, and in Picardy. In the pays de Caux alone they possessed the duchy of Longueville and the comté of Tancarville. In 1534 Marie de Lorraine, the eldest daughter of Claude I de Guise, married Louis II d'Orléans, duc de Longueville and comte de Dunois.[67] As with Claude's own marriage, the Guise aimed to marry into princely houses associated with the royal family. This process legitimised their own claims to be true-born French princes and not foreigners. In 1536 Louis died, leaving Marie de Lorraine a widow with an infant son, François. Marie and her father managed to obtain the wardship of the young duke.[68] Control of his vast landed wealth yielded substantial opportunities for patronage and financial rewards; both Marie and Claude took a keen interest in the accounts and administration of the duke's household. In 1542 the wardship accounted for 9 per cent of Claude's income.[69]

The ramifications of this inter-family relationship became apparent after Marie's second marriage in 1538 to James V, king of Scotland. In 1542 the unfortunate Marie was again widowed. James left a daughter, Mary Stuart, and a legacy that began fifty years of Guise involvement in Scottish and English politics. Marie de Guise remained queen of Scotland, acting as regent from 1554 until her death in 1560.[70] In the person of Marie de Guise the fortunes of the houses of Stuart, Guise and Orléans-Longueville became interwoven. The household and followers of the Longueville now owed at least a nominal loyalty to the Guise, and the Guise reciprocally had to defend the interests of their kinsmen. Control of the Longueville household enabled the Guise to extend their own clientele beyond their traditional power base.[71] Moreover, the regency in Scotland could be exploited to reward men from both their retinue and that of the Longueville. As with the Brézé

[65] See below, pp. 85–8.

[66] AN M 458, Longueville, fo. 2; La Roque, *Histoire généalogique de la maison d'Harcourt*, i, p. 63.

[67] Anselme, i, p. 218.

[68] BN Pièces Originales 2165 fo. 1020.

[69] AN Q[1] 1374. The account of 1541 for the barony of Manéhouville was scrutinised by Guise himself. In their own accounts the Guise included money for the upkeep of the duc de Longueville. Jacques Girard, *trésorier et receveur des finances* for the duc de Longueville, received a payment of 1,200*l* by order of Marie de Guise in 1549: ADSM C 8182, 'Compte du duché de Longueville, 1549–50'. In 1554 Marie was receiving 13,000*l* per annum from her dower alone: M. Wood, ed., 'Foreign correspondence with Marie de Lorraine, Queen of Scotland, 1548–57', *Scottish Historical Society*, 3rd ser., 7 (Edinburgh, 1925), pp. xlviii, 1.

[70] G. Donaldson, *Scotland: James V–VII* (Edinburgh, 1978), pp. 70, 80–131.

[71] The Guise attracted clients from the Beauce region, where the Orléans-Longueville were large landholders. Jean de Brezolles, *maître de logis* of Longueville's company, moved in 1556 to occupy the same position in the company of the duc d'Aumale: Vindry, p. 284.

inheritance, the Guise increased their following and credit through their ties with another established family.

This complex tripartite relationship is illustrated by the career of one man in particular. Jacques de La Brosse was made infamous by his role in the massacre of Vassy in 1562 and a contemporary called him, 'une des créatures le plus dévouées de la maison de Guise'.[72] Jacques filled the highest positions in the household of the young duc de Longueville. As tutor of the duke from 1547 until 1551 and as lieutenant of the ducal company of the *ordonnance* he furthered the careers of his kinsmen. But his early career owed little to the Guise and he was already a renowned captain by the 1540s. His appointment by Marie de Guise was made at the behest of her senior councillors: *maître d'hôtel* Jean de Beaucaire and his brother François, *précepteur* of the future cardinal de Lorraine and later *aumônier* of Mary Stuart. La Brosse was originally from the Bourbonnais and a neighbour of the Beaucaire. In 1548 he was entrusted with the mission to bring Mary back from Scotland.[73]

La Brosse's blossoming career was cut short by the death of François duc de Longueville in 1551, shattering the dominant relationship established by the Guise over the Longueville. There was now no male heir and the inheritance passed to a cadet line of the Orléans family, which involved tortuous lawsuits between several families, including the Guise. This suit was partially settled in 1553, in favour of the new duc de Longueville, Léonor d'Orléans (1540–73) and his mother, Jacqueline de Rohan, marquise de Rothelin.[74] Although Guise control of the Longueville household was brought to an end, Léonor remained close to the Guise. When the previous duc de Longueville died in 1551 his household was broken up and La Brosse was forced to look around for alternative forms of service. He was important enough to be offered the royal post of *maître des requêtes* but rejected this, hoping to be offered something by the Guise as he informed the dowager queen: 'Madame, apres avoir seu la plus maleureuse nouvelle qui me povet avenir, qui est la mort de feu Monseigneur votre filz, pour lequel j'avois abandonne toustes auctres esperances, me suis en chemin pour m'an aler ver Messieurs voz freres entendre se que dois devenir.'[75] La Brosse solicited her intervention with irony: 'si vous plest vous escripres effeccionement a Monsieur et Madame et Messieurs voz freres car ilon assez de moien, et tout homme qui a la barbe grise ne puit longuement actendre'.[76]

La Brosse eventually received a position in the household of the duc de Guise,

[72] De Thou, iii, p. 454.

[73] Vindry, p. 98. La Brosse's lands bordered the Beaucaire's seigneury of Puyguillon: J. de La Brosse, *Histoire d'un capitaine bourbonnais au XVIe siècle: Jacques de La Brosse 1485–1562* (Paris, 1929), pp. 24, 131. On the 1548 mission: A. Teulet, *Relations politiques de la France et de l'Espagne avec l'Ecosse au XVIe siècle* (5 vols., Paris, 1862), i, p. 159, n. 1; G. Dickinson, ed., 'Two missions of Jacques de la Brosse', *Scottish Historical Society* , 3rd ser., 36 (Edinburgh, 1942).

[74] La Roque, *Histoire généalogique de la maison d'Harcourt*, i, p. 735.

[75] Wood, ed., 'Foreign correspondence with Marie de Lorraine', pp. 100–1.

[76] *Ibid*, pp. 290–1.

becoming one of its most important members. He was a *conseiller gentilhomme* and *maître d'hôtel* from 1552 until 1557 and thereafter lieutenant of the duke's *ordonnance* company (1556–8).[77] In 1558, the year of Mary Stuart's marriage to the dauphin, he was appointed governor to the heir to the throne and was lieutenant of his *ordonnance* company in 1559. After the dauphin was crowned François II, La Brosse received his own company, employing François de Lorraine, *grand prieur* and fifth son of Claude I de Guise, as his lieutenant.[78] Throughout he remained closely involved with affairs in Scotland and was one of the councillors of the dowager queen sent to Scotland in 1559 to shore up her tottering regime.[79]

Of crucial importance to the Guise interest in Scotland was the need for good sea communications, especially for the rapid transportation of troops and provisions. Thus the position of François de Lorraine, *grand prieur*, as *capitaine-général des galères* had added significance. The post was no sinecure: François, with his younger brother René as lieutenant, was heavily involved in the seaborne support of Guise-inspired operations in Italy. As early as 1554, the two young men commanded an expedition to Corsica.[80] In 1560, when reinforcements were sent to bolster the regime of the queen dowager in Scotland, the land forces were commanded by René and the fleet by François. They were reinforcing an expedition similarly full of Guise clients: La Brosse had previously been sent with his son Gaston and was appointed governor of Leith.[81] There were plenty of captaincies available for the ambitious.[82] Normandy and its seafaring community were crucial to Guise ambitions in Scotland. To maintain a viable presence there the transport of men and materials had to be undertaken by those with local expertise and credit. The strategic importance of Normandy to Guise dynastic ambitions is a recurring theme of the period between the 1540s and the end of the Wars of Religion. Normans entered Guise service and benefited from the patronage and esteem which the enterprises to Scotland bestowed.

Another case also exemplifies the provincial ramifications of international dynastic alliances. In 1549 François de Guise married Anne d'Este, daughter of Ercole d'Este, duke of Ferrara and Renée de France, daughter of Louis XII. Since 1528 the Este had enjoyed the usufruct of the royal *vicomtés* of Caen, Bayeux and Falaise.

77 BN MS Fr 22429 fos. 130, 136–7.

78 Vindry, p. 98.

79 BN MS Clairambault 353 fo. 156; Dickinson, ed., 'Two missions of Jacques de la Brosse', p. 52.

80 BN MS Fr 20467, Elbeuf to Guise, Toulon, 30 Jan 1554. His maritime exploits provide the theme for the poetry of Remy Belleau, in *Larmes sur le trespas de Monseigneur René de Lorraine, et de Madame Louyse de Rieux Marquis & Marquise d'Elbeuf. Ensemble le tombeau de Monseigneur François de Lorraine Duc de Guyse* (n.p., 1566).

81 Dickinson, ed., 'Two missions of Jacques de la Brosse', p. 52.

82 Corbeyran de Cardilliac, seigneur de Sarlabous, a respected Gascon captain, first served in Scotland in 1549. In the early 1550s he was captain of Dumbarton, returning to France to fight under the duc de Guise at the siege of Thionville in 1558. He fought again in Scotland in 1560 as captain of Dunbar and *maître de camp* of the French forces and was later governor of Le Havre from 1563 until his death in 1584: E. Forestié, *Un capitaine gascon au XVIe: Corbeyran de Cardaillac-Sarlabous* (Paris, 1897), pp. 26–72.

The privileges of the incumbents included the right to farm out the revenues, collect all royal dues and nominate to all offices, except those of the *bailli* and captain of Caen and the governor of Falaise.[83] Ercole d'Este was already comte de Gisors in Normandy part of the dowry given to Renée by François I at the time of their marriage in 1531. Anne d'Este received the comté of Gisors in turn, as part of her own dowry, retaining it when she remarried Jacques de Savoie duc de Nemours in 1566. She was still countess on her death in 1607.[84] The influence of the Este, so far away in northern Italy, could be felt only indirectly in Normandy, since the duke of Ferrara had little concern for affairs in provincial France. His affairs in Normandy and the administration of his possessions were left to local officials, and more important tasks such as the nomination of offices were entrusted to a council headed by the Este ambassador at court and the Guise.

There exists evidence to illuminate the workings of the council. The *procureur-général* of the duke of Ferrara in his Norman *vicomtés* was an Italian named Giulio Ravilio Rosso.[85] He was a reviled figure who, during the first religious war, levied contributions on the locally strong and influential Huguenot community. The letters patent enabling him to raise these special taxes were obtained 'à la recommendation du duc de Guise'.[86] Rosso had committed a variety of sins in the eyes of the local population; he was not only a foreigner and a tax collector but also a servant of the Guise and their allies. Rosso was finally besieged by a Huguenot force in the château of Bayeux in February 1563 and after capture he was taken to Caen and executed along with his men. Other officials of the Este also met a bloody end, including the hated *contrôleur du domaine*, Thomas Noël, a repentant Calvinist.[87] After failing with the Este ambassador, Pierre Rémon, the *premier président* of the parlement of Rouen, solicited the duc de Guise about one of the viscomital offices in 1551: 'Je vous ai supply me vouloir estre aydant à recouvrir l'office de lieutenant du bailly de Caen en son siège de Falaise par le moyen de lambassadeur du duc de Ferrara pour ung des mes proches alliez.'[88] The office was venal and Rémon wished it to remain in his family, despite excessive relief taxes demanded by the Este on the death of the incumbent. Rémon protested that the office was in the king's gift and that the 400 *écus* demanded as payment were excessive. In the end, however, he appealed to Guise's honour: 'le feu pere du gendre de ma femme avoit tenu ledit office et que les parens dudit deffunct desiroient lung des siens ou filz du gendre en ceste succession. Jay mis en arrive mondit don pour l'honneur de vous et de

[83] BN Cinq Cents Colbert 53 fo.121. Although this was only a temporary grant it was continued by order of Henri III in 1577: ADSM 1B 92, 8 Feb 1577.

[84] AN AP 300 I 552.

[85] Charles de Bourgeville, sieur de Bras, *Les Recherches et Antiquitez de Neustrie à présent duché de Normandie* (Caen, 1588), p. 184.

[86] De Thou, iv, p. 245.

[87] *Histoire ecclésiastique des églises réformées au royaume de France*, G. Baum and E. Caunitz eds. (3 vols., Nieuwkoop, 1974), ii, p. 416.

[88] BN MS Fr 20541 fo. 70, Rémon to Guise, Paris, 24 Feb 1551. See also BN MS Fr 20533 fo. 17, Rémon to Guise, 11 Oct 1550.

vostres.'[89] He invoked the name of Diane de Poitiers to ensure an emotional response: 'Je vous supplie treshumblement non par la valloir dudit office mais pour lesdites causes me permectre avec vostre bonne grace poursuyvre la provision du don qu'il a pleu feu Roy me faire à la requeste de madame de Valentinois.'[90] Rémon owed much to the duchess and through her he began to establish links with the Guise which strengthened as the decade progressed.[91] In effect, Guise acted as a broker of the patronage in the *vicomtés* – a vital link between those in Normandy and the Este.[92] This example further reveals the way in which provincial affairs were interwoven with wider supranational dynastic relationships.

The three *vicomtés* assigned to the Este were strongholds of Calvinism.[93] The absence of the Este from Normandy and lack of seigneurial authority created a vacuum of authority in which protestant vassals and tenants worshipped unmolested. Moreover, the identification of the Este with the unpopular regime of the Guise during the reign of François II (1559–60) and the presence of foreign officials like Rosso represented a source of discontent which the protestants turned to their advantage.

The Este provided little succour for the champions of orthodoxy. Their court at Ferrara was one of the most brilliant in Italy and they were among the early princely protectors of Lutheranism outside Germany. Renée de France, the wife of Ercole d'Este, attracted reform-minded Frenchmen to her court and one of them, Marot, became her secretary. This tolerant policy ended in 1554 – Renée was even imprisoned by her husband for her faith during the subsequent backlash. In 1559 she returned to France on the death of her husband and continued to work for the reformed faith until her own death.[94] During the early years of her marriage to Guise, Anne continued to support the reform privately but in 1557 her *aumônier*, a heretic preacher, was finally removed at her husband's insistence. She was horrified by the massacre of Vassy.[95] Thus the spread of protestantism in the three *vicomtés* was aided by the weakness of seigneurial authority and the knowledge that the Este were favourable to reform.[96] As religious conflict intensified in the early 1560s,

[89] BN MS Fr 20541 fo. 70, Rémon to Guise, Paris, 24 Feb 1551.

[90] *Ibid.*

[91] Rémon, who came from a Parisian background, was *premier président* of the parlement of Rouen from 1543 to 1553. He received many favours and offices from the duchesse de Valentinois. At the accession of Henri II he was introduced to the *conseil des affaires*, almost certainly at the instigation of the duchess. Rémon soon became closely involved with her protégés, assisting the Guise in the parlement of Rouen when the judges blocked alienations of royal domain to the Guise: Frondeville, *Présidents*, p. 48.

[92] Guise showed an interest in appointments to offices in the comté of Gisors handled by the council of the duchess of Ferrara: BN MS Fr 20533 fo. 83, Fumée to Guise, Paris, 6 Jan 1549.

[93] J. Wood, *The nobility of the élection of Bayeux, 1463–1666: continuity through change* (Princeton, 1980), p. 161.

[94] *Biographie universelle ancienne et moderne* (83 vols., Paris, 1811–53), xxxv, pp. 426–7.

[95] L. Taylor, *Soldiers of Christ: preaching in late medieval and renaissance France* (Oxford, 1992), p. 193; De Thou, iv, pp. 167–8. Her attitude hardened after her husband's assassination in 1563.

[96] The Este did not neglect their Norman interests completely. When the *ordonnance* company of

protestants accused rapacious and hated seigneurial officials of being agents of the Guise.

The La Marck, princes of the Holy Roman Empire whose lands straddled the border with France, were also a part of the configuration of Diane de Poitiers designed to counter Montmorency's overwhelming influence on Henri II.[97] Like the Guise they were *princes étrangers* and fitted into the same model as the houses of Lorraine and Este, being all anti-Habsburg allies of the Valois. In 1539 Robert IV de La Marck, duc de Bouillon, married Françoise de Brézé, and through the intervention of Diane de Poitiers was given the office of *maréchal* in 1547 and made governor of Normandy in 1552. Awarding this governorship to Bouillon was certainly a shift in royal policy since the *gouvernement* of the province had traditionally been reserved for a member of the royal family or a Norman.[98] A royal favourite, whose only link to Normandy was through his wife, thus became governor. On his death in 1556 he was followed by his son, Henri-Robert (1540–74). Neither was to have much influence in the province, a factor compounded by the sale of a significant share of the Brézé inheritance to the duc d'Aumale.[99] These sales were forced upon the family by misfortune. In 1553 Robert IV was captured by the Imperialists and ransomed for 60,000 *écus*.[100] The family was further damaged by the Peace of Cateau-Cambrésis in 1559 when, as part of the treaty, Bouillon was divested of some of his lands and the promised compensation from the French king was never forthcoming.[101] It was to his uncle Claude, duc d'Aumale, that Henri-Robert sold the barony of Bec Crespin in 1562 to offset these debts.

In 1561 the close relationship with the Guise was complicated by Henri-Robert's conversion to Calvinism. During his lifetime Jametz and Sedan would become notorious safe havens for his co-religionists.[102] His failure to receive compensation after Cateau-Cambrésis was symptomatic of his loss of favour at court after the disgrace of his patron, Diane, in 1559. In Normandy his credit was even lower, because he was an inexperienced youth forced to sell his lands and without influence at court. He visited the province only seldom: in 1558 he was sent to reorganise the defences of Dieppe; returning in 1561 and ordered to restrict the growth of heresy, he seemed only to tacitly endorse Calvinism.[103] Bouillon's power

admiral d'Annebaut was broken up on his death in 1552 many of its officers found service in the duke of Ferrara's company, for example François de Plainville and Gabriel de Longuemare: Vindry, p. 25.

97 For this and following comments see, J. de Chestret de Hanneffe, *Histoire de la maison de La Marck* (Liège, 1898), pp. 75–182.

98 Harding, *Anatomy of a power elite*, pp. 225. The preceding governors were Charles duc d'Alençon (1515–25), Louis de Brézé (1526–31), François the dauphin (1531–6), Henri the dauphin (1536–47) and Claude d'Annebaut (1547–52).

99 Benedict, *Rouen during the Wars of Religion*, p. 33.

100 BN Dossiers Bleus 426 fo. 99.

101 Chestret de Hanneffe, *Histoire de la maison de La Marck*, p. 178; BN MS Fr 20646 fo.163, Jean de La Marck to Henri II, Jametz, 29 Mar 1559.

102 C. Buvignier, *Jametz et ses seigneurs* (Verdun, 1861), p. 26.

103 ACR A 17, 14 May 1558; Floquet, ii, p. 326.

base remained in the Ardennes and he made little effort to build up a clientage network in Normandy. Not one of the officers of his company of the *ordonnance* was a Norman.[104] Despite the religious divide, there was no animosity between the Guise and the La Marck families. This continued amity with the Calvinist magnates was to have adverse consequences for the consolidation of protestantism in Normandy.

It has long been remarked that Normandy was one of the most important centres of French protestantism, and that the number of adherents was growing rapidly prior to the Wars of Religion. It is less well known that the family most associated with the suppression of heresy was also growing in influence in the province at the same time. The Brézé inheritance in particular, as well as the close relations with leading Norman magnates and the exigencies of campaigning in Scotland, had extended Guise power beyond the confines of Champagne. On the eve of the Wars of Religion the Guise following was growing and it was not confined to a small section of the aristocratic elite.

[104] Vindry, p. 318.

2

Clients and servants

During the last decade the landed wealth and the fortunes of magnate families in the sixteenth century has begun to attract serious academic interest. Magnate power was reflected in the numbers of clients who followed them. Despite the voluminous literature on the structure of the patron–client relationship, there still remains much work to be done on the profile, development and dissolution of specific followings. Until further research is undertaken on the structure of affinities and the patterns of faction within institutions, gaps will remain in our understanding of political society. This chapter sets out to identify some of the families which constituted the Guise power base in Normandy. Some discussion of clients' careers and complex family networks is unavoidable, and many of the families discussed below played a crucial role in the formation and leadership of a catholic party during the civil wars. Most important were the *noblesse seconde*, for which the records are comparatively abundant; but it is possible to go beyond consideration of this group, to discuss petty nobles, lawyers, merchants and churchmen. Multiple ties of service and kinship were important, encouraging constant communication among the household, the Parisian councils and local servants. The Guise affinity was not a hierarchically ordered entity directed by the duke at its apex. Rather, he and his kinsmen were the *focus* of attention and the bonds of affinity were complex and multifarious. Horizontal ties of sociability and kinship were as important as vertical bonds of deference, loyalty and material security.

COUNCILS, COUNSEL AND FAMILY STRATEGY

Political history has traditionally placed great emphasis on the importance of relations among individual magnates and on their freedom of action. The concept that family strategy was largely formulated by autonomous individuals is a legacy of nineteenth-century epistemology, which placed insufficient emphasis on the context in which historical actors made decisions and formulated strategy. The role of conflict, debate and accommodation within family and household needs to be addressed. The status of a magnate depended on the sum of his honour and the strength of his following. The strategy of a magnate was likely to be most successful when it secured the support of his followers. An understanding of the concept of counsel and a knowledge of the competence and composition of councils are fundamental to the study of political society. Little has been written about the role of councils in the formulation of either royal or magnate strategy.[1] The Guise governed their household and created institutions to manage their affairs on a pattern, smaller than, but similar to, that of the crown. For example, judicial councils needed a formal structure in order to be able to deal with the mass of cases in which great landowners were always embroiled. But councils were not bureaucratic institutions, hierarchically ordered and with specialised functions. Counsel was not confined to particular specialists – anyone who had the ear of a particular lord was in a position to give counsel. All recognised that good counsel was a prerequisite for wise government, and the 'evil counsellor' was a commonplace image in late-medieval and early modern political discourse. It is also possible to envisage conflicting counsel being given and the existence of a variety of opinions and factions within the council and household of a nobleman, just as in the court of the king.

Councils not only tied clients closer to their patron by involving them in the decision-making process, but they also allowed the lord to come into contact with a variety of opinions and experiences – so crucial in an age of poor communications. Moreover, because ties of loyalty were multiplicitous and prone to breakdown, a conciliar decision was a means of reaching a broad consensus on strategy, thus facilitating the maintenance of loyalty. Councils provided a vital link to the uncoordinated and disparate web of contacts and information upon which the Guise family depended. In order to understand the remarkable solidarity of the Guise family, it should be appreciated that councils were the means by which all family members shared in the formulation of family strategy. The duc de Guise was head of the house but, in the final analysis, family unity could be maintained only by consensus.

At the apex of the various councils were the great family conferences convened in order to discuss family strategy and high politics; such events attracted the interest of contemporary commentators. It was at Joinville, the family seat where the matriarchal Antoinette de Bourbon resided until her death in 1583, where the largest and most important family conferences were held. Given the secrecy and risks which surrounded family councils it is little wonder that there is insufficient documentation on the proceedings. The partisans of the Catholic League (most of the leaders of which were members of the Guise family) met at Joinville to discuss strategy in December of 1584 and again at Nancy early in 1588.[2] Both these meetings were succeeded by periods of heated political activity, culminating in open revolt against the crown. In January 1564 the entire family left court amid

[1] For preliminary considerations: S. Carroll, 'The Guise affinity and popular protest during the Wars of Religion', *French History*, 9 (1995), pp. 126–30. On the council of the duc de Nevers: Jean de Chandon, *Vie et testament*, P. Chandon de Briailles, ed. (Epernay, 1857).

[2] Constant, *Les Guises*, pp. 128, 162.

great tension for a conference at Joinville to discuss its future strategy in the pursuance of admiral Coligny for the murder of François duc de Guise.[3] The attempt to create a consensus within the family diminished the likelihood of future discord.

At the court of a magnate or prince lived his closest advisers and confidants. In the household accounts of the duc de Guise in the 1550s these men are referred to as *conseillers gentilshommes* and *chambellans*.[4] The principal officers of the duke's company of the *ordonnance* were also close counsellors. The composition of the ducal household in the 1550s, for which records survive, suggest that long-serving Champenois and Picard families were among the most senior counsellors.[5] Although the appointment of a Norman, Jacques Du Val, seigneur de Mondreville, as *chef de conseil* in the early 1580s reflects the reorientation of family interests, he was married to a wealthy Champenois heiress.[6] Senior counsellors were concerned with the formulation of policy rather than its execution and they exercised an important role in brokering ducal patronage. The details of administration were left to the sedentary councils of finance and legal affairs based in Paris. The competence of the senior council included all important matters ranging from political strategy to the acquisition and sale of land, but it probably did not involve itself in technicalities. Due to the secrecy surrounding these meetings, little is known about what transpired while they were in session. No minutes of formal meetings have survived and it is not even known if written records were kept. It is clear that memoirs were drawn up in council in order to advise the duke on a course of action. The most notorious such document, the treasonous memoir found on the body of the murdered duc de Guise in 1588, was probably a royalist propaganda device concocted in order to justify his murder.[7] A more credible document entitled 'Advis donné a Mons. de Guyse quand il revint a la cour apres les barricades' dates from July 1588.[8] This document suggests how the duke should act on his return to the royal court. It dispassionately sets out Guisard strategy for ensuring dominance at court: the maintenance of royal favour, the securing of high office and 'le troisieme qui provient de deux, assavoir que tout le reste des courtisans deppendent ou de l'affection quilz Vous porteront, ou de la crainte quilz auront de vostre aucthorite et grandeur'. The advice was Machiavellian, urging the duke to keep the king 'entre lamour et la crainte'. The success of the duke was contingent on the

[3] Pimodan, *La mère des Guises*, p. 220.

[4] BN MS Fr 22429 fos. 130–8.

[5] The Foissy, the des Boves, the Choiseul, the des Essars and the Hangest were important. Jean de Choiseul, baron de Lanques, and René de Choiseul, seigneur de Benapré, were *gentilhommes servans* from 1552 until 1560: *ibid.*, fos. 130–61. Pierre de Choiseul, seigneur d'Isché, had previously been *guidon* of Claude de Guise in 1544: Vindry, p. 282.

[6] A. Margry, *Pierre Séguin: ligueur, reclus et écrivain, 1558–1636* (Senlis, 1896), p. 10. The father of Jean Péricard, another Norman counsellor during the 1580s and 1590s, was originally from Troyes.

[7] BN MS Fr 17302 fo. 108.

[8] BN Cinq Cents Colbert 30 fo. 177. Pierre d'Epinac, archbishop of Lyons, is usually attributed with its authorship.

views of his family and followers: 'faire entendre à tous Messieurs voz parens et autres qui tiennent vostre party'. Councils usually deliberated matters and drew up memoirs of a more mundane nature. In 1582 an ordinance of Henri de Guise for the administration of the duchy of Guise was drawn up 'apres avoir faict veoir en nostre conseil l'estat de nostre duché sur le rapport de M. Laurent Compagnon'.[9]

In addition to the councillors who followed the ducal court, there existed sedentary finance and judicial councils based in Paris, dealing with affairs in the capital and acting as intermediaries for correspondence and information emanating from the provinces and overseas. A number of secretaries were resident in Paris; they handled the duke's correspondence and enjoyed substantial influence. In the 1550s the legal councillors were paid members of the household and the judicial council typically consisted of four *avocats* of the parlement of Paris, one *procureur* and one *soliciteur* at the parlement, and one *procureur* at the *chambre des comptes*.[10] Among the most famous of these councillors was Pierre Versoris who first appears as a paid member of the judicial council in 1563 and as a *conseiller* of the cardinal de Lorraine in 1567.[11] Letters survive which outline the membership of the Guise council in the parlement of Paris in the late 1540s and early 1550s. It was convoked by one of the ducal secretaries who played a key role in conducting business affairs in the capital and liaising with the duke. The judicial council included members of the most important Parisian *robin* families, and later came to form the nucleus of the ultra-catholic faction in the parlement.[12]

As well as the peripatetic family council and the sedentary councils in Paris, there were provincial and seigneurial councils, such as those established in Normandy by the Guise cadets. Charles duc d'Elbeuf established a council in Rouen to pursue his rights and its workings can be seen in the prosecution of errant vassals from 1577 onwards.[13] Most of the councillors were lawyers at the parlement of Rouen, headed by Jacques des Boulletz, *practicien* in the parlement 'ayant la conduite des affaires de Monseigneur le duc d'Elbeuf'.[14] In 1584 he presented documents to 'consulter et deliberer au conseil de monseigneur le duc d'Elbeuf' concerning the vicomté of La Carnaille. The surviving documents show that he was assisted by Jean du Vivier who first appears as an *avocat* in the parlement for the duke in 1577 and then as councillor in 1580, rising to the post of *intendant* in 1589.[15] He profited from the patronage of more than one member of the family, acting on

[9] AMC D 3, 11 Sep 1583.

[10] BN MS Clairambault 1204 fos. 57–75.

[11] BN MS Clairambault 816 fos. 188–9; AN MC VIII 370 fo. 594, 3 Oct 1567.

[12] BN MS Fr 20543 fo. 43, Richet to Guise, 24 Sep 1549; 20513 fo. 134, Antoine Le Cirier to Guise, Paris, 20 Nov 1552. Christophe de Thou was a religious moderate and scion of the greatest of *robe* families. *Conseiller* Edmond Boucherat, a pensioner of the duc de Guise, and *conseiller* Jean de Longueil, *procureur* of the cardinal de Lorraine, were denounced by Condé in 1562: *Les recusations envoyees en la cour de Parlement de Paris, contre aucuns des Presidans & Conseillers d'icelle, Par Monseigneur le Prince de Condé & ses associés* (n.p., 1562).

[13] ADC E 237, 238, 353.

[14] ADC E 237, 18 Dec 1584.

[15] *Ibid.*, 5 Mar 1577 and 16 Dec 1580; ADSM G 2176 fos. 199–200, 9 Mar 1588; 1B 699, 16 Oct 1589.

behalf of both the duc d'Aumale and the cardinal de Guise.[16] So too did Guillaume Valdory, who first entered Guise service in 1568 as a *procureur* of Aumale at the parlement of Rouen, and occupied the same position for Elbeuf and the chevalier d'Aumale in the 1580s.[17]

In 1571 Claude duc d'Aumale mentioned that, having received a memoir from Dauphiné, 'jay incontinent envoyez à mon conseil pour y avoir advis'.[18] Unfortunately little is known about his council which presumably met in Paris. In Rouen during the 1560s, the legal affairs of the duke were handled by three lawyers – Maromme, Colombel and Ango – whose families belonged to the city elite.[19] The Colombel held a variety of municipal offices while serving the Guise. Romain was *avocat* of the duc d'Aumale in the parlement during the 1560s, as well as 'bailli de Mauny, pensionnaire et conseiller ordinaire' of the cardinal de Lorraine.[20] Evidence for the jurisdiction and business of Aumale's council is difficult to find. In 1587 the duchesse d'Aumale was present in Rouen in order to install a new *procureur*. Etienne de Verdun was entrusted with full power to oversee cases in both the parlement and the *table de marbre*. He was the great nephew of the previous incumbent and 'antien serviteur de la maison d'aumalle', associated with the family since 1555.[21] This continuity was valuable: Verdun was undoubtedly familiar with the cases pending and the local officials with whom he would have to work and occasionally prosecute. The contract stipulated that all cases were to be pursued after deliberation and decisions to be 'faict par conseil'.

COUNCILS AND SERVANTS AT WORK

In 1548 François de Guise obtained letters patent from Henri II authorising the sale of royal domain up to a value of 10,000*l* of *rente*. This grant was part of the conditions of the marriage contract drawn up between François de Guise (at this stage still duc d'Aumale) and Anne d'Este.[22] The pursuit of the grant, much of which was assigned on royal domain in Normandy, soon occupied more time and money than the raising of the comté of Aumale into a *duché-pairie* in July 1547, not

16 ADSM 2E1 934 fo. 244v, 14 Jun 1588; 1B 701, 22 May 1590.

17 ADSM 1ER 1589, 12 Oct 1568; 1B 3857, 15 Jul 1580; 1ER 1940, 6 Mar 1591; 1B 2153, 5 Aug 1589.

18 BN MS Fr 3188 fo. 60, Aumale to Gaspard de La Châtre, 16 Oct 1571. Regnauld de Loyseau, brother of the celebrated jurist, was certainly a member: AN 300 AP I 215 'liasses d'anciennes procedures et constitutions faictes par les seigneurs d'anet depuis 1582', 27 Nov 1585; 224 liasse 11, 11 Nov 1572. The composition of the council of the chevalier d'Aumale included several longstanding family servants: AN MC VIII 391 fo. 266, 16 Feb 1583.

19 ADSM 1ER 1589.

20 *Inventaire-Sommaire des archives communales antérieures à 1790. Délibérations de la ville de Rouen*, C. de Robillard de Beaurepaire, ed. (Rouen, 1887), pp. 168, 247–58; ADSM G 6595, 27 Apr 1561.

21 ADSM 2E1 931 fo. 404, 16 Nov 1587.

22 Bouillé, i, p. 204; *Catalogue des actes de Henri II*, 1548, p. 457. The edict of alienation was registered in Paris on 4 March 1549 'de l'expres commandement du roi'.

long after Henri's accession. The resources of the family were stretched even further after 1550, following the death of the duc de Longueville and the complicated inheritance which ensued. These matters generated a substantial corpus of documents which enable us to observe the function of councils in their conduct of Norman affairs. Their competence inevitably included many financial measures, such as the buying and selling of land and the enforcement of seigneurial rights. The role of Antoine Le Cirier, dean of the cathedral of Notre-Dame de Paris and *conseiller* at the parlement of Paris, is clear. Le Cirier had previously served the Orléans-Longueville and his switch to Guise service was eased by his kinship ties to other ducal servants.[23] It is perhaps premature to identify Le Cirier as the *chef de conseil* in Paris since few letters by other parlementaires survive, but his responsibilities were extensive and not confined to affairs in the parlement. Despite his promotion to the see of Avranches, he continued to sit on the council of the cardinal de Lorraine in the 1560s.[24] The relationship between the council in Paris and the ducal servants in Rouen is hinted at in the correspondence among ducal servants in the late 1540s and 1550s. Most notable is initial evidence of the existence of a council in Rouen conducting Guise affairs in Normandy. Witness the *bailli* of Aumale, Jean de Martimbosc, writing from Rouen concerning the jurisdiction of the *haute justice* of Aumale: 'Nous en avons delibere avecq le conseil et advise aprez avoir parlé à Monsieur le Premier President.'[25]

This letter also confirms the close relationship that existed between the Guise and the *premier président* of the parlement of Rouen, Pierre Rémon. In the years following this letter another senior magistrate, *président à mortier* Louis Pétremol, was to become closely involved in the affairs of the Guise. Pétremol, like Rémon, came to the attention of the Guise through their mutual links with the Brézé family, his father having been *receveur* of the comté of Maulevrier in 1490.[26] He was given a dispensation by his colleagues in Rouen, permitting him to help the duc de Guise with the lawsuits pending in the parlement of Paris. It is no surprise to find Pétremol giving the oration at the entry of the cardinal de Lorraine into Rouen in September 1550. After the ceremonies and the official banquet he was reported to have consulted the cardinal on several matters. In 1560 he was responsible for organising the *entrée* of Mary Stuart.[27] His brother, Antoine, *maître des comptes* in Paris, was named in the edict of alienation as a commissioner for the administration

[23] BN MS Fr 20470 fo. 73, A. Le Cirier to Guise, Paris, 3 Oct 1551. He had been a pensioner of the cardinal d'Orléans and the duc de Longueville. On their demise Le Cirier was compensated by receiving ecclesiastical benefices from the cardinal de Lorraine.

[24] Along with his godson Pierre Versoris: AN MC VIII 370 fo. 594, 3 Oct 1567; BN Dossiers Bleus 188 fo. 10.

[25] BN MS Fr 20548 fo. 59, Martimbosc to Guise, Rouen, 23 Mar 1548. 'Guise' in these letters refers to François de Lorraine who did not take the title duc de Guise until his father's death in 1550 – I have reduced his name and title to Guise for the sake of clarity.

[26] Frondeville, *Présidents*, p. 176.

[27] ADSM 1B 91 fo. 49; G. A. Prévost, ed., *Recueil des presidents, conseillers et autres officiers de l'échiquier et du parlement de Normandie par Bigot de Monville, 1499 à 1550* (Rouen and Paris, 1905), p. 48.

of the grant, facilitating communications between the ducal council in Paris and its agents in Rouen.[28]

The success of family strategy was dependent on the advice and the diligence of servants. The functioning of the Guise affinity in Normandy can be reconstructed from the correspondence of Pétremol and *conseiller* Augustin Le Cirier, brother of Guise's *chef de conseil* in Paris. The burden of work was further increased in 1551 with the death of the young duc de Longueville and the complicated succession which ensued. Nevertheless, the major issue remained the sale of the royal domain, beginning in 1548 and ending in 1556, when the relevant correspondence comes to an abrupt halt.

As early as August 1548 Roland Trexot was commissioned, at the instance of the council in Rouen, to measure and record the lands and rights for sale in the *vicomté* of Bayeux, pertaining to the royal gift to Guise.[29] Trexot was a *conseiller* at the parlement of Rouen and his appointment was partly due to his local knowledge, as he possessed lands near Bayeux. By November of the same year Louis Pétremol was receiving documents for the *procès-verbal*, concerning the sale of fiefs in the *bailliage* of Evreux.[30] It was also about this time, when the royal edict sanctioning the alienation of domain had to be sent for registration to the appropriate sovereign courts, that problems began to arise, forcing Guise to mobilise all his influence and resources in Rouen in order to achieve a satisfactory outcome. On 20 February 1549 Pétremol informed the duke that he had learned from his brother that the *chambre des comptes* had refused to register the royal command 'jusques à ce quelles soient verifées en ceste court de parlement à Rouen'.[31] The objections of the parlement of Rouen were outlined in its 'Remonstrance touchant le Domaine du Roy baillé a M. d'Aumale pour l'argent de son mariage'. The parlement put itself forward as the protector of the royal domain, which was inviolable since: 'le Roy ne peut bailler les terres en son domaine appartenans à sa Dignité Royale, qui sont inalienables . . . ladite obligation [the debt towards the d'Este] est personnelle et n'a peu abstraindre la Dignité Royale'.[32] Another factor which troubled the parlementaires was the transfer of so many tenants from the king to the Guise and the consequent increased power of seigneurial over royal courts. The parlementaires were less altruistic and uncompromising than their remonstrances to the king at first suggest and opposition was overcome by June.[33] The Guise faction in the parlement was able to ensure registration: undoubtedly some profited from bribes and others would benefit in the future from legal fees and as commissioners for the alienation.

[28] Another family associated with the Brézé, the Brevedent, was also playing a role in the legal and administrative affairs of the Guise: BN MS Fr 20534 fo. 45, Louis Pétremol to Guise, Rouen, 6 Jun 1549.

[29] BN MS Fr 20542 fo. 6, Trexot to Guise, Rouen, 26 Aug 1548.

[30] BN MS Fr 20553 fo. 22, Pétremol to Guise, Rouen, 6 Nov 1548.

[31] BN MS Fr 20538 fo. 69, Pétremol to Guise, 20 Feb 1549.

[32] BN Cinq Cents Colbert 54 fo. 70, 8 Feb 1549.

[33] BN MS Fr 20534 fos. 45–6.

The *chambre des comptes* in Paris was more stubborn in its protection of the royal domain. In September 1549 it was reported that royal *lettres de cachet* would be needed to obtain a satisfactory outcome. Although the parlement of Paris registered the edict in March, there continued to be opposition and obstruction six years later 'à la suscitation et menee de quelques ungs qui . . . ont trouvé moien pour interrompre vostre don et pensent vous envoyer de longue poursuicte et attente'.[34] The expenses of the council were high due to the need to pay the appropriate legal fees and to survey the land. Secretary Richet warned the duke that 'il fauldra faire quelques fraiz et despence pour aller sur les lieux qui voullez avoir et y mener gens de vostre conseil pour entendre que la valleur s'il y aura riens este allienė depuis l'an 1543'.[35] This work could be arduous. In July 1554 Richet visited each of the seven *vicomtés* of the duchy of Alençon, in order to check on the progress of the commissioners.[36]

The extent to which François de Guise became embroiled in the factional manoeuvring in Rouen is clear. He was able to build up support for the sale of the royal domain by outright bribery and by patronage involved in the lucrative contracts and commissions for the sale of the land. He was kept informed of developments but devolved details and appointments to men with local knowledge and contacts. Commissioners received royal letters and were ostensibly agents of the king but the sales of land were directed by the ducal council. Robert Vauquelin, for example, was made 'procureur-general sur le faict des fiefs en Normandie' and agents were allocated to different regions of the province.[37] These were lucrative offices and an important source of patronage. Nicholas Caillot was advanced 100 *écus* on his appointment as commissioner for Gisors and Trexot received 6,000*l* towards the costs of the *procès-verbaux* in his region.[38] The agents forecast that huge sums of money would accrue from the sales, exaggerations that were designed to maintain the duke's interest and entice him into spending more money with the sweet promise of fantastic returns. Estimates of the value of land in the *vicomté* of Rouen ranged from 80,000 *francs* to 120,000*l*.[39] This crock of gold obscured the problems posed by the many 'opposantz' of the sales and the 'subterfuges des contredisans' as Trexot called them.[40] Claims and counter-claims were made to

[34] BN MS Fr 20554 fo. 43, Richet to Guise, Rouen, 23 Dec 1555.

[35] BN MS Fr 20543 fo. 43, Richet to Guise, Paris, 24 Sep 1549.

[36] BN MS Clairambault 347 fo. 264, Richet to Guise, 15 Jul 1554.

[37] *Ibid.*, fo. 258, Vauquelin to Guise, Rouen, 2 Jul 1554. Trexot had been active in lower Normandy for some time. Vauquelin's kinsman, Antoine Caradas, bourgeois of Rouen, was designated as 'procureur du roy pour le faict des fiefs au bailliage de Gisors'. Nicholas Caillot, *avocat* at and later a *conseiller* of the parlement, was appointed commissioner for Gisors, and also acted as a financial agent for the duc d'Aumale. Montague du Vivier supervised land sales in the Perche and the lieutenant-general of the duchy of Alençon was appointed in Alençon: *ibid.*, fo. 264, Richet to Guise, 15 Jul 1554; BN MS Fr 20554 fo. 132, du Vivier to Guise, 24 Feb 1556; ADSM 2E1 313, 7 Sep 1556; 318, 25 Nov 1558; 323, 12 Aug 1561.

[38] BN MS Clairambault 347 fo. 264, Richet to Guise, 15 Jul 1554.

[39] BN MS Clairambault 348 fo. 136, Caradas to Guise, Rouen, 7 Jun 1555.

[40] BN MS Fr 20538 fo. 43, Trexot to Guise, Caen, 10 Feb 1549.

pieces of land and to their rights and privileges, in the hope of being bought off by the duke and sharing in his bounty. Problems were envisaged in the *bailliage* of Gisors as early as November 1548, since it formed part of the apanage of the duchess of Ferrara.[41] Trexot found himself 'bien empesché' by 120 *procès* he faced in lower Normandy.[42] The actual money received by the ducal treasury is impossible to estimate, but the returns seem to have been disappointing in relation to expectation and expenditure. A letter of June 1555 makes it clear that Trexot's sales had realised only 4,200*l* after four years of effort.[43]

By this date the duc de Guise had been pursuing the affair for nearly seven years. The whole matter was starting to cause more trouble and expense than it was worth. As 1555 drew to a close the continuing problems were exacerbated by the Longueville inheritance which had dragged on for four years. In December, Richet went to Rouen in person and wrote back in a worried manner: 'Monseigneur, jay entendu que luy vous a faict desgoulter de ces deux affaires et qu'estez sur le poinct de les quicter.'[44]

Little is known about the nature of the lawsuits fought out in the courts of Normandy concerning the land sales. The level of chicanery, deals and bribery can only be imagined. In protecting the royal patrimony the petty royal officials in the localities may have been more immune to Guise influence than senior magistrates. After all they were, in a sense, protecting their own livelihood. Jean d'Erneville, *lieutenant des gardes de forêts* of Evreux, Conches and Breteuil, was one of many royal officials who brought cases against the sale. This lawsuit dragged on especially after the case was evoked to the *chambre des comptes* in Paris. Pétremol was left in a quandary about how to proceed.[45] Occasionally a letter hints at more sinister activities. Secretary Brunet was sent from Paris to the aid of Guise agents, including a Norman household officer, Nicolas d'Osmont, who was being held prisoner by the parlement of Rouen:

> Jay veu le sieur d'Osmont prisonnier en la maison d'un huissier. Qui pour le desire et affection qu'il a de vous faire treshumble service m'a faict communiquer des faicts contenu en deux memoires . . . Et pour ce que ceulx qui les m'ont baillez craignent estre descouvertz de messieurs de la chambre des enquetes de Rouen . . . ils vous prient humblement . . . que lesdites memoires qu'ils m'ont baillez escripre de leur main ne viennent à la cognoissance de ceulz qui ont donné les arretz et jugements derniers.[46]

Osmont was one of the few Normans at the centre of the ducal entourage and had in conjunction with Pétremol originally presented the letters patent to the parlement

[41] BN MS Fr 20543 fo. 19, Richet to Guise, Melun, 8 Nov 1548.
[42] BN MS Clairambault 347 fo. 258, Vauquelin to Guise, Rouen, 2 Jul 1554.
[43] BN MS Fr 20545 fo. 37, Jesse Delalando, *receveur-général*, to Guise, Caen, 11 Jun 1554.
[44] BN MS Fr 20554 fo. 43, Richet to Guise, Rouen, 23 Dec 1555.
[45] BN MS Fr 20519 fo. 94, Pétremol to Guise, Rouen, 18 Feb 1553.
[46] BN MS Clairambault 348 fo. 141, Brunet to Guise, Paris, 9 Jun 1555.

of Rouen in 1549.[47] He was released from captivity and lost no time in writing to illustrate to the duke the great expense that he had undertaken, telling the duke that recently: 'il est vacqué ung greffe des esleuz de bernay ou il ne y a que xxv*l* de gaiges. Je vous supplye treshumblement votre bonté me le faire donner du Roy pour rescompense despertes et despences que je ay toutte ma vie faicte en son service.'[48]

Guise had to employ a circle of expert counsellors and a large group of servants due to the complexities of the land sales and the multitude of lawsuits. Magistrates in the sovereign courts had to be courted and bribed. Inevitably, he was the object of a host of requests for offices and favours. This was partly a reflection of Guise eminence at court after 1547. In addition, his need to employ agents directly in Normandy and the requirement to maintain a viable faction in the various law courts meant that he had to be especially sensitive to appeals for favour. These solicitations came both from those who were already in his service and from those who sought to exchange their goodwill for concrete rewards. The Pétremol, Pierre Rémon and Antoine Le Cirier were crucial to Guise fortunes in Normandy; their position gave them leverage to extract rewards. The duc de Guise secured the cooperation of *premier président* Rémon, whose chief patron was Diane de Poitiers, through patronage of his kinsmen. In 1550 Guise had procured an appointment to the *fauconnerie du roi*. Two years later Rémon beseeched the duke to intercede on behalf of his relative for a more lucrative post in the *fauconnerie* and to retain him as a *serviteur domestique*. As Rémon made clear, the bestowal of this office was both an exchange of honour and crucial to his kinsman's maintenance: 'acroistre et augmenter son estat par le moien dessusdict de votre bon plaisir sera affin qu'il ayt meilleur moyen de s'entretenir au service dudict seigneur [the king] et aussy vous en faire comme luy et moy desirans . . . en avoir le moien'.[49]

When Rémon died in 1553 the king was eagerly solicited by courtiers over the successor. Guise found himself faced with two conflicting candidates from amongst his own close contacts. Antoine Pétremol wrote in support of his brother, Louis, asking Guise to intercede with the king.[50] Antoine Le Cirier advanced another candidate, an official at the court.[51] In the event neither was successful. The family did not present a united front on the issue: Antoinette de Bourbon and François de Guise backed Pétremol, for which they were generously thanked with pledges of

[47] Osmont was one of the *gentilhommes servans* in the household from 1552 until 1557: BN MS Fr 22429 fos 130, 136, 140, having served in the household of the cardinal de Lorraine in 1547. Pierre d'Osmont, listed in the *arrière-ban* of 1552, was also in the household of the duke: E. Travers, ed., *Rôle du ban et de l'arrière-ban du bailliage de Caen en 1552* (Rouen and Paris, 1901), p. 110; BN MS Fr 20649 fo. 147, Osmont to Guise, Rouen, 6 Mar 1549; T. Courtaux and the marquis de Touchet, *Histoire générale de la maison de Touchet* (Paris, 1911), p. 45.

[48] BN MS Fr 20529 fo. 134, Osmont to Guise, 10 Jan 1558.

[49] *Ibid.*, fo. 142, Rémon to Guise, Villers-Cotterets, 9 Sep 1552.

[50] BN MS Fr 20544 fo. 73, A. Pétremol to Guise, Paris, 1 Jun 1553.

[51] *Ibid.*, fo. 75, Le Cirier to Guise, Paris, 1 Jun 1553.

future loyalty and service, but the cardinal de Lorraine was committed to another candidate.[52] Le Cirier also sought his own advancement. He put himself forward unsuccessfully for the office of *conseiller* at the parlement of Rouen; having previously received the support of Diane de Poitiers he solicited Guise.[53]

The Guise correspondence illustrates the symbiotic relationship between patron and client, evident from the tangible rewards accruing to both in the relationship.[54] The myriad obstructions facing the Guise meant agents had to be directly employed. A large affinity was not simply the reflection of a magnate's power but essential for the execution of any task. The power of local decision-making and appointment was devolved to a small group of *robins* in Paris and Rouen. Unfortunately, the correspondence dealing with the sale of land in Normandy ends in 1556 and it is not known what became of the royal gift, although after seven years the duke was beginning to despair. As late as February 1556 the parlement of Rouen was still blocking royal commands sponsored by the Guise, prompting Pétremol to ask the duke to seek more direct royal intervention.[55] Perhaps the duc de Guise was losing interest in the whole affair, as he prepared in the winter of 1556–7 to campaign in Italy. However, the status of the Guise at court and their close involvement with provincial Norman affairs raised the family's influence to new heights in the province.

HOUSEHOLD AND COMMENSAL OFFICERS

The core of an affinity consisted of those physically closest to the patron: those who served at his table and gave counsel and who were prepared to risk their lives for him or her. The two institutions which supported these noble servants were the household and the military retinue. It would be misleading to differentiate between household and military officers; the officers in a company of the *ordonnance* were effectively commensal officers, even if they did not hold formal office in the household. The major difference was that the household was supported by the lord, and the military retinue, whether company of the *ordonnance*, light cavalry bodyguard or company of foot, was funded primarily from royal coffers. In 1556 the formal paid household of the duc de Guise totalled some 159 persons, rising to 164 in 1561.[56] During wartime his company of the *ordonnance* numbered 100 lances or some 250 men. Such a retinue would have been further swelled by those who had

[52] *Ibid.*, fo. 117, A. Pétremol to Guise, Paris, 1 Aug 1553. Louis Pétremol always professed his loyalty: *ibid.*, fo. 40, Pétremol to Guise, Rouen, 20 Dec 1555, spending 'xxv ans au service du roy du vostre et de la justice'.

[53] BN MS Fr 20551 fo. 9, Le Cirier to Guise, Paris, 15 Jun 1553.

[54] Antoine Le Cirier also hoped to receive something from the spoils of the Longueville inheritance: BN MS Fr 20470 fo. 73, A. Le Cirier to Guise, Rouen, 3 Oct 1551.

[55] BN MS Fr 20554 fo. 103, Pétremol to Guise, Rouen, 10 Feb 1556.

[56] Harding, *Anatomy of a power elite*, p. 27. In 1561 there were 129 members of the household of the cardinal de Lorraine, costing 16,510*l*: BN MS Clairambault 1204 fos. 83–6.

never appeared on any payment roll: hangers-on and the host of professions from pages to prostitutes which serviced the lord's retinue.

The absence of accounts for Henri de Guise's household makes analysis of his patronage speculative. Normans occupied more senior positions in his household than under his father. In addition to the growing influence of Normans on his council, of three commensal officers identified in the 1570s two were of important Norman families and the other originated from the Norman–Picard marches. Nevertheless, the duke's *ordonnance* company was overwhelmingly Champenois in origin and recruitment of gendarmes in Normandy was left to his cousins.[57] The composition of the households of the cardinals de Lorraine and de Guise reflected their importance as great Norman lords.[58] A study of the household of Charles cardinal de Lorraine reveals how service was reinforced by kinship links and how client families benefited from the patronage dispensed by various family members.

In the 1560s the best paid and most intimate servants of the cardinal de Lorraine were the *camériers* who slept in his bedchamber.[59] This office perhaps reflects the cardinal's well-documented fears for his personal safety. Gabriel de La Vallée was the most senior of these men. Information concerning him is scarce but he was among the most important Guise servants during the Wars of Religion, and was the highest-paid member of the cardinal's household. Brantôme described him as the 'grand gouverneur' of the cardinal.[60] An examination of his kinship ties suggests that his origins were either Vexin or Beauceron. The earliest record of his service begins in 1540 when he appears as a *gentilhomme* in the household of Claude duc de Guise. Sometime after 1544 and before the beginning of the Wars of Religion he married the wealthy Briois heiress, Anne de Brinon. By this marriage he acquired a landed interest in the region to the north-east of Provins; he was *bailli* and captain of Sens until 1560, the same year as he first appears as a *camérier* in the cardinal's household.[61]

Gabriel had close kinship ties to his two fellow *camériers*, Gilles d'Abos and Denis des Fossez, both landowners in Normandy and the Vexin (see figure 2.1).[62] The three families were united by ties of common service and marriage. When his

57 Apart from the counsellors already mentioned, the Normans were Magdelon d'Espinay, lieutenant of the Guise company (1556); Etienne de Morainville, *maître d'hotel* (1540–50); Nicolas d'Osmont, *gentilhomme* (1552–6); Louis du Bosc, *chambellan* (1580–7); Guillaume Vipart, page (1570). The Picard, Jacques de Biencourt, *gentilhomme ordinaire* in 1575, was a vassal of the duchy of Aumale and son of the captain of Aumale.

58 For example: Jean de Rouville, *écuyer* of the cardinal de Lorraine (1561–4); François de Venois, *écuyer* (1564); Eustache d'Espinay de Saint-Luc, *protonotaire* (1561–4); Nicholas Martel, *gentilhomme* (1570); Pierre Morin, *écuyer* of the cardinal de Guise (1581).

59 BN MS Clairambault 1204 fos. 83, 89.

60 Brantôme, vii, p. 228.

61 BN MS Fr 8181 fo. 272v; C. Haton, *Mémoires*, F. Bourquelot, ed. (2 vols., Paris, 1857), i, p. 282. Royal letters sanctioning his resignation of the office of *bailli* were witnessed by the cardinal: *Catalogue des actes de François II*, M.-T. de Martel, ed. (2 vols., Paris, 1991), i, p. 216.

62 The governorships of Mantes and Meulan were dominated by these families in the 1560s and 1570s: BN Dossiers Bleus 1 fo. 1; 277 fo. 2; Collection du Vexin 17 fo. 150.

first wife died childless in 1569, La Vallée made a will instituting his nephew, Denis des Fossez, as principal heir on the condition that he adopt the La Vallée name and arms.[63] Des Fossez had begun his career as the *maître d'hôtel* of the cardinal de Lorraine in 1549 and in 1563 he married Gilles d'Abos's sister. By 1567 he was *sous lieutenant* of the young Henri duc de Guise.[64] Kinship ties continued to be strengthened during the 1570s. Sometime before 1577 La Vallée and Abos became brothers-in-law when they married two of the heiresses of a Norman–Vexin family, the Morainvilliers-Vipart.[65] Following the death of the cardinal de Lorraine in 1574, the tripartite grouping remained an important component of the affinity. La Vallée continued his close contacts; he bought *rentes* from the duc de Guise and appears in a contract of 1577 as his *procureur-général*. Denis des Fossez acted as guarantor for the duke in 1582. Gilles d'Abos was the governor of the future Louis II cardinal de Guise in the 1560s, and by 1580 was *gentilhomme ordinaire* in the cardinal's household.[66]

The geographical diversity of the households of the senior line may be underlined by reconstructing the careers and kin networks of these men. La Vallée remained involved in Briois society throughout the Wars of Religion, being elected to represent Provins at the Estates-General in 1588. But on the death of his wife most of the Briois possessions passed to her daughter by her first marriage. Thereafter, he divided time between his remaining possessions in the Brie and his kinsmen living in the Vexin and the Beauce.[67]

The kinsmen of senior commensal officers formed the nucleus of the households of the Norman branches of the house of Guise. The socialisation of the young princes took place in an environment dominated by the loyal familiars of their parents and elder brothers. On the death of Claude de Guise in 1550, Etienne de Morainville was appointed tutor of René d'Elbeuf. Etienne had been one of the few Norman members of the Guise household. He began his career as a man-at-arms of the duc de Guise in 1534, rising to *maître d'hôtel* in the 1540s. His lands bordered those of the marquis in the Roumois and his election to the provincial estates in 1551 suggests a man who enjoyed local influence. During the Wars of Religion his relatives formed a subgroup in the marquis's gendarmerie company.[68] Thus René

63 AN MC VIII 373 fo. 600, 16 Aug 1569. Gabriel died in 1596.

64 BN MS Fr 32867 fo. 1110; Dossiers Bleus 277 fos. 1–6; Pièces Originales 1207 nos. 3–12.

65 AN MC VIII 382 fo. 871, 21 Dec 1577.

66 AN MC VIII 388 fo. 718, 17 Aug 1581; 390 fo. 370 12 Sept 1582; 391 fo. 609, 16 May 1583; Chenaye-Desbois, i, p. 24. These families were not exclusively servants of the Guise. Montmorency influence was also strong in the Vexin. Gilles d'Abos left Guise service in 1581 to become an officer in the company of Montmorency-Damville, and his father had served as a man-at-arms of Coligny in 1557 and later as the ensign of Montmorency-Méru: BN Dossiers Bleus 1 fos. 1–24.

67 Haton, *Mémoires*, i, p. 639. In 1577 he was living at Etampes, near to his de L'Isle cousins. The following year he was residing at Montainville which bordered the lands of the des Fossez in the Vexin. In 1581 he was living near Provins: AN MC VIII 382 fo. 871, 21 Dec 1577; 386 fo. 296, Apr 1579; 387 fo. 129, 23 Feb 1581.

68 *Délibérations de la ville de Rouen*, p. 174; BN Pièces Originales 2041 no. 8; ADSM 2E1 304, 9 Oct 1550; 877, 11 Jul 1560; 350, 19 Feb 1575.

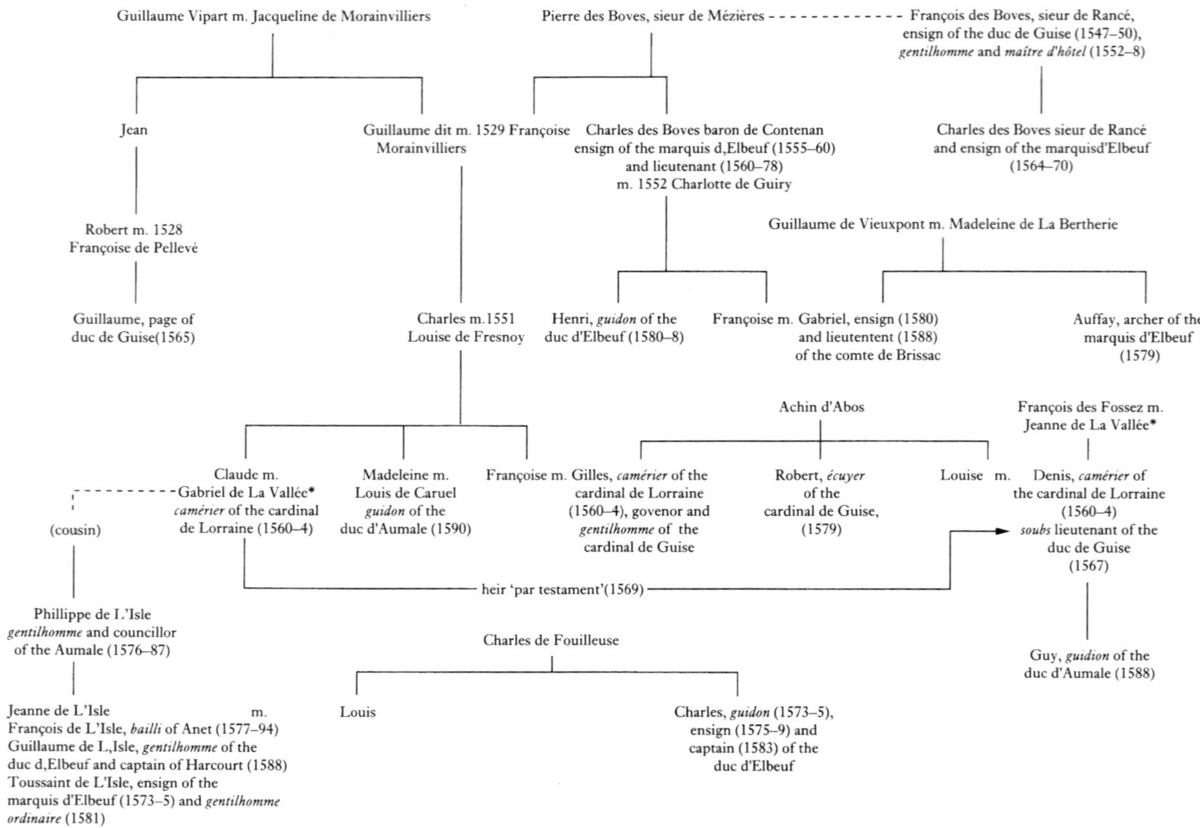

Figure 2.1 Some kinship networks in the various households of the house of Guise

not only received the lands of his father, but he also inherited established networks of clients and influence.

Figure 2.1 demonstrates that the household of the young René marquis d'Elbeuf was a focus for many longstanding Guise servants. After the death of Morainville, his household was dominated for the remainder of the sixteenth century by a single family, the des Boves. Originally from Champagne, they constituted a key component of the ducal household in the 1540s. The marriage strategy of the des Boves orientated them to other client families in the Vexin. Françoise des Boves married Guillaume de Morainvilliers-Vipart, *bailli* and captain of Mantes, who died in 1533.[69] Her younger brother, Charles baron de Contenan, married a Vexin heiress and soon rose to prominence, first as ensign (1555–60) and then as lieutenant (1560–78) of the Elbeuf gendarmerie company. The Champenois branch of the des Boves was represented by Charles, seigneur de Rancé and ensign of the company from 1564 to 1570.[70] The structure of Elbeuf's household thus supported and extended the traditional interest in eastern France, as well as symbolising the growing influence of the family in the Vexin. Indeed, his household and company of the *ordonnance* initially provided patronage opportunities for his mother and elder brothers.

René's son, Charles, inherited and continued to employ the servants of his father. But after reaching his majority in the mid-1570s, he established a council and household which reflected his Norman connections. From the early 1580s Charles de Sarcilly, sieur d'Ernes, *premier maître d'hôtel* and *intendant* of the duc d'Elbeuf was the most important ducal representative in Normandy.[71] His entry into ducal service was not fortuitous. He claimed descent from the house of Lorraine, being the son of Jean and Catherine, *batârde* de Lorraine. The family was well patronised by the Lorraine. The younger sister of Charles, Marguerite, was *fille d'honneur* and *dame d'atours* of Louise de Lorraine, daughter of the duc de Lorraine, and on her marriage at Nancy in 1573 she received 6,000 *florins* from the duc de Lorraine and a total of 10,000 *florins* from the cardinals de Guise and de Lorraine.[72] The office of *intendant* was increasingly important in the later sixteenth century: Sarcilly was expected to oversee and work with the duke's council and officials in Normandy, though no documentation concerning his duties survives before 1589 when he resided in Rouen in order to supervise the affairs of his patron. In 1593 Jacques des Boulletz, head of the judicial council in Rouen, brought a lawsuit against him for non-payment of 100 *écus*. Good lordship required the

[69] Guillaume Vipart, a Norman, was the sole heir of his uncle Louis de Morainvilliers, assuming his name and arms in 1512. He held lands close to Anet and Ivry in the Vexin Français and Vexin Normand. As illustrated in figure 2.1, the granddaughters of Guillaume and Françoise all married high-ranking Guise servants: E. Réaux, *Histoire des barons de Maule* (Paris, n.d.); F.-A. de Vipart, *Généalogie de la maison de Vipart* (n.p., 1751).

[70] Vindry, p. 304; BN Dossiers Bleus 127 fo. 7v.

[71] ADSM 2E1 365, 14 Feb 1582. He was especially important during the Catholic League and the reconstruction of the duke's estates after the Wars of Religion. Charles's younger brother, Philippe, was *maître d'hôtel* in 1588.

[72] ADC 2E 882, 'Généalogie de la Maison de Sarcilly'.

accommodation of disputes between client families.[73] Despite being an exclusively Norman lord, Charles d'Elbeuf maintained his historic ties to eastern France by marrying a Burgundian and employing 'easterners'. This policy ensured the continued interdependency between his following and those of his cousins. For example, the captain of Elbeuf's bodyguard was the brother-in-law of the captain of the duc de Guise's bodyguard, and both men were Burgundians.[74]

The independent household established by the duc d'Aumale in the 1550s reflects his position as a major landholder in Normandy. His most senior Norman councillor Charles de La Menardière, *maître d'hôtel* from 1551 until 1568 and *intendant* in 1568, provides further evidence of the large Brézé component in his retinue. La Menardière's appointment was at the recommendation of Aumale's mother-in-law, Diane de Poitiers.[75] The Aumale household shrank on Claude's death in 1573. In 1574, when his young heir Charles was a student at the University of Pont à Mousson, it comprised only thirty-two persons, including two *gentilhommes de la chambre* and one *maître d'hôtel*, at a cost of 15,000 *francs.* It was then being run by the duke's uncle and guardian, the cardinal de Lorraine, who appointed the *bailli* of the bishopric of Metz (of which the cardinal was bishop) as *gouverneur et surintendant.*

Once again the composition of the household of a cadet line of the house was largely determined by the interests of the senior line. The origin of the household members is difficult to establish since only the toponymics are listed, but only one man represented the ducal power base in Normandy. The most important member of the household was his *valet de chambre* Charles de Lorraine, second son of the duc de Mercoeur.[76] The two men were to remain close friends after university, an alliance that had begun when the duc de Mercoeur took Catherine de Lorraine, daughter of Claude duc d'Aumale, as his third wife in 1569. On his majority duke Charles augmented the Norman contingent in his household, reflecting his landed power base and political interests. In the 1580s, of seven men identified four were Norman.[77]

[73] ADSM 1B 706, 11 May 1593. The duc de Guise brokered an accord between René de Maugiron and Charles des Boves in 1560: Brantôme, vi, p. 369.

[74] Jean de Boyer was raised as a page in the household of the cardinal de Lorraine, rising to become *maître d'hôtel* and captain of the bodyguard of Elbeuf. In 1588 he married Minerve de Sémur, sister of the captain of the guards of the duc de Guise: BN Dossiers Bleus 127 fo. 2; AN MC VIII 401 fo. 228, 28 Feb 1588.

[75] ADSM 2E1 313, 7 Sep 1556; 323, 12 Aug 1561; 341, 11 Sep 1570, Nov 1570. Charles's father, Bertrand, had been *bailli* and captain of Caen: Chenaye-Desbois, x, pp. 609–10. In 1548 Diane had appointed Pierre to a curacy in her gift, and another member of the family was a senior commensal officer during the 1550s: ADSM G 9536, 1548–9; C. Chevalier, ed., *Comptes des receptes et despences faites en la chastellenie de Chenonceau par Diane de Poitiers* (Paris, 1864), pp. 169, 192, 230, 287.

[76] BN MS Fr 22441 fos. 82–107, 'Estat faict par nous Charles cardinal de Lorraine de nostre trescher et honnore nepveu Charles de Lorraine'. The sole Norman was the *maître d'hôtel* and vassal, Robert de Bailleul, sieur d'Anserville.

[77] Richard Bahuet, *maître d'hôtel* (1580); Antoine du Mesnil, *gentilhomme servant* (1587); Louis de Serre, *maître d'hôtel* (1588); Guillaume Petit, *gentilhomme ordinaire* (1590).

MILITARY RETINUES

Associated with the core of senior counsellors and household servants at the heart of the affinity was the military retinue. Companies of the *ordonnance* were recruited by a captain and paid for by the crown. The pivotal role of the companies in the patronage system of the French monarchy in the late fifteenth and sixteenth centuries has attracted much attention and controversy. Robert Harding saw the gendarmerie as the key institution of the French Renaissance state, maintaining the equilibrium between the crown and the magnates through patronage in return for loyalty. The breakdown of this harmonious relationship, especially the decadence of the gendarmerie was, according to Harding, a major factor in fuelling noble discontent during the Wars of Religion.[78] Harding's theory aims to demonstrate the failure of the clientage system upon which society was founded and which had, until the Wars of Religion, maintained some sort of equilibrium by acting as a hierarchical conduit for patronage and favour in return for service. Harding's conclusions derive from a study of the changing size and composition of the gendarmerie throughout the Wars of Religion. He states that the number of *ordonnance* companies declined to a meagre twelve in 1585, having reached the large number of one hundred in 1569. Most damaging to the ethos of the permanent nature of the companies was the edict of 1579 which provided for the adoption of a rota system, in which each company was operative for one-third of a year only. Moreover, at the same time the traditional unit of the companies, the lance (composed of three archers for every two men-at-arms) had become meaningless and now simply corresponded to the number of men in a company. Thus he was able to conclude that 'as an institution for the maintenance of noblemen, it was dead in 1579, when it ceased to provide them with permanent careers'.[79]

Harding's functionalist approach, which sees the Wars of Religion largely as a crisis of the nobility, has found support elsewhere, notably from Orlea.[80] Paradoxically, the excellent list of figures on the gendarmerie's strengths during the Wars of Religion provided by Orlea plainly contradicts both his own case and the piecemeal evidence offered by Harding.[81] Orlea's data shows that during the 1570s the crown was still willing and able to expand its complement of gendarme companies, their nominal strength reaching a wartime high of 170 companies and 6,290 lances in 1578.[82] The evidence from twenty muster rolls held from 1559 to 1585 shows that the lance maintained its numerical strength of three archers to every two men-at-arms, and that companies were largely up to strength.[83]

[78] Harding, *Anatomy of a power elite*, pp. 71–80. [79] *Ibid.*, p. 74.

[80] M. Orlea, *La noblesse aux Etats généraux de 1576 et de 1588: étude politique et sociale* (Paris, 1980), pp. 50–67. [81] *Ibid.*, p. 57.

[82] *Ibid.*; BN MS Fr 3209, 21543. These figures are supported by recent research: J. B. Wood: *The king's army: warfare, soldiers and society during the French Wars of Religion, 1562–76* (Cambridge, 1996), pp. 129, 144–52.

[83] See appendix C. The lance was usually slightly under strength (on average 2 men-at-arms to 2.88

Harding's evidence would still have some credence if these same companies were being employed on a rota basis after 1579. But the political anarchy of the 1580s and the frequency of campaigns suggests that this policy was of temporary duration. Harding's assertion that there were a mere twelve companies in royal service in March 1585 ignores the nature of the civil war, involving three factions each of which could muster their complement of *ordonnance* companies. The gendarmerie was not dead but the control of patronage was out of the hands of the king because of political and fiscal decentralisation. Companies continued to exist without royal pay – employed by the Catholic League, the duc d'Anjou and the Huguenots and living off the land and expropriating royal revenues. In February 1589 the royalists forces alone mustered 103 companies.[84]

Far from being in decline the gendarmerie maintained its strength, since the embattled monarchy, despite its edicts and good intentions, could not check the spiralling increase of military expenditure and the proliferation of units, including the maintenance of the number of *ordonnance* companies at high levels. A chronically weak crown could not afford to cut off the supply of patronage at will simply to ease its financial difficulties. Indeed, in order to maintain political stability it had to buy support with patronage. It is not possible that the widespread violence and indiscipline which characterise the gendarmerie companies in the reign of Henri III, and which Harding is right to emphasise, can have been the work of so few units. In reality there was a huge expansion of military patronage and offices during the Wars of Religion. The crown and the provinces were burdened with increasing military expenditure for which they simply could not pay. Honours and offices failed to bring financial reward and their very abundance devalued all honorific and virtuous worth.

The expansion of military units is also evident in other arms. Light cavalry and infantry commands proliferated in each locality and every small bourg had to have its garrison. From the late 1560s onwards important noblemen began to receive, in addition to the *ordonnance*, units of light cavalry paid for by the crown as a bodyguard and officered from among their own retinue.[85] The continuing tactical value placed on cavalry over infantry even in the 1590s was perhaps one reason why the gendarmerie survived into the wars of the Catholic League. The effects of the expansion and devaluation of patronage were to have widespread political and fiscal implications. An early casualty was the chivalric order of Saint-Michel which

archers) but there is no significant change in the proportion of archers to men-at-arms over the decades. From 1560 to 1576 the company of the ducs de Longueville increased from 73 to 146 men. In 1579 the marquis d'Elbeuf had more men in his company than ever before. In 1581 the duc d'Aumale had only six fewer than in 1572. More significantly the two lieutenant-generals in Normandy, Jean de Moy and Tanneguy Le Veneur, increased the size of their companies consistently throughout the 1570s until their numbers rivalled the units commanded by the magnates.

84 BN MS Fr 3413 fo. 74.

85 For example: BN MS Fr 21536 fo. 2193, 'Role de trente arquebusiers a cheval ordonne par le roy a M. la Meilleraye', 1 Jun 1576; BN MS Fr 25809 fo. 273, 'Monstre a Rouen de trente arquesbusiers a cheval soubs Berthrand de la Braize estant pres de M. de Carrouges', 1577.

became a virtually worthless dignity because it was awarded with reckless prodigality.[86]

The stigma attached by nobles to serving in the army as archers, infantry officers or light cavalrymen declined throughout the sixteenth century. Social prejudice should never be confused with social reality. Most archers in the muster rolls were classed as *sieurs*, some as *écuyers* and even occasionally *chevaliers*. In 1579, Jean baron de Vieuxpont, from an ancient Norman family, was an archer in the company of the marquis d'Elbeuf. Orlea's presumption that 'tous les archers étaient roturiers', is incorrect.[87] The patronage opportunities for noblemen in the infantry and light cavalry units during the Wars of Religion increased. Two of the most important upper Norman noblemen, Adrien de Bréauté and Jean de Clères, had such commands in the 1550s before progressing on to command their own *ordonnance* companies in the 1560s, perhaps a reward for their loyalty to the crown.[88] One of the largest and most celebrated infantry regiments in France was that commanded by the comtes de Brissac. In time of war this regiment would have numbered in the thousands and provided many commands for the Brissac to fill.[89]

The continuing vitality of the *ordonnance* companies into the seventeenth century confirms their central role in the formation of affinities during the Wars of Religion. The military retinue of a nobleman was further strengthened by the proliferation of infantry, light cavalry and garrison offices. Political and fiscal decentralisation meant that local notables did not depend so heavily on the crown for the upkeep of their retinues. The Huguenots and the Catholic League, as well as a host of provincial potentates, were able to plunder localities or take over entirely the local royal fiscal machinery. If there was a failure of clientage it came not as a result of royal edicts but because the bonds of clientage were more complex and unstable than has hitherto been assumed. Moreover, local notables faced the same problems as the crown in terms of decentralised political authority and financial constraints when trying to control a province or even finding the resources to support their own affinity or military retinue.

The huge numbers of company musters permit the study of noble followings until the 1580s, when the lists become rare. Muster lists should be analysed with caution, since the geographic distribution of the company depended on the region in which the muster was held. Subgroups within a company included integrated and long-serving clients as well as groups of mercenary *roturiers*. Companies

86 Orlea, *La noblesse aux Etats généraux*, p. 61.

87 *Ibid.*, p. 58.

88 Clères was captain of 560 foot: ADSM 7J 3, 23 Jun 1553 and 12 Jun 1554. Bréauté was captain of 300 foot in 1557: BN MS Fr 32369 fo. 225.

89 This regiment grew out of the Piedmont regiment commanded by the maréchal de Brissac in the 1550s. For a list of his lieutenants in Piedmont: François de Boyvin, sieur de Villars, *Mémoires*, Michaud and Poujoulat, 1st ser., x, pp. 389–90. In 1567 Pierre du Bosc, sieur de Préaux, was 'enseigne-colonel de M. le comte de Brissac': ADSM 2E1 335, 21 Aug 1567.

contained landless adventurers such as those identified by Kristen Neuschel, but most of the men-at-arms and archers owned fiefs. They pursued the profession of arms and could afford the expensive equipment; they were 'vivant noblement' and therefore *de facto* noblemen. In 1586 complaints were made to the parlement of Rouen about Pierre Morin who:

> soubs pretexte de noblesse [fait] plusieurs exces et outrages de coups de baston à plusieurs pauvres labourers et hommes de bras de la parroisse de mondeville [near Caen] . . . mesmes faict loger icel soldatz en leurs maisons faict piller les pauvres et iceux inthimidé pour les empescher de le mettre à la taille . . . ladite quallite de noblesse est usurpé par ledit morin.[90]

Morin possessed sufficient resources to live nobly, having served as a *gentilhomme de la chambre* of the cardinal de Guise in 1581. The complaints made by his neighbours were evidently irksome, as he obtained letters of nobility in 1587 which confirmed rather than transformed his juridical status.[91] Gendarmes were not impoverished *hobereaux*, and the muster lists rarely report that horses or equipment were substandard. François Darandel, man-at-arms of the duc d'Aumale from 1575 until 1592, was a typical gendarme, although his length of service was longer than most. The family was not part of the provincial elite and it seems to have played no role in provincial high society and politics. Nevertheless, the dowry of 4,000*l* that Darandel provided for his daughter in 1592 suggests a family which belonged to the comfortable if not distinguished gentry. During this period the kinsmen of Darandel and his wife, Marie Lasnier, held a number of royal offices in the *vicomté* of Neufchâtel, such as *contrôleur* of the *magasin à sel*, *tabellion* and *grenetier*. By embarking on a military career Darandel was ascending the social ladder. His credit was geographically limited but nonetheless significant in the region of Neufchâtel.[92]

While recognising the high turnover of personnel in companies and the brief careers of many gendarmes, it is important to emphasis the enduring structures of companies. Each company had its distinctive regional character and a measure of stability was provided by the enduring networks of kinship and artificial kinship.[93] By analysing subgroups and by following the fluctuation in company structure, a clear picture of the changing composition of a clientele emerges. In 1565 Claude duc d'Aumale could boast a company of the *ordonnance* composed of noblemen from all over northern and eastern France. There were men in his company from Picardy, Normandy, Champagne, the Beauce, Burgundy and the Bourbonnais.[94] By 1572 the diversity of Aumale's company was somewhat reduced. The contingent from Normandy had swelled, making up 40 per cent of the company, while only 5 per cent were now coming from his *gouvernement* of Burgundy.[95] The

[90] ADSM 1B 3206, 11 Oct 1586.

[91] P.-F. Lebeurier, *Etat des anoblis en Normandie de 1398 à 1687* (Evreux, 1866), pp. 25–6.

[92] ADSM 2E1 2293, 17 Jun 1592.

[93] Bourquin, *Noblesse seconde et pouvoir*, pp. 32–3, 228. Bourquin's definition of family ties is highly circumscribed. [94] See appendix C.

changing geographical composition was not without reason or political consequence. In the case of the company of the duc d'Aumale the changes were due to the elevation of a new lieutenant. François Chabot, seigneur de Brion, a Burgundian, was replaced in 1569 by Claude Vipart, baron de Becthomas, promoted from ensign.[96] One man would have taken his followers with him and they would have been replaced from among the kin and servants of his successor.

Subgroups, formed around officers and senior men-at-arms, were able to move easily between one company and another, between one patron and another. This happened within the affinity of the Guise family. In March 1573 Claude duc d'Aumale died at the siege of La Rochelle. Since his children were minors, his company was left in the hands of its officers. These men were comparatively fresh-faced, a new lieutenant, ensign and *guidon* having made their appearance only a few months earlier at a muster in October 1572. Most important among these was a new lieutenant, Jacques de Tiercelin, seigneur de Possé, of a family with a strong power base in Picardy.[97] During the next few years an influx of Picards began to replace the Burgundians. The company was increasingly drawn from Normandy, Picardy and the *pays* which constituted the northern borders of the Ile de France. Although no musters exist for the crucial period of the late 1580s, officer posts in the company were monopolised by Picards and Normans. Of nine officers identified as serving in the 1580s, four were Picard and three Norman. In a number of cases officers had interests in both provinces.[98] The changing structure of Aumale's company reflects both his position as a landowner on the Norman–Picard border and his desire to build a following in order to support his claim to the governorship of Picardy. Despite the changing composition of the officer elite there remained ties to the past, such as Guy des Fossez and Louis de Caruel, kinsmen of the most senior councillors of the cardinal de Lorraine (figure 2.1).[99] The landholding base of these two men in the Vexin and the *bailliage* of Evreux complemented that of their patron who owned lands in the Eure valley, which formed the boundary between Normandy and the Ile de France. The continued importance of vassalage, not in terms of dues and services to be rendered but as a point of physical contact and

95 This contradicts Harding's assertion that 90 per cent of the men in a company originated in the *gouvernement* of the captain if he was a lieutenant-general or governor: *Anatomy of a power elite*, p. 23, n. 15. Lower down the social scale (i.e. lieutenant-generals) captains had a more parochial interest and the composition of companies reflects this.

96 Vindry, p. 285.

97 Originally a Tourangais-Norman lineage, the Tiercelin had married into an important Amienois family in 1520: Orlea, *La noblesse aux Etats généraux*, pp. 131–7.

98 Antoine de Runes, captain of Amiens since 1567, *guidon* (1588) and ensign (1591) of the company, was a fiefholder of the duchy of Aumale and a landholder in Picardy: *Deux ligueurs de Picardie. Documents historiques sur un maieur d'Amiens et un gouverneur de Gerberoy* (Paris, 1874), p. 43. Anne Tiercelin, *guidon* in 1581, represented the Norman line of a largely Picard lineage. His fellow Normans were Guillaume de Bigars, ensign (1588–91), and Louis de Caruel, *guidon* (1590). The other Picard officers were: Jacques d'Applaincourt, lieutenant (1581); Antoine du Hamel, ensign (1581); and Jean de Caron, ensign (1588).

99 BN Dossiers Bleus 277 fo. 2; ADSM 2E1 2291, 3 Feb 1590.

mutual recognition, cannot be underestimated as a means of entry into service or a reason for fidelity.[100]

Quantitative analysis of the geographic distribution of the company of the marquis d'Elbeuf shows that it was dominated by men from the Vexin Français and Champagne during the 1560s; this reflects the landed interest of his officers. The des Boves, who had lands in these regions and who were elevated by René's mother, dominated the household. In 1565, just before René's death, 45 per cent of the men identified came from Champagne, 32 per cent from the Vexin Français but a mere 13 per cent from Normandy, where the majority of René's lands were situated.[101] The lieutenant and ensign of the company, both from the des Boves family, seemed to have as much influence over the composition of the unit as the captain. In fact, they would have recruited men from among their own clients, servants and contacts.

The company of the seventeen-year-old Charles, marquis d'Elbeuf, demonstrates that he formerly absorbed men with his uncle, Claude duc d'Aumale. Charles was a more forceful character than his father and was anxious to establish a more independent household, closer to his landholding base. Fifty per cent of his company in a muster taken in October of 1573 had, only one year previously, been serving under the banner of his uncle. Although the des Boves family continued to monopolise the officers' posts there were changes in the geographic composition of the company. The same muster shows that 24 per cent of the company now came from Normandy and 18 per cent from the Bourbonnais. Companies were thus not created or changed by recruiting individuals but by the exchange and movement of different subgroups. However, the ability of subgroups to move to a different patron while remaining in the service of the Guise clan reveals one of their major strengths as a family.

The complexion of Elbeuf's company in the 1570s changed as the number of Normans increased. The last surviving muster held in 1579 shows that the Norman contingent now constituted one-third of the company, along with significant numbers of men from the Vexin and Picardy. During the 1580s the complexion of the company reflected Elbeuf's growing political interest in Normandy, but continuity with the past was maintained with the appointment of the son of Charles des Boves as *guidon* in 1588.[102] Disruption caused by the changing character of the company was minimised by the employment of men from the Vexin, which had traditionally been a recruiting ground for the Guise.[103] Charles de Fouilleuse,

[100] Neuschel, *Word of Honor*, pp. 132–85. Olivier de Cartula *écuyer*, man-at-arms of the duc d'Aumale (1572–5) and *maître d'hôtel* of the duchesse d'Aumale (1587–91), held the fief of Amaulry de Serez valued at 20*l* of *rente* per annum from the duke's barony of Ivry: Maudit, *Ivry-la-Bataille*, p. 499.

[101] 2ee appendix C.

[102] The ensign of the company in the late 1580s was the important Norman lord Jean de Vieuxpont: AN AB xix 3117, p. 415; ADSM 2E1 2007, 27 Aug 1588.

[103] Gilles de Crèvecoeur, *guidon* in 1573, was from the Vexin. Two Vexin men-at-arms during the 1570s, Pierre d'Aigrefeuille and Louis de Silly, married into the Morainville family which had a history of service to the Guise dating back to the 1530s: ADSM 2E1 350, 19 Feb 1575.

seigneur de Flavacourt, was the descendant of an important Vexin family which could claim a former *bailli* of Rouen among its number. His elevation into the company of the marquis d'Elbeuf as *guidon* (1573–5) and then ensign (1576–9) coincided with the influx of Normans into the unit. Fouilleuse probably owed his elevation to the fact the he was a distant relation and neighbour of the des Boves. Charles d'Elbeuf was inclined to focus his household on Normandy, but until 1576 he was still a minor who had spent most of his youth at Joinville. He therefore relied heavily on Fouilleuse for his Norman connections with which to begin the restructuring of his company. Fouilleuse remained a faithful companion of Elbeuf, being present at his wedding in 1583 in the capacity of 'capitain de cent hommes darmes soubz le command du duc d'Elbeuf'.[104]

The bonds among the noblemen in a company were multifarious. Fouilleuse established his position in the company by arranging marriages into the families of his comrades. His younger brother Louis's match to Jeanne de L'Isle inscribed his family into a complex network of kinship ties (see figure 2.1).[105] The Beauceron L'Isle family illustrates the web of family ties and multiple service which characterised the Guise affinity. No less than five members of the family held senior positions in the households and companies of the branches of the Elbeuf and Aumale in the 1570s and 1580s. They filled the posts of *bailli* of Anet and captain of Harcourt, as well as sitting on formal councils.[106]

The composition of the Guise retinues was determined by traditions of service and by patterns of landholding. In the Vexin and the Seine valley the estates of the family ensured that it was among the most important foci for the aspirations of local nobles. Traditions of family service which began in the 1540s continued throughout the Wars of Religion. These traditions and the bonds of kinship among local families ensured that magnate affinities, though constantly mutating, possessed elements of continuity. Vicinage and kinship inextricably bound the retinues of the various branches of the house of Guise. The ascendancy of the L'Isle family in the households of the Elbeuf and Aumale owed much to the fact that their cousin was Gabriel de La Vallée, the senior counsellor of the cardinal de Lorraine. Likewise, the contract of 1579 between Charles de Fouilleuse, ensign of the marquis d'Elbeuf, and Robert d'Abos, *écuyer* of the cardinal de Guise, hints at the mundane

104 Vindry, p. 304; BN Cabinet d'Hozier 216 fo. 101.

105 E. Morel, *Houdencourt: seigneurie et paroisse* (2 vols., Compiègne, 1878–82), i, p. 299.

106 Toussaint de L'Isle was a man-at-arms in the company of the marquis d'Elbeuf (1565–9), ensign (1573–5) and one of his *gentilshommes ordinaires* in 1581. Guillaume de L'Isle was a man-at-arms in the same company (1573–9) and captain of Harcourt in 1588. Philippe began his career as a man-at-arms for the marquis d'Elbeuf in 1565, he then served in the company of the duc d'Aumale (1572–5) and later held prominent positions in the households of the duke and his brother the chevalier d'Aumale. François was *bailli* of Anet from 1577: Vindry, p. 304; ADSM 6F 11, 'Recueil des capitaines de Normandie', 12 Sep 1588; ADSM J 138, 'Documents conçernant le comté de Maulévrier, 1468–1779', 1576; AN MC VIII 381 fo. 684, 4 Dec 1576; 391 fo. 266, 16 Feb 1583; 400 fo. 139, 8 Aug 1587; AN 300 AP I 219, 28 May 1577.

interaction among the Vexin servants of the Guise and demonstrates further the recondite ties of kinship and vicinage.[107]

SEIGNEURIAL OFFICIALS

Seigneurial officials were a key component of an affinity, since they were intimately connected to the elite of rural society. They had an important role to play in local politics and they often appear as representatives of the Third Estate at the Norman Estates. All the larger territorial jurisdictions, such as the comté of Eu in Normandy, were run by a council of seigneurial officials.[108] In 1580 Henri de Guise ordered the principal officials of the duchy of Guise to assemble every fortnight and to keep a record of their deliberations. The ordinance of the duke was designed to re-establish a procedure begun by his grandfather that, in recent years, had fallen into abeyance. The purpose behind re-establishing the council was to increase efficiency by ensuring participation, cooperation and consensus among the senior ducal *officiers*.[109]

It is easy to underestimate the importance of seigneurial officials as components of an affinity. Officials were not merely petty judges and collectors of taxes. Judicial officials had a legal training and boasted multiple contacts with the local legal community. Financial officials were usually merchants whose relationship to the lord was more complex than the terminology of financial contracts and leases suggest. They invariably enjoyed high status in mercantile circles and were an important source of credit for nobles. Moreover, all of the most senior seigneurial officials possessed independent local influence.

At the apex of the seigneurial hierarchy were the governors and captains of towns and châteaux. The most important offices at the disposal of the Guise would often go to a trusted and longstanding family servant. Charles de La Chaussée was governor of the comté of Eu from 1579 to 1583, having previously served in the household of the cardinal de Lorraine in the capacity of *pannetier*. His father, François, had served as governor of Joinville and *surintendant des maisons* of Claude duc de Guise.[110] These offices conferred proprietal rights like any other and the incumbent had to be reimbursed before surrendering his charge. In 1588 Guillaume de L'Isle, who had been made captain of Harcourt by the duc d'Elbeuf, resigned his office to a local nobleman on payment of 200*l*.[111] The level of remuneration depended to a large extent on the rights attached to the office. Thus the apparently minor captaincy of Toucques was resigned on payment of the sum

[107] BN Dossiers Bleus 278 fos. 67–8.

[108] In 1600 there was mention of the 'conseil . . . estably en la ville d'Eu': AN 300 AP I 102, liasse 2, 'Estat par estimation de la recepte et despence a faire pour Madame la duchesse de Guyse'.

[109] Carroll, 'The Guise affinity and popular protest', p. 129.

[110] ADSM 1E 486/2 fo. 83; BN MS Clairambault 1204 fo. 84; Chenaye-Desbois, v, p. 527.

[111] ADSM 2E1 936, 12 Sep 1588.

of 4,000 *écus* in 1580.[112] It would be misleading to suggest that all military office was dominated by sword nobles. Jacques Blondel, for example, *procureur fiscal* of the duc d'Elbeuf, was also captain of Lillebonne in 1590.[113]

The large number of *procès* in which the Guise had an interest in the royal courts in Normandy necessitated a close degree of cooperation between paid household servants and the lawyers whom they instructed. It was, after all, the *bailli* of Aumale, Jean de Martimbosc, who wrote to François de Guise mentioning the meeting of a council in Rouen to discuss the *haute justice* of the duchy in March 1548. Growing territorial influence in the 1550s and 1560s increased the amount of patronage available. The inheritance imposed a greater burden on those lawyers employed to pursue and protect rights. When the legal and administrative tasks had been much lighter the Le Roux had been able to combine their duties as seigneurial officers of the Guise with those of *conseillers* in the *échiquier* or the parlement of Rouen. By the second half of the sixteenth century few seigneurial officials were recruited from the magistracy but the *officiers* of the landed estates more often than not had a legal background. Those employed by the Guise often acted as *avocats* and *procureurs* for their patrons in the parlement or in the lesser courts of the *bailliage* or the *présidial*. Jean de Martimbosc was an *avocat* in the parlement of Rouen as well as *bailli* of Aumale in the 1550s. The family was not of lowly status: Louis de Martimbosc was abbot of Chartres and Marion was later abbot of Jumièges, *grand vicaire* of the cardinal de Bourbon in the archbishopric of Rouen (1575) and *conseiller* at the parlement of Rouen (1568–93).[114] It would be wrong to see seigneurial office as in irrevocable decline in the face of the inevitable triumph of royal offices. A letter from Antoinette de Bourbon to her daughter Marie de Guise suggests some of the considerations to be made when appointing to an office:

> I have had news with many requests for the [office of] vicomte de Longueville, who is dead. I have written as you told me . . . to the officers of the place, to inform me in your father's absence of the most sufficient and capable [person] to exercise the office conscientiously for the good of the duchy and the solace of the people. Many offer money for it, but this should not be allowed for a judicial office. The bearer said you made some promise to the controller Janot, and I would not hinder him, but give it for money I will not, and I think he would not offer it. The procureur of Longueville has asked for it, offering his office of procureur 'pour faire proufit'. A good procureur is indeed required, and if he were vicomte all the more.[115]

112 ADSM 2E1 919, 12 Jan 1580.

113 ADSM 1E 462, 28 Mar 1590.

114 Jean de Martimbosc was *bailli* of Aumale from 1551 to 1561: ADSM 2E1 304, 11 and 17 Oct 1550; 305, 5 Aug 1551; 323, 7 Sep 1556. Like other servants of the Guise, Martimbosc found his way into service through mutual links with the Orléans-Longueville, having been a pensioner of and having acted as *avocat* for the duc de Longueville. René de Martimbosc was also in the service of the Longueville as *procureur-fiscal* of Gournay and La Ferté: ADSM 2E1 305, 5 Aug 1551; 339, 22 Aug 1569. On Marion: Frondeville, *Conseillers*, p. 450.

115 *Letters and papers, foreign and domestic, of the reign of Henry VIII*, J. S. Brewer *et al.*, eds. (21 vols., London, 1864–1932), 1538, p. 49. Antoinette de Bourbon to the Queen of Scotland, 18 Aug 1538.

This letter dates from a time when venality had not yet become the norm or when offices had to be sold for financial expediency. It does show that offices were conferred after a collective process of consultation. Antoinette, who had a great influence in the administration of family affairs, cooperated with her own daughter and with their local servants. In July 1552 René des Buaz, *conseiller* at the parlement of Rouen, wrote to Antoinette in favour of Jean Lambert, already a servant of the Guise: 'Madame aiant sceu l'indisposition de vostre bailli d'Ellebeuf vous aye adverty pour vostre service et M. le marquis le personage lequel pour la provision dudict office luy est necessaire: M. Jehan Lambert advocat en ce parlement procureur-general de monseigneur le cardinal de Lorraine en ce pays de normandie.'[116] She replied that such a decision would have to be taken in council with 'l'advis de mes enffans que j'attends bien tot icy'.[117]

Seigneurial officials were linked by ties of kinship and vicinage to office holders and nobles in the localities of upper Normandy. The memoir written by Adrien Miton, which covers the years from 1520 to 1640, offers an insight into the small world of a minor office holder and reveals the routine interaction of a closely knit group of office-holding families.[118] Miton, an *élu* since 1569, recorded the significant events in Neufchâtel-en-Bray which usually centred upon the family life-cycle of birth, baptism and death. His kinship ties bought him close to the seigneurial officials of the comté of Eu and the duchy of Aumale. The boundaries of sociability were delineated by his ties to these officials, and by his relations to the bourgeois of Neufchâtel and the local gentry. Robe and sword in the region coexisted in relative harmony.[119] Adrien refers to his cousins who dominated the administration of the comté of Eu. Richard was *receveur* of Eu (1581–92) and his son, Richard II, was *lieutenant-général* of the *bailli* from 1585. Laurent was *greffier du conseil.*[120] Adrien was also related to the *bailli* of Aumale, and in 1590 conferred on him the honour of naming his son at baptism. In the small world of the pays de Bray these families ranked among the local elite.

The posts of *bailli* or *vicomte* required legal knowledge and so those with such a background were preferred. Similarly, those with a commercial background were best suited to manage the financial affairs of the estates. Only merchants and bourgeois possessed the ready cash and expertise to accept the farm of a given revenue. They were also to be found heavily involved in the wider financial affairs of the Guise, lending money, constituting *rentes* and acting as proxies and guaran-

[116] BN MS Fr 20515 fo. 73, des Buaz to Antoinette, Rouen, 16 Jul 1552. Lambert seems to have been successful as he qualified as *bailli* of Elbeuf in 1559 and 1560: ADSM 2E1 319, 4 Aug 1559; 321, 26 May 1560. He was *bailli* of both Aumale and Elbeuf in 1561: ADSM 2E1 323, 12 Aug 1561.

[117] BN MS Fr 20515 fo.74, Antoinette to des Buaz, n.d. The councils of Antoinette and the cardinal de Lorraine are also mentioned in connection with the administration of Elbeuf, in BN MS Fr 20649 fo. 157, Le Picart to Antoinette, Paris, 1 May 1551.

[118] F. Bouquet, ed., *Documents concernant l'histoire de Neufchâtel-en-Bray* (Rouen, 1884).

[119] In 1594 three sword nobles attended the baptism of Miton's son, Georges.

[120] They attended the baptism of Guillaume Miton in 1581.

tors in financial transactions. They provided the Guise with the local knowledge, expertise and contacts which facilitated links with the commercial community in Rouen. Nicholas Rogy, *bourgeois marchand* and *receveur* of Mauny, performed many other tasks for the duc d'Aumale outside the scope of his office, involving himself particularly in the duke's financial affairs. As a merchant Rogy had both the capital and the financial contacts to facilitate these transactions. His name appears regularly in notarial records as a guarantor and witness for the duke.[121] As well as arranging transactions, acting as cautions and witnessing contracts in Rouen, seigneurial officials were also expected to advance loans to their lords. The need for specie was at its most pressing during times of political crisis. The ability of Richard Miton to advance 5,000 *écus* to the duchesse d'Aumale during the early 1590s is further evidence of his family's standing in the Bray.[122]

Minor seigneurial offices were occupied by lesser nobles and bourgeois. Families such as the Franqueville were employed by the marquis d'Elbeuf and lived in the seigneurial domicile at La Saussaye, having served the comtes of Harcourt since the mid-fifteenth century.[123] The local significance of forest offices should not be underestimated, although they may have been venal or enfeoffed like their royal equivalents. Mathieu de Montpellier was *verdier* of Lillebonne before rising to become *bailli* and captain of the château in 1589.[124] Richard Marsollet, *verdier* of the duchy of Elbeuf in 1582, was sufficiently prominent to represent the Third Estate of the *vicomté* of Pont de l'Arche at the provincial Estates in 1585. He came from a Rouennais merchant background and was heavily involved in the financial affairs of his master.[125]

THE FINANCIAL FOUNDATIONS OF AFFINITY

Financial officials played a different role from that of judicial and noble counsellors; they were creditors and bankers as well as advisers and were bound to their employer by strict contracts, stipulating the duration and terms of employment. Financial affairs were also devolved to local *receveurs* and *fermiers*. A central finance council seems to have operated as a means of investigating and redressing financial maladministration. The senior financial councillors of the duc de Guise resided in Paris.[126] The best-documented career relates to Alphonse de

[121] Florimond Mallet, *receveur* of Aumale, also appears frequently: ADSM 2E1 323, 12 Aug 1561; 304, 11 and 17 Oct, 6 Nov 1551.

[122] AN 300 AP I 102, Jun 1591.

[123] ADSM 2E1 330, 4 Oct 1565. Claude Poiseau, *verdier* of Elbeuf, was ennobled in 1595 'sans payer finance': Lebeurier, *Etat des anoblis*, p. 31.

[124] Nicolas de Montpellier had been *receveur* of the comté of Lillebonne in 1575. Eustache Trevache succeeded him and married his widow: ADSM 2E1 362, 8 Oct 1580; 352, 14 Feb 1576; 1E 462, 11 Apr 1589.

[125] ADSM 2E1 365, 19 May 1582; 920 fo. 234, 10 Nov 1583; 924 fo. 230, 31 Oct 1585; 2294, 26 Jul 1592.

[126] Claude Lyonne was *conseiller, trésorier* and *receveur-général* of the duc de Guise from 1579: AN MC VIII 386 fo. 466, 30 May 1579. He was succeeded by the wealthy Parisian merchant, Jean Mérault,

Maugarny, *conseiller* and *intendant* of the duke during the 1580s. The office of *intendant* became increasingly common in the second half of the sixteenth century, and *intendants* had investigatory powers as well as overseeing financial matters. Maugarny's apprenticeship had been spent in the service of Catherine de Clèves before her marriage to Henri de Guise. He first appears in ducal service in 1575 and by the end of the decade was responsible for restoring the chaotic ducal finances.[127] This entailed considerable labour, involving investigations into the seigneurial administration and the debts of the duke. It is likely that these issues were addressed by a council directed by Maugarny. In 1580 Maugarny visited the duchy of Guise with a longstanding servant and *surintendant* of the duke, François de Pilla, abbot of Saint-Méen, in order to investigate seigneurial maladministration. They drew up a number of detailed suggestions, seeking to reduce corruption and improve administrative efficiency, which were presented to the senior ducal council.[128] In 1583, as a result of the *recherche*, the duke issued an ordinance to all his officers, requiring them to keep accurate financial records which were to be checked and verified by Maugarny.[129] Jacques Belleau, vicar-general of the cardinal de Lorraine, seems to have held similar responsibilities regarding his master's finances. He appears regularly in the Parisian notarial archives approving mundane tenurial contracts, as well as large financial transactions. The families which managed the financial administration were closely related. Belleau was a relative of Pierre Hotman, *trésorier-général* of the cardinal between 1559 and 1575, who was also responsible for overseeing leases and constituting *rentes* for his patron. His brother, Jean Hotman, was a member of the cardinal's household in 1561 and his son, Thibaut, was *trésorier-général* of the marquis d'Elbeuf in the 1570s.[130]

Senior financial officials were paid higher wages than other household servants, and they also received non-monetary rewards.[131] The position of financial officials in the household was anomalous since they were obligated by contracts for a fixed term of years. Contracts stipulated the advances that were to be made. *Trésoriers-généraux* were expected to provide credit and had to be capable of raising large sums of money. In 1579 Claude de Lyonne lent the duc de Guise 12,000 *écus* and in the

whose son, Pierre, fulfilled the same function for the duc d'Aumale in the late 1580s: Carroll, 'The Guise affinity and popular protest', p. 141.

127 AMC A 14 liasse 6, 13 Jun 1567; AN MC VIII 380 fo. 580, 6 Jul 1575. His investigations encompassed the purchase and sale of land and *rentes* between 1554 and 1584: BN MS Fr 8182.

128 The investigations and recommendations are collected in AMC D 3.

129 AMC D 3, 6 Jul 1583, 'Ordonnance sur fait de nostre finances que nous voullons et entendons estre inviolable'.

130 Belleau was the godfather of Jacqueline Hotman: AN MC VIII 372 fo. 234, 3 May 1568; 380 fo. 207, 23 Mar 1575; BN Dossiers Bleus 361 fo. 34. Jean was 'commis du trésorier à la suicte de monseigneur': BN MS Clairambault 1204 fo. 84.

131 The annual wage of a *trésorier-général* in the 1560s and 1570s was 1,200*l*: BN MS Clairambault 1204 fo. 84; AN MC VIII 361 fo. 217, 23 Feb 1574. Maugarny either purchased or was granted a number of fiefs in the duchy of Chevreuse. Belleau was abbot of Cheminon, Saint-Martin de Choisy and canon of the Sainte-Chapelle in Paris.

following three years advanced him at least 23,000 *écus*.[132] The many contracts involving Pierre Hotman demonstrate the wide variety of tasks he undertook on behalf of different members of the Guise family. His most important roles were as banker and financial broker. His extensive contacts in Paris facilitated the sale of *rentes* and of royal offices granted to the Guise. Parisian *robins* and bourgeois, as well as commensal officers, eagerly speculated in *rentes* sold by the family.[133] Hotman advanced huge sums of money to the cardinal de Lorraine. On the cardinal's death in 1574 he was owed 92,800*l*. By an accord of September 1576 Henri duc de Guise agreed to pay the remaining sum of 58,232*l*, but the financial crisis of the Guise ensured that the debt was not liquidated until December 1583. The forbearance of the Hotman family in this matter demonstrates how trust and familiarity helped to sustain family finances.[134] The relationship between the Guise and their servants was not devoid of affective bonds. In death Belleau wished to continue his association with his deceased masters, bequeathing 666 *écus* to ensure that masses were said for him and for the souls of Charles cardinal de Lorraine and François duc de Guise.[135]

Although Paris was the major source of credit, the Rouen money market was an important subsidiary source of credit since the Guise possessed local contacts and their lands provided collateral.[136] Aumale's residence in Rouen was a focus for financial meetings. Alternatively he could lodge in the house of his *procureur*, Robert Raoullin, as he did in 1565 whilst completing the buying of some land.[137] The duke maintained a treasury in Rouen overseen by Etienne Houdry 'recepveur des deniers de mondict seigneur en la ville de Rouen', to whom tax farmers and the fiscal officers of the duke paid the seigneurial revenues.[138] Commerce and the exchange of specie in the sixteenth century were facilitated by kinship connections, and Rouen and Paris had strong commercial connections sustained by family networks. The relationship between the financial officials in Paris and the servants in Normandy was intimate. Jean Hinselin was *trésorier-général* of the duc d'Aumale from 1581 to 1586 and his brother was secretary and later *intendant*. He was Parisian and in 1584 was living in the house of Etienne de Bray, later one of the leaders of the Catholic League in Paris.[139] Hinselin had business interests in

[132] AN MC VIII 394 fos. 191–4, 24 Jul 1584.

[133] During the third War of Religion Hotman was active in helping the cardinal to sell *rentes* on the hôtel de ville: AN MC VIII 372 fos. 296, 351–5, 443, 596, 597, 780–2. On the Guise affinity in Paris: Carroll, 'The Guise affinity and popular protest', pp. 138–44.

[134] AMC A 14 liasse 7, 1 Sept 1576, 23 Dec 1583.

[135] AN Y 124 fo. 459, 12 May 1583.

[136] Borrowing was more expensive in Rouen. The rate of interest was 10 per cent compared to 8 per cent in Paris.

[137] A. Héron, ed., *Deux chroniques de Rouen* (Rouen and Paris, 1900), p. 315. The comte de Maulévrier also had a residence in the parish of Saint-Godard.

[138] ADSM J 138, 1576, 'Ferme du comté de Maulevrier'.

[139] AN 300 AP I 223, 13 Feb 1584, 9 May 1584; R. Descimon, *Qui étaient les Seize? Mythes et réalités de la ligue parisienne* (Paris, 1984), p. 112.

Normandy and responsibility for certain royal tax farms in the province. His agent in Rouen was Martin Houdry, *greffier héréditale* of the *magasin à sel* and husband of Louise de Bray, a relative of Etienne.[140]

Marriage, war and the purchase of offices and land all required nobles to raise large sums of cash. The Rouennais notarial archives show that land was regularly mortgaged to raise capital quickly. The Norman cadet branches of the house of Guise procured large sums on the Rouen money markets in this manner. The borrowing undertaken by both the Aumale and the Elbeuf from the 1550s to the 1590s divides into two distinct phases.[141] Unlike his son Charles, Claude duc d'Aumale was a heavy borrower in Rouen. Conversely, Charles duc d'Elbeuf borrowed heavily in the 1580s whereas his father, René, never seems to have constituted *rentes* in Rouen. This financial pattern reflects the political strategy of each man. In the case of the Aumale, the father was more concerned with Norman affairs and establishing a clientele in Normandy than the son who pursued his political career almost exclusively in Picardy. René marquis d'Elbeuf was never a significant figure in the province but his son became the commander of the Catholic League there in 1585. The borrowing of money can be traced to distinct periods of activity (usually military). In the 1550s Claude d'Aumale raised money for the campaigns against the Habsburgs. In the 1580s Charles d'Elbeuf borrowed heavily in order to finance his contingent in the expedition led by the duc d'Anjou into the Low Countries, and later he needed money as a commander of the Catholic League.

Troops had to be raised and paid for in advance, thereafter recouping money from the royal treasury. If indebtedness rose and intervention by the king was not forthcoming land had to be alienated in order to meet obligations. In 1557 Claude d'Aumale was granted the office of the *bailli* of Caen, which he sold two years later to offset debts incurred during the wars against the imperialists.[142] The advent of the Wars of Religion meant no respite from spiralling military expenditure for both crown and nobility. Aumale was forced to sell the seigneuries of Estouteville and Plainbosc in 1570 for 30,000*l* to a creditor, and his son was compelled to sell the entire barony of Bec Crespin in 1579 to another, Nicholas Romé, in order to ease the legacy of debt bequeathed to him.[143]

When a large amount of money needed to be raised a legal document was drawn up empowering a chosen servant or client to act as an agent. Armed with the *procuration*, which detailed the sum required, the servant would set off to Rouen to sell the *rentes*. In some cases the borrower had made preliminary contacts and was aware of whom to approach. In other cases the agent would have used his own

[140] Likewise, the family of Etienne Brice, *receveur-général* of the duke from 1574 to 1581, had both Parisian and Rouennais branches: Carroll, 'The Guise affinity and popular protest', p. 141.

[141] See appendices A and B.

[142] ADSM 2E1 323, 28 Jul 1561. The original agreement was reached in April of 1559 by which the purchaser agreed to meet the debts of the duke totalling 2,170*l* of *rente*. The office was probably granted by the king in lieu of money he owed the duke.

[143] ADSM 2E1 341, 11 Sep 1570; Lechevalier, *Notice historique sur les barons et la baronnie du Bec*, p. 12.

personal contacts and knowledge to find those willing to buy. Seigneurial officials usually acted as guarantors for the repayments and contracts often specified the revenues for repayment. Up to four seigneurial officers with legal and financial expertise would normally be present to discuss and witness contracts and pledge their chattels and goods as guarantee.[144] Discussions and legal formalities took place in the residence of the duc d'Aumale in the parish of Sainte-Croix de Saint-Ouen in Rouen. The duc d'Elbeuf conducted his own financial transactions at his cousin's residence in 1582.[145] Sometimes a trusted client might figure among the signatures.[146]

Constituting *rentes* had political as well as financial implications. Examining these transactions as purely financial and legal documents underestimates the personal bond of the contract. The parties were either familiars, or brought together by a mutually recognised third party. These personal links provided some degree of insurance and trust. The buying of *rentes* was not a purely individual decision or commitment. It was a family investment to provide an income for future generations. Those who bought *rentes* from the Guise often had personal contact with them. Many of the creditors of the Elbeuf and Aumale were supporters of the ultra-catholic faction during the Wars of Religion, and some the most important Rouennais financiers, such as the Puchot and the Hallé, played a significant role in financing the Catholic League and in installing a leaguer regime in 1589.[147] The correlation between financial assistance and political support is illustrated by the Bauquemare. Between 1556 and 1582 the Bauquemare and their close kinsmen bought 1,870*l* of *rentes* from the Aumale and Elbeuf.[148] Jacques de Bauquemare, *premier président* of the parlement of Rouen from 1565 until 1584, was a towering figure in the city during the civil wars. A confirmed catholic but at the same time a moderate concerned with keeping order in the city, he was personally known to the Guise by 1551 when he solicited the duke for a favour.[149] In the years that followed

144 A *procuration* established by Charles duc d'Elbeuf in May 1588 stipulated the alienation of 600*l* of *rente*, and named Jacques Vernier as proxy for the sale. The guarantors included Mathieu Dupont *receveur* of the duchy of Elbeuf, Imbert Le Peinteur *receveur* of the comté of Harcourt, Pierre Le Danois *receveur* of the comté of Brionne and Jean Michel *adjudicateur* of the forests of Elbeuf: ADSM 2E1, 2003, 9 May 1588.

145 ADSM 2E1 365, 19 May 1582.

146 Throughout the 1550s, Robert Raoullin, sieur de Longpaon, the *procureur* of Aumale in the parlement, was entrusted with the task of finding buyers of *rentes* and in 1561 he paid off arrears and outstanding debts. Jean de Brevedent, lieutenant-general of the *bailliage* of Rouen and Nicholas Caillot, a lawyer and later *conseiller* of the parlement of Rouen, appeared as witnesses for the duke: ADSM 2E1 304, 11 and 17 Oct 1550; 305, 4 Sep 1551; 313, 7 Sep 1556; 314, 30 Sep 1556; 323, 12 Aug 1561.

147 See below p. 217.

148 Frondeville, *Conseillers*, p. 360; *Présidents*, p. 54. This figure includes 630*l* bought by Jean Le Febvre d'Escalles, a *conseiller* at the parlement of Rouen (1544–71) and brother-in-law of Jacques de Bauquemare. His son, Charles, maintained the family alliance by marrying Marguerite de Bauquemare: Frondeville, *Conseillers*, p. 528.

149 Frondeville, *Présidents*, pp. 54–5; *DBF*, v, pp. 942–3; BN MS Fr 20533 fo. 108, Bauquemare to Guise, Rouen, 15 Jan 1551.

he bought *rentes* from the Guise and acted as witness, intermediary and guarantor in transactions between the Guise and other members of his family.[150] This kin group were not dependants, but a relationship with the Guise was forged by financial dealings over the decades. These personal contacts were to be useful during political crises. By the 1580s the Bauquemare clan was in sympathy with the political and religious convictions of the Catholic League, and it was a powerful force behind the hegemony of the League in Rouen. Jacques de Bauquemare's two sons sat on the local provincial council of the League.[151] There were further connections with the Guise through mutual links with the Croismare family. Jacques de Bauquemare was married to Catherine de Croismare whose cousin, Charles de Croismare, sieur de Saint-Just, was 'attaché à la maison de Claude de Lorraine, duc d'Aumale'.[152] It is possible to come full circle since Charles de Croismare was married in 1550 to Anne Jubert, the younger sister of Jean Jubert, vicar-general of the cardinal de Lorraine for the abbey of Bec and also sister of Jacques, a *conseiller* in the parlement and a major creditor of the Guise.[153]

A longstanding relationship with the Guise should not be seen as synonymous with joining the Catholic League. Huguenots and others opposed to catholic extremism were purchasers of Guise *rentes*. The elite of Rouen society was capable of pursuing independent family strategies. When Charles d'Elbeuf needed to raise funds for the duc d'Anjou's expedition to the Low Countries in 1581 he turned to Louis Le Mercier, sieur de La Bretesque, *vicomte* of Evreux and Anjou's *maître des requêtes*.[154] Le Mercier was a trustworthy contact, having been involved with the financial affairs of the Guise as early as 1550. He raised money for Elbeuf by selling *rentes* among his own family and friends.[155] The link between this kin grouping and the Guise was merely financial; they were on the periphery of the Guise affinity and remained royalists during the Catholic League.[156] Other catholic moderates, such as *conseiller* Pierre du Quesne, and even some Huguenots such as Alonce de Quintanadoines, François de Civille and Catherine Le Gras bought *rentes* from the Elbeuf.[157] The complexities of faith took second place to raising cash. Elbeuf could

150 See for example: ADSM 2E1 334, 13 Jan 1567.

151 Frondeville, *Présidents*, pp. 65–6, 258. Their cousin Charles Le Febvre d'Escalles was also a leaguer.

152 Frondeville, *Présidents*, p. 206. It was due to Bauquemare's influence that Jean de Croismare was received as a *président* of the parlement in 1567.

153 Frondeville, *Conseillers*, p. 136. Jacques de Bauquemare married his nephew Jean du Bosc, sieur de Coquéreaumont, to Anne Jubert in 1581 at which a large gathering of both families was present: ADSM 2E1 364, 25 Oct 1581.

154 ADSM 2E1 363, 12 Jul 1581.

155 ADSM 2E1 304, 11 and 17 Oct, 6 Nov 1550. Barbe and Anne Le Mercier bought 800*l* between them. Pierre Le Cornier, son of Barbe Le Mercier and a *conseiller* in the parlement of Rouen, acquired 1600*l*. A *consul des marchands* of Rouen in 1574 and future *conseiller* in the parlement, André Bonnissent, who was married to Louise Le Mercier, bought 150*l*.

156 Frondeville, *Conseillers*, pp. 561, 598–9.

157 On the Quintanadoines and Civille: G. K. Brunelle, 'Immigration, assimilation and success: three families of Spanish origin in sixteenth-century Rouen', *Sixteenth Century Journal* 20 (1989), 205–19. In *The New World merchants of Rouen, 1559–1630* (Ann Arbor, 1991), p. 150, Brunelle argues that confessional differences did little to hinder commercial relationships between families.

turn to the Huguenot community because he was preparing to join the head of the *politique* faction identified with religious compromise.

Despite such nuances political and religious loyalty correlated with financial interdependence. Personal bonds often developed from financial dealings and financial transactions reinforced existing ties. Although *rentes* were constituted on property or revenues, the buyer gambled on the solvency of the seller in order to receive prompt repayment. During times of political and fiscal instability the purchaser relied on the future financial solvency and social success of the seller. Both parties preferred to deal with someone they could trust. Financial difficulties during the 1570s and 1580s forced the ducs d'Aumale, d'Elbeuf and de Guise to sell land. Personal bonds permitted them to reschedule arrears and delay payments by agreement, and to find trustworthy buyers for property. Thus when the duc d'Elbeuf was forced to sell the seigneury of Quatremares in 1584 for 80,000*l* to meet debts incurred in the Netherlands campaign, he did so to one of his lieutenants in the Catholic League, Jean de La Haye.[158]

PRELATES AND CHURCHMEN

The power of the Guise in the French church was extensive and a detailed analysis is beyond the scope of this study.[159] Clients in the church can be divided into three categories. First, there were those prelates who acted as councillors of the family and who enjoyed a privileged position in the household. Second, there were those who administered ecclesiastical affairs in the localities, a group which included important officials, such as vicars-general and *receveurs-généraux*. In addition, the Guise were significant brokers of ecclesiastical patronage which ensured that they were continually solicited for favour.

The cardinals de Lorraine and de Guise were great temporal as well as spiritual lords. The household of the cardinal de Lorraine thronged with sword nobles. Likewise the lay members of the family employed clerics in their household and provided benefices on their temporal lands. The elevated position of the Guise within the French church afforded them a bounty of patronage. The bishopric of Avranches was dominated by two clients families – the Le Cirier and the Péricard – from 1561 to 1639.[160]

The cardinal de Pellevé, a Norman, was the senior councillor of the cardinal de Lorraine. According to Castelnau 'ce prélat ne parvint aux dignités ecclesiastiques que par un dévouement servile à la maison de Guise, & surtout au cardinal de Lorraine qui lui ouvrit le chemin de la fortune, en le nommant son

158 ADSM 2E1 367, 28 Oct 1586.

159 For a fuller discussion: J. Baker, 'The House of Guise and the church'.

160 A. Le Canu, *Histoire du diocèse de Coutances et Avranches* (2 vols., Coutances, 1877–8), i, p. 458. Temporal lords sometimes employed ecclesiastics. François de Pilla, abbot of Saint-Michel en Thiérache, was *surintendant* of the duc de Guise in 1581: AN MC VIII 388 fo. 52, 25 Jan 1581.

intendant'.[161] Pellevé's rise to eminence was indeed due to Guise patronage. In 1561 and 1564 his name preceded all other commensal officers in the household accounts of the cardinal. He began his career in the parlement of Paris and by 1553 he was bishop of Amiens. In 1559 he served on the council sent to Scotland to bolster the regime of Marie de Guise and in 1563 he was chosen as archbishop of Sens on the resignation of the cardinal de Guise. He was raised to the cardinalate in 1570 and was later archbishop of Reims during the League.[162] Pellevé was far from being the *créature* that Castelnau depicted. Little is known about his role on the Guise council, although his legal training made him 'un homme forte versé aux affaires'. The Pellevé were a ramified family, belonging to the Norman *noblesse d'épée* elite. The elder branch, represented by the cardinal and his siblings, possessed a large landed interest in the Vexin. Their elevated position in local society ensured that they served a number of competing magnate families.[163] However, the Pellevé were especially attracted to Guise service and marriages to other clients families were common. One of the cardinal's nephews followed him to Scotland and died at the siege of Leith in 1559, and another died thirty years later defending Paris against Henri de Navarre. His sister married Robert Vipart, cousin of the lieutenant of Claude duc d'Aumale (see figure 2.1). The cardinal de Lorraine took a close interest in the couple's son Guillaume. He was present in 1566 at the establishment of Guillaume's wardship, and the boy entered the household of the duc de Guise as *gentilhomme page*, going on to become a leaguer captain in Normandy.[164] Françoise, Anne and Roberte de Pellevé, nieces of the cardinal, contracted marriages to men associated with both the Guise and the Catholic League.[165]

In Normandy, the most senior clerical clients oversaw the administration and religious life of the two greatest abbeys, Bec and Fécamp, and were drawn from important local families. Jean Jubert, *protonotaire* of the cardinal de Guise and vicar-general of Bec (1558–70), was closely integrated into the local ecclesiastical hierarchy. He was dean of the cathedral of Notre-Dame de Rouen in the 1560s and prior of Mont-aux-Malades (near Rouen). His elder brother Jean, a *conseiller* in the parlement, was a considerable buyer of *rentes* from the duc d'Elbeuf.[166] The kinsmen of ecclesiastical servants also appeared regularly in military retinues. Three kinsmen of Artus Damerval, a Picard and grand prior of the abbey of Fécamp (1559–92) for the cardinals de Lorraine and de Guise, saw service as archers in the company of Charles duc d'Aumale in the 1570s. The ties of Georges de Boscregnoult, grand prior of Bec in the 1580s, were more clearly Norman. His family originated from the Roumois and held land from the duc d'Elbeuf, and his

[161] Michel de Castelnau, *Mémoires, Collection universelle des mémoires relatifs à l'histoire de France* (67 vols., Paris, 1786–91), xli, p. 299.

[162] Anselme, ii, p. 74; Brantôme, vi, p. 38.

[163] Gilles de Pellevé, younger brother of Nicholas, served as the ensign of the constable de Montmorency in 1567 and was married to Geneviève de Montmorency-Fosseux.

[164] Anselme, ii, pp. 77–8; BN Pièces Originales 3029 fo. 46; Dossiers Bleus 674 fos. 20–1.

[165] They were married to Michel d'Estourmel, Nicholas de Moy and Robert de Monchy respectively.

[166] ADSM 2E1 316, 14 Mar 1558; 364, 25 Oct 1581; Frondeville, *Conseillers*, p. 137.

kin network extended to both the local nobility and the Rouennais bourgeoisie. His kinsmen were patronised by the Guise: Jean de La Houssaye was sacristan of Bec between 1548 and 1553, and Pierre de La Houssaye was archer in the company of the duc d'Elbeuf in 1579. Another relative, Michel Le Nepveu, a lawyer at the parlement, had been appointed to the office of *sénéchal* of Esié by the cardinal de Lorraine in 1557. Le Nepveu's family contained both merchants and lawyers and continued to provide servants for the Guise throughout the Wars of Religion: Raoullin was *receveur-fermier* of Fécamp in 1588.[167]

Revenue farmers and financial agents of monastic lands acted as brokers and creditors. They were recruited from among higher-status families than their counterparts in seigneurial administration, suggesting that the great value of ecclesiastical benefices attracted the most important Rouennais *robin* and bourgeois families. Nicolas Romé, *intendant* of the abbey of Fécamp, was of an important Rouennais banking family, creditors of the Guise. Ennobled before 1577, he had already served as a *conseiller* in the parlement of Rouen (1567–75) then as *maître des requêtes* (1575–84). Louis II cardinal de Guise supervised Romé's activities closely. In 1577 he lectured his servant on the evils of indebtedness: 'I will always find it better and more expedient to sell out than to borrow money'.[168] The Aumalé were less judicious and by the late 1570s could no longer meet their obligations. One of the chief beneficiaries was Romé, whose acquisition of the barony of Bec Crespin from the duke in 1579 confirmed his entry into the elite of Norman society.[169] Jean Ballue, *receveur-général* of the abbey of Bec, was of less elevated stock. A middling Rouennais bourgeois, he also used his Guise connections to further his family, marrying his daughter to Robert de Bailleul, later a gentleman in the Aumale household. In 1562 Jean's son, Adrien, was appointed to the curacy of Routout by the chapter of the abbey of Bec. He was already a canon of the cathedral of Rouen, a position he continued to occupy during the period of the Catholic League.[170]

Minor positions could easily be found for the kinsmen of servants. Louis de La Menardière, cousin of the *intendant* of the duc d'Aumale, was a monk at Bec and two of the younger sisters of Charles de Sarcilly, *intendant* of the duc d'Elbeuf, were nuns in the convent of Renée de Guise at Reims. Serving the Guise offered the chance to provide for cadets while maintaining the integrity of inheritances. The influence of the family reached into the rural hinterland of the Caux. In 1586 the cardinal de Guise allocated small sums to four 'prebstres pensionnaires'.[171] The

[167] Chenaye-Desbois, i, p. 439; ADSM 1B 590, 7 Feb 1562; 2152, 24 Nov 1588; M. Charpillon, *Dictionnaire historique de toutes les communes du département de l'Eure* (2 vols., Les Andelys, 1868), i, p. 439; *Inventaire-Sommaire des archives départementales de l'Eure, antérieures à 1790*, ser. E, E. Lebeurier *et al.*, eds. (Evreux, 1899), pp. 148, 193.

[168] Quoted in Dewald, *The formation of a provincial nobility*, p. 234.

[169] Frondeville, *Présidents*, p. 424; AN MC VIII 398 fo. 494, 18 Sep 1586; ADSM 2E1 934 fo. 224v, 14 Jun 1588.

[170] ADSM, G 9550, 9568; ADSM 2E1 877, 12 Jul 1560; 12 Feb 1561. Geoffrey Ballue was *receveur* of the city in 1569 and *conseiller-échevin* in 1584.

[171] ADSM 2E1 934, 14 Jun 1588.

captaincy of Fécamp and the possibility of placing younger sons in the abbey also attracted the Cauchois lesser nobility.

On the eve of the Wars of Religion, servants of the Guise belonged to every section of the Norman elite. The various branches of the house of Guise offered multiple and complementary avenues for advancement, especially in upper Normandy. The geographic composition of the affinity was largely determined by the spatial distribution of the family estates. The nucleus of the Guise following in Normandy was drawn from the marches of upper Normandy and from the regions which bordered the Seine: vicinage and tradition were fundamental in shaping its identity. Provincial boundaries were transparent to the social links between neighbouring regions: the Guise affinity was strong throughout the Vexin, and the nobilities of Ponthieu and the Vimeu in Picardy and the Caux and Bray in Normandy were closely integrated. The concentration of lands and benefices in upper Normandy guaranteed opportunities for Rouennais lawyers, magistrates and merchants. The employment of Rouennais families to conduct business and the borrowing on the city money market extended family influence among the ecclesiastical and lay hierarchy of the city. Nevertheless, the growth of the Guise affinity needs to be placed in the contemporary political context. In the 1550s the Guise were one of a number of magnate power brokers in the province. The campaigns of the 1550s distanced magnates from provincial affairs but this changed in 1559 with the coming of peace and the unexpected death of the king. After 1559 local power bases became increasingly important in the struggle for power. The Guise affinity was fluid in composition, and developed and strengthened during the Wars of Religion.

3

Faction, religious schism and dynastic strategy, 1558–1562

On the night of 15 April 1562 fighting erupted on the streets of Rouen between protestants and catholics. This was a response to tension within the city, inflamed by the massacre of Vassy and the dramatic political events which were unfolding in and around Paris. The Huguenots in Rouen were well prepared and the authorities taken completely by surprise. The strategically important convent of the Célestines was seized, shortly followed by the hôtel de ville itself. The following day the keys of the town were secured and the beleaguered *bailli*, Jean d'Estouteville, seigneur de Villebon, forced to hand over the château. His lieutenant in the Vieux Palais, Louis de Bigars, sieur de La Londe, was compelled to do likewise. By the morning of 17 April the Huguenots were in control of the third largest city of the kingdom.[1]

The motives behind this successful *coup de main* were rooted in the fear of impending religious repression. Immediately following Vassy, the Huguenots in Rouen mounted an armed guard to protect their assemblies. The massacre was seen as the beginning of a premeditated plot to eradicate protestantism. The subsequent march of the Triumvirs on Paris and the virtual imprisonment of the defenceless Charles IX and his mother only lent further credence to this conspiracy theory. On 19 April the duc de Bouillon, governor of Normandy, arrived in Rouen from court to pacify the rebels. The Huguenot leaders represented their actions as a defensive measure to ensure the safety of 'the people' against the machinations of malevolent factions and to defend royal edicts protecting protestant worship. Their remonstrance directly accuses the duc de Guise, linking Vassy and his seizure of the king's person with attempts to mobilise catholic forces in Normandy.[2]

Huguenot fears were as much the product of local circumstances as of the massacre and events in Paris. The apologia had nothing to say in favour of the prince de Condé but did voice anxiety about the Guise and suspicion about the threat posed locally by Villebon and others. The rise of confessional conflict in Normandy has already been thoroughly analysed, notably by Benedict. In focusing

[1] Benedict, *Rouen during the Wars of Religion*, pp. 96–7; *Histoire ecclésiastique*, ii, p. 715; 'Relation des troubles excités par les calvinistes dans la ville de Rouen depuis l'an 1537 jusqu'en l'an 1582', *La revue de Rouen et de la Normandie* (Rouen, 1837), p. 14; 'Discours abbregé et memoires d'aulcunes choses advenues tant en Normandye que en France depuis de commencement de l'an 1559, et principalement en la ville de Rouen', in Héron, ed., *Deux chroniques de Rouen*, pp. 194–5. The Huguenot insurgents reportedly numbered 500 compared to the handful of men at the disposal of Villebon.

[2] *Histoire ecclésiastique*, ii, pp. 716–18.

on anti-protestant activists and their relationship to ultra-catholic magnates, this chapter illustrates the relationship between court faction and local politics.

COURT FACTION AND FAMILY STRATEGY, 1558–1559

The death of Henri II on 10 July 1559 separates the glories of the Renaissance monarchy from the ignominy of the introverted and chaotic civil wars. The sense of dramatic change is heightened because it ushered in the weak rule of François II when 'the ultra-catholic Guise took control of the government'.[3] Yet this is an artificial historical watershed for, in terms of policy, there was little difference between the two reigns. The Guise were conventional in pursuing family interests rather than devoting themselves to a simple religious ideology.

The Guise assumption and control over royal patronage in the summer of 1559 generated changes of personnel at court. The virtual bankruptcy of the monarchy heightened the need to dominate the patronage network by limiting the number of offices available. Yet the Guise were shrewd enough to realise the dangerous consequences of alienating too many important families. There was no series of wholesale disgraces such as had happened on the accession of Henri II. Evidence for the unpopularity of the regime and its mistreatment of the princes of the blood is often derived from unfavourable protestant sources. The Guise had to accommodate their new ally the queen-mother, with her antipathy to the *connétable*, and to her husband's late mistress. Diane de Poitiers was sacrificed, but the Montmorency were too powerful: the *connétable* was deprived of the office of *grand maître* but this took place only after his eldest son François was compensated with the office of *maréchal*.

Far from altering the designs of the dead king, the Guise showed themselves to be highly conservative. Their policies did not herald the dawn of a new era. They implemented the policies of Henri and his most trusted and faithful friend Anne de Montmorency in maintaining a viable peace with Spain while at the same time pursuing French dynastic claims in Scotland.[4] At home religious persecution was to be intensified, as Henri II had intended.

In the weeks before Henri's death, the Guise were present at council meetings, though Montmorency had been the major power broker at court. The origins of his ascendancy began two years previously. In the 1550s the Montmorency–Guise rivalry had intensified as François, duc de Guise, sought to capitalise on his growing military reputation first gained at the defence of Metz in 1552. Montmorency, with one eye on the royal finances and the other on his rival, increasingly represented a more pacific faction at court. The difference between the two men was magnified by the humiliation of the *connétable* at the battle of Saint-Quentin in August 1557. While Montmorency languished in Spanish captivity, Guise embar-

[3] J. H. M. Salmon, *Society in crisis: France in the sixteenth century* (New York, 1975), p. 118.

[4] *CSPF*, 1558–9, p. 305. There was a council meeting to formulate a Scottish policy on 7 June 1559.

2. Francois de Lorraine, duc de Guise.

ked on the capture of Calais, which fell in January 1558.[5] Henri himself became suspicious of the reputation of Guise, and Montmorency's return to France in October 1558 stiffened his resolve to seek peace.[6] Henri's freedom for manoeuvre was hampered by the parlous state of the royal finances and the growing confidence and assurance of the protestants. The imprisonment in May of Montmorency's nephew, François de Coligny, seigneur d'Andelot, on suspicion of heresy was a Guise initiative motivated by factional advantage. They were determined to capitalise on their ascendancy at court. The pinnacle of Guise influence came in April when Mary Stuart, niece of the duc de Guise, married the dauphin – a reward for the capture of Calais. Success breeds jealousy and Diane de Poitiers, the former

[5] This victory was due to the cooperation between the duke and the cardinal de Lorraine at court: Potter, 'The duc de Guise and the fall of Calais, 1557–8'.

[6] For this and following: Baumgartner, *Henry II*, pp. 197–230.

3. Charles cardinal de Lorraine, archbishop of Reims and abbot of Fécamp.

mentor of the Guise, realigned herself with her old antagonist Montmorency by arranging a marriage between her granddaughter and Henri de Montmorency-Damville.

The winter of 1558–9, with Montmorency safely back at court, witnessed a more vigorous pursuit of peace and a colder royal attitude to the Guise. The request of the duke for further rewards for his victory at Calais, especially the office of *grand maître*, was refused and, realising his increased isolation, he left court on 1 December 1558. With the Montmorency ascendant, peace negotiations began in earnest in February 1559, six miles from Cambrai.[7]

At the same time another event of significance was unfolding. Mary Tudor died in November 1558 and immediately Mary Stuart assumed the arms and titles of the

[7] De Thou, iii, p. 350.

sovereigns of England.[8] Although peace was concluded with Philip II by the treaty of Cateau-Cambrésis in April 1559, it would be wrong to see this as a comprehensive renunciation of war. Montmorency and the treasury gained peace while the king, the Guise and thousands of other noblemen would be able to continue their martial feats on another front.[9]

The traditional depiction of Guise strategy is that of the family using all its resources in the destruction of protestantism.[10] This is an inaccurate reading of the events of the period 1559–60. We should not see the 1560s from the perspective of either their opponents or the Catholic League of the 1580s. The cardinal de Lorraine was the most powerful ecclesiastic in the French church and had a great stake in its future. But this was not the only determinant of family strategy, and Lorraine was not a pro-papal ideologue in the same mould as the hawkish cardinal de Tournon.

Ultra-catholicism itself was never the sole preserve of the Guise, even when the family became synonymous with the defence of catholicism in the 1570s and 1580s. When the edict of Compiègne established inquisition tribunals in July 1557 the Guise family were campaigning in Italy. Henri needed to hold a *lit de justice* to enforce the publication of the edict. The inquisition was to be run by representatives from the three leading families in France: the cardinals de Bourbon, de Châtillon (nephew of Montmorency) and de Lorraine.[11] Diane de Poitiers and the maréchal Saint-André also had a significant influence on the king's hardline policy. The edict which reinforced measures against heresy after Cateau-Cambrésis was drawn up and signed at Montmorency's château of Ecouen when the *connétable* was once again ascendant at court.

Henri II's preoccupations at the end of his life – religion, finance and Scotland – set the agenda for his son's reign.[12] The real problem was that Guise dominance at court and of patronage ensured that policy was perceived as the work of a single faction rather than the result of a consensus reached during the previous reign. The battle for supremacy at court destabilised France as excluded magnates sought a constituency among those opposed to the policies of Henri, among them protestants and unpaid soldiers.

From the summer of 1559 until the drama of the *Conjuration* of Amboise (March 1560), which severely shook the regime, a firm grip was maintained on the flow of royal patronage.[13] Guise acquired the office of *grand maître* at the expense of Montmorency, who retired to his estates. He also wrested the office of *grand*

[8] *CSPF*, 1558–9, pp. 314, 324, 346. The English ambassador Throckmorton became obsessed with this affront.

[9] De Thou, iii, p. 254, lamented this continuation of hostilities when France was exhausted.

[10] Injudicious reading of the 'historical' works of Regnier de La Planche would certainly give this impression: H. Hauser, *Les sources de l'histoire de France: Le XVIe siècle, 1494–1610* (4 vols., Paris, 1912), iii, pp. 66, 82.

[11] *Histoire ecclésiastique*, i, pp. 136, 163.

[12] *CSPF*, 1558–9, p. 307. The council sat 'very hard on matters of finance, whereof they have much lack, notwithstanding the great sums they have borrowed'.

[13] Harding, *Anatomy of a power elite*, pp. 34–5.

chambellan from his young kinsman Léonor d'Orléans, duc de Longueville.[14] The control of François II's household which these offices afforded complemented the preponderance of the cardinal de Lorraine in the church. In the royal council Guise conducted military affairs while Lorraine looked after finance. Andelot was replaced as colonel-general of the infantry by Sébastian de Luxembourg, vicomte de Martigues, a distant kinsman of Antoinette de Bourbon.[15] Obviously any invasion of Scotland would require the full cooperation of the officers involved. Andelot was suspect because of his religion and family ties.

Diane de Poitiers and her closest relatives also suffered. Despite the protests of her son-in-law, Claude duc d'Aumale, she was forced to retire to her lands in an effort to appease the queen-mother.[16] Diane's daughter, Françoise de La Marck, was also banished from court and her husband the duc de Bouillon came close to losing his governorship of Normandy. The mistress without a king had become a political liability. Guise relations with Bouillon soon thawed, leaving him dependent on them to maintain his governorship.

The problem of the Bourbon claim, as princes of the blood, for a leading role on the royal council made Catherine de Médicis a very useful ally, and great efforts were made to accommodate her. Nevertheless the Guise attitude to both Montmorency and Antoine de Bourbon was one of cautious deference. The two Bourbon brothers, Antoine de Navarre and Louis prince de Condé, and their cousin Charles prince de La Roche-sur-Yon were all offered seats in council. In addition, Condé, who had not been thought of as worthy of a governorship before, was offered that of Picardy in place of Gaspard de Coligny.[17] However, the Bourbons, jealous of the rights and honours due to them as princes of the blood, came under pressure from those discontented with the present regime. Navarre was in contact with the English ambassador, Calvinist ministers and Montmorency who all counselled Navarre to press his rights which, of course, would benefit them. Young hotheads in Condé's retinue were eager to make their own reputation through action. Nonetheless, on his return to the south from a family conference at Vendôme, Navarre reaffirmed his loyalty to the king and adherence to catholicism.[18] He was accused by Calvinists, and by subsequent historians, of indecision and for being seduced by both the Guise and Philip II with the mirage of compensation for the loss of Spanish Navarre from his kingdom. In fact, Navarre occupied an excellent bargaining position from which to extract favours from the Guise.[19] Poitou was thus added to his already large *gouvernement* of Guyenne. On

[14] La Roque, *Histoire généalogique de la maison d'Harcourt*, i, p 735; *La légende de Charles cardinal de Lorraine et de ses frères, descrite par François de L'Isle* (Reims, 1576), p. 34.

[15] L. Romier, *La conjuration d'Amboise* (Paris, 1923), p. 4.

[16] Diane's nephew, Louis de Brézé, bishop of Meaux, was compelled to vacate his office of *grand aumônier*: *CSPF*, 1558–9, p. 338.

[17] Romier, *La conjuration d'Amboise*, p. 20. [18] *Ibid.*, pp. 20–3.

[19] For a traditional evaluation of Navarre's role: N. M. Sutherland, *Princes, politics and religion* (London, 1984), pp. 55–72.

25 November 1559 Navarre, La Roche-sur-Yon and the cardinal de Bourbon began their mission to accompany Elisabeth de Valois to Madrid, there to wed Philip II in accordance with the Franco-Spanish peace.

Condé, furious at the inactivity of his brothers, began to plot against the Guise. There was certainly sufficient scope and enough disaffection on which to base a conspiracy. Patronage emanating from court was sharply curtailed in desperate economy measures. Pensions were cut back or left unpaid and thousands of disbanded soldiers swelled the ranks of the discontented.[20] Henri II's generous grants of royal domain were revoked, 'chose qui despleut grandement à beaucoup de Princes, grandes seigneurs & personnes notables qui se voyoyent frustrez de leurs bienfaitz'.[21] Religious tensions and violence now affected every province of France. In Paris the burning of parlementaire Anne du Bourg (a prosecution begun in the reign of Henri II) made the cardinal de Lorraine even more unpopular with moderate opinion.[22]

A PROVINCE IN EUROPEAN POLITICS: NORMANDY AND THE SCOTTISH CAMPAIGN, JULY 1559 –JULY 1560

Normandy faced similar problems to the rest of the kingdom in 1559. A forced loan of 800,000*l* levied on the province in the previous year still remained unpaid. Twenty years later Charles de Bourgeville recalled vividly the hardships that this particular tax caused.[23] In the region surrounding Rouen, peasants fled their villages in order to escape the exactions.[24] It is against a background of religious, political and economic uncertainty that the preparations of the Guise for the Scottish expedition must be considered.

The Scottish expedition of 1548–9, undertaken at the behest of the house of Lorraine, had received the full support of Henri II. Supporting the Guise regime in Scotland proved to be expensive. Debts of over 275,000*l* remained unpaid on Henri's death.[25] Peace had been concluded with England in 1550 and Marie de Guise became regent in April 1554. An able politician like her mother Antoinette de Bourbon, she reconciled disaffected noblemen by pursuing a lenient policy towards protestantism. This strategy was hampered by the presence of Frenchmen in her household and French troops on Scottish soil. Her precarious position obviated a policy of repression as advocated by the royal council, but fears of repression and loss of independence, following the French marriage of Mary

[20] Romier, *La conjuration d'Amboise*, pp. 6–8; *L'Histoire de l'Estat de France, tant de la republique que de la religion sous le règne de François II* (n.p., 1576), p. 5.
[21] *Histoire de l'Estat de France . . . sous le règne de François II*, p. 39.
[22] De Thou, iv, pp. 400–1.
[23] Bourgeville, *Les recherches et antiquitez de la province de Neustrie*, p. 162.
[24] Floquet, ii, p. 277.
[25] M.-N. Baudouin-Matuszek, 'Henri II et les expéditions françaises en Ecosse', *Bibliothèque de l'Ecole des Chartes*, 145 (1987), p. 352.

Stuart, provoked open revolt against the regency.[26] By August 1559 Marie de Guise was clinging to the strongholds of Dunbar and Leith, awaiting assistance from her brothers.

The reports from the many English spies in Normandy provide an unparalleled picture of a provincial polity during the reign of François II. In the beginning the campaign had not been perceived as solely in the sectional interests of the Guise. When Henri II was still alive he had seen Scotland as a crown for his eldest son. As early as 29 June 1559 Throckmorton, the English ambassador, reported the imminent dispatch of Jacques de La Brosse, 'accounted one of the best men of war in France', and Nicholas de Pellevé bishop of Amiens. They were among the most senior Guise counsellors. La Brosse was a veteran of the Scottish campaign of 1548–9 and Pellevé, who was accompanied by three theologians from the Sorbonne, was entrusted with the task of combating heresy. The 2,000-strong expedition force landed in August 1559.[27] English intervention in support of the Confederates counterbalanced French support for the regency. Peace was finally concluded in July 1560 after Marie de Guise's death, indecisive campaigning and amid increasing turmoil in France.[28]

Interest lies less in the political narrative than in the effects of the logistics and preparations for the campaign and their specific relation to the Guise position in Normandy. The problem of supplying an army over such long distances, even one as small as 3–4,000 men, was a major problem for the early modern polity.[29] The logistical problem was exacerbated by the English threat to French shipping. The difficulties of traversing the North Sea are illustrated by the frustrated attempts to send René de Lorraine, marquis d'Elbeuf, and François de Lorraine, *grand prieur*, to Scotland with reinforcements. This expedition was first mooted in July 1559 but not realised until spring 1560. Indeed, the *grand prieur*, who was entrusted with the task of leading the Levant galley fleet from Marseilles, was still in transit along the western seaboard of France when peace was eventually concluded. The operation, of which the Guise assumed full control on Henri II's death, not only had to deal with the perennial problems of distance, bad weather and corsairs but also the political instability in France, shortage of money and war weariness. Nowhere were these factors more evident than in upper Normandy where the major preparations were sited.

After the first expedition had departed in August 1559 the Channel ports were occupied with the victualling of ships and fresh troops awaiting transport. The disruptions of war signified continuing hardship to Honfleur, Le Havre, Dieppe and Fécamp which were dependent on fishing and commerce. These problems were exacerbated by the very nature of the Scottish campaign itself, which was

[26] Donaldson, *Scotland: James V–VII*, pp. 80–99.
[27] *CSPF*, 1558–9, p 346; De Thou, iii, p. 454.
[28] Donaldson, *Scotland: James V–VII*, pp. 96–9; De Thou, iii, pp. 456–66.
[29] These troop figures include those men already based in Scotland before the arrival of reinforcements.

increasingly perceived as of benefit only to a narrow factional interest. Normandy's expanding Calvinist community could only look on apprehensively at the attempts to suppress their religion in Scotland. Huguenot communities were already strong in Le Havre and Dieppe. The latter became home to one of the largest Calvinist congregations in France. The first pastors had arrived in January 1558 and the town had strong trading links with Scotland. John Knox visited the town in February and March 1559, baptising several important local noblemen. The expansion of the reform was encouraged by the captain of Dieppe, Charles de Ponsard, sieur de Fors, a Poitevan appointee of the admiral, Gaspard de Coligny.[30]

As admiral, Coligny had a role to play in campaign preparations and at the beginning of the new reign there is little evidence for his enmity of the Guise. He was not stripped of his governorship of Picardy until early 1560. Thereafter he began to use the office of admiral to build up support in Normandy. He spent more time than ever before in the province, cultivating links with the reformed community. He was sent to Normandy by the queen-mother to enquire into the state of religious feeling. This culminated in the celebrated petition signed by 50,000 Norman Huguenots, presented to the king at Fontainebleau in August 1560.[31] Despite his hostility to the confessional policies of the regime, Coligny acted diligently in his military duties.[32] He may have seen the expedition as an opportunity to expand his credit and reputation in the province and increase his authority at the expense of the vice-admirals who were usually responsible for naval logistics. In July 1560 the office of vice-admiral fell into abeyance and the captaincy of Le Havre passed to Coligny's Languedocian client Jean de Cros.[33]

There was no nobleman in Normandy who had the requisite local credit and the complete trust of the Guise family able to organise the expedition and maintain smooth relations between court and locality. The two most important Normans in the Guise retinue, Tanneguy Le Veneur, seigneur de Carrouges, and his brother the bishop of Evreux, lacked significant local office and were dispatched on an embassy to England in September 1559.[34] The expedition was to be directed largely by the family itself. On 2 December René marquis d'Elbeuf was created lieutenant-general of Scotland by the king. Although as a Norman landowner René could expect to have some leverage in Norman society, if this was the rationale behind his appointment it was flawed by his inexperience and the composition of his clientele, which was recruited largely from the traditional Guise strongholds in eastern France. Moreover, the commission was drawn up against a background of rising discontent among the townsfolk of Rouen and Dieppe:

30 A. Borély, *Histoire de la ville du Havre et de son ancien gouvernement* (3 vols., Le Havre, 1880–1), ii, p. 18; G. and J. Daval, *Histoire de la réformation à Dieppe* (2 vols., Rouen, 1878), i, pp. 7–17; ADSM 6F 11, Recueil de capitaines de Normandie; *CSPF*, 1559–60, pp. 142–4.

31 L. Romier, *Le royaume de Catherine de Médicis* (2 vols., Paris, 1922), i, p. 215; De Thou, iii, p. 526.

32 *CSPF*, 1558–9, pp. 432–3, 454–5.

33 H. Amphoux, *Essai sur l'histoire du protestantisme au Havre et dans ses environs* (Le Havre, 1894), p. 44; Borély, *Histoire de la ville du Havre*, ii, p. 24.

34 *CSPF*, 1558–9, pp. 541, 570, 586.

They are not in good quietness; they grudge and murmur at the Cardinal of Lorraine's proceedings and his government of their King. They fear not so much the war, and think the Cardinal of Lorraine has cause to fear the people, who (as the voice is) does not lie far from the King, and has a guard for his more assurance.[35]

Reports like this from English spies, however subjective and anecdotal, provide eye-witness accounts of the preparations for the Scottish campaign. The contacts of the English agent probably included many Huguenots, obviously concerned more about the continuing policy of repression than the war at this time. This report is contemporaneous with the controversial trial of protestant magistrate Anne du Bourg in Paris. Indifference to the war in Scotland might have continued in Normandy if Elbeuf's relief expedition had been able to leave port. Instead the marquis was driven back by storms and only two vessels completed the hazardous voyage.[36]

The misgivings of the Huguenot minority about the Guise were expressed by a wider section of the community for different reasons. Normandy now had to suffer the host of idle soldiers and the re-fitting of storm-damaged ships. Supplying and equipping the relief expedition in Normandy cost 166,454*l*, and the local population was now burdened with the army in the depths of winter.[37] On 5 January 1560 Elbeuf established his residence in Dieppe, thus adding to the chagrin of the indigenous protestant community who found the public exercise of their religion proscribed for the next two months.[38] On 13 March Francis Edwards, an English agent, informed London about the sentiments of the Dieppois:

Arrived at this town of the 7th [March], and received a letter from a friend at Rouen, who wrote that he had seen a letter from Dieppe, mentioning that d'Elbouef had departed into the country. The merchants are glad of the same, for he was right noisome unto them; few men can say well by him or the Cardinal of Lorraine, and think there will be some stir before they bring their matters to pass. All men draw back and get themselves out of the way, in order not to go with him on this voyage [to Scotland]; some say they are sick and other[s] they lack money. There is much talk of the Queen. The poor merchants would be sorry to have war of her making; they say it is too great a price for them, they will not be able to wear it out; they will be content with peace, they have no money for war at present; 'whishing the Cardinal of Lorraine were bound to a stake and all the dogs of the Pallis Garden were upon his back'.[39]

Merchant concern about the effect of continued war on trade merged with the acute Huguenot hatred of the Guise. Soldiers antagonised the townsfolk of Le Havre: 'they would have meat and drink without money, wherefore the townsmen and they can scant agree'.[40] The tension inside Dieppe, where Elbeuf was physically present with troops, was only relieved when he departed:

[35] *Ibid.*, 1559–60, p. 184.
[36] C. de La Roncière, *Histoire de la marine française* (6 vols., Paris, 1899–1932), iv, p. 26.
[37] *Ibid.*, p. 28, n. 1.
[38] Daval, *Histoire de la réformation à Dieppe*, i, p. 13.
[39] *CSPF*, 1559–60, p. 446. [40] *Ibid.*, p. 493.

On the 26th [March] M. de Foesse [Fors], Captain of Dieppe, came to the castle of Dieppe and proclaimed that noone should call the people there Lutherans on pain of death. The people of Dieppe every night in the market-place and afterwards, going through the streets, sing the Psalms of David, and some days have sermons preached to them in the fields.[41]

This example demonstrates that royal edicts could not be carried out when the local royal officers had no interest in the enforcement. The cardinal de Lorraine was beginning to realise that religious repression was counter-productive because, far from ensuring religious uniformity and peace, it only served to destabilise the body politic. Peace negotiations under the auspices of the queen-mother went forward in the spring of 1560 in tandem with preparations for a further expedition, to include the Levant galley fleet.[42] A large force of nobles gathered at Dieppe in early May to hasten preparations. This time the Guise called on men of local influence to facilitate preparations. Elbeuf was now accompanied by the rehabilitated governor of Normandy, the duc de Bouillon, who, as a Calvinist himself, offered the hope of improved relationships with the Huguenots. Accompanying them were Jean d'Estouteville, seigneur de Villebon, *bailli* of Rouen, and Claude de Lorraine, duc d'Aumale.[43] This council comprised the two most important royal office holders in the province and the two members of the Guise family who were also large landowners in upper Normandy. It was hoped that these men would have the necessary influence, as the Venetian ambassador reported: 'M. d'Aumale has been dispatched to Normandy that his presence and authority may hasten the outfit of ships, and the supplies of ammunition and victuals.'[44]

Preparations continued through the summer. The admiral was at Le Havre supervising the transport for the troops who were arriving daily.[45] All prospective voyages to Guinea, Brazil, Biscay and Canada were halted and the captains ordered to prepare for royal service. On 20 June Coligny held a council of war at Le Havre with all the sea captains.[46] These measures belied the continuing problems of the expedition. The peace negotiations dragged on and the limit of Guise power in Normandy was evident as the fleet was unable to sail. François d'Andelot, no friend to the Guise, refused to embark with troops under his command in Marseilles, whereupon many other captains and soldiers followed his example.[47] He and his brother, the admiral, had little to gain from going to Scotland in person. Even as they celebrated the peace treaty in Edinburgh it was clear to the English that the Guise had been forced into peace by internal circumstances:

The ten hulks stayed for the French king have been discharged, because the mariners would not serve . . . The Admiral having consulted all the captains for the sea at Newhaven,

[41] *Ibid.*, pp. 493–4. [42] *Ibid.*, pp. 521–2, 531. [43] *CSPF*, 1560–1, p. 39.

[44] *Calendar of State Papers, foreign series, Venetian*, R. Brown et al, eds. (9 vols., London, 1867–97), 1558–61, p. 180.

[45] Five vessels were readied for the embarkation of 800 men, and stores were laid in at Caudebec, Harfleur and Le Havre itself for a long campaign: *CSPF*, 1560–1, p. 143; La Roncière, *Histoire de la marine française*, iv, p. 27. [46] *CSPF*, 1560–1, pp. 166–7. [47] *Ibid.*, p. 105.

received answer that the ships were not meet for any enterprise and the men were not willing to serve . . . It is thought that [in Marseilles], as about Dieppe the people and mariners are so evil satisfied that they dare not trust them.[48]

Lack of money and internal instability prevented the Guise from devoting adequate attention to Scotland. The obstacles in the way of a successful military intervention may well have been insurmountable, but they also say much about Guise authority in Normandy. The campaign foundered on their inability, despite their dominance at court and the help of the admiral, to mobilise the Norman ports for sustained relief operations. The admiral's role became more ambiguous as he strengthened his own provincial power base, especially among members of the local reformed community hostile to the enterprise. The governor, Bouillon, had little credit that could be of use to the Guise. Despite their landed interest René and Claude de Lorraine lacked the major office, patronage and affinity to facilitate the departure of the relief force. The Scottish campaign illustrates the limits of Guise power even at the height of their mastery of the patronage resources of the crown.

THE GUISE AND THE RESPONSE TO PROTESTANTISM IN NORMANDY, 1559–1560

After the death of François II in December 1560 Guise influence at court declined. The Guise counteracted this by cultivating their provincial links and by increasingly identifying themselves with ultra-catholic opinion. In Rouen there was already an ultra-catholic faction in the city which looked for support and leadership from the catholic aristocracy. The coterie of men who represented the ultra-catholics among the Rouennais city elites had maintained definite and traceable links to the Guise going back many years and a number were paid servants. Nevertheless it would be wrong to see these men as the pawns of some higher authority. The Guise were more ambivalent towards ultra-catholicism than has been assumed hitherto and the people who moved into their orbit did so because of their own beliefs and strategies. Alliance and empathy with the Guise interest was at once a means of combating heresy and a way of furthering an individual's career ambitions.

Normandy had long protestant traditions. In 1528 Pierre Bar became the first person to be executed for heresy. In 1531 an *inquisiteur de la foi* was established in the province.[49] This tribunal was installed in the convent of the Jacobins in Evreux in the diocese of Gabriel Le Veneur – a close *fidèle* of the cardinal de Lorraine. However, it functioned for only a short time, its prosecution record uneven and its efficacy questionable.[50] Despite the inadequacies of judicial repression, it did have an impact: Evreux was to remain largely untouched by the growth of Calvinism in the 1550s.[51] Elsewhere in the province heresy spread rapidly. In Rouen protestant

[48] *Ibid.*, p. 182. [49] Floquet, ii, pp. 223–4.

[50] Bonnenfant, *Histoire générale du diocèse d'Evreux*, i, p. 133.

[51] On the issue of repression: Benedict, *Rouen during the Wars of Religion*, p. 49.

cells became embedded, though it was lower Normandy which led the way in the establishment of churches. The congregations of Saint-Lô, Vire and Bayeux had churches by 1557 and Caen followed suit in 1558.[52] Lower Normandy was far enough away from the surveillance of the parlement of Rouen and too jealous of its own autonomy to permit the efficient prosecution of royal edicts. The most striking and politically dangerous aspect of the growth of Calvinism was its success in attracting the nobility. The rate of conversions was particularly noticeable in lower Normandy. The conversion of the elite of the local *noblesse d'épée* encouraged and influenced those of lesser status. At its peak in the late 1560s Calvinism could claim to be the religion of 40 per cent of the nobility of the *élection* of Bayeux.[53]

In upper Normandy Calvinist nobles were less numerous and less self-assured, although Dieppe had had a church since August 1557 and the village of Luneray in the pays de Caux provided a centre of worship for Huguenots from the neighbouring bourgs and villages. The great temporal lordships were located along the right bank of the Seine. Inhibiting the growth of rural Calvinism may have been the reluctance of the great magnates to support reform openly. One of the largest landowners and upper Norman magnates was Léonor d'Orléans, duc de Longueville. His mother, Jacqueline de Rohan, won a legal action against the Guise in 1554 which gave her sole wardship of the young duke when he succeeded his cousin, François d'Orléans, in 1551. The Guise were uncles and guardians of the late duke and despite the legal wrangles maintained a close interest in the affairs of his successor.[54] Thus in 1560 the cardinal de Lorraine was named as guardian for the administration of the young duke's estates until he attained his legal majority.[55] At the same time preparations were under way for the marriage of Longueville to the eldest daughter of François duc de Guise. However, the relationship between the duke and Jacqueline de Rohan was soured in the same year when Guise took the office of *grand chambellan* from his prospective son in law. Relations between the two families continued to deteriorate, as the English ambassador reported in May 1561:

> The King [Charles IX] was sacred at Rheims on 15th . . . The Prince of Condé, the Admiral, the Duke of Longueville, the Mareschal of Montmorency and his brother Damville, were not at the sacre, because they would not assist at the Mass. The said Duke is clean fallen from the other side and from his marriage that was in hand with the Duke of Guise's daughter; he is now altogether on this side, which has greatly increased the Protestants, he being one of the greatest of this realm.[56]

52 M.-S. Lamet, 'Reformation, war and society in Caen, lower Normandy, 1558–1610', unpub. Ph.D. thesis (University of Massachusetts, 1978), pp. 144–54; *Histoire ecclésiastique*, i, p. 252.

53 Wood, *The nobility of the élection of Bayeux*, p. 161. For a list of Protestant noblemen: E. Laheudrie, *Recherches sur le Bessin: histoire du Bessin des origines à la revolution* (2 vols., Caen and Bayeux, 1930), ii, pp. 10–14.

54 La Roque, *Histoire généalogique de la maison d'Harcourt*, i, p. 735; BN Pièces Originales 2165 fo. 1053; ADSM C 8182, 'Comptes du duché de Longueville, 1549–50'. The duc de Nemours was also close to the new duke even though only distantly related.

55 BN MS Fr 20176 fo. 195, Letters Patent of Charles IX, 15 Mar 1562.

56 *CSPF*, 1561–2, p. 121.

This rupture with Guise over religion was not as obvious as it seemed. At this particular juncture the major influence over Longueville was his mother, who was a correspondent of Calvin. Nevertheless, Longueville's conversion was a major boost to the protestant cause, especially in upper Normandy where he had many tenants and because the chapel at Luneray was surrounded by his lands. Longueville's château at Tancarville on the Seine acted as a haven for Huguenots escaping persecution.[57]

Among the *moyenne noblesse* of upper Normandy the most important Calvinist was Charles de Martel, seigneur de Bacqueville. As early as 1534 Bacqueville was suspected of harbouring heretics. He held many of his lands from the duc de Longueville and like his lord his attitude to protestantism was ambivalent. He signed Condé's association for the defence of the Gospel in 1562 but never took up arms. He was a moderate, and his seven children were a mix of both protestants and catholics. His links to the church hierarchy were strong. His kinsman Etienne, perhaps a brother, was bishop of Coutances between 1552 and 1560 and one of his sons was a pensioner of the cardinal de Lorraine in 1561.[58]

Bacqueville's faith did not therefore determine his political affiliations. The ducs de Longueville and de Bouillon were also Calvinists but both followed highly individual strategies. Both men were kinsmen of the Guise and this, as much as their religion, coloured their strategy. Neither had much in common with the Calvinist faction except religious conviction. Indeed, in November 1561, during Coligny's ascendancy at court, Bouillon was in danger of losing his office because he was 'well affected to the House of Guise'.[59] Bouillon was undoubtedly devout and during a sojourn in Normandy in July 1561 he gave great heart to the reformed community with his sympathetic attitude to their plight.[60] But the failure of magnates like Bouillon and Longueville to provide anything more than compassionate concern would prove a severe handicap to the formation of an armed protestant party in upper Normandy. Though a major stronghold in terms of numbers, Norman protestantism lacked a leader of sufficient status to defend its early gains. The essentially egocentric mentality of both Bouillon and Longueville should not simply be seen as the lost opportunity of Norman protestantism. Rather, their strategies were perfectly logical within the context of noble culture: collaborating with the Guise to further their respective houses. Indeed, Bouillon was probably dependent on Guise support to retain his office, as he lacked other means of support at court after the death of Diane de Poitiers.

Until 1559 Calvinism was the concern of a small, if growing, minority of the French elites. Likewise the repression of heresy and attempts to foster catholic piety was the domain of a few zealots. The catholic hierarchy in Rouen made little

[57] A. Deville, *Histoire du château et des sires de Tancarville* (Rouen, 1834), p. 260.

[58] A. Hellot, *Essai historique sur les Martels de Basqueville et Basqueville-en-Caux* (Rouen, 1879), pp. 159–88; *DBF*, iv, pp. 1128; BN MS Clairambault 1204 fo. 83.

[59] *CSPF*, 1561–2, pp. 401–2. [60] Floquet, ii, p. 363.

attempt to revive popular devotion to catholicism in the 1550s and 1560s.[61] Etienne de Bacqueville-Martel, bishop of Coutances, made no effort to visit his diocese for six years, despite the growth of heresy. In 1558 he remained only seven months in the face of Calvinists threats.[62] The response of the ecclesiastical authorities in the diocese of Rouen to the reform movement was equally languid and ineffectual.[63] The secular arm of repression was represented by the parlementaires in Rouen who were, by and large, catholic moderates with a distaste for harsh measures.

The small group of Rouen magistrates active in defence of orthodoxy is of most interest. It is possible to trace the links between the Guise family and this clique. The most zealous anti-protestant activists in Rouen in the 1550s included two *conseillers* in the parlement: Robert Raoullin, sieur de Longpaon, and René des Buaz, canon of the cathedral of Notre-Dame de Rouen and vicar-general of the diocese of Rouen, who was, in the absence of the cardinal de Bourbon, the principal ecclesiastical representative in the diocese. Both men were sometime counsellors of the Guise. The des Buaz were important lower Norman *officiers* and remained stalwarts of the ultra-catholic faction throughout the Wars of Religion. René had been appointed to an extraordinary judicial council by the Guise in 1545. He corresponded with the family and in 1550 had the honour of announcing to the parlement the impending arrival of the cardinal de Lorraine in the city. In 1561 he pressed strongly for the compilation of lists detailing Easter observance.[64] Longpaon's was a more single-stranded career, first in the service of Diane de Poitiers and then as the *procureur* of the duc d'Aumale.[65] In 1554 he accused *conseiller* Antoine de Croismare of heresy during a full session of the parlement, and his endeavours resulted in the purge of five suspect *conseillers* in 1556.[66] These ardent anti-protestants were undoubtedly motivated largely by religious zeal, but in the absence of documents the possibility remains that they were supported by or hoped to attract the approbation of their patrons.

Tensions in Rouen increased after the establishment of the protestant church in 1557. During the period 1560–1 there were no fewer than nine serious public order disturbances.[67] The *bailli* Jean d'Estouteville, seigneur de Villebon, was an ultra-catholic who became notorious for his harshness towards the Huguenots. In 1560 he drew up a list of those who did not take part in catholic rituals and processions.[68] Far from being a Guise placeman, Villebon had risen in the service of Anne de

[61] Benedict, *Rouen during the Wars of Religion*, p. 192. [62] *DBF*, iv, p. 1128.

[63] D. Nicholls, 'Inertia and reform in the pre-Tridentine French church: the response to protestantism in the diocese of Rouen, 1520–62', *Journal of Ecclesiastical History*, 32 (1981), 185–97.

[64] Prévost, ed., *Recueil des presidents, conseillers . . . du parlement de Normandie*, p. 48; ADSM 1B 92, Sep 1550; 1 Mi 345 fo. 345. René's brothers held a plethora of royal posts in lower Normandy during this period, including the offices of *vicomte* of Falaise, *vicomte* of La Carnaille, captain of Toucques and *receveur-général* of Caen. [65] BN NA Fr 21165 fo. 74.

[66] Floquet, ii, pp. 295–6; G. Le Hardy, *Histoire du protestantisme en Normandie depuis son origine jusqu'à la publication de l'édit de Nantes* (Caen, 1869), p. 16.

[67] Benedict, *Rouen during the Wars of Religion*, p. 58.

[68] Floquet, ii, p. 297; *Histoire ecclésiastique*, i, p. 348.

Montmorency and had donated several pieces of territory to the *connétable* 'pour la bonne amitié qu'il a à Monsieur Anne duc de Montmorency'.[69] The ultra-catholics, in the 1560s especially, were at no time a monolithic faction. Rather, Villebon consistently neglected the wishes of the Guise. In June 1560 the inhabitants of Dieppe, Le Havre and Rouen presented a confession of faith to the parlement of Rouen. This was publicly burnt in front of the cathedral on the 12th. The following day the religious procession of the *fête-dieu* turned into religious riot. Following this episode some 2,000 Huguenots marched on the parlement to demand justice. Not to be outdone by this show of strength Villebon rode through the streets of Rouen 'en grande compagnie' demanding that all citizens celebrate the festival for the full eight days on pain of death.[70] This action did not necessarily make him a Guisard and he remained unresponsive to Guise concerns.

Royal policy at this time, formulated largely by the cardinal de Lorraine, was designed to defuse religious tension as much as possible in order to stabilise the tottering Guise regime.[71] The impending assembly of notables at Fontainebleau (21–26 August 1560) was the beginning of the search for some solution to instability. Lorraine had realised well before the unsettling and disruptive Conspiracy of Amboise that religious repression would only exacerbate dangerous factionalism.[72] Villebon was more concerned about his own authority than that of the Guise. Indeed, the activities of Villebon and other provincial zealots like him threatened Lorraine's attempts to secure the monarchy:

> I am also told that the cardinal greatly complains of Villebon accusing him of too much zeal and inquisitiveness in having caused such great turmoil, and that he ought rather to have dissembled and pretended not to see what did not please him, than to proceed to such extremities for the discovery of what was kept hidden, whereby he has done nothing but place all his Majesty's Ministers in danger and anxiety.[73]

On 7 July 1560, in line with Lorraine's strategy, a general pardon was published at the parlement of Rouen and prisoners involved in the recent disturbances were released.[74] But court directives had little effect on the tensions in the provinces. In August Rouen was again the scene of further violence. The lieutenant-general of the *bailliage*, Jacques de Brevedent, found it increasingly difficult to pursue the functions of his office, since he 'n'osait sortir de sa maison; craignoit tout de la haine de certains malveillants qui voulaient faire le contraindre à mettre en liberté un de leurs, détenu prisonnier'.[75] Brevedent's reputation was tarnished in the eyes of the

[69] P. des Forts, *Le château de Villebon, Eure-et-Loire: étude historique et archéologique* (Paris, 1914), p. 32.

[70] *Histoire ecclésiastique*, i, pp. 351–2.

[71] His elder brother may have been more hawkish. For a more detailed analysis of court politics and changes in family strategy during these years: S. C. Shannon, 'The political activity of François de Lorraine, duc de Guise (1559–1563): from military hero to catholic leader', unpub. Ph.D. thesis (University of Boston, 1988).

[72] Romier, *Conjuration d'Amboise*, p. 150.

[73] *CSP*, *Venetian*, 1558–80, p. 226.

[74] Floquet, ii, p. 314.

[75] ADSM G 2164, 15 Aug 1560.

reformed community by his connections with Diane de Poitiers and then the Guise. Along with Longpaon he was involved with the efforts of the Guise to sell *rentes* in Rouen, and enjoyed the occasional favour of the cardinal de Lorraine. In addition, his family was influential in the Rouennais ecclesiastical hierarchy.[76]

Those attempting to combat heresy in 1560 included members of the ecclesiastical hierarchy who counted on the support of a small number of lay zealots.[77] They were an intimate and unorganised group of individuals united by confessional zeal and by personal ties to the Guise family and the cardinal de Bourbon. The actions of this handful of priests and royal *officiers* were largely ineffectual, since there was little support at court for a policy of unrestrained repression – in fact, more the opposite. The activities of the *bailli* Villebon were at odds with the policy of the cardinal de Lorraine. Nevertheless, the nucleus of ultra-catholics in Rouen would grow in the following year and the Guise, increasingly displaced at court, sought to strengthen their affinity in Rouen and to reaffirm their commitment to the fight against heresy.

THE GUISE AND THE DEFENCE OF CATHOLICISM, DECEMBER 1560 – APRIL 1562

François II's ailing health exacerbated the debilitating political and religious fissures. He died on 5 December 1560, only eight days before the opening of the Estates-General convoked at Orleans to debate the ills plaguing the kingdom. The accession of a minor strengthened the hand of Catherine de Médicis and the princes of the blood. The Estates-General of Orleans presaged those of 1576 and 1588 in its generally favourable attitude to the Guise. A reaction against the defunct regime failed to materialise, though the perennial problem of taxation and the religious question were high on the agenda.[78] The concern of delegates about these issues did not lead to the scapegoating of the Guise. Although it is difficult to verify the accusations that the Guise worked to prevent the election of Calvinist deputies, it is clear that many of their own followers were returned. The deputies of Dauphiné and Burgundy, provinces governed respectively by the ducs de Guise and d'Aumale, demanded that the princes of the house of Lorraine enjoy the same rank as the princes of the blood at the Estates.[79] Although this request was rejected, and

[76] Brevedent was deputed by the town council of Rouen to go to Paris and lobby the cardinal de Lorraine for a reduction of the town's tax contribution in 1555. The cardinal obtained him an audience in front of the king and the privy council: ACR A 17, 14 Aug 1555. His uncle had been a priest and his son Denis was abbot of La Trappe and canon and deacon of the cathedral of Rouen: Frondeville, *Conseillers*, p. 244.

[77] On the activities of the priest, Adam Sécard, see below, p. 110.

[78] De Thou, iv, pp. 2–8; G. Picot, *Histoire des Etats généraux considérés au point de vue de leur influence sur le gouvernement de France de 1355 à 1614* (4 vols., Paris, 1872), iii, pp. 24–32.

[79] De Thou, iv, p. 16. The deputies were urged to give 'aux princes de Lorraine, les mêmes titres qu'on donne aux Princes du sang'.

despite widespread dissatisfaction with the regime and distrust of the cardinal of Lorraine, condemnation of the family was muted.[80] Guise clients were also elected to represent the Second Estate in Champagne. Despite the Guisard caucus, the First Estate, presided over by Gabriel Le Veneur, bishop of Evreux, was isolated in its vehement denunciation of protestantism.[81] It is possible that clients in the Second Estate did not see the issue as imperative. Jean de Bailleul, seigneur de Renouard, deputy for Alençon, was a Guise agent who had been responsible for the arrest of Madeleine de Mailly, Condé's mother-in-law and a stalwart of the reformed cause.[82] He was either unwilling or unable to press for a conservative agenda in defence of orthodoxy, the *cahier* of his *bailliage* calling for a 'bon concile generale' to heal schism. Such a *cahier* reflected the concerns of the majority, especially in its desire to reform the clergy and the judicial system and to reduce taxation.[83]

Overall, the problems for the Guise were not in the Estates but at court, where they found themselves out of favour. The ducs d'Aumale, de Longueville and de Nemours all took leave of the court in January 1561 and the cardinal de Lorraine departed on 1 February.[84] On 24 March 1561 Antoine de Navarre was made lieutenant-general of the kingdom, although Catherine was the real influence at court as regent. Catherine's attempt to manage court affairs on a Bourbon–Montmorency axis was doomed to failure. The ageing Anne de Montmorency was irked by the influence of the Calvinists at court and the behaviour of his own nephew, admiral Coligny. During Easter 1561 the formation of the Triumvirate for the defence of catholicism set the seal on the Guise–Montmorency *rapprochement*. Strictly speaking the Triumvirate was an association led by Guise, Montmorency and maréchal Saint-André. It resulted from their loss of influence at court but its strength was drawn from the range of opinions it embraced. It encompassed the ultramontane cardinal de Tournon, no friend to the Guise, and important nobles like the duc de Montpensier and the comte de Brissac.[85] The formation of the catholic party had as much to do with factional manoeuvring as religious convictions. Constituted by magnates, it lacked a coherent ideology or programme and disdained appealing to a wider audience.

80 When the Estates reconvened in August 1561 the Huguenots were better organised and more effective in promoting their cause: N. Valois, 'Les états de Pontoise, août 1561', *Revue Historique de l'Eglise de France*, 29 (1943), 237–56.

81 Lacourcé and Duval, eds., *Recueil des pièces originales et authentiques concernant la tenue des états-généraux* (11 vols., Paris, 1789), i, pp. 9–15, 125, 137–45.

82 *Histoire de l'estat de France . . . sous le règne de François II*, p. 624; De Thou, iii, p. 569; *DBF*, iv, p. 1296; Travers, ed., *Rôle du ban et de l'arrière-ban du bailliage de Caen*, p. 117. Bailleul had served in Italy under the Guise as the lieutenant of the *ordonnance* company of Jean d'Annebaut.

83 C. Fierville, 'Le cahier des doléances des trois ordres du duché et bailliage d'Alençon en 1560', *Mémoires lus à la Sorbonne dans la séance du comité imperial* (1876), p. 3.

84 L. Romier, *Catholiques et Huguenots à la cour de Charles IX* (Paris, 1924), p. 54; Shannon, 'The political activity of François de Lorraine', p. 245.

85 Romier, *Catholiques et Huguenots*, pp. 104–5.

François de Guise left court in April, not wishing to be seen to condone tolerant attitudes to worship. Guise also broke off the engagement of his daughter to the duc de Longueville, following his refusal to attend mass at the *sacre* of Charles IX. The cardinal de Lorraine, however, pursued a more tolerant line, culminating in the colloquy of Poissy in September. Whether this was driven by political manoeuvring or a sincere desire for doctrinal reconciliation is not at issue here. The fact is that the Guise family was not presenting a monolithic ultra-catholic front.[86] In defence of family interests the Guise were politically flexible and were not united in their search for a solution to the religious question. The duc de Guise stood firm against any concessions that would undermine the position of the catholic church but did not interfere with his brother's plans. His image as a popular military and catholic hero had begun to take root in the imagination of the Parisian *menu peuple*. His uncompromising beliefs made him the focus of attention during the procession of the *fête-dieu* in Paris on 5 June 1561. An eye-witness remembered the vast crowds: 'la presse empeschoit le chemin; et la clameur et la voix du peuple applaudissoit sa venue par une joye extrême, qui démonstroit la fiance et l'assurance qu'on avoit de luy'.[87]

The queen-mother sought to stabilise her regency by defusing religious and factional tensions. The edict of 30 July 1561 was the result. It aimed at stopping the escalating violence in the provinces in order to lay the groundwork for an accommodation at Poissy. Most significantly it proscribed all leagues and associations. On the surface the edict only recognised catholicism but it ended the death penalty for heresy, and governors, like the duc de Bouillon in Normandy, were told privately to show leniency in its application.[88] The new mood of conciliation was crowned when, at the reopening of the Estates-General at Pontoise in August, a formal public reconciliation was staged between Guise and Condé. On 9 September 1561 the first debates of the colloquy of Poissy began.

The colloquy failed but Catherine continued to search for a solution, summoning an assembly of notables to convene at Saint-Germain in the coming winter. On the other hand, the failure of Poissy undoubtedly damaged the credit of the cardinal de Lorraine and probably convinced his brothers that moderation was a failure. Moreover, the Huguenots were beginning to dominate the *conseil du roi*. Condé's rising star was crowned with his acquisition of the governorship of Picardy in place of the Triumvir, the comte de Brissac. Aumale was the first to leave court on 9 October, rapidly followed by the cardinal de Lorraine and the bishop of Evreux. Ten days later the duc and cardinal de Guise, accompanied by the ducs de

86 For a discussion of the religious question in 1561: Shannon, 'The political activity of François de Lorraine', pp. 286–99; H. O. Evennett, *The cardinal of Lorraine and the Council of Trent* (Cambridge, 1930); D. Nugent, *Ecumenism in the age of reformation: the colloquy of Poissy* (Cambridge, Mass., 1974).

87 Brantôme, iv, pp. 233–4. Significantly, Joachim du Bellay's *Hymne au roy sur la prinse de Calais* was reprinted the same year.

88 Romier, *Catholiques et Huguenots*, p. 163.

Longueville, Nemours and 'other great personages' in a train including 700 men, departed.[89] Longueville's presence in this cortège suggests that religion was not the sole motive for this exodus. Rumours of plots circulated and both Catherine and Navarre pleaded for Guise to return to court. When Montmorency left court two days after Guise, the rump *conseil du roi* was controlled by one faction. The council was dominated by Catherine, chancellor Michel de l'Hôpital, Navarre, Condé and Coligny. The former favourites of Henri II were absent from the centre of royal patronage but all the more dangerous for it. The projected assembly of notables, bereft of the most powerful men in the kingdom, would have little authority

The Guise family remained in eastern France from October 1561 until March 1562, ignoring Catherine's persistent appeals to return to court. Unfortunately little is known about their movements. Christmas spent at the family seat at Joinville provided a good opportunity to formulate strategy and take counsel. Thence the duc de Guise and the cardinal de Lorraine moved on to Nancy where they were entertained by their cousin the duc de Lorraine. From here the two brothers, accompanied by the duc d'Aumale, travelled to Saverne to discuss doctrinal reconciliation with the duke of Württemberg and his Lutheran theologians. From Saverne, where the Guise hoped to neutralise Lutheran opinion or even create an anti-Calvinist alliance, they returned to Joinville. Aumale's return to court on 6 March was probably to facilitate information-gathering.[90] The Guise were either plotting to frighten Catherine into acceding to their wishes or aiming to seize power. As an English commentator wryly noted: 'the Court fears the Guise more than the Guise fear the Court'.[91]

Attempts at reform and reconciliation at court were in stark contrast to the escalating violence in the provinces; here catholics and Huguenots dispensed their own justice. In Normandy in August the great horse fair at Guibray was the scene of disorder.[92] Just as the Triumvirate was a response to the growing influence of the Huguenots at court, steps were being taken in the same direction in the provinces. Growing catholic activism was forming out of the kernel of the zealots of the 1550s. Guise plotting in the winter of 1561–2 correlates with the renewed vigour of ultra-catholics in Normandy, culminating in the raising of catholic forces in March 1562 by Guise clients.

On 19 September 1561 Pierre Quitard of Bourges was executed in Rouen for possessing papers listing the names and detailing the wealth of the 400 leading Rouennais Huguenots. This affair gives credence to the not unbiased claims of the *Histoire ecclésiastique* that there was an anti-protestant plot being hatched in Rouen.[93] Quitard's links to the Guise are a possibility. On his arrest he was reported

89 *CSPF*, 1561–2, pp. 360–2, 396–403.
90 *Ibid.*, p. 547.
91 *Ibid.*, p. 479; Shannon, 'The political activity of François de Lorraine', p. 326.
92 Benedict, *Rouen during the Wars of Religion*, pp. 56–7.
93 *Histoire ecclésiastique*, i, pp. 858–61.

to be in possession of correspondence from the cardinal de Lorraine and Catherine. The duc de Bouillon was sent with a special commission to try Quitard in the *présidial* courts and justice was quickly dispensed. The *Histoire ecclésiastique* implicated a number of local men who seem far more likely candidates for a projected *démarche* in Rouen.

The nascent ultra-catholic faction was formed largely from members of the influential parlementaire community. The author of the *Histoire* may have been expressing his prejudices in compiling this list of miscreants. It could be argued that these men were easy targets for protestant propaganda since they were high-ranking royal officials and enforcers of unpopular royal policies. However, in the sixteenth century the royal will depended completely on the diligence of local officials. The systematic destruction of their property during the protestant hegemony in Rouen in 1562 is further evidence of the existence of an identifiable ultra-catholic faction.

Conseiller Robert Raoullin, sieur de Longpaon, and Louis Pétremol, *président* of the parlement, had long been associated with the Guise. As early as December 1560 Pétremol, perhaps identified in the popular imagination with the Guise, was the subject of threats and attacks, and in July 1561 suffered 'des injures et voyes de faict commises contre luy et ses domestiques en sa maison située au faubourg Cauchoise'.[94] These men were joined by ultra-catholics who had no previous connection with the Guise, but who had played a prominent role in the persecution of heretics. Jean Péricard, *procureur-général*, and Nicolas Damours, *avocat-général* of the parlement had served on anti-heresy commissions in lower Normandy in 1559 and 1560 respectively.[95] The Péricard, in particular, prospered from their association with the Guise, attaining major offices in the Norman judiciary and ecclesiastical hierarchy. Henri de Guise awarded Jean three seigneuries 'in consideration of the services which the said Péricard had rendered him and the late lord duc de Guise, his father'.[96] Jean's eldest son became secretary and later counsellor to Henri de Guise. Three younger sons sat in the parlement of Rouen in the late sixteenth century and the family controlled the bishopric of Avranches from 1583 to 1639.[97]

As in Paris the *basoche* was an important component of the radical catholic community. For Richard Papillon, *avocat*, and Louis Marc, *huissier*, of the parlement, association with the grandees legitimised political intrigue and religious violence. Papillon was a fanatic and later arrested for his part in the murder of a Huguenot *officier*. In 1561 Marc was a founding member of the general confratern-

[94] Frondeville, *Présidents*, p. 176; ADSM 1 Mi 346 fos. 238–58.

[95] Le Hardy, *Histoire du protestantisme en Normandie*, p. 30.

[96] Dewald, *The formation of a provincial nobility*, p. 89.

[97] Frondeville, *Conseillers*, pp. 501–2. Damours also remained closely identified with the Guise interest during the Wars of Religion. He counselled the duc d'Aumale on campaign in Normandy in 1562, and his house was destroyed by the Huguenots in retaliation. His elder brother, Pierre, later joined the Catholic League: Floquet, ii, pp. 397–410; Frondeville, *Présidents*, p. 238.

ity of the Holy Sacrament in Rouen. Established to defend the doctrine of the real presence, it was an early indication of the popular lay response to the mounting threat of heresy.[98] Both men were communicants of the same parish church, signifying the role played by ties of vicinage and sociability in uniting ultra-catholics.[99] That the ultra-catholic cause was nurtured by networks of zealots in parish communities is illustrated by the presence of the dean of the cathedral and vicar-general Adam Sécard, *curé* of Saint-Maclou, among the conspirators.[100] The Sécard were to play an important role in the development of radical catholicism in Rouen throughout the second half of the sixteenth century. Adam was intimately tied to the cardinal de Bourbon, who held Saint-Maclou in his gift. In the 1550s he attempted to lead the combat against heresy from his parish by reviving devotional activity and preaching.[101] He was censured by the parlement for the virulence of his language in 1552, but enjoyed the support of wealthy and sympathetic parishioners, including servants of the Guise.[102]

In 1543 the wealthy parishioners of Saint-Maclou established a confraternity of the Holy Sacrament. Although confraternities honouring the eucharist were a common feature of late-medieval Norman piety, the founding of the confraternity of Saint-Maclou coincided with the growing awareness of heresy and the first concerted royal crackdown on protestantism. The organisation of services was on a pattern similar to the statutes drawn up at the founding of the general confraternity in 1561, which was designed to promote devotion throughout the city. Membership of the confraternity of Saint-Maclou was restricted and attendance by lay brothers at the services was not compulsory, but it was formed 'aussi pour inciter le peuple' to revere the eucharist.[103] At Pentecost 1562 – a time of great tension in the city – Sécard, referred to in the registers as the 'terreur des hérétiques', was elected *procureur* of the confraternity of Saint-Maclou.[104] The ultra-catholic faction in

98 Benedict, *Rouen during the Wars of Religion*, pp. 116, 172–3.

99 Papillon was treasurer of Saint-Vivien in 1562–3 and again in 1573–4: ADSM G 7755; 7758.

100 *Histoire ecclésiastique*, i, 229.

101 In 1553 he received permission to preach every day in the nave of the cathedral: ADSM G 2161, 14 Feb 1553; 2164, 27 Oct 1560; *Histoire ecclésiastique*, i, pp. 229, 354. During the Corpus Christi procession of 1560, the parishioners and clergy of Saint-Maclou were showered with garbage by protestants: Benedict, *Rouen during the Wars of Religion*, p. 61.

102 J. Loth, *Saint-Maclou de Rouen: l'église –la paroisse* (Rouen, 1913). The Ballue were treasurers of Saint-Maclou between 1538 and 1541 and again in the 1570s. They were part of the ecclesiastical hierarchy and servants of the Guise, Claude being *receveur* for the abbey of Bec in 1560: ADSM G 6884; 6888. A priest named Colombel was also identified by the *Histoire ecclésiastique* as one of the chief aides of Sécard in the campaign against heresy. The Colombel family was also closely associated with the Guise and, like the Sécard, were associated with radical catholicism throughout the Wars of Religion. Nicolas Damours was treasurer of the church in the mid-1560s: ADSM G 6887.

103 Both statutes called for a weekly mass, followed by an *Ave Verum* and a short procession in the vicinity of the church. The constitution of 1561 provided for services to be heard in churches on a rota basis: Benedict, *Rouen during the Wars of Religion*, p. 68; Loth, *Saint-Maclou*, pp. 148–51. On Norman confraternities in general: C. Vincent, *Des charités bien ordonnées: les confréries normandes de la fin du XIIIe au début du XVIe siècle* (Paris, 1988).

104 Loth, *Saint-Maclou*, p. 151.

Rouen was united by shared religious zeal and by common ties of sociability and *amitié*. There is no doubt that the conspirators were in communication with the Guise and the cardinal de Bourbon, and that many of the families identified contributed consistent support to the ultra-catholic cause throughout the Wars of Religion.

Potential Guise support in the winter of 1561–2 went beyond a small coterie of the Rouennais elite. On 7 April 1562 two catholic captains of Norman origin, Nicolas Le Gras and Nicolas Maze, marched through the streets of Rouen drumming up recruits. This was provocation to the Huguenot community and the recruiters were promptly set upon; Maze was wounded and Le Gras slain.[105] They had been commissioned to raise forces for the Triumvirs. Maze was a veteran infantry captain of the civil wars who had served under the baron de Clères.[106] The complicity of the baron is confirmed by the remonstrance presented to the duc de Bouillon in April 1562 by the Huguenots, who explained their rebellion as a defensive measure against an all-encompassing catholic attack. They specifically referred to the raising of troops for Guise:

> Est aussi notoire, que ledit sieur de Guyse, par les commissions qu'il a fait expedier sous le nom du Roy, a fait lever gens en plusieurs & en divers lieux, afin d'estre le plus fort a executer son entreprinse & de saccager ceux de la religion, voire jusques à envoyer à ceste fin capitaines en ceste ville de Rouen.
>
> Davantage on sait de certain que le sieur de Clere & le sieur d'Ozebost & autres gentilhommes de ce païs levent & font amas de gens de guerre, pour aller trouver ledit sieur de Guyse & ceux de sa ligue.[107]

Jean baron de Clères was an experienced captain of an ancient and powerful upper Norman lineage. He played an active role in Norman affairs, being elected to the provincial Estates for the *bailliage* of Rouen in 1549 and 1556.[108] Well before the spring of 1562 he was a familiar of the ducs d'Aumale and de Guise.[109] Clères' kinship ties ensured that he was no friend of the Montmorency, but Diane de Poitiers was a greater influence on his orientation to the Guise.[110] This is indicated by the case of his nephew François de Bricqueville, seigneur d'Auzebosc, who came from a powerful and ramified Norman lineage. Auzebosc, along with his uncle,

105 *Histoire ecclésiastique*, ii, pp. 714–15.

106 ADSM 7J 43, Chartrier de la famille Martel, 25 Sep 1554. Significantly, he was ennobled during the reign of François II: Lebeurier, *Etat des anoblis*, p. 190.

107 *Histoire ecclésiastique*, ii, p. 717.

108 He commanded an infantry company in 1554 and captained 100 *chevaux-légers* in 1557: ADSM 7J 3, Chartrier de la famille Martel, 23 June 1553; 12 June 1554; BN MS Clairambault 1087 fo. 134; F. Farin, *Histoire de la ville de Rouen* (6 vols., Rouen, 1738), ii, pp. 400–2.

109 Aumale was in the process of buying horses from Clères in January 1558 while recuperating from illness at his residence of Mauny near Rouen: BN MS Fr 20536 fo. 113, Claude d'Aumale to François de Guise, Mauny, 8 Jan 1558.

110 Clères had married the granddaughter of *maréchal* Odart du Biez, a notable enemy of the Montmorency.

came to the attention of the Guise through their mutual ties to the Brézé.[111] Auzebosc, for whom it was said that 'ladict dame a telle affection', was held in the highest regard by Diane de Poitiers.[112] In 1557 she urged the chapter of Rouen cathedral to avail one of Auzebosc's men of the privilege of Saint-Romain, by which the canons could pardon a single convicted murderer each year, 'pour le désir que j'ay de faire plaisir en ce que me sera possible, à mon nepveu d'Ozebosc'.[113] This supplication was successful and Auzebosc thanked the canons personally. Clearly these ties of kinship, however tenuous to modern eyes, could be activated at any time as part of a reciprocal relationship. When the duc d'Aumale married Louise de Brézé he became part of this complex Norman kinship network, which could be exploited when need arose.

Clères and Auzebosc were more likely to aid the Guise in 1562 because of their historical kinship links rather than their religious zeal. Both men also possessed strong affiliations to the Norman Huguenot nobility. Auzebosc was a first cousin of the leading Huguenot captain, François de Bricqueville, seigneur de Colombières – ties which were not ruptured by the civil war. The wives of both men appear from wardship records to have either been protestant themselves or from families strongly identified with the reformed faith. Adrien de Bréauté, tutor to the young Jacques de Clères, petitioned the king in 1565: 'd'ordonner jusques à . . . ledit sieur de Clere ait attaint son age porté par la loy, il ne sera mis presche selon la Religion pretendue reformée ès terres et seigneuries dud. sieur de Clere . . . eu esgard que ses predecesseurs ont tousjours vescu suivant les statutes de l'eglise Romaine Catholique'.[114] The seventeen-year-old baron's adherence to catholicism was obviously perceived as being tenuous, although he fought on the catholic side in the ensuing years. Bréauté was most concerned about the influence of the other tutors on the impressionable young man. These included Huguenots like his uncle, Guy de Bricqueville, seigneur de Sainte-Croix, and his step-mother, Marguerite de Louvigny. Auzebosc and his wife, Françoise de Chenevelles, had a son christened Isaac, an Old Testament name popularised by Calvinists.[115]

The close ties of both men to the Huguenot community make it unlikely, as the *Histoire ecclésiastique* and the Rouennais Huguenots claimed, that Auzebosc and Clères saw their mission as part of a premeditated offensive against the reformed church. It is clear that the two nobles were dispatched into Normandy in order to elicit support from their friends and kin for the Guise family in the expected military confrontation with the prince de Condé. The rigid division of parties into protestant and catholic obscures the reality of loosely constructed factions built around kinship, affinity and religion. The ultra-catholics, like all factions, were a

[111] Jean, son of Georges baron de Clères, was the product of his father's second marriage. Georges had originally been married to Anne de Brézé, daughter of the comte de Maulevrier, and was lieutenant of the company of Louis de Brézé in 1525. François d'Auzebosc was Georges's grandson from his first union: BN Cabinet d'Hozier 97 fo. 5; MS Clairambault 1087 fo. 134.

[112] A. Floquet, *Histoire du privilège de Saint-Romain* (2 vols., Rouen, 1833), i, pp. 270–4.

[113] *Ibid.* [114] BN MS Clairambault 1087 fo. 140. [115] ADSM 2E1 360, 2 Mar 1575.

broad church built on the constantly shifting foundations of individual and family interests. Appeals to religious belief and attempts to control the royal patronage network were different ways of strengthening and broadening support. Religious and political ideology, especially in the short term, gave identity to what were volatile and dynamic entities. The very diversity of interest within a faction or affinity militated against control from above. The support that the Guise family received in March and April 1562 was based on common interest born of the bonds of service and patronage, religion and kinship. The mobilisation of catholic troops in the provinces was executed through intimates and their trusted contacts.

The subterfuges of the duc de Guise in the winter of 1561–2 were motivated by the political domination of the court by the Huguenot faction and its allies. The duke solicited potential followers in the French provinces and cultivated foreign princes, notably the Lutheran duke of Württemberg. The imbalance in royal counsel was soon manifested in the liberal interpretation of royal commands, originally designed to prevent large assemblies. The new interpretation effectively sanctioned public Calvinist worship in provinces like Normandy and Guyenne.[116] By November 1561 the Huguenots of Rouen were sufficiently confident of immunity from the authorities to hold services publicly in the Halles.[117] On 3 January 1562 the assembly of notables convened at Saint-Germain to discuss solutions to the religious question. The absence of the greatest catholic magnates rendered the atmosphere more favourable to the Huguenots, resulting in the Edict of Toleration (17 January 1562). Theodore de Bèze could even contemplate the conversion of the royal family.[118] However, the lack of urgency that the parlements showed in registering the edict illustrates the widespread catholic despair at such a measure. The crown had little chance of enforcing the edict without the support of the parlements. Paris was the most recalcitrant of all, waiting until 6 March and a royal *lettre de jussion* before complying with the wishes of the royal council. Conversely the parlement of Rouen was the most amenable of all the sovereign courts, being the first to register the edict. This indicates the weakness of the ultra-catholic faction in Rouen, which consisted largely of a few magistrates, often personally linked to the Guise. The vast majority remained, until the outbreak of the civil wars, part of a moderate catholic and essentially erastian elite.[119]

Having returned to Joinville at the end of February from his meetings with Württemberg, the duc de Guise was fully aware of Parisian anxieties, as his brother Aumale was resident at the court at Saint-Germain. Antoine de Navarre, who was leading the vocal opposition against the Edict of Toleration, summoned him to Paris and the Coligny brothers had already considered it wise to retire from the

[116] Romier, *Catholiques et Huguenots*, pp. 264–6.
[117] Benedict, *Rouen during the Wars of Religion*, p. 52.
[118] Romier, *Catholiques et Huguenots*, p. 286.
[119] Dewald, *The formation of a provincial nobility*, p. 48; Benedict, *Rouen during the Wars of Religion*, pp. 78–9.

4. The massacre of Vassy. The role of the duc de Guise was more ambiguous than this piece of Huguenot propaganda by Tortorel and Perisson suggests.

fiercely orthodox capital.[120] The Triumvirate had only to march on Paris and take control of the king and his mother, but the massacre perpetrated by Guise's retinue on 1 March 1562 at Vassy made protestant resistance and civil war inevitable. The reaction to Vassy in Paris and the triumphal entry of the Triumvirate and thousands of their supporters on 16 March provide some of the earliest evidence that Guise was perceived in the capital as the leader of the catholic magnates and champion of the cause. Having entered the porte Saint-Denis in quasi-regal fashion he was met by 'infini peuple, et plusieurs crioyt qu'il fut le bienvenu et qu'il estoit venu ancores assés à temps pour chasser les huguenots. Beaucoup de gens luy allèrent au devant, entre aultres le Provost des merchans'.[121] If the *Chanson sur le massacre de Vassy* is an indication of popular feeling, the killings at Vassy were believed to be not only justified but exemplary.[122] Such sentiments are distinguishable from Guise's own account of the massacre. He expressed regret at the 'accident' which he blamed on the provocations of the Calvinists and on hotheads among his own retinue.[123] Whether he felt remorse at the killing of innocent women and children is immaterial – his apologia was probably intended to repair the damage caused to his relations with moderate allies at home and abroad – for the justification of his actions reveals a discrepancy between his public image and his family strategy. The differing interpretations of Vassy provide an early indication of the ambiguous relationship between the Guise and their partisans among the lower orders which manifested itself most clearly during the massacre of Saint Bartholomew.

Despite the hostile atmosphere, Condé remained in the capital with 1,000 men. There was no bloodshed between the opposing camps, and the prince rejected the calls from the helpless regent for assistance and left the capital on 23 March.[124] The way was now open for the Triumvirs to take control of the king. Condé eventually raised his standard at Orleans and called on all of France to sign his Treaty of Association (11 April 1562) in defence of the Edict of Toleration and against the unjust imprisonment of the king. Four days later Rouen was seized by the Huguenots. This coup was mounted by local residents profoundly disturbed by events in Paris. However, these conflicts were not their immediate concern. They were justified in their anxieties about the intrigues of the ultra-catholics in Normandy guided by the duc de Guise himself.

120 *CSPF*, 1561–2, pp. 525, 547; Romier, *Catholiques et Huguenots*, pp. 311–15; De Thou, iv, pp. 166–9.

121 P. de Paschal, *Journal de ce qui s'est passé en France durant l'année 1562*, M. François, ed. (Paris, 1950), p. 8; *CSPF*, 1561–2, p. 558.

122 A. Le Roux de Lincy, *Recueil de chants historiques français depuis le XIIe jusqu'au XVIIIe siècle* (2 vols., Paris, 1841–2), ii, pp. 269–72.

123 *Discours au vray et en abrege de ce qui est dernierement à Vassi, y passant Monseigneur le Duc de Guise* (Paris, 1562).

124 Romier, *Catholics et Huguenots*, pp. 322–5.

4

Civil war and blood feud, 1562–1574

The radical catholic faction in Normandy had proved ineffectual in arresting the alarming progress of protestantism. In Rouen the city authorities were powerless to stop the Huguenot coup. The strength of protestantism in Normandy was evident in 1562. The most important towns were either seized or declared for the rebels and large numbers of noblemen rallied to the Calvinist cause. As elsewhere in France, coordinating such a disparate faction proved difficult. The protestant party comprised a number of competing factions. Military strategy was conditioned by local feud and the search for plunder as well as by planned strategy. However, the dynamism of the protestant activists was in contrast to the impotence of the catholic–royalist cause in the summer of 1562. In lower Normandy the royalist forces, isolated and outnumbered, awaited salvation from their distrusted Breton neighbours. The first War of Religion was an important turning point for local society. In Rouen the ignominy of the protestant takeover radicalised previously moderate institutions such as the parlement. During the 1560s the ultra-catholic faction in the city grew larger and more vociferous. Likewise, the provincial Estates began to articulate the demands of the catholic majority. Although protestantism remained numerically strong during the 1560s, the number of activists among its enemies was growing. Politics at the court was also changing. The commencement of the Guise–Montmorency feud in 1563 cut across the confessional divide, ensuring the break-up of the broad catholic faction which was symbolised by the Triumvirate. The *maréchal* de Montmorency, who became head of his house in 1567, was widely distrusted by catholics as too moderate. The ultra-catholic faction was represented by the Guise, the duc de Nevers and, increasingly, by the heir to the throne, Henri duc d'Anjou. The fortunes of the Guise in court politics had a particular resonance in the political society of Normandy, for it was during the 1560s that the family hugely expanded its landed interest in the province and the cadet Norman branches began to employ more Normans in their households and retinues.

CIVIL WAR IN NORMANDY, 1562–1563

It is neither intended to present an analysis of the protestant party during the first War of Religion, nor necessary to give a detailed account of the military campaign in Normandy. The task of establishing the composition of the respective catholic and Huguenot adherents in Normandy during the first War of Religion is complicated by two factors. First, a consideration of the ease with which lesser nobles acted independently of any higher authority or overall strategy is required. Allegiance was often ephemeral and military activity carried out for no other purpose than pillage and plunder. The fluidity of noble relationships was a product of noble culture; noblemen changed sides or remained neutral in accordance with individual strategies. It did not mean, however, that there were no distinct factions in Normandy based on religious faith and around identifiable affinities. Second, the Calvinist governor of Normandy, the duc de Bouillon, endeavoured to assemble a third party in the province. It has been suggested that this was an early attempt to form a party composed of both religions, thus reconciling them in the political sphere along the same lines as the *politiques* were to attempt later.[1] In fact, Bouillon had no concern other than to bolster his own flagging authority.

The narrative of events can be divided into a number of distinct phases. From the fall of Dieppe on 22 March until late August 1562 the Huguenots took control of the major urban centres in the province. Claude de Lorraine, duc d'Aumale, was dispatched thither with a special commission as lieutenant-general of Normandy to rectify the breakdown in royal authority. He was supported by Jacques de Matignon as his lieutenant in lower Normandy. Bouillon, furious that his own position was being undermined, established his own base at Caen. He cooperated with the local Huguenot forces and succeeded in effectively besieging Matignon in Cherbourg. The catholic nobility was surprised, unorganised and often indifferent to the tide of protestant success.

The next major development witnessed the arrival of a large royal army in Normandy and the subsequent seizure and sacking of Rouen on 26 October 1562. A few weeks earlier Breton troops had entered lower Normandy and the short-lived Huguenot hegemony began to crumble. The final phase of the war took place in February and March 1563. Admiral de Coligny marched from Orleans to Le Havre in order to secure English subsidies for his mutinous German mercenary *reiters*. During this brief campaign he was able to retake several key strongholds, including Caen.[2]

The urban character of protestantism is evident from the rapid success of the rebellion. In May 1562 Saint-Lô, Bayeux, Falaise, Vire, Lisieux, Carentan, Pont de l'Arche and Le Havre all followed Rouen and Dieppe in falling under the control of the Huguenots. The corollary of urban protestantism was the spread of the new faith among the provincial noble elite. A list dating from September 1562 details

[1] De Thou, iv, p. 240.

[2] The best accounts of the first civil war in Normandy are: *Histoire ecclésiastique*, ii, pp. 712–884; Michel de Castelnau, *Mémoires*, Michaud and Poujoulat, ix, pp. 462–8; 'Discours abbregé', pp. 712–884; Daval, *Histoire de la réformation à Dieppe*, i, pp. 22–46.

the leading protestant nobles.[3] There were large numbers of Normans. For example, the seigneur de Rouville was captain of 'cens gentilshommes Normans'. The list corresponds to a roll call of the provincial elite. Some, like the comte de Montgommery and the baron de Colombières, could claim kinship ties to the Huguenot leadership; others, such as Ponsard, captain of Dieppe, were clients of Coligny.

Noble strategy might marry religious faith to financial gain. On 5 May 1562 Louis baron d'Orbec, *bailli* of Evreux, and his kinsman Jean d'Aché, captain of Tancarville for the duc de Longueville, pillaged the cathedral town of Lisieux.[4] This sort of localised violence and iconoclasm had little to do with the ambitions of the prince de Condé. The Wars of Religion were more the product of these local acts of violence and the virtually autonomous depredations of bands of soldiery than of grand strategy. The Huguenots did not constitute a monolithic party. Moderates like Charles de Bacqueville-Martel and the duc de Bouillon had little success in tempering their more zealous co-religionists. Bouillon arrived at Rouen on 19 April 1562 to treat with the rebels but, realising his own impotence, was forced to retire, leaving Martel there as his lieutenant. Martel had been a protector of protestants since the 1530s and two of his sons joined Condé's army. He remained loyal to the crown and was forced to withdraw from Rouen early on 14 May in response to the increasing level of iconoclasm which he was powerless to prevent.[5] Superseded by the duc d'Aumale as the principal royal officer and with few links to the Calvinist leadership, Bouillon tried to establish his own power base in Caen, which he entered in June 1562. He cooperated with the Huguenots who were strong in the locality and tried to prevent the outbreak of religious violence which would further destabilise his position. The seizure of church plate was useful for supporting a small army but not enough to offset the loss of financial support from the crown, which Bouillon estimated at 35,000*l*.[6]

On 5 May 1562 Claude de Lorraine, duc d'Aumale, was created royal lieutenant-general in Normandy, which conferred upon him widespread powers of authority. This followed the inability of Bouillon to reason with the rebels in Rouen and the deterioration of the political situation in Normandy. Aumale was an obvious choice. He was an experienced soldier and, as a large local landowner, could be expected to possess more local political and financial influence than Bouillon. Moreover, as Bouillon's uncle he was less likely to offend his nephew's honour and drive him openly into the arms of his fellow Calvinists.

Aumale's key problem was to contain widespread revolt with limited resources.

[3] PRO SP Elizabeth 70/41 no. 436, 'Estat des parties . . . qui ont resolu de vivre et mourir ensemble pour mantenir lEvangille en France'. This is a more comprehensive document than that printed in *Correspondence de Theodore de Bèze*, H. Meylan *et al.*, eds. (Geneva, 1960–), vi, app. vii.

[4] M. Sauvage, 'Les troubles de 1562', *Etudes Lexoviennes*, 1 (1915), pp. 53–4.

[5] Hellot, *Essai historique sur les Martels de Basqueville*, pp. 166–72.

[6] BN MS Fr 15876 fo. 245, 14 Jul 1562; Le Hardy, *Histoire du protestantisme en Normandie*, pp. 91–131.

The main catholic–royalist army, gathering in and around Paris, took priority in resources and the local elites were completely unprepared to deal with the Huguenot threat. Jacques de Matignon was dispatched from the court to lower Normandy in order to rectify the situation. A locally important man but also a *fidèle* of Catherine de Médicis, he was expected to act as a counterbalance to Aumale's extensive powers.[7] It was immediately apparent that neither man had the resources to conduct a vigorous offensive campaign. Local credit and specie for the payment of troops were at a premium. Matignon, like his protestant counterparts, relied heavily on church plate and contributions from local churches to maintain his troops.[8] Nevertheless he remained on the defensive, strengthening Cherbourg and awaiting the arrival of reinforcements. Aumale complained strongly about his lack of money and his weakness was revealed by the failure of an attack on Rouen. He summoned the city on 28 May 1562 but, after a few days of ineffectual bombardment, he was compelled to break camp and withdraw when the garrison was reinforced by the seigneur de Morvillier. Aumale's army numbered no more than 3,000 men and he possessed no siege guns.[9] To combat the strong protestant forces in Normandy the duke mobilised the local catholic nobility by using the patronage at his disposal and by summoning his own clients and *amis* to serve him. Less conventionally, he also attempted to deploy the catholic peasantry as an armed militia against Huguenot troops.

Aumale was able to give leadership to a disorganised band of catholic noblemen, in arms before his arrival. Most notable of these was the displaced *bailli* of Rouen, Villebon d'Estouteville, and the Guise agents in Normandy, Clères and Auzebosc, who had been actively recruiting for some time. In order to galvanise these forces, and provide the offices these men expected for their service, commissions were quickly dispatched by Aumale.[10] He also relied on the following of his fellow Triumvir and Norman landowner, the comte de Brissac, whose lands and clientele in Normandy were extensive and whose connections to the Guise and the ultra catholic faction are well documented.[11] A handful of veterans of the Italian wars who had fought under the count were given commissions by Aumale. Their

7 J. de Caillières, *Histoire du mareschal de Matignon* (Paris, 1666).

8 BM Y 102 fo. 32, Charles IX to Matignon, 27 May 1562.

9 *Lettres de Catherine de Médicis*, H. de La Ferrière and Comte Baguenault de Puchesse, eds. (9 vols., Paris, 1880–99), i, p. 317; Paschal, *Journal de ce qui s'est passé en France durant l'année 1562*, pp. 25–50.

10 Adrien de Bréauté was invited to raise 100 mounted arquebusiers and 200 foot. He was captain of Gisors for the duke of Ferrara, father-in-law of the duc de Guise: BN MS Fr 32369 fos. 227, 255; Pièces Originales 496 fo. 17.

11 Brissac served under the duc de Guise in the Italian campaign of 1556–7. The trust and cooperation of Brissac was of vital assistance in the pursuit of dynastic claims in Italy. After the end of the Italian wars in 1559 the relationship began to blossom, especially when the Guise recalled Brissac from Piedmont to bolster the regime of François II. He was appointed governor of Picardy in 1560 and became a leading figure in the ultra-catholic faction until his death in 1563: C. Marchand, *Charles Ier de Cossé, comte de Brissac et maréchal de France, 1507–1563* (Paris, 1889).

exploits in the defence of the monastery of Saint-Philibert against the protestants in 1562 were later commemorated by royalist propagandists.[12]

The motives of the royalist activists in 1562 were various. The case of Antoine de Vieuxpont, sieur de Saussay, demonstrates the inter-relationship between patterns of affinity and confessional zeal. Antoine and his elder brother Jean, baron de Vieuxpont, had previously served under Brissac in Italy. In 1562 he was given command of 300 foot by Aumale, in turn filling the company with his own clients and servants.[13] The precipitous response of the Vieuxpont to the Huguenot coup in Rouen suggests that their loyalties were determined by more than ties of fidelity. On 21 April 1562, barely six days after the fall of Rouen, Jean and Antoine met at the house of their sister Nicole, dame d'Ouville-la-Rivière, in the pays de Caux, to organise an abortive attack on the nearby Huguenot chapel and stronghold at Luneray.[14] This seems to have been an autonomous action by the family and an early demonstration of the ardour which made the Vieuxpont one of the pillars of Norman catholicism. Their antipathy to the reform may have stemmed from Coligny's removal of the baron from the governorship of Dieppe in 1553. The new incumbent, Ponsard was, like his patron, both a Huguenot and an outsider. The Vieuxpont were prepared to aid the Guise against a mutual enemy. This laid the foundation for the Vieuxpont to become one of the most faithful followers of both the Brissac and the Guise throughout the entire Wars of Religion.[15]

Aumale could rely on a measure of support from the local catholic nobility but he was severely short of the money to conduct an aggressive campaign. The Huguenots held the urban centres and they did not hesitate to expropriate local revenue or extort money from the inhabitants. From August 1562 Montgommery, on the basis of Condé's commission, was paying his gendarmerie companies out of the *taille* collected in the *élections* of Carentan and Saint-Lô.[16] Montgommery had no reservations about levying large sums upon his co-religionists. His undisciplined troops committed acts of violence against the friendly population of Dieppe and imposed a forced loan of 15,000*l* on the inhabitants. As a lower Norman, Montgommery was an outsider; townsfolk complained to Coligny and clamoured for the reinstatement of a moderate local man, Charles de Bacqueville-Martel.[17]

[12] 'Histoire contenant le vain effort des Huguenots assiégans le prieuré de Sainct-Philibert', Cimber and Danjou, v, p. 34. Louis Le Pellerin and Martin du Bosc had served as men-at-arms in Brissac's *ordonnance* company. Aumale appointed Le Pellerin captain of 200 foot, governor of Harfleur and captain of the *arrière-ban* of the *bailliage* of Evreux: François de Boyvin, *Mémoires*, Michaud and Poujoulat, 1st ser., x, p. 389; Sauvage, 'Les troubles de 1562', p. 63; Vindry, p. 501.

[13] The ensign of the company, Guillaume Bernard, was wealthy enough to lend his captain 500*l*, presumably towards the upkeep and pay of the company: ACR A 19, 26 Jul 1562; ADSM 2E1 327 *bis*, 31 May 1564. This document was witnessed by Jean Lambert, *avocat-général* of the cardinal de Lorraine. Jean de Vieuxpont had previously served in the Annebaut *ordonnance* company: Travers, ed., *Rôle du ban et de l'arrière ban du bailliage de Caen*, p. 120.

[14] *Histoire ecclésiastique*, i, p. 796.

[15] D. Asseline, *Les antiquitez et chroniques de la ville de Dieppe* (2 vols., Dieppe, 1874), i, p. 250.

[16] BN Cinq Cents Colbert 24 fo. 4.

[17] Daval, *Histoire de la réformation à Dieppe*, i, pp. 41–6.

Aumale also had considerable powers to expropriate local sources of revenue. The *décime* of the diocese of Rouen was used for the payment of troops. Aumale was able to raise loans on the strength of the anticipated revenue of these taxes and the administration of finance provided further opportunities to dispense patronage. Jean de La Vache, *procureur* of the *bailliage* of Gisors, and Jacques Bellier, *élu* of Rouen, were commissioned to collect the *décimes* from three deaneries in upper Normandy to pay the duke's gendarmerie.[18] In transactions such as this the commissioners advanced cash to Aumale and his subordinates in return for the farm of such potentially lucrative contracts.[19] As his brothers were great ecclesiastical lords, the duke could exploit existing credit networks. He borrowed 2,000*l* from the former *trésorier-général* of the abbey of Fécamp and his artillery train was sustained by a loan of 800*l* from the abbey's *receveur*, who was later reimbursed from local royal revenues.[20] Temporal revenues were also assigned for the upkeep of specific units. After the end of the first War of Religion the troops of Adrien de Bréauté, for example, were maintained from the *grenier à sel* of Saint-Valéry-en-Caux.[21] During the second religious war the same captain was 'charge de prendre les deniers du Roy qui se severoient a l'arriere-ban pour payer les troupes qu'il avoit levées'.[22] Aumale made the baron de Clères, already the captain of 100 mounted arquebusiers, not only *colonel du ban et arrière-ban* but also *receveur du ban*, which involved him in the collection and distribution of royal revenues. He received a wage for his office as well as handling cash that came from the *aides* of the *arrière-ban*.[23] Disbursements of royal revenue at source in the localities strengthened an interdependence between provincial elites and local royal fiscal administration outside the crown's control, and forced an increasing decentralisation of power. Local elites were able to circumvent the royal will effortlessly and act independently of authority because they were able to appropriate provincial patronage and revenues.

Wartime expediency determined that Aumale employed methods little different from plunder. He seized cloth belonging to Rouennais merchants which was at Brionne waiting to be fulled:

Aumale, auquel la Royne avoit refusé argent pour [avoir] mal executé sa commission, cottisoit les villes au plus haut qu'il pouvoit, n'oubliant son proufit particulier, deliberant de

[18] ADSM G 5670, Chambre du clergé, 27 May 1562.

[19] In July 1562 Aumale directed these men to forward 1,200*l* to the seigneur d'Alègre: ADSM G 5668, Chambre du clergé, 13 Jul 1562.

[20] AN 300 AP I 223, 31 May 1562; ADSM 1B 591, 2 Sep 1562.

[21] BN MS Fr 32369 fo. 227, May 1564.

[22] *Ibid.*, fo. 229, 7 Oct 1567.

[23] Between 25 October and 14 November he received 1,450*l* from a subordinate *receveur* responsible for the *bailliage* of Caux: BN Pièces Originales 781 fos. 66–70. Another Guise client to enjoy a command was François de La Menardière, elder brother of the *maitre d'hôtel* of the duc d'Aumale, who was given a commission to muster the *ban* of Alençon, Caen and the Cotentin: BN Dossiers Bleus 442 fo. 3, 22 May 1562.

faire transporter par charroy à Amyens les toiles susdites des marchans de Rouen, pour les vendre si les marchands ne vouloient racheter à haut prix, pour à quoy les attirer, il leur promettoit pardon & sauveguarde, dont Péricard, Procureur du Roy, faisoit les despeches moyennant un escu pour sa signature.[24]

One major consequence of the Huguenot *coup d'état* in Rouen and the unleashing of iconoclasm was the radicalisation of the attitudes of the parlementaires towards protestantism. The absence of leading moderates in the parlement, such as *premier président* Saint-Anthot, who spent the duration of the troubles at his residence in Burgundy, and the trauma of the flight of the parlement from Rouen, raised the profile and credit of the minority ultra-catholic faction. Leadership now passed to the militants involved in the ultra-catholic conspiracy of the previous year.[25] The parlement, which reconvened at Louviers on 22 July 1562, liaised closely with Aumale through the Guisard *procureur-général*, Jean Péricard, who seems to have sat on the ducal council.[26] The property of many catholic exiles was ransacked, but the extent of the losses incurred by a small group of individuals implies that Guisards and other perceived ultra-catholics were targeted by the Huguenots.[27] Amidst bitterness and escalating violence it is hardly surprising that attitudes hardened and that the *arrêts* of the parlement became increasingly severe towards heretics. A number of laws sanctioned the detention of all heretics and their summary execution should they resist. In August a spate of hangings of ordinary and harmless Huguenots led Michel de Castelnau to be dispatched by the royal council in order to restrain the new-found zeal of the parlement of Rouen.[28]

Aumale thus utilised his contacts among both the *noblesse de robe* and the *noblesse d'épée* in his campaign. He also called on assistance from a more surprising quarter: the Norman peasantry. He urged local peasants to defend themselves against attack and where possible to harass and hinder Huguenot troops and worshippers. Accusations of appealing to the peasantry to take up arms was a common literary device for denigrating opponents. Nonetheless, these reports should not be dismissed out of hand, since reports from English spies verify the claims made in the *Histoire ecclésiastique*. A local tradition of peasant resistance to authority may have underlain the confrontation between bands of peasants and admiral Coligny at Bernay in February 1563. Insurrection flared in this region in the 1570s and 1580s.[29] The organisation of the peasantry, which later facilitated open armed revolt, began during the violent summer of 1562:

[24] *Histoire ecclésiastique*, ii, p. 738.

[25] *Ibid.*, i, p. 858.

[26] *Ibid.*, ii, pp. 724–5, 733 n. 3; Floquet, ii, pp. 410, 415.

[27] Among others Raoullin de Longpaon and Nicolas Damours were victims: ADSM 1B 592, 27 Feb –8 Mar 1563; 593, 2 Apr 1563; Floquet, ii, p. 397; Frondeville, *Conseillers*, p. 327.

[28] Michel de Castelnau, *Mémoires*, Michaud and Poujoulat, 1st ser., ix, pp. 462–5.

[29] The correlation between the peasant leagues of 1562–3 and those of the 1570s and 1580s is strong. The Catholic League summoned the peasantry to its aid in 1589 in much the same way as Aumale in 1562. See below, chapter 7, pp. 222–8.

Ces assemblées de paysans avoient continuée depuis le siege mis devant Rouen par Aumale, tellement que chaque paroisse avoit son capitaine, qui contraignoit les paysans d'acheter des armes, lesquels se voyans ainsi enbastonnés, traittoient ceux de la religion fort inhumainement, jusques à piller les maisons de leurs propres seigneurs.[30]

The author of the *Histoire ecclésiastique* undoubtedly exaggerates the degree of control exercised by Aumale over the rural population. He was only encouraging what the peasantry had done for centuries: protecting itself against rapacious soldiery. Inter-communal religious violence was not exclusively confined to the larger urban centres: in June 1560 the Huguenots of Luneray came under attack from a local confraternity led by priests from neighbouring parishes. When this centre of protestant worship faced similar threats in 1562, the Huguenots of Dieppe came to the aid of their more isolated co-religionists.[31] They attacked the settlements of Cany, Veules and Saint-Valéry-en-Caux, on hearing that 2,000 armed catholic peasants had gathered in the region.[32] A similar convocation of peasants at Bernay in February 1563 was easily scattered by the veteran troops of admiral Coligny. The prejudices of the author of the *Histoire ecclésiastique* are evident: he wanted to represent the Huguenots as the party of social order and high social status. Despite this bias, there is much truth behind the polemic. In June 1562 an English agent writing from Dieppe noted not only the arrears of pay owed to the troops of Aumale, but also the number of peasants in the train of his army.[33] Another English informant reported to London the following month:

Last Thursday arrived at Dieppe and spake with M. De Force [de Fors], the captain here, concerning his coming and going to the Prince [de Condé], who doubted the same, considering the dangers abroad from men of war, and the peasants, whose disorders are increased. This proceeds from the Duke D'Aumale, who has promised them not only the sack of their Lords, but also to enfranchise them from all tasks and taillages for ever.[34]

No evidence exists to suggest that the duc d'Aumale was intending to establish a catholic league organised at parish level. The reports of English spies were a mixture of truth, rumour and speculation. It is unlikely that Aumale made specific promises to abolish taxation and he did not have control over the movements of the Norman peasantry. Nevertheless, he was in a position to sanction and encourage the peasant resistance to heretical lords, though the motivation was military necessity and neither he nor his kinsmen attempted to revive this embryonic anti-protestant association after 1563. Whether Aumale's leadership of the Norman peasantry passed into folk memory and contributed to peasant support for the Catholic League in 1589 remains speculation.

30 *Histoire ecclésiastique*, ii, p. 334; De Thou, iv, p. 509.
31 *Histoire ecclésiastique*, i, p. 355; ii, pp. 830–2.
32 *Ibid.*, ii, p. 801. The sieur de Veules was a protestant and lieutenant of Dieppe.
33 *CSPF*, 1562, pp. 91–2.
34 *Ibid.*, p. 178.

PURSUING A BLOOD FEUD

The Edict of Amboise brought the first religious war to an end on 19 March 1563. Admiral Coligny's winter campaign in lower Normandy retrieved the Huguenot losses sustained there the previous autumn. The assassination of François duc de Guise on 24 February forestalled the *coup de grâce* about to be delivered to the beleaguered Huguenot forces in Orleans. The deaths of Guise, Saint-André and Antoine de Navarre, the capture of both Montmorency and Condé and the absence of the cardinal de Lorraine at the Council of Trent left Catherine ascendant at court. Consequently, the Guise suffered a loss of influence at court which was to last, with some interruptions, until the accession of Henri III in 1574.

Although not politically impotent, the Guise could not wield the same authority or enjoy the same favour that they had experienced under Henri II and François II, or more recently during the first religious war. One reason for this was the trauma that affected the family in the aftermath of the first War of Religion. The death of the duc de Guise was rapidly followed in the same year by that of François de Lorraine, the *grand prieur*, and that of René marquis d'Elbeuf in 1566. The next generation of the Guise family, whose hopes were chiefly represented by Henri, the new duc de Guise, were mere youths who possessed only the potential of high birth, combined with the residual credit and honour that radiated from the late duke's glorious reputation. These young men were not in a position to make an impact at court, so leadership of the family devolved to the cardinal de Lorraine and the duc d'Aumale, both of whom possessed ability but lacked the charisma of their illustrious brother.

The political strategy of the Guise family between 1563 and the Saint Bartholomew's Day massacre was dictated less by an all-encompassing desire for the eradication of heresy than by a quest for justice against Coligny, whom they held responsible for the duke's assassination. The murder had a significant impact on the psyche of the family. It had the profoundest effect on the cardinal de Lorraine who completely abandoned his moderation over religion and began to display the ultramontanism previously associated with men like the cardinal de Tournon. He displayed more vigour in promoting catholic renewal. However, the Guise did not compromise their interests for the catholic cause; religion and family strategy had a complex interdependent relationship and were not always reconcilable.

François de Guise was praised throughout Europe for his martial abilities and chivalric deeds. After Condé was captured at the battle of Dreux, Guise had offered his own apartments and bed to his prisoner. His penitential behaviour after the massacre of Vassy and the death-bed pardon of his assassin had lent added mystique to his legend, and contrasted sharply with the delight expressed publicly by Coligny on hearing news of the assassination.[35] This did little to assuage the seething hatred of the Guise family for the admiral.

[35] E. Lavisse, *Histoire de France*, vi, pt 1, *La Réforme et la Ligue*, by J. H. Mariéjol (Paris, 1904), p. 82.

Entreaties to the king for redress over the murder were hampered by the absence of the cardinal de Lorraine at Trent.[36] During August some supporters swore vengeance and pledged themselves to pursue the culprits up to the fourth generation of descent.[37] It was not until 26 September that the king was formally petitioned for justice.[38] The petition itself would have been drawn up after counsel had been taken and support solicited from allies and kinsmen. The signatures attached to the petition give a good indication of Guise supporters at court. The document was signed by all of the surviving members of the family except the cardinal de Lorraine. Support was forthcoming from ultra-catholic magnates, such as the ducs de Montpensier and de Nemours and the cardinal de Bourbon. The signature of the duc de Longueville indicates that kinship solidarity cut across religious conviction. He had abjured Calvinism before July 1563, for in that month he married the catholic heiress, Marie de Bourbon, duchesse d'Estouteville. She was the niece of Antoinette de Bourbon and a first cousin of the Guise brothers. This match was engineered by the Guise to reward Longueville's loyalty to the catholic cause and to open channels to Condé.[39] The marriage was part of a Guise plan to rebuild the traditionally good relations with the Bourbon-Vendôme and isolate admiral Coligny. Thus Condé, the prince de La Roche-sur-Yon, the cardinal de Bourbon, the duc de Montpensier and the duc de Nemours witnessed the marriage contract as counsellors of the betrothed.[40]

In reply to the Guise petition, Charles IX sought to defuse the heated political situation by evoking the lawsuit from the parlement of Paris to the jurisdiction of the royal council and furthermore to suspend any judgement for three years. Shortly afterwards the king in council rejected the demand of the cardinal de Lorraine, who had recently returned to court, that the Tridentine decrees be implemented in France.[41] The cardinal was interested in catholic religious renewal: he encouraged the Jesuits, strengthened ecclesiastical discipline in his diocese of

[36] Lorraine was a reformer, advocating the primacy of the council and sceptical of the pope's sincerity about reforming abuses. However, by the summer of 1563 he had forged a more conciliatory line with the pope in order to ensure that a reform programme was decided upon: L. von Pastor. *The history of the popes from the close of the middle ages* (40 vols., London, 1891–), xv, pp. 303–35.

[37] The documents printed in R. Knecht, *The French wars of religion, 1559–1598* (London, 1989), p. 107, are unsigned copies, difficult to interpret and require more detailed analysis than can be given here. Signatory Guy de Daillon, a powerful provincial lord, is not usually identified as a Guisard. The oaths pledged support to the recently formed anti-protestant league in Guyenne, suggesting that the Guise wished to harness their cause to local catholic initiatives.

[38] *Mémoires-journaux de François de Lorraine duc d'Aumale et de Guise, 1547 à 1563*, Michaud and Poujoulat, 1st ser., vi, pp. 538–9.

[39] For example: BN MS Clairambault 346 fo. 303, Marie de Bourbon to François de Guise, 10 Oct 1553; 351 fo.119, Adrienne d'Estouteville to François de Guise, Gaillon, 13 Oct 1557. Originally, François de Lorraine, *grand prieur*, had been offered as a suitable husband until his untimely death.

[40] G. de La Morandière, *Histoire de la maison d'Estouteville* (Paris, 1903), pp. 623–31; BN MS Clairambault 726 fo. 67. The marriage hugely increased the wealth of Longueville and, after his minority ended, he became more independent and was able to distance himself politically from the Guise as their influence waned at court.

[41] *CSPF*, 1564–5, pp. 39–40; Lavisse, *Histoire de France*, vi, pt. 1, p. 84.

Reims and founded a university at Pont à Mousson in 1571. And yet the main interest of the Guise family lay not in the reforms promulgated at Trent but in their pursuit of Coligny. It was the 1580s which saw the dawn of a catholic religious revival. Implementation of the decrees of Trent was not seriously on the political agenda in the 1560s and Lorraine was well aware that many catholics, notably in the sovereign courts, were as suspicious of the Council of Trent as they were of the Jesuits.[42]

The pursuit of Coligny took precedence over all other matters, although his position as one of the leaders of French protestantism served only to intensify the religious convictions of the Guise. The feud threatened to destabilise the uneasy peace that Catherine de Médicis had brokered. Coligny was a member of the Montmorency clan and the feud rekindled the enmity between the Guise and the Montmorency. At the end of the first civil war, Anne de Montmorency saw his opportunity to regain some of his former influence. Navarre and Guise were dead and Catherine's antipathy to her former rival had abated as she was desperately in need of support. Not surprisingly the whole Montmorency family rallied to the defence of their kinsman: 'Here is no bruit so great as the demanding of the death of M. de Guise, which M. D'Aumale purchases against the Admiral. The Constable is a friend to the Admiral, who has great propos with M. d'Aumale.'[43]

In 1563–4 the rehabilitation and influence of the Montmorency-Châtillon were plain for all to see. In contrast, the Guise failed utterly in their quest to obtain satisfaction over the death of the late duke or the implementation of the Tridentine decrees. The outcome was the public reconciliation of Henri duc de Guise and Coligny on 5 January 1564. More significant than this sham was the ensuing retirement of the Guise family to Joinville soon afterwards. Louis cardinal de Guise was the only member of the family to remain in regular attendance at court on its celebrated tour through the Midi. Henri de Guise appeared briefly in June 1565 at the festivities in honour of the Spanish plenipotentiaries at Bayonne, thereafter departing to fight the Turks in Hungary. The cardinal de Lorraine spent most of 1564 at Reims overseeing the enforcement of diocesan reform, culminating in a provincial synod in November.[44] Guise impotence at court and indeed their absence from the heart of patronage and influence is inconsistent with the preponderant role in politics often assigned to the cardinal de Lorraine.[45] Between 1563 and 1567 the attendance of the Guise on the *conseil du roi* declined dramatically.

[42] For the religious beliefs and political manoeuvres of the cardinal: Evennett, *The cardinal of Lorraine and the Council of Trent*.

[43] *CSPF*, 1563, p. 552.

[44] Bouillé, ii, pp. 318–19, 339–40; *CSPF*, 1564–5, pp. 35–6; V. Graham and W. McAllister Johnson eds., *The royal tour of France by Charles IX and Catherine de' Medici: festivals and entries 1564–6* (Toronto, 1979), pp. 35, 77; D. Cuisiat, 'Lettres du Charles cardinal de Lorraine, 1525–74', thèse de IIIe cycle (2 vols., University of Nancy, 1970), ii, p. 422.

[45] N. M. Sutherland, *The massacre of Saint Bartholomew and the European conflict, 1559–1572* (London, 1972), p. 32. Sutherland's misunderstanding stems from her reliance on and uncritical reading of protestant texts and her failure to understand noble aspirations within their cultural context.

Councils were dominated by the resurgent Montmorency–Châtillon and especially the chancellor, Michel de L'Hôpital.[46] It was the duc d'Aumale who took the leading role in counter action. He personally quarrelled with the *connétable* towards the end of 1563 and left court well before his siblings. When the royal cortège reached Champagne (of which Aumale was temporarily governor in place of his late brother) at the beginning of its tour, he quarrelled with the prince de Porcien, a leading Huguenot and enemy of the Guise.[47]

Retirement from court did not entail an end to political intrigue: loss of favour at court could be offset by the cultivation of allies, away from the public glare of court life. The death of the princesse de Condé in August 1564 allowed the cardinal de Lorraine to offer a marriage alliance to the prince. Condé, jealous of the status now enjoyed by the admiral, was eager to expand his political and social contacts. Consequently, the cardinal and Condé met at Soissons at the end of 1564.[48] A marriage alliance would bind those unfavoured at court against the Montmorency. Lorraine suggested a number of candidates: his nieces, Mary Stuart and Catherine de Guise, and Anne d'Este, widow of the late duke. Despite the many obstacles to such a union the preliminary talks were enough to alarm the Montmorency.[49] Nothing came of these plans but amity between Condé and the Guise continued for some time because this unholy alliance was in the interests of both families. In September 1565 the English ambassador noted the amicable relations that existed between the prince, the cardinal de Guise and the marquis d'Elbeuf.[50] The marriage of Condé to Françoise d'Orléans, Calvinist and sister of the duc de Longueville, fortified this amity. Family networks easily traversed the religious divide. At a time of civil war these networks could permit a leading Huguenot like Jacqueline de Rohan, mother of Françoise and Léonor d'Orléans, to appeal directly to the Guise for help. In 1569 she appealed as 'vostre tante' to Anne d'Este to exert her influence in obtaining a *mainlevée* on the dower lands of her daughter, presumably confiscated along with all other lands belonging to those outlawed by the crown.[51]

In terms of blood relations, Condé was much closer to the Guise family than to the Montmorency; Antoinette de Bourbon was his aunt and François de Guise had been his first cousin. Condé's departure from court in July 1567, which precipitated the Huguenot attempt to seize the king at Meaux and the outbreak of the second civil war, was the result of the perceived threat to Huguenots from French catholics and from the arrival of the duke of Alva in the Low Countries. However, Condé was also under pressure at court from ultra-catholics independent of the Guise,

[46] N. Valois, *Le conseil du roi au XIVe, XVe, et XVIe siècles. Nouvelles recherches suivies d'arrêts et de procès-verbaux du conseil* (Paris, 1888), p. 192. During these years the cardinal de Guise appeared ninety times on different councils and the cardinal de Lorraine a mere twenty-four. He was surpassed by L'Hôpital (196), Anne de Montmorency (128) and admiral Coligny (forty-one).

[47] *CSPF*, 1564–5, p. 121.

[48] *Ibid.*, p. 248: Lavisse, *Histoire de France*, vi, pt. 1, pp. 89–90.

[49] Brantôme, iii, pp. 356–7; De Thou, v, p. 12.

[50] *CSPF*, 1564–5, p. 465.

[51] BN MS Fr 3237 fo. 37, Jacqueline de Rohan to Anne d'Este, 27 Jul 1569.

stemming from his rivalry with the great hope of radical catholics, the sixteen-year-old heir to the throne, Henri duc d'Anjou. Their conflict came to a head over command of the army being prepared in response to the turmoil in the Low Countries. Catherine had been willing to accommodate the Huguenots in 1563 but there was no doubt that she would support her favourite son in this dispute.[52] The antipathy between the two princes would not abate and it is likely that Anjou ordered the murder of Condé after his capture at the battle of Jarnac in 1569. Significantly, it would be Longueville who reclaimed possession of the mutilated corpse which had been put on public display by the victorious Anjou.[53]

Having established cordial relationships with Condé in the winter of 1564–5, the cardinal de Lorraine travelled to Paris with a large retinue of armed men. Although he had a dispensation from the royal prohibition on carrying arms, this was highly provocative because François, maréchal de Montmorency, was governor of Paris and the Ile de France. Tolerant towards the reformed church, he hated the Guise even more than his father and was in charge of a volatile capital city. In the light of subsequent events it seems that the interview between Lorraine and Condé was designed to ensure the neutrality of the latter in any potential Guise–Montmorency conflict.[54]

The cardinal's entry was a show of strength in Montmorency's *gouvernement*.[55] To this end he summoned his *amis* and the duc d'Aumale from his residence at Anet. The brothers joined forces at Nanteuil, a Guise estate situated between Paris and Soissons.[56] The force appears to have been led by commensal officers of the cardinal, two of whom were widely noted for their militant catholicism.[57]

The maréchal de Montmorency went to the parlement of Paris on 8 January 1565 to declare that he could not ignore the cardinal's flouting of royal edicts banning the carrying of arms (he later claimed to have no knowledge of the cardinal's dispensation). Lorraine ignored his order not to enter Paris, coming through the porte Saint-Denis. Aumale arrived through a different gate, leaving the cardinal to face Montmorency and the Calvinist prince de Porcien alone. In the ensuing skirmish one or two of Lorraine's men were killed and the cardinal and his nephew forced to take ignominious refuge in a nearby house. Eventually, they reached the safety of

[52] *DBF*, ix, pp. 444–6; Lavisse, *Histoire de France*, vi, pt. 1, p. 95; P. Chevallier, *Henri III: roi shakespearien* (Paris, 1985), p. 143. [53] Brantôme, iv, p. 348. [54] De Thou, v, p. 19.

[55] For the narrative of events: De Thou, v, pp. 12–19; Michel de Castelnau, *Mémoires*, Michaud and Poujoulat, 1st ser., ix, pp. 512–13; Agrippa d'Aubigné, *Histoire universelle*, A. de Ruble, ed. (9 vols., Paris, 1886–97), ii, pp. 214–17.

[56] Henri de Guise was at Nanteuil but played only a minor role in the affair.

[57] 'Lettre de M. le mareschal de Montmorency à M. le duc de Montpensier, prince de sang au sujet de la querelle avec le cardinal de Lorraine', Cimber and Danjou, vi, pp. 256–7. The retinue included Nicolas Durand, seigneur de Villegagnon, originally a protégé of admiral Coligny who had abjured protestantism and was now vilified by his former allies, and Gautier de Foissy, seigneur de Crenay, *premier maître d'hôtel* of the duc de Guise from 1550 to 1562 and thereafter *surintendant* in the household of the duke's widow: Haton, *Mémoires*, i, pp. 33–6, 170, 448, 507, 547, 560, 622–4; ADSM 2E1 304, 4 Oct 1550; Bouillé, ii, p. 584.

the hôtel de Cluny, where Aumale awaited them. Lorraine thought himself safe in this strongly catholic quarter, some distance from the governor's residence.[58] Instead, Montmorency surrounded and menaced the cardinal in his refuge; tension spread throughout Paris and the parlement became desperate to prevent an escalation of the violence. The Guise withdrawal from Paris on the parlement's intercession contrasted with the rapturous reception they had received in 1562. If the cardinal had expected to receive popular acclaim when he entered, he was sorely disappointed. In the exchange of vitriolic pamphlets which ensued, protestant writers satirised the cardinal's behaviour and mocked his lack of support.[59]

In the two best-known pro-Guise tracts there is little evidence of an attempt to appeal directly to popular elements. The incident had damaged the honour of the Guise family, and the intention of these pamphlets was to exculpate the family and denounce the Montmorency. Protestantism was not denounced as a creed but religion is used to highlight the distinction between the two families. Whereas Montmorency's men are said to be protestants, the cardinal and his nephew are saved by 'un evident miracle, & par le toute puissance de Dieu'. These appeals were directed at potential noble allies rather than urban supporters, highlighting the damage done to the honour of the house of Guise and emphasising the lowly status of the Coligny.[60]

Vindication of the family in print was one strategy in the continuing Guise–Montmorency feud. Both families petitioned the court for redress of their grievances, in the meantime summoning their kinsmen and allies. The cardinal retired to his château at Meudon outside Paris and thence to Champagne. According to the protestant, Regnier de La Planche, Aumale retired with his men to his seat at Anet where his call to arms went unheeded. Montmorency felt threatened enough to call on the support of his cousin, admiral Coligny, who arrived in Paris on 22 January accompanied by seventy gentlemen. While the court toured Guyenne, civil war between the two leading magnate families threatened to break out in northern France.

Aumale was preparing for action by attempting to form a league.[61] Leagues and associations were not new phenomena in 1565. Royal troops were used to disperse a catholic defence association in Guyenne the previous year, and the duke had encouraged associations of peasants in Normandy in 1562.[62] Once again he turned to Normandy for support. He entered Rouen on 17 February 1565, ostensibly on private business. In the Norman capital 'se presenterent par devers luy plusieurs de

[58] De Thou, v, p. 16.

[59] *La légende de Charles, cardinal de Lorraine*, p. 95; Aubigné, *Histoire universelle*, ii, p. 216.

[60] *Lettre d'un gentilhomme champenois escrivant a un sien ami Parisien, pour responce à certains libelles fameux nouvellement publiez* (Orleans, 1565); *Lettre d'un seigneur du pays de Haynault envoyée à un sien voisin et amy suyvant la cour d'Espaigne* (Antwerp, 1565). Although the first pamphlet argues that matters of faith should be left to theologians, the second accuses Coligny of striving to break the pacification edict and introduce *prêches* into Paris.

[61] De Thou, v, p. 32.

[62] Aubigné, *Histoire universelle*, ii, p. 213.

la ville pour luy faire la reverance et le saluer de la part tant de l'eglise que de l'hostel de ville et aultres particulliers. Le lendemain, aprez disner, il alla visiter le Vieil Pallaiz à Rouen, et au reste on ne peult entendre par quoy il y estoict venu.' The captain of the Vieux Palais, Louis de Bigars, a man of ultra-catholic sympathies, was a familiar of men in the duke's retinue, although it is not known whether he pledged his support in the event of civil war.[63] From Rouen, the duke headed for his *gouvernement* of Champagne in order to continue sounding out potential supporters. The object of the duke's peregrinations after the tumult in Paris is revealed by a letter he wrote to his brother, René marquis d'Elbeuf, from Champagne on 26 February 1565:

> J'en ay par plusieurs fois cydevant escript à Messieurs de Montpensier, d'Estampes, Cehavigny: par où ils avoyent peu juger la volonté que j'ay tousjours de nous venger, et combien je desirerois l'association que vous dites prevoyant assez combien elle estoit necessaire non seulement pour nous, mais aussi pour tous les gens de bien à qui l'on en veult plus que jamais.
>
> Et pour ceste cause, mon frere, je trouverois merveilleusement bon que les dicts Sieurs y voulussent entendre, laissant les villes, d'autant qu'il n'y a nulle asseurance en peuple, comme je l'ay dernièrement encore cogneut. Mais avec la Noblesse, de ma part je suis tout resolu et prest.[64]

The authenticity of this letter was contested by pro-Guise pamphlets, but it makes no specific mention of Calvinists or religion and it is known that Aumale did try to establish a league. The reference to 'the people' suggests that the Guise were expecting some show of popular support when they entered Paris, and provides further evidence that popular identification of the Guise with the catholic cause was still incomplete. That the Montmorency were concerned about the growth of Guise influence among the bourgeois elites is illustrated by the production of pamphlets designed to emphasise the special relationship between the capital and the Montmorency and to portray the Guise as *parvenus* in the region.[65] It is probable that the popular adoration of the Guise family only developed fully after the Saint Bartholomew's Day massacre, and indeed during the crisis of the 1580s. Until then little was done to exploit popular support. In the 1560s Aumale placed his faith entirely in the nobility.

Many other nobles were canvassed besides those named in the letter.[66] Those mentioned were united by nothing more than their catholicism and their attachment to the north-west – the Maine, Anjou, Touraine and Brittany.[67] Elbeuf

[63] In 1547 he assisted at the marriage of a sister of Aumale's ensign, Claude Vipart: Charpillon, *Dictionnaire historique de l'Eure*, ii, p. 474.

[64] Printed in *La légende de Charles cardinal de Lorraine*, pp. 97–8.

[65] *Du grand & loyal devoir fidelite et obeissance de Messieurs de Paris envers le Roy* (Paris, 1565).

[66] Monluc rejected these overtures: A. de Ruble, ed., *Commentaires et lettres de Blaise de Monluc maréchal de France* (5 vols., Paris, 1864–72), iii, pp. 80–2.

[67] Besides the duc de Montpensier the conspirators included François Le Roy, seigneur de Chavigny, Montpensier's lieutenant-general in the *gouvernement* of Anjou, Touraine and the Maine. Jean de

received the letter from his brother while in Touraine, where he had a small landed interest, strongly suggesting that the regional component of a larger anti-Montmorency league was under discussion.[68] The king acted quickly to proscribe all leagues and associations and in January 1566 a reconciliation between Coligny and the cardinal de Lorraine was staged at the assembly of notables at Moulins. Coligny was also formally exonerated from any complicity in the assassination of the duc de Guise. The real sentiments of both parties were unmistakable; Aumale refused to acknowledge the admiral and Henri de Guise was not even present at the ceremony. When he eventually arrived at court the admiral withdrew.[69]

THE MASSACRE OF SAINT BARTHOLOMEW AND THE RESOLUTION OF THE GUISE–MONTMORENCY FEUD

In recent years N. M. Sutherland's interpretation of the background to the Saint Bartholomew's Day massacre has received renewed attention following its belated endorsement by J.-L. Bourgeon.[70] She contends that the cardinal de Lorraine was gaining influence at court from 1566 and unravels the conspiracy which began by ensnaring the duc d'Anjou into Lorraine's ultra-catholic faction, and culminated in an attempt to assassinate all the Huguenot leaders in the summer of 1568. Though he had ultra-catholic sympathies, Anjou was far from being the tool of the cardinal, and Lorraine was not the puppet-master that ill-informed protestant observers, both English and French, believed. It was a natural and a common literary device to portray the heir to the throne as misled by evil counsel. No individual in early modern society could have mounted 'a nationwide campaign of harassment and violence against the Protestants'.[71] The Guise were still only part of a larger ultra-catholic faction, composed of families that had differing strategies, and the main feature of the later 1560s was not the return to power of Lorraine, but the rise at court of new personalities patronised by Catherine, many of whom gathered around the heir to the throne – a catholic prince in better health and with greater potential than his siblings.

The rise of this faction took place against the breakdown of Spanish authority in

Brosse, duc d'Etampes, governor of Brittany, was a catholic but not essentially a Guisard; his nephew and lieutenant-general in Brittany, Sébastian de Luxembourg, vicomte de Martigues, was also a party to the negotiations, and his services to the Guise and his ultra-catholic connections are apparent from at least 1560 when he was briefly colonel-general of the infantry and a captain in the Scottish expedition. De Thou, in his history, also adds the name of Charles d'Angennes, bishop of Le Mans, who was introduced to the royal council by the Guise in 1559 and accompanied the cardinal de Lorraine to Trent in 1563: *DBF*, ii, pp. 1087–8.

68 Elsewhere the support of the ducs de Nevers and de Longueville was counted on: *Lettres de Catherine de Médicis*, ii, p. 288.

69 Bouillé, ii, pp. 373–4; Salmon, *Society in crisis*, p. 151.

70 J.-L. Bourgeon, 'Les légendes ont la vie dure: à propos de la Saint-Barthélemy et de quelques livres récents', *Revue d'Histoire Moderne et Contemporaine*, 34 (1987), 102–16.

71 Sutherland, *The massacre of Saint Bartholomew and the European conflict*, p. 76.

the Low Countries and the bloody repression instituted by Alva. Lorraine may have sympathised with Alva and he supported the decline of Huguenot magnate influence at court but he was not dominant in council and did not have a European strategy. In 1566 Guise influence at court was at its lowest ebb. When Tavannes arrived at court in early 1567, the Guise family was conspicuous by its absence.[72] According to the English ambassador, decisions were made by a small council consisting of the queen-mother and her protégés, none of whom was a native magnate.[73] Lorraine's impotence was most obvious in his failure to persuade his niece to choose the husband of his choice or to aid her during her difficulties in the period 1564–8. Even as the fortunes of the family improved following the recommencement of the civil wars in 1567, it did not attain its former heights. As the cardinal de Guise lamented in 1568 'je n'ayme guere la plus part des compagnies qui sont an cest court pour estre ainsy facheuse qu'il est possible'.[74]

The Guise had no monopoly as champions of catholicism and in the provinces the religious parties needed no prompting from the cardinal to engage in violence; royal authority was ineffective in preventing plots, assassinations and massacres. In this atmosphere it was not only the protestant leaders who feared for their safety; the Guise too feared assassination.[75] The dominance of the religious moderates on the royal councils between 1564 and 1567 angered many provincial catholics, and a number of local catholic defence leagues came into existence. The most celebrated of these was the Confrérie du Saint-Sacrement organised by Tavannes in Burgundy, and leagues were especially strong in Guyenne, Languedoc and Provence, where protestantism was most entrenched.[76] The local leagues were autonomous and do not provide evidence of a vast catholic conspiracy. They were alliances of bourgeois, ecclesiastics and nobles and thus seem far removed from the noble association envisaged by the duc d'Aumale – aimed more against the Montmorency than the protestants.

The lack of knowledge about factional politics in the mid-1560s is compounded by the nature of the evidence. The paucity of the data means it is very hard to follow the movements of the Guise. Protestant propaganda has to be treated with caution as it was much easier to attack and accuse the Guise than the crown. Condé had to justify his resort to arms by showing that he was protecting the crown against evil counsel. The confused events which led to the third civil war in September 1568 exemplify the problems of interpreting the evidence. Histor-

[72] Tavannes, *Mémoires*, Michaud and Poujoulat, 1st ser., viii, p. 291.

[73] N. M. Sutherland, *The French secretaries of state in the age of Catherine de Medici* (London, 1962), p. 146.

[74] BN MS Fr 3231 fo. 27, the cardinal de Guise to the duc de Nemours, 27 Oct 1568.

[75] Bouillé, ii, pp. 385–6.

[76] Tavannes, *Mémoires*, pp. 289–94; J. de Serres, *Recueil des choses memorables avenues en France sous les regnes de Henri II, François II, Charles IX, Henri III et Henri IV, contenant infinies merveilles de nostre siècle* (n.p., 1599), p. 297; Lancelot du Voisin, seigneur de La Popelinière, *L'Histoire de France . . . depuis l'an 1550 iusques à ces temps* (2 vols., n.p., 1581), ii, pp. 10–15.

ians and contemporaries have traditionally identified the cardinal de Lorraine as the most militant member of the royal council. His correspondence demonstrates that the depredations of the Huguenots in Champagne had badly affected the family's estates. Though he feared for his own safety, he welcomed the Peace of Longjumeau in March 1568, in the hope that 'chacun fasse comme lui même et oublie les injures passées'.[77] The conspiracy theory put forward by Sutherland, in which the renewal of the civil war was the consequence of the failed attempt by the cardinal de Lorraine to eliminate the protestant leadership, places too much stress on protestant sources and uncorroborated English reports, eager to defend their return to conflict.[78] If there was an attempt to eliminate the Huguenot leaders in 1568 both Catherine and her acolyte Birague bore as much responsibility as Lorraine.[79]

The protestant *démarche* at Meaux in 1567 and the third civil war which began in 1568 discredited the moderate catholics represented by the chancellor, L'Hôpital, who lost Catherine's confidence and was forced to leave court in May 1568. The influence of the cardinal de Lorraine at court was resurgent but this was due more to his capacity for raising money on behalf of the crown than the affection of the royal family. As the Venetian ambassador shrewdly observed: 'le cardinal de Lorraine est en faveur à présent; mais c'est par accident ou par nécessité, car tant que la reine n'a pas eu besoin de lui, elle n'a pas été fâchée qu'il restât longtemps de la cour'.[80] War did provide opportunities for the family to display its noble virtues: Aumale received important military commands and the young duc de Guise achieved a seat on the privy council after his stirring defence of Poitiers between July and September 1569.[81] Attempts to portray the politics of the 1560s simply in terms of the struggle of distinct ultra-catholic, Huguenot and *politique* parties confound reality. It is too simplistic to see the Guise simply as 'chefs du catholicisme intransigant'.[82] Henri d'Anjou's determination to establish himself as the leading defender of catholicism was manifested in his antipathy to Condé, which precipitated the latter's departure from court in July 1567. Anjou was made lieutenant-general of the kingdom in November 1567 following the death of the connétable de Montmorency. His fame was spread as the new hero of the catholic cause after his two crushing victories over the Huguenots at Moncontour and Jarnac.

The discrediting of the politics of moderation did not see the victory of the Guise

77 Cuisiat, 'Lettres du Charles cardinal de Lorraine', pp. 485, 493–4.

78 Sutherland, *The massacre of Saint Bartholomew and the European conflict*, pp. 75–105.

79 Tavannes, *Mémoires*, p. 303.

80 M. N. Tommaseo, *Relations des ambassadeurs vénitiens sur les affaires de France au XVIe siècle* (2 vols., Paris, 1838), ii, p. 151. In the early months of 1568 he advanced 50,000*l* to pay for troops, and he encouraged the buying of *rentes* on the hôtel de ville in Paris to pay for the war. He bought huge amounts of bonds and then resold them to his clients in smaller sums. The feverish financial activities of the cardinal during 1568 and 1569 can be followed in AN MC VIII 372, 373.

81 Bouillé, ii, p. 445. 82 Lavisse, *Histoire de France*, vi, pt. 1, p. 133.

but the elevation of a new group of Catherine's protégés. The 'new men' at court were united by their Italian ancestry, mistrust of the Huguenots and loyalty to Catherine. René de Birague entered the royal council in 1568, was made *garde des sceaux* in 1570 and became chancellor the following year.[83] Albert de Gondi, comte de Retz, was a longstanding servant of Catherine. His star waxed with his patron and he was named a governor of the king in 1566.[84] Louis de Gonzague, duc de Nevers, also began to receive favour in the mid-1560s. His marriage to the heiress Henriette de Clèves, duchesse de Nevers, in 1566 required a special royal dispensation which allowed the title of the *duché-pairie* of Nevers to pass through the female line. He was made governor of the marquisate of Saluces, followed by Piedmont in 1567 and the Nivernais in 1569.[85] Catherine was careful to check Guise aspirations: ultra influences on Anjou's council were counterbalanced by the appointment of *politiques* and Aumale was refused command of the vanguard of the main royal army.[86]

Guise influence on the royal council increased following the renewal of the civil wars, but soon dissipated. In June 1570, Charles IX discovered the amorous attentions displayed by Henri de Guise towards his younger sister, Marguerite de Valois. Charles became so furious at the thought of such a union that Guise's life was in danger. Anjou's relations with the Guise became frosty. The family was in disgrace and hurriedly left court, a departure which facilitated the conclusion of peace between Catherine and Coligny. A new edict of pacification was signed at Saint-Germain (8 August 1570) and talks began on the marriage between Marguerite de Valois and the heir to the Huguenot leadership, Henri de Navarre. Even the duc de Montpensier, a staunch catholic and recently married to the sister of the duc de Guise, found it expedient to be 'pas plus ami des Guises'.[87]

This situation threatened to push the Guise further into the political wilderness. Indeed, one of the preconditions of peace was their removal from court.[88] Only the agitated condition of Paris, furious at the pacification, prevented the admiral from benefiting from the fall of his rivals. As his safety could not be guaranteed he was unable to remain at court.[89] The cardinal de Lorraine made no attempt to return to court, complaining to his kinsman the duke of Ferrara that:

[83] *DBF*, vi, pp. 509–10.

[84] *Ibid.*, xvi, pp. 549–54. Sutherland, *The massacre of Saint Bartholomew and the European conflict*, p. 70, is wrong to suggest that Gondi was essentially pro-Guise.

[85] *DBF*, xvi, pp. 606–7. Allowing the *duché-pairie* to pass through the female line was vital to the status of Nevers and was also highly contentious. There ensued a spate of disputes over precedence at court stemming from this royal decision: Anselme, iii, pp. 667–711.

[86] *Lettres de Catherine de Médicis*, iii, p. 79; Michel de Castelnau, *Mémoires*, *Collection universelle des mémoires particuliers rélatifs à l'histoire de France*, xlv, p. 60.

[87] De Thou, vi, pp. 62–3; Lavisse, *Histoire de France*, vi, pt. 1, p. 113; Chevallier, *Henri III*, pp. 143–5.

[88] *CSPF*, 1569–71, pp. 263, 291; *Négociations diplomatiques de la France avec la Toscane*, G. Canestri and A. Desjardins, eds. (5 vols., Paris, 1859–75), iii, pp. 634, 637.

[89] Tensions were running high in Paris well before the massacre: Diefendorf, *Beneath the cross*, pp. 84, 88–92.

> La cour a bien changé depuis le temps où le duc [Ferrara] y était élevé; maintenant on cherche à défavoriser les anciens serviteurs de la couronne, à ne dire jamais la verité, à essayer d'entretenir les grands en division et rompre, s'il est possible les bonnes alliances et amities, pour mettre chacun en défiance de son compagnon.[90]

From May 1572 Lorraine was absent in Rome at the conclave to elect a new pope. He took no part in the dramatic summer of that year.

On 31 January 1572 Henri de Guise petitioned the king to rescind the 1566 *arrêt* exculpating Coligny. His failure left the alternatives of open revolt or reconciliation. In May 1572 Guise, Mayenne and Aumale formally recognised Coligny's innocence. This was a part of Catherine's wider policy of reconciliation and the admiral was able to return to court on 6 June. It was a humiliating climbdown after nine years of bitterness, and Henri de Guise received little in the way of influence at court as compensation. The indignity of his position increased as Coligny reached the zenith of his power in the summer of 1572. Coligny's encouragement of Charles IX's fantasies of military glory in the Spanish Netherlands underlay his downfall. The resolve of the Huguenot leadership to support their co-religionists in the Low Countries led to a *rapprochement* between Anjou and the Guise, and disturbed Catherine's appointees on the royal council.[91] After the defeat near Mons of French protestant troops acting on their own by the Spanish on 17 July 1572, Coligny prepared to march north regardless of royal approval. The council was left with the stark alternatives of moving against Coligny, thus precipitating civil war, or war with Spain.

It is unnecessary to present a detailed analysis of the events of 24 August, which have been the subject of lively debate in recent years. Most historians would now agree that the murder of Coligny and the other protestant leaders ordered by the crown should be differentiated from the uncontrollable general massacre which it sparked.[92] After Coligny's decision to leave for the Low Countries, it seems that the royal council sanctioned the Guise to proceed with their feud and murder Coligny. This is substantiated by the identity of the assassin who wounded the admiral. Maurevert was a Guise servant and awarded a large pension by the duke a few months later.[93] To the Guise, the assassination of Coligny was a just retribution, an attack motivated by revenge rather than religious passion.

[90] Cuisiat, 'Lettres du Charles cardinal de Lorraine', p. 555

[91] Sutherland, *The massacre of Saint Bartholomew and the European conflict*, pp. 251–9; Bouillé, ii, p. 488.

[92] There is an ever expanding historiography on the massacre fuelled by the recent debate over its causes. A good introduction to the controversy is M. Venard, 'Arrêtez le massacre!' *Revue d'Histoire Moderne et Contemporaine*, 39 (1992), 645–61. On the difficulty of reconstructing the events: D. Crouzet, *La nuit de la Saint-Barthélemy: un rêve perdu de la renaissance* (Paris, 1994). The version presented here owes much to Diefendorf, *Beneath the cross*. The controversial views of J.-L. Bourgeon are summarised in *L'assassinat de Coligny* (Paris, 1993).

[93] Maurevert began his career as a page in the household of François de Guise. In 1573 he was awarded a pension of 2,000*l* by Henri de Guise and was a member of his household in 1581: BN MS Fr 8182 fo. 321; AN MC VIII 388 fo. 445. He had previously been a Huguenot and changed sides in 1569: Crouzet, *La nuit de la Saint-Barthélemy*, pp. 463–8.

5. Henri de Lorraine, duc de Guise and comte d'Eu.

After the initial attempt on Coligny's life, enraged Huguenots demanded an inquiry, which could only have led to royal complicity being revealed. On the evening of 23 August a secret royal council was summoned, where it was decided that Coligny had to be killed. However, this would entail the deployment of larger forces, as the wounded admiral was heavily guarded. It is not clear who was present at this midnight council – certainly it was dominated by men close to Catherine and Anjou: Nevers, Retz, Tavannes and Birague. The ducs d'Aumale and de Guise were either party to the deliberations or called in by the council to be personally informed of the plan.[94]

The following morning the ducs de Guise and d'Aumale and the young Charles

[94] Constant, *Les Guises*, pp. 317–38.

d'Elbeuf set out to fulfil their honourable duty to exact revenge in blood.[95] His mission accomplished, the duc de Guise rode directly to Saint-Germain where he hoped to apprehend the vidame de Chartres and the comte de Montgommery. Thus he was absent from the city when the general massacre began. Horrified by the scenes he witnessed on his return he headed for the hôtel de Guise which 'servit de refuge à un très grand nombre de huguenots, qui, sans cette resource, auroient été assassinés comme les autres'.[96] An English report, a source hardly biased in the Guise favour, clearly exonerates him from involvement in the mass killings: 'The Duke of Guise himself is not so bloody, neither did he kill himself, but saved divers; he spake openly that for the Admiral's death he was glad for he knew him to be his enemy, but for the rest the King had put to death such as might have done him very good service.'[97] The Guise were perfect scapegoats for the beleaguered monarchy but the duke refused to accept sole responsibility for the carnage and the protestants blamed the crown. The tract *Reveille-Matin* reserves its hostility for the monarchy and is aware of the duke's role in rescuing protestants and his refusal to accept blame for the popular fury.[98] The actions of the duke suggest a man of honour rather than a religious fanatic. In private he was careful to differentiate between his duty to his father's memory and the aftermath of the murder of Coligny which was not his responsibility. While many protestant *amis* of the Guise were saved, their catholic enemies in the Montmorency clan, like Montmorency-Thoré and the maréchal de Cossé, went in fear of their lives.[99]

The Guise were never the prisoners of religious principle and conviction. Family solidarity often came before religious principles. In 1572, for example, the duke supported his Calvinist kinsman the duc de Bouillon in a dispute with the bishop of Verdun, despite the bishop's protestation that he was defending the catholic religion.[100] In public, however, the duke failed to counter royalist propaganda with his own version of events. Perhaps he felt no need to justify himself. Public misunderstanding of his role on 24 August was to have far-reaching consequences, contributing to the myth of the uncompromising foe of heresy. His reluctance to publicise his actual role strengthened the crude image of a zealous warrior and guaranteed his popularity in Paris. Nevertheless, the Guise cannot be exonerated from contributing to the atmosphere of heightened religious feeling in the city in August 1572. Several historians have underlined the role of Catholic preachers,

[95] Mayenne had left France to join the Holy League against the Turks.

[96] Bouillé, ii, p. 508; De Thou, vi, pp. 411–12; Diefendorf, *Beneath the cross*, pp. 104–5.

[97] *CSPF*, 1572–4, p. 185.

[98] *Le Reveille-Matin des François et leurs voisins* (Edinburgh, 1574). On the Guise as scapegoats: 'Lettres du Roy au gouverneur de Bourgogne, par lesquelles il charge ceux de Guise du meurtre commis en la personne de monsieur l'amiral et de la sedition advenue à Paris, et mande qu'il veut que l'édict de pacification soit entretenu', Cimber and Danjou, vii, p. 137.

[99] De Thou, vi, p. 411.

[100] Buvignier, *Jametz et ses seigneurs*, p. 32. This is even more striking when it is considered that Guise's father had been 'the protector' of the bishopric of Verdun: Evennett, *The cardinal of Lorraine and the Council of Trent*, p. 414.

and in particular the combative sermons of Simon Vigor, in exciting the emotions of the populace.[101] Vigor's intolerant fulminations may have echoed the views of the Guise family but there is no evidence to suggest that he acted as its mouthpiece. It is quite clear, however, that Vigor rose to prominence through the patronage of the cardinal de Lorraine and Gabriel Le Veneur, bishop of Evreux. He came from the Evrechin and it was in Evreux, where he was *grand penitencier*, canon of the cathedral and priest of a nearby parish, that François I had established the inquisition in Normandy. In order to progress, clients such as Vigor needed the support of patrons, but this does not imply that his identity and freedom of action were effaced. By August 1572 he had achieved an elevated position in the Parisian church hierarchy; this gave him the opportunity and made it his duty to speak out on matters of conscience.[102]

Henri de Guise may have boosted his popularity in Paris but he was hated more than ever by Charles IX. The extent of Guise popularity with the masses (and thus the increased danger to the monarchy) is hard to assess. François de Guise had been the object of admiration during processions in Paris but, if contemporaries are to be believed, the cardinal was never loved. The juxtaposition of glorious and honourable military hero with scheming and greedy prelate is a stereotype which requires circumspection of the historian. Nonetheless, at the height of Guise unpopularity in 1559 it was the residences of the cardinal at Meudon and Marchais which were the object of the anger of rioters and not the hôtel de Guise itself, and when Lorraine entered Paris in 1565 there was no ecstatic welcome and seemingly no popular support against the maréchal de Montmorency.[103]

The Guise could also claim popularity for negative reasons. With the exception of the cardinal de Lorraine, their influence on the royal council was minimal. They represented neither the distastefulness of compromise with the Calvinists nor did they belong to the circle of Italian courtiers who were increasingly blamed for the woes of the kingdom. The Guise were perceived as being outside government and therefore irreproachable as the crisis of the civil wars continued into the 1570s and 1580s. On the other hand, there were continual reminders of their military prowess, such as Henri de Guise's defence of Poitiers in 1569. The contrast of martial vigour with court corruption became an even more powerful image during the reign of Henri III.

It would also be a mistake to regard the Guise family as the ducal house

[101] B. Diefendorf, 'Simon Vigor: a radical preacher in sixteenth-century Paris', *Sixteenth Century Journal*, 18 (1987), 399–410; J.-L. Bourgeon, 'Quand la foi était révolutionnaire: les sermons d'un curé parisien, Simon Vigor, en 1570–1572', *La vie, la mort, la foi, le temps. Mélanges offerts à Pierre Chaunu*, J.-P. Bardet and M. Foisil, eds. (Paris, 1993).

[102] On his Evrechin links: M. Charpillon, *Dictionnaire historique de l'Eure*, ii, p. 309; M. Castilla, *Bulletin de la Sociéte Historique et Archéologique de l'Orne*, 31 (1912), p. 350. In 1560 he represented the First Estate of Evreux at the Estates-General.

[103] *Correspondence des nonces en France: Lenzi et Gualtiero, légation du cardinal Trivultio, 1557–1561*, J. Lestocquoy, ed. (Rome, 1977), p. 231.

supported by insignificant cadets. Their strength lay in a remarkable solidarity. Claude duc d'Aumale was a major political figure in his own right. When in March 1573 he became, at the siege of La Rochelle, the second member of the family to be killed by the Calvinists, Charles IX was aware of the emotion that the news might unleash in Paris:

> considerans que sur la nouvelle de la mort de feu nostre cousin le Duc d'Aumalle, le peuple pourra prendre occasion de se esmouvoir . . . a ceste cause, nous avons advisé vous faire ceste lettre pour vous dire et mander que vous regardiez et tenir la main de vostre part qu'il ne se face aulcun esmotion populaire en nostre ditte ville.[104]

The Guise remained distrusted and out of favour at court until Charles IX's death in May 1574 and were not fully rehabilitated until the return of Henri III from Poland in September 1574. The Guise–Montmorency feud remained unabated: when François de Montmorency had arrived at court in December 1573, the duc de Guise promptly retired. The influence of the cardinal de Lorraine on Catherine reached a low point as the authority of the comte de Retz increased. As the king's health declined, both the cardinal and the duc de Guise left court fearing the complete ascendancy of the queen-mother and her favourites.[105] She was delighted to hear of the death of the cardinal in December 1574. With only the cardinal de Guise remaining of the male offspring of the first duke, the fortunes of the family now rested in the hands of a new generation, though watched over as ever by Antoinette de Bourbon. The despondency which had been cast over the family by the death of François de Guise had faded by the time of Lorraine's death. The arrival of the new king at Lyons in September 1574 gave the family great cause to hope. Henri III had a military reputation, was considered an indomitable foe of heresy and had been close friends with the duc de Guise for many years. All members of the Guise family were present at the council meetings that took place in Lyons. The Montmorency were in disgrace: Damville was in open alliance with the Huguenots and the maréchal Montmorency had been imprisoned for his part in *politique* plots. Henri's decision to prosecute the war against Damville and his Huguenot allies gave the Guise an opportunity to press home their advantage.[106]

THE IMPACT OF CALVINISM ON THE GUISE AFFINITY

Historians have traditionally viewed the relationship between religion and clienteles in functionalist terms. According to Lucien Romier, magnates could count on the loyalty of vast client networks. Robert Harding has argued that religious ideology was employed by governors as a means of bolstering their provincial power. Clientage was undoubtedly an important convector of religious affiliation,

[104] *Registre des délibérations du bureau de la ville de Paris*, F. Bonnardot *et al.*, eds. (10 vols., Paris, 1883–1903), vii, p. 54. [105] Bouillé, ii, pp. 529, 554–5. [106] De Thou, vii, pp. 136–52.

and evidence exists to suggest that magnates used religious ideology to solicit both noble and popular support. However, these approaches fail to take into account the complex nature of patron–client relations and ignore the strategies and actions of clients, whose support was contingent.

The Guise attitude to heresy was more ambiguous than hitherto assumed; their affinity in the 1560s was not uniformly ultra-catholic and was evolving at a time of political and religious uncertainty. The development of the Guise following mirrored the turmoil of high politics. Religious differences might abruptly terminate a longstanding relationship but equally confessional disagreements might be no barrier to *amitié*. The very structure of personal ties ensured that the bonds of affinity often remained latent, until activated during a crisis. Yesterday's enemies could become tomorrow's allies in the fluctuating allegiances of factional politics, and the Guise proved adept at attracting and integrating former Huguenots into their following.

So widespread was the appeal of Calvinism to the French nobility that many Guise clients had protestant relatives. Occasionally, the Guise were forced to break with senior commensal officers. François de Hangest, a prominent Picard household officer during the 1550s, enjoyed favour during the reign of François II. In 1559 he was *maître d'hôtel* in the ducal household and in July 1560 he was awarded a gift by the king of 1,100 *écus* in the presence of François de Guise. After the fall of the Guise from power he disappears from the household accounts, a break which may have been due to opportunism, but was more likely motivated by conscience. Though a follower of Condé, he was a notably unreliable ally, and his relative, Charles, remained a paid member of the Guise household during the first War of Religion.[107] The household of the cardinal de Lorraine was also 'contaminated' by heresy. It is unclear whether this affected his political strategy, although it could have influenced his moderate stance in 1560–1. The case of the Huguenot Gilles de Hattes, *conseiller* of the parlement of Rouen and 'superintendant des affaires du cardinal' in Normandy in 1561, demonstrates the obstacles to overseeing servants, and the possible means by which the conspiracies of the cardinal's ultra-catholic servants in Rouen were exposed.[108] Heresy penetrated into the heart of Lorraine's household when the first wife of his *camérier* Gabriel de La Vallée converted to Calvinism. According to Claude Haton, 'elle se fust volontiers meslée de la religion huguenoticque, n'eust esté le peu de respect qu'elle portoit à son mary . . . car elle n'estoit des plus religieuses et scrupuleuses, touchant la vraye religion catholique'.[109]

Repentant protestants also entered Lorraine's service. Durand de Villegagnon had been the leader of the ill-fated mission to establish a protestant colony in Brazil. His conduct in the Americas and his subsequent apostasy was vitriolically condem-

[107] BN MS Fr. 22429 fo. 150; 3942 fo. 27; Neuschel, *Word of Honor*, pp. 41–51.
[108] Frondeville, *Présidents*, p. 223; ADSM G 6595.
[109] Haton, *Mémoires*, ii, pp. 619, 639.

ned by protestant commentators. That a fellow student of Calvin and former associate of Coligny should become so close an ally of their bitterest enemy infuriated Calvinists. Villegagnon and other apostates took advantage of Guise patronage to denounce the errors of the reformed faith.[110] The first patron of Remy Belleau, poet and scholar, was René, marquis d'Elbeuf, whom he followed on the Naples campaign in 1557. By 1560 he had become an adherent of Condé and subsequently became a protestant. His relapse into catholicism coincided with his appointment as preceptor to the young Charles d'Elbeuf in 1563. Reintegration into the Guise entourage was perhaps due to the influence of his relative Jacques, who was *surintendant* of the cardinal de Lorraine. By 1574 Remy had risen to the position of *surintendant* of Elbeuf's household.[111]

According to his biographer, Belleau's religious belief remained ambiguous. Perhaps his convictions were transmitted to his young charge, since Charles d'Elbeuf's attitude to protestantism was moderate when compared to his cousins. In the 1570s Charles employed former Norman Huguenots in his household, such as members of the Fouilleuse and Sarcilly families.[112] The numerical strength of protestantism in Normandy was such that Huguenot vassals, tenants, neighbours and servants had to be accommodated. The pragmatic attitude of René and later Charles d'Elbeuf is best explained by their affective ties to protestants. René's wife, Louise de Rieux, may well have harboured protestant sympathies like her sisters. Her mother, Suzanne de Bourbon, guardian of René and Louise's children on their deaths in 1566, seems to have been a protestant. In 1561 she permitted the establishment of a chapel at Lillebonne, which she held in dower. Naturally she showed little inclination to encourage catholic worship, and her vassals in the parish of Troispierres demanded a resident priest 'attendu qu'il y a longtemps que le curé dudict . . . n'ayant faict aulcune residence'.[113] The chapel did not survive the death of its patron in 1570, but the Coligny, as joint administrators of Lillebonne with the marquis d'Elbeuf, later tried to revive protestant worship. The marquis was unconcerned by these developments. When the cathedral chapter attempted to prevent the reintroduction of protestant worship to Lillebonne it was not Elbeuf but Jean de Moy, governor of the pays de Caux and an ultra-catholic, to whom the canons protested. When Lillebonne and Brionne, which also had a chapel in the

110 A. Heulhard, *Villegagnon: roi d'Amérique. Un homme de mer au XVIe siècle, 1510–72* (Paris, 1897), p. 188; T. Wanegffelen, 'Le plat pays de la croyance: frontière confessionnelle et sensibilité religieuse en France au XVIe siècle', *Revue d'Histoire de l'Eglise de France,* 81 (1995), 391–411. Mathieu Launay, one of the founders of the Catholic League, was another convert and anti-protestant polemicist patronised by the Guise: P. Ascoli, 'The Sixteen and the Paris league, 1585–1591', unpub. Ph.D. thesis (University of California, Berkeley, 1971), p. 4.

111 A. Echkhardt, *Remy Belleau: sa vie – sa bergerie* (Budapest, 1917); ADSM 2E1 904, 16 Jun 1574.

112 The elder line of the Sarcilly had been close to the house of Lorraine since the 1550s; their cousins provided two Huguenot captains in 1562: H. de La Ferrière-Percy, *Histoire du canton d'Athis* (Paris, 1858), pp. 31–7. Charles de Fouilleuse, officer in Elbeuf's gendarmerie company in the 1570s, was a Huguenot as a youth and related to prominent protestant families of the Vexin.

113 ADSM 1E 481, 31 May 1565.

1560s, were definitively inherited by Elbeuf in 1584 on the eve of the Catholic League, open protestant worship did become more dangerous. More difficult to explain is the existence of chapels at Elbeuf and Ancenis in the 1560s which had been in the family's possession since the previous decade.[114]

Although the gradual transference of much of the Harcourt inheritance to the Elbeuf must have alarmed the local protestant community, its joint administration by the Guise and the Coligny was handled amicably despite mutual hostility. The career of Eustache Trevache, Rouennais merchant and Huguenot, is indicative of Elbeuf's ambivalent attitude to heresy. In 1574 the cardinal de Lorraine ratified the farm of the comté of Lillebonne, a lease renewed by Elbeuf in 1581. The contracting with a Huguenot was uncontroversial, since Trevache worked jointly for the Guise and the Coligny.[115] More difficult to resolve is Trevache's position as a financial agent of Elbeuf in the 1580s, culminating in his efforts, at the height of the Catholic League revolt, to raise 10,000 *écus* for his master on the Rouen money markets. Trevache was either poorly informed of political events or, more likely, received personal guarantees of his safety. Following the accommodation between the League and the king in July 1585, these assurances must have seemed empty and Trevache fled to London. The relationship between Trevache and Elbeuf had been mutually beneficial and uncomplicated by ideology. The duke was more concerned with the efficient running of his estates than any contradiction between his employment of a Huguenot and his desire for the extermination of heresy, as his membership of the Catholic League required. Thus, when Trevache belatedly fled the League, the duke's first concern was that Trevache had left without paying the money he owed.[116]

Royal edicts ordering the destitution of protestant office holders and the sequestration of Huguenot assets disrupted seigneurial administration. Adrien Bridou, *vicomte* and *receveur* of Aumale in 1567 and *vicomte* of Neufchâtel-en-Bray for the king, was a protestant.[117] In 1569, following a royal edict which dispossessed protestant office holders, Bridou lost his royal office and seemingly his seigneurial office too. Perhaps the duke had appointed Bridou unaware of his religious convictions, and thereafter failed to remove him because either the office was venal or his religion inconsequential. Business was hampered more by royal interference than by confessional animosity. In 1570 the new *receveur* of the duchy of Aumale was arrested by royal officers demanding payment of sums owed to protestants,

[114] ADSM G 2174, 22 Jul 1581; S. Mours, *Les églises réformées en France* (Paris and Strasbourg, 1958), pp. 73, 99.

[115] Charles marquis d'Elbeuf was a minor until 1576 and Guy-Paul de Coligny was a minor until 1584. Thus the lands were administered by their relatives.

[116] Brunelle, *The New World merchants of Rouen*, pp. 155–6; ADSM 2E1 360, 13 Jun 1580; 365, 14 Feb 1582; 1er meubles, 24 Feb 1586; 2E1 2283, 27 Mar 1585. Trevache had been *receveur-général en la province de Normandie*: ADSM 2E1 351, 9 Jul 1575; ADC E 353, 13 Nov 1585. Trevache returned to Normandy between 1586 and 1588 but fled again as the political situation once more deteriorated.

[117] His predecessor was also a protestant: Bouquet, ed., *Documents concernant l'histoire de Neufchâtel-en-Bray*, p. 11.

including 4,500 *écus* due to Jean du Moucel, *contrôleur* in the chancery of Rouen. Du Moucel was a prominent opponent of orthodoxy. During the first religious war he raised troops for the protestant cause and was accused of the murder of a priest, and in 1557 his nephew had scuffled with a leading ultra-catholic member of the parlement of Rouen, disrupting a session of the court. There was every reason for du Moucel to despise the duc d'Aumale. In January 1563 one of the duke's leading counsellors was implicated in the murder of du Moucel's father-in-law, a protestant royal officer in Rouen.[118] Two years later the duke sold du Moucel 300 *écus* of *rente*, illustrating that public confessional hostility was tempered by private contacts and transactions. The Guise relationship with many Huguenots in the 1560s was ambivalent and unconstrained by religious ideology. The rhetoric of religious hatred belied the complexity of the family's response to protestantism.

THE FOUNDATIONS OF A PROVINCIAL POWER BASE, 1562–1574

As the fortunes of the family oscillated at court, influence in Normandy increased steadily during the 1560s. On the death of Diane de Poitiers in 1566 the duc d'Aumale collected the last of the Brézé inheritance. He established his residence at Anet and began to recruit Normans for his *ordonnance* company. The duke's identity as a Norman would be confirmed by his burial at Aumale, becoming the first member of the house of Lorraine to be buried in Normandy since Jean de Lorraine, comte d'Harcourt, in 1472.[119] The rising Norman profile of the family had serious implications for local protestants. The proximity of René marquis d'Elbeuf's lands to Rouen must have been a source of great anxiety to the reformed community. In the same way that the property of leading ultra-catholics was attacked during the Huguenot interregnum in Rouen, Elbeuf's lands were subjected to pillage in May 1562.[120]

The death of the prince de Porcien had even more serious ramifications for upper Norman protestantism. The inheritance of the comté of Eu in 1564 by right of his wife, Catherine de Clèves, had made him one of the greatest of Norman magnates. Porcien was a celebrated Calvinist captain who vigorously pursued the rights granted to him by the Edict of Amboise in 1563 to establish a chapel at Roumare, an appurtenance of the comté of Eu situated near Rouen. This caused great bitterness with the chapter of Rouen cathedral which had bought Roumare, save for the high justice which remained with the count. Porcien was legally within his right according to the pacification but his action was provocative and revealed the difficulties of enforcing the peace. In 1566 the parlement set out to investigate

118 'Journal d'un bourgeois de Rouen depuis l'an 1545 jusqu'à l'an 1564', *Revue de Rouen et de la Normandie* (Rouen, 1837), p. 6; ADSM 1B 593, 22 Apr 1563.

119 N. Potin de La Mairie, *Recherches historiques et biographiques sur les possessions des sires Normands de Gournay, Le Bray Normand et Le Bray Picard* (2 vols., Gournay, 1852), i, p. 307.

120 Saint-Denis, *Notices historiques sur les communes et environs d'Elbeuf*, iv, p. 52.

the dispute, Porcien complaining bitterly of the machinations of the stalwarts of the ultra-catholic faction in the court, namely Péricard, Bigot and Damours.[121] Local disputes which involved Guisard clients exacerbated the existing animosity between the Guise and Porcien. The Guise had a particular antipathy for Porcien, since they had supported his family in the 1550s in its disagreements with Anne de Montmorency. They felt he was obliged to them and by becoming a protestant had betrayed their trust. They disputed the original Clèves succession which passed to Porcien; he then supported the Montmorency in their feud with the Guise. In September 1566 the cardinal de Lorraine denied complicity in an injury committed by his servants on the prince, and when the prince died in May 1567 the cardinal was widely believed to have poisoned him. Whether this story is apocryphal or not the cardinal was uncharacteristically frank in his correspondence: 'Quel bien, utilite et bonheur ce serait pour le chretiente si beaucoup d'autres de semblable humeur jouaient ce meme tour.'[122] Porcien's death-bed wish that his wife should refrain from marrying the duc de Guise was in vain, as in August 1570 Guise married his widow, by then a repentant Calvinist. Eu was an immensely important, wealthy and compact territory in upper Normandy, located between the *bailliage* of Caux and the provincial boundary with Picardy. One of the largest lordships in Normandy, it comprised 270 fiefs and *arrière* fiefs and in the 1580s had an annual revenue greater than the duchies of Elbeuf and Aumale combined. The marriage brought the landed interest of the family in Normandy to the level of the ducs d'Alençon and de Longueville.

The expansion of the Guise affinity in Normandy in the 1560s was closely associated with the rise of catholic militancy, symbolised by the resistance to Porcien. The shift of parlement and city council away from moderation after the Huguenot coup was of most benefit to the Guise.[123] In the wake of the ephemeral Huguenot hegemony in Rouen came the first instances of popular catholic retribution. The impending publication of royal letters of grace for refugee Huguenots provoked protests, and in January 1563 400 people besieged the parlement demanding the execution of several protestant leaders. The success of the Guisard, Raoullin de Longpaon, in placating the crowd demonstrates the influence he enjoyed among the zealous. In Rouen the popular disturbances of the 1560s cannot be studied in isolation from the machinations of those elites opposed to moderation. When further disturbances led to the murder of a leading Huguenot official, the maréchal de Vieilleville, a moderate who had been sent to maintain order in the city, accused Longpaon and the *bailli*, Villebon d'Estouteville, of complicity, precipitating a confrontation in the streets in which Villebon was supported by the

121 Floquet, iii, pp. 23–7.

122 Cuisiat, 'Lettres du Charles cardinal de Lorraine', ii, pp. 439, 447; De Thou, v, p. 307.

123 This did not mean, however, the domination of the ultra-catholics. In April 1570 the parlement turned down requests to expel Huguenots who failed to observe Easter: BN MS Fr 15551 fo. 176, Bauquemare to the seigneur de Morvillier, Rouen, 9 Apr 1570.

Rouennais.[124] The duc d'Aumale maintained close contact with Longpaon, who acted as his *procureur* in the parlement. He visited his client, who was in financial difficulty, while in Rouen in February 1565. He paid off the huge debts that Longpaon had incurred and provided him with an annual pension in return for inheriting Longpaon's lands when he died.[125]

The Norman provincial Estates also became an arena for protest against royal religious policy. The Estates met annually to vote taxes and present grievances to the king. Its convocation each November was an important social event and deputies mingled with a 'grand nombre de barons et gentilshommes signalez'.[126] Before the first civil war representatives to the Estates, in common with the parlementaires, showed little interest in the persecution of heretics. By the beginning of the second civil war, a more radical outlook is discernible. In 1567 the *cahiers* of the three upper Norman *bailliages*, and that of the Cotentin, called for a profession of faith for all royal officers.[127] In 1570 objections to many of the clauses contained in the Peace of Saint-Germain contrasted with the parlement's swift ratification.[128] Following his acquisition of Eu in 1570, the duc de Guise took a much closer interest in the deliberations of the Estates, for it was this body which voted on the level of the *taille* and the proportion that each *élection* was liable to contribute. However, Eu was outside the jurisdiction of the Estates and Guise fought a continual battle to maintain the status quo. Taxes levied on Eu were better apportioned at court, where Guise could expect to have more bargaining power and spend less money in bribes, than by a large elected body like the Estates which would have been difficult and more expensive to influence.[129] Extant documents pertaining to the deliberations and the election process for the *bailliage* of Rouen reveal that in the First and Second Estates, whose members are more easily identifiable than the deputies of the Third, there was an increasingly large number of electors and deputies linked either directly to the Guise or connected with the ultra-catholic faction. In this way the Estates were, like the parlement, taking a more active role in politics.[130] The Guise were thus party to the information,

[124] Benedict, *Rouen during the Wars of Religion*, p. 113; *Histoire ecclésiastique*, ii, pp. 789–92; François de Scépeaux, seigneur de Vieilleville, *Mémoires*, *Collection universelle des mémoires particuliers rélatifs à l'histoire de France*, xxxii, pp. 112–19.

[125] ADSM 2E1 329, 19 Feb 1565.

[126] *Cahiers des Etats de Normandie sous le règne de Henri III*, C. de Robillard de Beaurepaire, ed. (2 vols., Rouen, 1887–8) i, p. 310.

[127] H. Prentout, 'Les Etats provinciaux de Normandie', *Mémoires de l'Académie Nationale des Arts et Belles Lettres de Caen* (3 vols., Caen, 1925–7), i, pp. 291–8.

[128] *Cahiers des Etats de Normandie sous le règne de Charles IX*, C. de Robillard de Beaurepaire, ed. (Rouen, 1891).

[129] Prentout, 'Les Etats provinciaux', ii, pp. 38–41.

[130] For a list of deputies attending the provincial Estates: Farin, *Histoire de la ville de Rouen*, iii, p. 381. Adam Sécard, in the forefront of the battle against heresy from the 1550s, was deputy for the First Estate of the *bailliage* of Rouen between 1562 and 1565 and again in 1571. Catholic captain Antoine de Vieuxpont, sieur de Saussay, was returned for the Second Estate in 1562 and again in 1568. Nicolas Maze, elected to the Estates of 1567, had sparked the Huguenot uprising in Rouen in 1562 by recruiting for the Triumvirate.

opinions and gossip that circulated both during the sessions of the Estates and the social engagements and meetings that accompanied them.

In order to maintain the fragile peace the crown sought the support of the nobility by dispensing patronage. Those who had supported the crown naturally expected rewards.[131] The inflation of honours that damaged the authority of the crown during the Wars of Religion began in the first civil war. From the early 1560s the dissatisfaction of local elites with the devaluation of office, both financially and honorifically, was a crucial factor in the crumbling authority of the monarchy. Moreover the control of patronage devolved, more than ever, into the hands of the local elites. This decentralisation of power, allied to existing discontent with the crown, undermined monarchical authority and contributed to political instability. In Normandy the impotence of the governor, Bouillon, further undermined royal authority, but this was counteracted by the growing power of the office of lieutenant-general. The relationship between the lieutenants-general in Normandy and the Guise demonstrates the limits of royal authority and the growth of Guise influence in the province. Two of these men, Jean de Moy, seigneur de La Meilleraye, and Tanneguy Le Veneur, seigneur de Carrouges, owed their rise during the first civil war to Guise patronage, thereafter becoming loyal servants of the crown before adopting different strategies during the rise of the Catholic League. They were loyal to more than one patron but the strength of loyalty depended on specific circumstances – it was never constant. Their relationship to the Guise was complex and reveals that the links of affinity remained latent, and could be activated at any time.

The Le Veneur were an important Norman ecclesiastical family in the early sixteenth century, possessing close ties to the most powerful of Norman families, the Brézé and the Annebaut (see figure 4.1) The Brézé connection explains the intimate relationship between Gabriel Le Veneur, bishop of Evreux, and the cardinal de Lorraine. By this means Gabriel's elder brother, Tanneguy, seigneur de Carrouges, became a familiar of the Guise and by 1559, according to English reports, a 'devoted' friend of their faction. Under François II the Le Veneur brothers performed important services for the Guise. In 1560 Carrouges was appointed *gentilhomme ordinaire du roi* and charged with the sensitive mission to arrest Condé's mother-in-law.[132]

Carrouges was first sent to Rouen in February 1563 to quell the disturbances caused by the showdown between the maréchal de Vieilleville and Villebon d'Estouteville. He remained there and, on Villebon's death in 1565, assumed the

[131] In 1563 Jean baron de Clères was made captain of fifty lances of the *ordonnance* and François, seigneur d'Auzebosc, became the *colonel de légionnaires de Normandie*: ADSM 7J 8, Chartrier de la famille Martel, 26 Jul 1564.

[132] *CSPF*, 1558–9, p. 570. He had fought with François de Guise at Metz and succeeded his father as captain of Vire and Avranches in lower Normandy: BN Pièces Originales 2958 fo. 47, Apr 1559; BN MS Fr 32866 fo. 69; *Catalogue des actes de François II*, i, 386; *Histoire de l'Estat de France . . . sous le règne de François II*, p. 624; De Thou, iii, p. 569.

functions of *bailli* with the support of the city council. From 1563 he was a lieutenant-general in Normandy, responsible for the *bailliages* of Rouen and Evreux.[133] On his appointment Carrouges was in possession of the best ultra-catholic credentials which, allied to his ability to keep order in the city, endeared him to all shades of catholic opinion. Over the next twenty-five years he played a shrewd and ultimately dangerous game of remaining loyal to the crown but reinforcing his historic links to the Guise. In a time of peace and stability having more than one patron was highly beneficial, but during a time of crisis it became perilous when a particular side had to be chosen or it was decided to remain neutral.

Carrouges did not immediately have complete authority in his new jurisdictions. In June 1564 the duc de Bouillon was reinstated as governor of Normandy.[134] Bouillon's Calvinism, and his dubious record in the war, made this decision controversial at a time when anti-protestant feeling was so high. However, the appointment was not made at the insistence of the Huguenots, but rather at the behest of the ultra-catholic ducs d'Aumale and de Montpensier. Kinship was again the motive behind their lobbying: Aumale was the uncle and Montpensier the father-in-law of Bouillon. His reinstatement did not pass without complaint from catholics. Tension in Rouen was further increased during Bouillon's sojourn with a protestant retinue in the city from 18 June to 12 July 1564. Huguenot residents flocked to the duke to demand redress for the tribulations that they had suffered since the fall of the city to catholic forces. In the face of growing catholic opposition, he left Rouen on 5 September 1564 and, although he remained nominal governor, real power now lay with the three resident lieutenants-general of Normandy.

Benedict has found little evidence to suggest that Carrouges was a Guisard client, demonstrating how he was loyal to the throne and scrupulous in carrying out royal commands.[135] This was probably the picture that Carrouges would have chosen to leave for posterity. Like all noblemen, he was egotistic in pursuing his own family interests and highly opportunistic in his relations with both the crown and his other major patrons, the Guise. He had originally risen in Guise service but, having gained significant royal office, his strategy was aimed at protecting his precarious position by maintaining order in the city and cultivating links at court. Above all, this meant stabilising the volatile religious situation in Rouen. The enforcement of edicts designed to keep the religious peace reinforced his own grip on power. Furthermore, he bolstered his own position by rewarding his servants and expanding his affinity, ensuring that men from his company of the *ordonnance* monopolised the military offices in Rouen and filled captaincies in the surrounding

[133] Floquet, ii, p. 512; Benedict, *Rouen during the Wars of Religion*, p. 32. He was also *bailli* and captain of Evreux between 1567 and 1585.

[134] For this and following: Benedict, *Rouen during the Wars of Religion*, p. 116; 'Discours abbregé', pp. 307, 315; *CSPF*, 1564–5, p. 184.

[135] Benedict, *Rouen during the Wars of Religion*, p. 118.

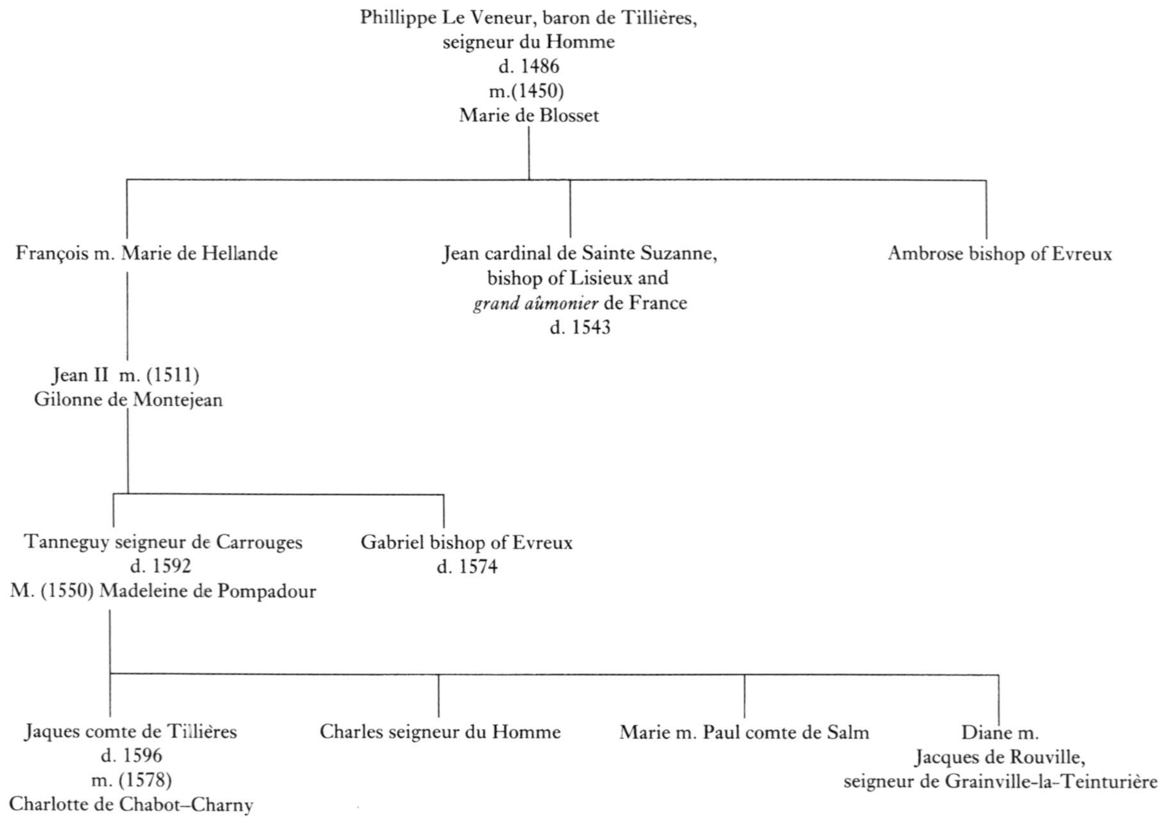

Figure 4.1 The Le Veneur in the sixteenth century

bourgs.[136] He also pursued a policy of marrying his children into the local elite and obtained offices for his sons.[137] Royal patronage failed to weaken his ties to the Guise. In 1577 and 1578 Jacques Le Veneur was the *guidon* of Charles duc de Mayenne and in 1583 his wife's half-sister married the duc d'Elbeuf. Finally, Carrouges married his remaining daughter to Paul comte de Salm, *chambellan* of the duc de Lorraine.[138]

Carrouges's desire to maintain his links to the Guise was due only partly to affection for and historical identification with the family, sentiments which, however much a part of noble culture, were not crucial in determining strategy. By cultivating patrons other than the crown, Carrouges broadened his contacts and channels of communication. Moreover, the influence of the duc d'Alençon (duc d'Anjou from 1576) in Normandy was another good reason for amity with the ultra-catholics. Alençon, leader of the *politiques*, had a large clientele in Normandy and an *échiquier* at Alençon. His power necessarily impinged on the authority of the lieutenants-general. In February 1570 Catherine de Médicis had to write to reassure Matignon and Carrouges that Alençon's authority was restricted to his apanage, and that the duke only had the right:

> pour commander en ce qui est de son domaine et sans toucher à ce qui est de vostre autorité; et pour ce il ne faut pas que vous cragniez qu'il ait voullu aucunes choses entreprendre en vos gouvernemens, lesquelz tant s'en fault que je voulisse conseiller de diminuer ou en distraire aucune chose, que je les voudrois accroistre et augmenter; et vous pouvez assurer que je tiendrai toujours la main que vous soiez favourablement traictez non seulement en ce qui concerne l'auctorité de vos charges, mais en toutes autres choses.[139]

In his relations with the crown Carrouges was interested in improving his bargaining position. His correspondence with the monarchy was dictated by two themes: the maintenance of peace in Rouen and complaints about money. It seems unlikely that these complaints reflected his true financial health. They do reveal the growing power of provincial governors and lieutenants-general, and the need for the crown to appease their grievances in order to maintain stability. Brantôme was close to Carrouges and commented at some length on his friend's resentment of the favourable treatment accorded to one lieutenant-general, Jacques de Matignon, at the expense of himself and Jean de Moy, in 1574: 'madame, respondit Carrouges, mais à l'un vous luy donnez du bon foing et bonn' avoyne, et aux autres deux vous ne leur donnez que de la paille, et les traictez à coups de fourche'.[140]

It is necessary to treat Brantôme's tales circumspectly, but his narrative corresponds with many of Carrouges's surviving letters. In April 1567 Carrouges

[136] For example, Nicholas de Pommereul was the ensign of his company of the *ordonnance* (1569–76) and captain of the château and Vieux Palais of Rouen in 1576: Vindry, p. 501; BN MS Fr 25809 fo. 250.

[137] Jacques, comte de Tillières, became captain and *bailli* of Rouen in 1576: ACR A 19, 14 May 1576.

[138] Vindry, p. 301; La Roque, *Histoire généalogique de la maison d'Harcourt*, ii, p. 1180.

[139] *Lettres de Catherine de Médicis*, iii, p. 299.

[140] Brantôme, v, p. 164.

complained to one of the secretaries of state for finance that he was receiving a pension totalling a mere 200 *francs* per month, while Matignon was in receipt of 300. In the same letter he went on to say that he was maintaining a household that included twenty gentlemen at a cost of 1,000 *francs* per month.[141] During the third civil war he was forced to advance from his own pocket the pay of his company of mounted arquebusiers because royal finances were so stretched.[142] It is no wonder that men like Carrouges were eager to maintain their links to the Guise, since magnates could pressure the royal treasury to pay. The need for the crown to satisfy the patronage aspirations of local elites, in order to maintain stability, was the major cause of the diffusion of power. Loyalty was conditional upon reward. In Normandy this prompted the innovation of dividing the governorship among the three lieutenants-general in 1575, following the death of the duc de Bouillon. There was a further expansion of office as lieutenants-general and lieutenants were now created under each of the three new governors. The decentralisation of royal authority increased the power of the local *noblesse seconde*. However, as the number of offices multiplied and the ability of the local economy to support these offices decreased, so the traditional competitiveness of the nobility for honours was heightened. As the Wars of Religion progressed, the deterioration of the traditional structure of patronage compounded the political and religious crisis.

The most dangerous consequence of the decentralisation of authority was the ability of the local elites to control the royal tax administration. Long before the Huguenots established an independent taxation system in the south-west local commanders were expropriating royal taxes in time of war. In 1567 Carrouges was a commissioner appointed by the crown to oversee the farming out of the *aides* of the *bailliages* of Rouen and Evreux. Carrouges asked Catherine de Médicis that the arrears of his pension be paid out of the increase in the farm. He added that he had already spent 400 *écus* and hoped to recoup his money when further transactions were concluded, assuring the queen-mother that the profits of the tax farmers would be 'fort petit'. Catherine readily agreed to all these demands.[143] There was a great potential for taking money out of the royal taxation system at source and bypassing official accounting procedures and, of course, this only concerned the money that Carrouges was prepared to account for.

The political calculation of the Moy family on the eve of the Wars of Religion was conditioned by its traditional ties to the Bourbon and antipathy to the Montmorency-Châtillon.[144] Charles de Moy (d. 1567), seigneur de La Meilleraye,

[141] BN Pièces Originales 2958 fo. 58, Carrouges to Bourdin, Rouen, 8 Apr 1567.

[142] BN Ms Fr 15548 fo. 51, Carrouges to Charles IX, Rouen, 16 Sep 1568.

[143] *Lettres de Catherine de Médicis*, iii, p. 2; BN Ms Fr 23193 fo. 7, Carrouges to Catherine, Rouen, 12 Jan 1567.

[144] Charles de Moy began his career in 1515 as a man-at-arms in the company of François de Bourbon, comte de Saint-Pol, brother of Antoinette de Bourbon. His elder brother Nicolas was lieutenant of the *ordonnance* company of Charles de Bourbon, duc de Vendôme. In the marriage contract of Anthoine de Moy, son of Nicolas, to Charlotte de Chabannes in 1539, one of the signatories was

governor of Le Havre (1528–60) and vice-admiral of France (1532–60) (see figure 4.2), was one of the most important figures in Normandy, despite a brief period of disgrace during Anne de Montmorency's first period of ascendancy in the 1530s. He fell foul of the Montmorency again in 1560 when his hopes of resigning his offices to his eldest son were frustrated by the accession of Charles IX, who awarded admiral Coligny the governorship of Le Havre. The new governor went in person to take up his command, instituting a Languedocian client as his lieutenant.[145]

Vice-admiral Moy was responsible for hiring vessels, sending out commissions and supervising the logistics during the Scottish campaign of 1548–9. His correspondence with the duc de Guise demonstrates that he was trusted and laboured hard to ensure that the venture, in which the duke had invested much money and matériel, was successful. Moy's infirmity was a severe handicap to preparation for the expedition of 1560.[146] He expected favours in return, and although he undoubtedly solicited several patrons at court, only letters written to the Guise survive.[147] Significantly, it was to Guise that Moy turned for a position for his relative Jacques de Moy, sieur de Vereins:

> Monsieur le sieur de Vereins present porteur que vous cognoissez avoir esté lieutenant de ma compagnie [since 1548] a tres bien obey de remectre ceste charge entre les mains de mon filz suivant le commandement du Roy et daultant Monseigneur que led. Vereins a deslibere de la parte que sera led. seigneur pour luy faire service à vous. Je vous supplye treshumblement Monseigneur qu'il vous plaise l'avoir pour recommande en estre moyen qu'il s'en employe en l'estat auquel led. seigneur l'a pourveu en vostre faveur vous assurant Monseigneur qu'il est homme de bien.[148]

The developing relationship between the two families was illustrated when the cardinal de Lorraine and the duc de Guise stayed at La Meilleraye on one of their rare visits to Rouen.[149]

This growing rapport, which owed much to Antoinette de Bourbon's presence at the head of the Guise clan, began to confuse the traditional loyalties of the Moy. During the crisis years between 1559 and 1562 their support was solicited first by the Guise and then by Condé.[150] The activity of Charles de Moy's eldest son, Jean, during the first civil war demonstrates how traditional ties of service and

Marie de Luxembourg, widow of François de Bourbon, comte de Vendôme and mother of Antoinette de Bourbon: R. Rodière and E. Vallée, *La maison de Moy* (Le Mans, 1928), pp. 48–75.

145 *Catalogue analytique des chartes, documents historiques composant les archives du collège héraldrique* (2 vols., Paris, 1866), ii, p. 191; Borély, *Histoire de la ville du Havre*, ii, p. 24; Rodière and Vallée, *La maison de Moy*, p. 75.

146 BN MS Fr 3118 fo. 15, 'Estat des vivres qui ont esté faict chargé par Monseigneur de La Meilleraye', 21 Jul 1549; MS Clairambault 341 fo. 209, Moy to Guise, Le Havre, 24 Mar 1548; MS Fr 20549 fo. 141, Moy to Guise, Leith, 11 Jul 1548; MS Clairambault 344 fo. 226, Moy to Guise, Brest, 16 Sep 1548.

147 For example: BN MS Clairambault 348 fo. 92, Moy to Guise, 27 Mar 1557.

148 BN Ms Fr 20545 fo. 3, Moy to Guise, La Meilleraye, 5 Jul 1554.

149 Floquet, ii, p. 194; Cuisiat, 'Lettres du Charles cardinal de Lorraine', i, p. 59.

150 Charles was created a *gentilhomme ordinaire du roi* on the accession of François II and received the collar of the order of Saint-Michel in December 1561: BN MS Fr 32764 fo. 73; 32866 fo. 17.

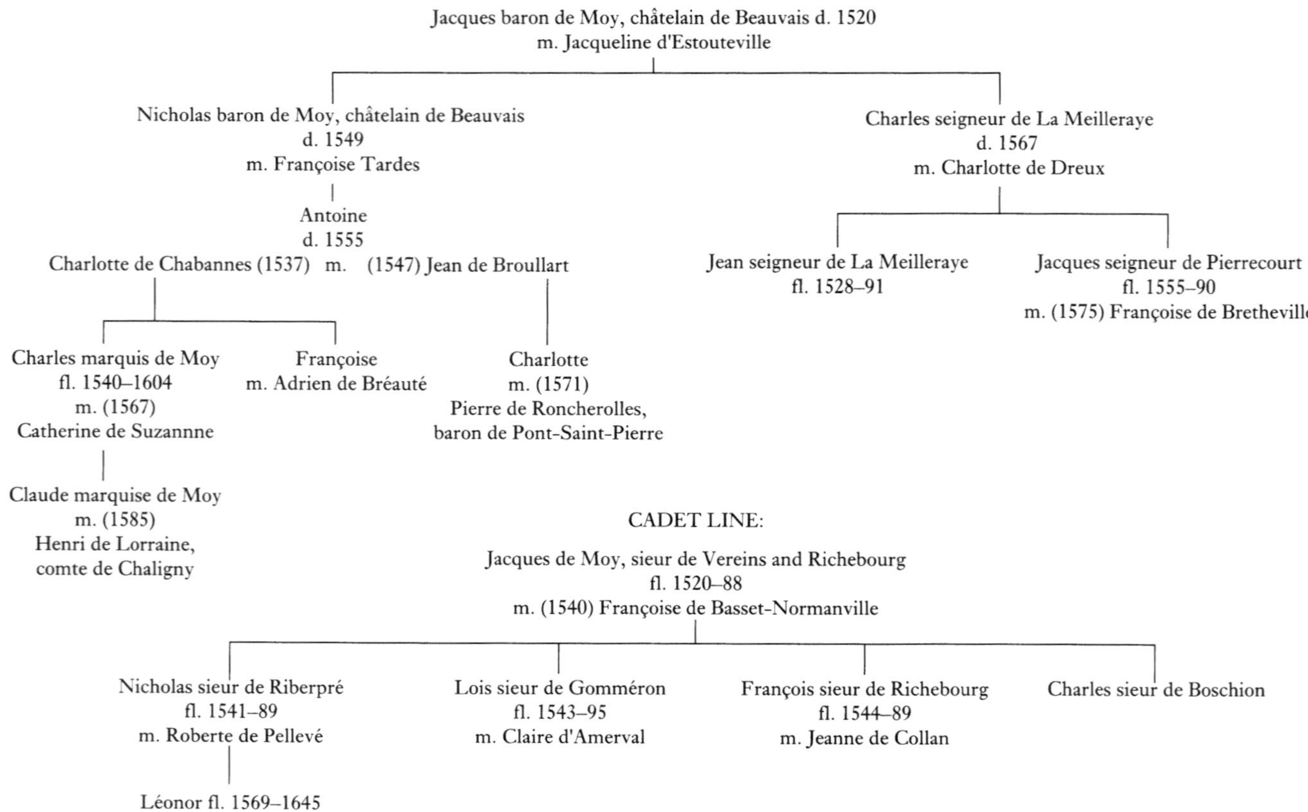

Figure 4.2 The Moy in the sixteenth century

aristocratic egoism combined to influence individual action. Jean initially rallied to Condé and the protestants in May 1562, but by the end of July he had changed sides, accepting the captaincies of Honfleur, Lisieux and Pont-Audemer from Aumale.[151] His opportunism brought high rewards, and his subsequent shift to ultra-catholicism in the mid-1560s indicates that he was not primarily motivated by religion. There is no evidence to suggest that either father or son was protestant. Condé's revolt and the subsequent collapse of royal authority improved Jean's bargaining position. His decision to join Condé at Orleans in May 1562 was a significant boost for the protestant cause in upper Normandy. But the captaincies of such places as Dieppe and Le Havre were already in the hands of Coligny's clients, and his family had every reason to expect little favour from a member of the Montmorency clan. Moy's rapid return to the catholic party was a consequence both of his ambivalence to the protestant cause and the satisfactory accommodation of his wishes by the royalists. When appointing him to the three captaincies, Aumale passed over a number of committed catholic candidates. Moy did not have to wait much longer to regain the 'family' offices: he became vice-admiral on 1 September 1562 and lieutenant-general of Normandy in July 1563, which post he occupied until 1590. He was not a half-hearted turncoat and in early September 1562 attacked the advancing comte de Montgommery near Dives. Satisfied for the time being with the honours of royal service, Moy began to cement a relationship with the Guise and the ultra-catholic faction, in order to consolidate and build on his recently accumulated offices.[152]

Unlike the supra-provincial magnates, Jean de Moy drew recruits to his company of the *ordonnance* almost exclusively from his native province. The geographic base of the clientele of the provincial elites was much narrower than that of a great lord, being drawn largely from a single *pays* or *bailliage*. On average nearly 50 per cent of his company came from the Caux, particularly around La Meilleraye, between Le Havre and Rouen: most of his officers were both neighbours and kinsmen. The forty-five men in his company who came from the Caux represented 11 per cent of the 398 nobles found to be holding fiefs in this region in 1575, and must represent a greater percentage of nobles in the *vicomtés* of Caudebec and Montivilliers which bordered his lands.[153] The officers of his company were substantial local men in their own right and were the locus of subgroups shaped by patterns of kinship and sociability. Membership extended to Rouen, with cadets of Rouennais notable families appearing in his muster lists.[154]

Local military office had long been part of the infrastructure of provincial power relations. During the civil wars military office continued to be lucrative and its importance increased. Officially non-venal, it was in fact subject to the same

[151] Sauvage, 'Les troubles de 1562', p. 64.

[152] BN Pièces Originales 2078 fo. 50; De Thou, iv, p. 245.

[153] Orlea, *La noblesse aux Etats généraux*, p. 54.

[154] Claude du Four, man-at-arms from 1569 to 1581, was of a wealthy bourgeois lineage.

proprietary rights as other offices. In 1585 Tanneguy Le Veneur resigned the captaincy of Evreux for 1,200 *écus*. The very low figure suggests that he was selling the office below the market price to a client – another form of patronage.[155] The local nobility also benefited from Jean de Moy's positions as vice-admiral and lieutenant-general. Men from his retinue were granted local offices such as the lieutenancies and captaincies of Honfleur, Harfleur and Pont-Audemer.[156] The offices of captain of the gendarmerie and vice-admiral appear to have been complementary: Pierre Sécard was firstly a man-at-arms in the Moy company (1580–5) and then *commissaire ordinaire en la marine du ponant* in 1588. His brother Michel occupied the office of lieutenant of the admiralty (1581–3). There are many other examples which elucidate the corollary between membership of the Moy *ordonnance* and the tenure of local naval office.[157] These clients were related by ties of sociability and kinship; they were neighbours and companions of Jean de Moy, highlighting the importance of community and physical proximity in establishing an affinity.

By the late 1560s Jean de Moy had become conventionally catholic: in 1569 he obtained papal authority to build a chapel at La Meilleraye in honour of the soul of his late brother.[158] The revival of his faith was undoubtedly genuine but it was not unconnected to his desire to strengthen his position in upper Normandy with appeals to religious solidarity. It is no coincidence that his power base in the pays de Caux had a large protestant population, and that many of his potential rivals for hegemony in the region were Huguenots.

Moy was as jealous of his status as his fellow lieutenants-general, although his rivalry with the Matignon, traditionally lieutenants-general in lower Normandy, was more deep-seated than Carrouges's.[159] He was particularly suspicious of the potential strength of Charles de Bacqueville-Martel, a major landowner in his *gouvernement* and a former lieutenant in the province for the duc de Bouillon. Bacqueville died in 1566 but was succeeded by his son Nicolas, a protestant, and also like his father loyal

155 ADSM 2E1 923, 6 Jul 1585. The minor captaincy of Toucques was sold for 4,000 *écus* in 1583, and was most likely the market price since the purchaser, a Montmorency, was of higher status than the vendor: ADSM 2E1 919, 12 Jan 1583.

156 The examples are numerous: Jean de Moy's younger brother, Jacques, was captain of Honfleur from 1565 to 1589; Gaspard de Coullarville was a neighbour and ensign in Moy's company (1570–1) and appointed by Moy as *commissaire extraordinaire des guerres* (1568–78), and lieutenant of Harfleur; Charles d'Ercambourg was a man-at-arms in the Moy company (1569–81) and his brother, François, was captain of Pont-Audemer; Pierre Le Doyen, man-at-arms in 1570 and *maître de logis* in 1574, went on to become lieutenant of Honfleur from 1581 until 1590.

157 H. de Frondeville, *Les conseillers du parlement de Normandie sous Henri IV et sous Louis XIII, 1594–1640* (Rouen and Paris, 1964), p. 296. Pierre was a household officer and acted as proxy in financial matters: ADSM 2E1 2013, 23 May 1590; 2015, 24 Nov 1590. Other examples of this sort of patronage include Adrien de Filières, man-at-arms from 1570 until 1581, who occupied a position in the *armée navale* in 1588 and Jean d'Osterel who was also a gendarme during the same period and appointed *capitaine ordinaire en la marine*. Although Osterel was captain of Ardres and the comté of Guines, he was resident in the household of Jean de Moy in 1574.

158 Rodière and Vallée, *La maison de Moy*, p. 80.

159 *Correspondence de Joachim de Matignon*, L.-H. Labande, ed. (Monaco and Paris, 1914), p. 83.

to the crown. Moy distanced himself from his rival by espousing a more aggressive catholicism. Conflict came to a head between them over the exemptions obtained by Bacqueville's gendarmes from paying the *aides* of the *arrière-ban*. Moy alleged that a deception had been perpetrated because there was no record of their service. Charles IX reprimanded him and ordered him to ensure payment of the men.[160] When the king moved Bacqueville's company out of the Caux the following month, Moy dryly commented that 'Quant à celle du sieur de Bacqueville Jay entendu que vostre maiestie a ordonne qu'elle s'achemine en vostre camp là ou à la verite pour beaucoup de raisons sera trop mieulx que par deca.'[161]

A more vigorous anti-Huguenot stance brought opportunities to gain credit among wider catholic opinion. The greatest threat to Moy's authority came from Huguenot-dominated Dieppe, and from the Huguenot nobility of rural upper Normandy. Moy was lobbied by the catholics of Dieppe and following the Peace of Longjumeau in 1568 he supported their demand that protestant worship be proscribed in the town.[162] His nascent radicalism was thus mirrored, indeed spurred, by local catholic feeling. In 1567 during the second civil war he had met with the captain of Dieppe, René de Beauxoncles, seigneur de Sigognes, to discuss ways of preventing a protestant uprising.[163] Subsequent attempts by the garrison of the château to secure the town on 26 and 27 October 1567 were humiliating failures. The irate townsfolk soon turned the tables and besieged the garrison. When order was finally restored Moy was determined to repair his damaged honour. Soldiers were billeted on Huguenot residences, houses were burnt and pillaged and a tax of 16,000*l* was levied on the town. Destruction was not carried out at random by the soldiery but ordered directly by a vengeful Moy; among the victims was a prominent Huguenot *conseiller* at the parlement of Rouen, Jérôme Maynet.[164]

In common with his counterparts Moy was deeply involved in the problems of collecting royal revenue. After the Peace of Longjumeau large numbers of troops had to be paid off. Units that were to be retained also clamoured for their pay. Moy estimated the cost of troops in his jurisdiction (principally for the defence of Le Havre and Dieppe) to be 12,000*l* per month, payable from contributions levied on the countryside. The crown's financial chaos meant that Moy's pension was unpaid and the pay of the garrison of Dieppe was five months in arrears.[165] He asked permission to use loans made to the crown in the pays de Caux for his own purposes, which effectively meant siphoning off revenue before it came under the scrutiny of royal fiscal officials.[166] The increasing powers delegated to local com-

[160] BN MS Fr 26291 fo. 396, 26 Jan 1568.
[161] BN MS Fr 15554 fo. 176, Moy to Charles IX, Caudebec, 4 Feb 1568.
[162] BN MS Fr 15608 fo. 123, Moy to Charles IX, Dieppe, 7 Apr 1568.
[163] Daval, *Histoire de la Réformation à Dieppe*, i, p. 69.
[164] ADSM C 1228, Registres du Bureau des Finances de la Généralité de Rouen, 26 Nov 1585.
[165] BN MS Fr 15608 fo. 87, 'Instruction envoyee au Roy par monseigneur de la meilleraye pour les affaires de son gouvernement', 24 Mar 1568.
[166] BN MS Fr 15608 fo. 143, Moy to Charles IX, Dieppe, 11 Apr 1568.

manders signified that only they had the local resources and credit to sustain the war effort. As Moy had feared, there were few people prepared to lend money to the crown and so Charles IX asked his lieutenant-general to forward 20,000*l* of his own money to pay troops.[167] A shrewd nobleman could raise money locally, speculate in his financial dealings with the crown and reap substantial rewards. By August 1568 there was little improvement in the financial situation and Moy pointed out that few captains were prepared to follow the king's wishes: 'Je ne voy personne qui veuille resider ordinairement aux places et entrer en ceste despence sans y attendre aulcune recompense.'[168] At the height of the third civil war Moy, in his capacity as vice-admiral, requested that he be able to raise his own extraordinary tax on salt vessels arriving in his marine jurisdiction.[169]

In his efforts to support the local war effort Moy was commissioned to raise revenue and loans in conjunction with Michel de Vialar, *président* of the parlement of Rouen. They worked closely together during the third civil war (1568–70). The statement of the seventeenth-century historian of the parlementaires, Bigot de Monville, that Vialar 's'attacha aux intérêts de la Maison de Guise et exécuta plusieurs commissions contre ceux de la RPR [religion prétendue réformée]' is supported by contemporary evidence.[170] Vialar had been a signatory of the will of Claude duc de Guise in 1550, was a financial agent for the family in Italy in 1557 and related to other major Guise creditors.[171] Originally Parisian *robins*, the family also possessed property in Rouen which had been severely damaged during the Huguenot occupation in 1562.[172] Vialar was a zealous catholic whose friendship with the cardinal de Bourbon is confirmed by the free lodging provided for him by the abbey of Saint-Ouen. Both he and Moy displayed a particular antipathy towards Huguenot *conseiller*, Jérôme Maynet; Moy destroyed his property and Vialar urged the cardinal de Bourbon to exclude him from the parlement once peace was established in 1570.

Vialar was therefore the perfect choice for the commission to seize Huguenot property as outlined in the Edict of Saint-Maur (September 1568) – confiscations which had brought in 40,000*l* by May 1570.[173] Moy also became involved in this dubious method of raising revenue and both men acquired a major financial stake in the catholic cause. Even as he pleaded poverty, Moy was able to invest in land in

167 BN MS Fr 15546 fo. 122, Charles IX to Moy, Paris, 29 May 1568.

168 BN MS Fr 15547 fo. 308, Moy to Charles IX, La Meilleraye, 24 Aug 1568.

169 BN MS Fr 15550 fo. 130, Moy to Charles IX, Caudebec, 15 Nov 1569.

170 Frondeville, *Présidents*, p. 221.

171 Bouillé, i, p. 584; BN MS Fr. 20529 fos. 17–18, Vialar to Guise, Venice, 3 Oct 1557; Carroll, 'The Guise affinity and popular protest', p. 142.

172 ADSM 1B 592, 3 Mar 1563. It is noteworthy that both his predecessor and successor, Jean de Lallement and Nicholas Damours respectively, were closely identified with the ultra-catholic faction, suggesting that offices were resigned with some discrimination.

173 BN MS Fr 15551 fo. 256, Vialar to Charles IX, Dieppe, 1 May 1570. Vialar hoped to raise another 40,000*l* in the same way but was furious that peace negotiations were hindering his activities: *ibid.*, fo. 258, Vialar to Catherine, Dieppe, 1 May 1570.

1569 and 1570 to the value of 3,800*l*.[174] In a pessimistic letter to Moy on the eve of peace in August 1570, Vialar spoke in favour of an end to hostilities but was worried that peace would strengthen his enemies:

Je vous advertir d'aultre chose si non que je vous faictz bancqueroute et léssion de biens et vous prie ne fonder à l'advenir aulcune esperance sur les deniers procedans de mesdites commissions. Vous savez quelle inimitie me portent deux grandes seigneurs de la court de parlement qui ne cessent pour chacun jour de m'apeller 'galant' et dire qu'il me faut tuer dont l'execution sera facile puys que je nay receu aulcun accroisement en honeur et authorité pout avoir tant de foys exposé ma vie pour le service de leurs Maiesties.[175]

Clearly Vialar feared the wrath of the expropriated. After the Peace of Saint-Germain he clashed with protestant judges. In one incident he swapped insults with the unfortunate Jérôme Maynet while the court was in full session.[176]

During the third War of Religion Moy's drift towards a more extreme position continued. He was ruthless in breaking up Huguenot conspiracies to betray Le Havre and Dieppe, plots in which senior local rivals were implicated.[177] One of the men was François de Bacqueville-Martel, seigneur de Lindboeuf, hitherto Moy's friend even though he was the brother of Moy's main local rival. His appearance in person to defend himself against treason charges before the parlement was unusual and confirms contemporary reports that he was counting on Moy's testimony to exonerate him. His execution on 5 March 1569 indicated the hardening line being taken by the parlement.[178] The role played by Moy's sacrifice of a friend was widely acknowledged: 'L'action de la Meilleraye fut interpretée differement: bien de gens condamnèrent sa séverité, comme outrée; mais le plus grand nombre le loüa, d'avoir eu assez de vertu, pour sacrificier un ami particulier aux intérêts de la République.'[179] In serving the commonweal, Moy dealt a severe blow to a rival family in the pays de Caux. His obduracy was shared by his cousin Jacques, sieur de Riberpré, who pillaged Huguenots indiscriminately in the Caux.[180] During the civil wars of the 1560s the Moy used royal office to build a substantial clientele in upper Normandy, and become the leading ultra-catholic family in the region. Their marriage strategy confirmed their political and religious orientation. In 1565 Nicolas de Moy married the niece of the cardinal de Pellevé, chief counsellor of the cardinal de Lorraine.[181]

Both Jean de Moy and Tanneguy Le Veneur had a longstanding affiliation with the Guise and their success in royal service did not end the vitality of these links. By

174 BN MS Fr 15550 fo. 81, Moy to Charles IX, Caudebec, 26 Oct 1569; 26414 fo. 153.

175 BN Cinq Cents Colbert 7 fo. 247, Vialar to Moy, Rouen, 24 Jul 1570.

176 Floquet, iii, p. 82–5.

177 In February 1569 Moy was informed of a conspiracy to seize Le Havre. He captured the château which acted as the refuge of the plotters and hanged the defenders. The leading plotters were then condemned to death *in absentia* for treason: 'Discours abbregé', p. 356; Daval, *Histoire de la réformation à Dieppe*, i, p. 100.

178 Daval, *Histoire de la réformation à Dieppe*, i, p. 126.

179 De Thou, v, p. 566

180 Daval, *Histoire de la réformation à Dieppe*, i, p. 105.

181 BN Cabinet d'Hozier 252 fo. 3.

cultivating contacts they counterbalanced dependence on royal patronage. Their autonomy increased as royal authority weakened: in 1570 Moy simply refused to obey when the king ordered his *ordonnance* company out of Normandy.[182] The crown could not buy complete loyalty with offices and honours, since the pressure on resources and the inflation of honours devalued their financial and honorific value. In March 1569 the garrisons of Tancarville, Pont de l'Arche, Château Gaillard, Honfleur and Fécamp had received no pay for six months and no one was prepared to advance the necessary cash.[183] The burden of office, caused by the upkeep of troops and the need to support clienteles and buy favour, was exacerbated in Normandy by the open favouritism displayed by the queen-mother to Jacques de Matignon. Carrouges expressed his bitterness to Catherine in 1574:

> Madame, je pense que M. de la Mayleraye et moy l'avons mieux servy; car nous luy avons très bien conservé ses places, que nul n'y a osé attenter ny prendre; et Matignon a laissé perdre et prendre vilainement les siennes; et puis, pour les reprendre, il a ruyné tout le pays, et faict despendre au roy pour son armée combien de cent mill' escus, qui lui fairoient bien besoin ailleurs; et ast' heure, pensez donc madame, à qui le roy a plus obligation, ou à luy ou à nous.[184]

Their growing landed interest and recruitment of Normans into their military retinues were part of the expansion of the Guise power base in Normandy in the 1560s, though the radical catholic faction remained small, especially in the parlement. Even ultra-catholic *gens de bien* feared the kind of popular sedition which greeted the Peace of Saint-Germain in Paris, Rouen and other provincial cities. The parlement of Rouen encountered great difficulty in implementing the peace edict. The court was powerless to prosecute the perpetrators of serious anti-Huguenot disturbances in March 1571. The Guise had no direct involvement but their associates were among the leaders of the catholic mob. One of these, Laurent Maromme, was a wine merchant, captain of the city militia and petty tax collector, a substantial member of the bourgeoise who had seen his property ransacked by protestants in 1562 and he had lost a relative killed at Dieppe while fighting under Jean de Moy. The sentence of death passed on him by an extraordinary royal commission was commuted to banishment, but even this was not enforced, and the following year he was involved in the Saint Bartholomew's killings in Rouen. Maromme's immunity implies powerful protectors. His kinsman, Louis, was legal counsel to the duc d'Aumale, one of a number of ties which suggest the existence of a network of supporters among the Rouennais ultra-catholic faction, ensuring that his pleas for clemency were heard at the highest levels.[185]

182 BN Ms Fr 15552 fo. 71, Moy to Charles IX, La Meilleraye, 23 Jun 1570.

183 BN MS Fr 15549 fo. 90, maréchal de Cossé to Charles IX, Rouen, 13 Mar 1569; fo. 180, maréchal de Cossé to Charles IX, Rouen, 27 Mar 1569.

184 Brantôme, v, p. 164.

185 BN MS Fr 16621, 20 Feb 1567; Floquet, iii, pp. 91–124; ADSM 1ER 1589, 12 Nov 1563, 12 Oct 1563, 1574; ACR M fo. 13; Frondeville, *Conseillers*, p. 578–9.

As in Paris, some of the worst disturbers of the peace were officers of the militia responsible for maintaining order.[186] The leaders of mob violence were usually zealous men of means such as Maromme. Although he moved in the orbit of the Guise affinity, this did not predispose him to commit acts of violence. Nobles usually saw popular unrest as seditious and as a threat to order and hierarchy, and there is little evidence to suggest that the Guise actively sought to encourage and exploit popular protest in the 1560s and early 1570s. Nonetheless, it would be rash to dismiss the connection between faction politics and popular protest. The religious disturbances of 1571 revealed to the Rouennais the extent to which the Montmorency had abandoned the catholic cause. It was commented bitterly that the maréchal de Montmorency and his retinue, who had arrived to restore order, 'estoient de la couleur des Calvinistes et ne vallent rien'.[187] Dissatisfaction with the failure of the monarchy to protect catholicism, already evident in the early 1570s, would grow during the reign of Henri III, while taxation and the proliferation of offices would reach unprecedented heights. The Guise, with their great landed interest and sizeable affinity and their identification with the catholic cause, were ideally placed to take advantage of the discontent and catholic radicalism which began to destabilise France in the 1570s.

[186] On the role of militias in popular disturbances: Diefendorf, *Beneath the cross*, pp. 159–71; Benedict, *Rouen during the Wars of Religion*, pp. 42–5; Carroll, 'The Guise affinity and popular protest', pp. 80, 149.

[187] 'Relation des troubles excités par les calvinistes', p. 43.

5

Malcontents and defenders of the faith: the building of a political power base

The disintegration of royal authority was not interrupted by the accession of Henri III in May 1574. The crown had virtually lost control of the south, continued to be threatened by Huguenot–*politique* plots, and was unable to deploy military force effectively. The return of the new king from Poland was eagerly awaited by the Guise, who anticipated restoration to the privy council. But catholic expectations of a more vigorous prosecution of the war were to be disappointed. The arrival of the king in September and the return to favour of the Guise did little to ameliorate the desultory performance of the royalist armies, and only the exorbitant demands of the Huguenot–*politique* alliance – unlimited demands for freedom of worship and the trial of those responsible for the Saint Bartholomew's Day massacre – prevented the king from settling. The Guise interest dictated war, since peace would ensure the return of the Huguenots and the Montmorency to court at the expense of their newly recovered prominence. The campaign of autumn 1575 was therefore crucial to the security of the Guise family.

Royal ineffectiveness contrasted with the vigour of the duke, who left court in early September 1575 to organise the defence of his *gouvernement* against an invading Huguenot and *reiter* army led by Guillaume de Montmorency-Thoré.[1] The ducal lands were threatened and Antoinette de Bourbon was forced to flee Joinville for the safety of Saint-Dizier. The penury of the crown meant that the duke had to rely on his own resources and local credit. He borrowed heavily and his army was constituted largely from his kinsmen and their followers. Commissions were handed to clients and heralds were dispatched all over Champagne summoning the duke's *amis* to the standard. The battle of Dormans, at which Montmorency-Thoré was defeated, may have been only a minor action but it was a credit to Guise's organisational and military abilities. Guise's battle wound, proudly paraded in Paris, earned him the popular soubriquet *le balafré* ('scar-face') and contributed to his burgeoning reputation as a military leader.[2]

In May 1576 the king had little choice but to meet the demands of his adversaries

[1] On this and following: Bouillé iii, pp. 13–17. Aubigné, *Histoire universelle*, iv, pp. 380–1, puts Guise's forces at 10,000 men, although this included units raised by the crown and other nobles. The depredations of this army can be followed in Haton, *Mémoires*, ii, pp. 779–800.

[2] 'During the king's absence the duke of Guise has showed himself much in the place and about town to have the favour of the common people': *CSPF*, 1575–7, p. 210.

at the Peace of Monsieur, the tolerant religious provisions of which were enshrined in the Edict of Beaulieu. Catholics everywhere were dismayed at the political and religious concessions to the Huguenots. Guise felt aggrieved by this surrender after his feats the previous autumn and was now concerned at his status and personal safety at court. Adverse reaction to the settlement coalesced in Picardy, where Condé was confirmed as governor of Picardy, receiving Péronne as a surety for the fulfilment of the terms of the peace.

THE ORIGINS OF THE CATHOLIC LEAGUE

The founding of the Catholic League, or League of Péronne, has received less attention from historians than it deserves. The Bourbon dynasty was haunted by its spectre, since it demonstrated the weakness of the monarchy in the face of disparate interest groups united by ideology. In 1665 the *intendant* of the *généralité* of Rouen questioned the loyalty of one family merely because its fortune had been considerably enhanced by involvement in the League.[3] There exists no adequate investigation of the League's origins and consequently misconceptions and prejudice remain. Contemporary opponents of the Guise saw their 'Machiavellian' designs behind the crisis and nineteenth-century nationalist historians stressed the danger to the *patrie*, since 'Henri de Guise voulut devenir maître en France, en se plaçant au dehors dans la dépendance du roi d'Espagne.'[4] The still-conventional belief that the Guise were the leaders of the League from its inception is based on tendentious evidence. The Guise made no secret of their disappointment at the Edict of Beaulieu, but they swore to uphold it and evidence of their complicity with the League is based on hearsay, non-contemporaneous reports and, most questionably, Huguenot propaganda.[5] Hostility to the peace came from diverse quarters and was strongest among those likely to lose office as a result of the articles of pacification.[6]

The origins of the League, its cooption by the crown and subsequent prohibition should be viewed in the context of the establishment of local defence leagues in the 1560s. But our understanding of its genesis remains fragmentary and little attention has been devoted to the manuscript evidence. Only careful attention to the narrative of the events and to the surviving sources will illuminate its development and composition in 1576–7. Contemporary accounts, such as that of the Parisian, Pierre de l'Estoile, should be treated with caution as the League was a clandestine

[3] Voysin de La Noiraye, *Mémoire sur la généralité de Rouen*, 1665, E. Esmonin, ed. (Paris, 1913), p. 73.

[4] E. C. Davila, *Historie of the civill warres of France* (London, 1647–8), p. 445; J. de Croze, *Les Guises, les Valois et Philippe II* (2 vols., Paris, 1866), i, p. 227.

[5] For the case against the Guise: Orlea, *La noblesse aux Etats généraux*, p. 39.

[6] The seigneur de Ruffec, captain of Angoulême and one of the earliest of Henri III's *mignons*, and Claude de La Châtre, captain of Bourges and until recently a supporter of François duc d'Alençon, were among the earliest adherents of the League: Constant, *Les Guises*, pp. 81–2.

organisation.[7] Traditionally, the League has been seen as the creation of Jacques d'Humières, lieutenant-general of Picardy and governor of Péronne, Roye and Montdidier, who succeeded in galvanising the local catholic nobility. Historians have seen the League as a largely parochial movement with little impact in other provinces but, in fact, the League of Péronne was a coalition of different interest groups and its support was not confined to Picardy.[8] Moreover, the League was a much greater threat to monarchical authority than the local leagues of the 1560s. First, the strength of support among the lesser nobility made it a formidable force. Secondly, after its cooption by the king, the League leadership succeeded in retaining local control of the organisation and corresponded in secret in order to minimise royal interference.

As lieutenant-general of the province, Jacques d'Humières was the natural leader of the groundswell of Picard noble distaste for the Edict of Beaulieu. The restoration of Condé to the governorship of the province would ensure the return of protestant émigrés and the channelling of patronage to his followers. Humières' family was noted for its loyalty to the monarchy and longstanding rivalry with the Bourbon-Vendôme.[9] The faultlines of local political allegiance ensured that the Humières looked elsewhere for protection; they were traditionally allied to the Montmorency. However, the influence of the Montmorency, once so pervasive in northern France, was in decline. Henri de Montmorency-Damville remained powerful in Languedoc but his elder brother, the maréchal de Montmorency, had seen his influence at court damaged by involvement in malcontent plots and subsequent imprisonment. Moreover, Humières was locked in a bitter legal dispute with his brother-in-law, Guillaume de Montmorency-Thoré.[10] By 1576 Humières probably felt the lack of influential contacts and he may have turned to the Guise for support, though there is no reliable evidence. Humières and other Picard town captains were concerned about their authority on Condé's return; their association was formed due to the absence of magnate influence, not because of it.

On 13 May 1576 an assembly gathered at Péronne to discuss the terms and implications of the peace. It dispatched a delegation to the king with a letter of recommendation from the lieutenant of Péronne, Michel d'Estourmel.[11] After the return of this unsuccessful mission Humières, as the man most likely to receive some form of compensation, counselled acceptance of the royal will. It is clear from the surviving correspondence with Humières that it was Estourmel, his lieutenant, and another local nobleman, Jacques d'Applaincourt, who were responsible for

[7] Pierre de L'Estoile, *Journal du règne de Henri III*, L.-R. Lefèvre, ed. (Paris, 1943), p. 117, exaggerates its urban support.

[8] Benedict, *Rouen during the Wars of Religion*, p. 153; Dewald, *The formation of a provincial nobility*, p. 48 n. 1.

[9] The Humières had always sought to assert the independence of Péronne from the *gouvernement* of Picardy: D. Potter, *War and government in the French provinces: Picardy, 1470–1560* (Cambridge, 1993), pp. 95–6. [10] De Thou, vii, p. 425.

[11] For this and following: J. Dournel, *Histoire de la ville de Péronne* (Péronne, 1879), pp. 213–16.

defying the king. The Péronnais held firm and refused to give up the keys to the town or the magazine to royal agents. On 5 June a group of noblemen gathered at Applaincourt's residence, five kilometres from the town, to sign the articles of association which he had drawn up the day before. They were later signed by nearly 200 nobles, soldiers and leading inhabitants of Péronne. Humières also signed but tactfully retired to his château at Becquincourt. On 8 June Henri wrote both to Humières and to Applaincourt, demanding that royal orders be carried out and that Estourmel and Applaincourt leave Péronne immediately.[12] The role of the lesser nobility was greater than hitherto recognised. It was they who journeyed throughout the towns of Picardy, urging adherence to the League: Applaincourt went to Abbeville and the sieur de Sainte-Marie to Amiens.[13] The Péronnais stood firm against royal threats and overtures and the king was soon forced to rescind his promise to Condé, offering him Cognac and Saint-Jean d'Angély as places of surety instead. By then the League had spread to Ham and Doullens.[14]

The manifesto of the League and the appended articles of association only survive as they were presented in protestant propaganda.[15] The demands of the rebels require analysis. The first article of the manifesto, which states that the association is under the authority of the king, is the only reference to royal authority, and the willingness to associate with the defence of catholicism elsewhere in Europe (article 11) encroached on the king's prerogative. The other articles elaborate a constitution headed by a noble council and an elected provincial commander and include a call for the return of provincial rights enjoyed at the time of Clovis. In their discussion of the fundamental laws and in the role assigned to conciliar government and popular sovereignty, these principles foreshadowed the political ideology developed by the Catholic League during the late 1580s. The major difference between the nascent League and its fully developed successor lay in the progenitors' ambivalence to heresy. It was essentially a defensive organisation pledged to protect catholicism and said little about the extermination of heresy.

The League of Péronne should not be confused with the Catholic League which was established by the king on 2 December 1576. Having spent the summer attempting to prevent the spread of the association, Henri now outflanked the leaguers by coopting their movement. A list of the signatories of the original League does not survive, but Guise clients were deeply involved in its promotion in the summer of 1576. Jacques d'Applaincourt began his career in the household of

[12] *Lettres de Henri III*, ii, pp. 444–5.

[13] E. Prarond, *Histoire de la Ligue à Abbeville, 1576–1594* (3 vols., Paris, 1873), i, p. 147; *Inventaire-Sommaire des archives de la ville d'Amiens antérieures à 1790*, ser. BB, *Délibérations de l'échevinage*, P. Durand, ed. (Amiens, 1894), 24 Jul 1576.

[14] Dournel, *Histoire de la ville de Péronne*, pp. 216, 219–21. The sieur de Sainte-Marie was governor of Doullens.

[15] *Conspiration faicte en Picardie sous fausses & meshcantes calomnies contre l'edict de pacification* (n. p., 1576); *Articles de la ligue & association de quelques Catholiques ennemis de la paix establie en France* (n. p., 1576). These documents are discussed in Orlea, *La noblesse aux Etats généraux*, p. 38.

the cardinal de Lorraine and by 1575 he was the ensign of the duc d'Aumale, rising to lieutenant in 1581. In the 1580s he was captain and governor of Guise.[16] Documents detailing those who signed the royal version of the League in 1577 have survived.[17] These lists can only provide clues to the identity of the original conspirators, whose numbers had now been diluted by religious moderates and royalists. A study of the names enables one major conclusion to be drawn.[18] Support for the League of Péronne demonstrates the declining influence of the Bourbon-Vendôme in Picardy and the analogous growth of the Guise affinity in the region. The traditional following of the Bourbon-Vendôme had been weakened by Condé's attachment to protestantism. Neuschel has shown how volatile was the relationship between Condé and his clients in the 1560s – evidence of a following in flux.[19] Applaincourt is paradigmatic of this transformation. Once a servant of the Bourbon and a follower of Condé in 1562, by 1576 he was a *fidèle* of the duc d'Aumale and one of the chief opponents of Condé's return. Religious fissures among the Bourbon in the 1560s led to the atrophy of their traditional support in the province. During the 1560s some clients followed Condé, some Navarre; some were attracted to royal service and others still preferred to follow no lord. The period between 1562 and 1577 saw a reordering of political society in northern France, as the traditional Montmorency and Bourbon followings were disordered by family and religious divisions. The Guise were well placed to exploit the vacuum in Picardy, where they were major landowners. The family was closely related to the Bourbon and Antoinette de Bourbon retained an interest in the fortunes of traditional Bourbon servants. Following the disgrace and execution of Jacques de Coucy for treason in 1549, largely at the behest of the Montmorency, she provided for the welfare of his children and was instrumental in obtaining *lettres d'abolition* for the family in 1576.[20] The duc d'Aumale's arms were quartered Lorraine-Guise and Bourbon and even before the crisis in Picardy his retinue was becoming increasingly Picard in complexion. The lists of signatories of the League in 1577 reveal a substantial number of Guise clients, as well as men who would be patronised by the Guise and serve as Catholic League captains in the 1580s and 1590s. The king was fully aware of Picardy's strategic importance and took steps to augment the royal affinity in the province after 1577.[21]

The appearance of former servants of the house of Bourbon as signatories of the League of Péronne suggests neither a dramatic switch to Guise service nor the outright rejection of the Bourbon as patrons. There was a catholic Bourbon to

[16] BN MS Clairambault 1204 fo. 83; Vindry, p. 285.

[17] BN Collection de Picardie 53 fos. 9–12; BN MS Fr 3329 fos. 17–18.

[18] See appendix D. [19] Neuschel, *Word of Honor*.

[20] D. Potter, 'A treason trial in sixteenth-century France: the fall of marshal du Biez, 1549–1551', *English Historical Review*, 105 (1990), 595–623; ADSM 2E1 304, 4 Oct 1550.

[21] It is well known that the duc d'Epernon was made governor of Boulogne by the king. It is less well known that by 1582 the duc de Joyeuse's ordonnance company had a large Picard contingent, including two officers of Picard origin: BN NA Fr 8633 fo. 82.

whom the Picard nobility could look to for leadership: the cardinal. In the 1570s the cardinal de Bourbon strove to maintain the family inheritance in northern France for his catholic nephews and wards, the comte de Soissons and the prince de Conti. The strategy of the cardinal, his support for the Catholic League and his close relationship with the Guise are crucial to understanding the success of the League in the 1580s. This coalition was largely forged in the 1570s and manifested by the number of men who served both the cardinal and the Guise. In this case, multiple allegiance ensured a durable alliance. The beginning of this alliance and its ramifications are best studied by an analysis of the senior counsellors of the cardinal de Bourbon and by analysing the development of the League of Péronne after its cooption by the king.

The re-ordering of traditional allegiances in upper Normandy and Picardy between 1562 and 1577 is symbolised by the career of André de Bourbon-Rubempré and his relatives. Rubempré was a cadet of the house of Bourbon who fought for Condé in 1562 but, like so many others, his loyalty was tested by the civil war and his conservative religious convictions. He continued to serve the Bourbon as *premier chambellan* of the cardinal in the late 1560s, by which period his conversion from proto-Calvinist to militant catholic was complete, though due as much to factional manoeuvring as religious conviction. The chief opponent among his fellow councillors, Louis de Mainteternes, Bourbon's vicar-general and *trésorier*, advocated cordial relations with the cardinal's protestant relatives. Relations with these relatives cooled further in the early 1570s as Mainteternes' moderating influence waned. At the same time Rubempré entered Guise service.[22] In 1572 the duc de Guise trusted him enough to sell him land to the value of 18,000*l* in the comté of Eu and make him governor of the comté at the same time.[23] Rubempré was a natural choice and as a landowner in Picardy and upper Normandy he had credit in both provinces.

As he rose in the cardinal's service, Rubempré advanced his Norman brothers-in-law. Pierre de Roncherolles, baron of Pont-Saint-Pierre, became first his lieutenant and then his successor as captain of Abbeville; François de Roncherolles, seigneur de Maineville, was a member of the retinue of the cardinal de Bourbon in the 1570s and 1580s, and promoted to the lieutenancy of the company of the cardinal's nephew, the comte de Soissons, in 1578. The Roncherolles were among the most important ultra-catholic families in Normandy. François's soubriquet 'menneligue' reflected his role as the chief agent of the Guise in the 1580s. It is no exaggeration, therefore, to describe the marriage that took place in 1572 between Pierre de Roncherolles and Charlotte de Moy as the most significant Norman marriage of the Wars of Religion. This family alliance formed the axis around which the ultra-catholic faction in Normandy, and later the Catholic League, coalesced. Like Rubempré, Jean de Moy, had joined Condé briefly in 1562 only to

22 Saulnier, *Le rôle politique du cardinal de Bourbon*, pp. 96–7. De Thou's account, viii, pp. 553, is chronologically incorrect.

23 BN MS Fr 8182 fo. 277.

abandon the protestant cause and embrace the Guise and ultra-catholicism. His cousin Louis, governor of Ham, was an early supporter of the League of Péronne.[24]

The cardinal de Bourbon was shocked by the leniency of the Edict of Beaulieu. As opposition was fomenting in Picardy he made one of his rare visits to his archdiocese. As archbishop of Rouen he soon came under pressure from his congregation to prevent enforcement of the Edict of Beaulieu. The cathedral chapter petitioned the cardinal to use his influence in order to prevent the return of protestant worship. A delegation was dispatched to urge the cardinal to 'venir en ceste ville et y estre quelque temps pour en expedier les hereticques et faire ce qui sera necessaire'.[25] The edict had also been badly received by the *échevins* of Rouen, who asked the king for an exemption from its tolerant clauses.[26] In contrast, the parlement was more accommodating and registered the edict quickly, but fears about the return of protestantism to Rouen were not assuaged and a special assembly of the parlement was convened in July 1576.[27] Among those present were fifteen senior magistrates and two *maître des requêtes* representing the crown. Also present were opponents of the edict, among them the cardinal de Bourbon and Pierre de Roncherolles who, as *premier baron de Normandie*, had the right to sit in the court. Bourbon failed to persuade the assembled judges to restrict the exercise of protestant worship. He was forced to act on his own initiative, confronting the protestant congregation during worship on 23 July, six weeks after the signing of the League of Péronne.[28] Bourbon's attempt to emulate the League of Péronne in defying the edict was made against a background of continued fear and uncertainty in Normandy. Sightings of troops caused a number of alarms in Rouen.[29] On 11 August Carrouges informed the parlement that the king had sent him warning of a conspiracy against the city. The king 'vouloit qu'il fust pourveu a ce que ses sujects ne se distraissent de son obeissance sans entrer en quelconque ligue et que de luy lier la corde de dessus la teste si ils entreprennent telle ligue'.[30]

Elections for the Estates of Blois in October were keenly fought. The manifesto of the League of Péronne had called for the election of sympathetic deputies. The king made vain attempts to ensure the election of reliable men. On 15 November 1576 he ordered the replacement of Emery Bigot, deputy of the Third Estate of Rouen, following: 'quelque soupcon seroit intrevenu entre aucuns de ses subjectz mal affectionnez au bien de son service iceulx voyans de nos principaulx officiers, desquelz la fonction n'a autre esgard que à desirer et à rechercher, ce qui nous est de plus particullier, estre employez à faire les plainctes et dolléances de son peuple'.[31]

[24] Orlea, *La noblesse aux Etats généraux*, p. 37. On the Roncherolles, see J. Dewald, *Pont St-Pierre, 1389–1789* (Berkeley, 1987). [25] ADSM G 2171, 26 Jun 1576; Floquet, iii, pp. 160–1.

[26] ACR A 19, 12 May 1576. [27] ADSM 1B 93, 22 May 1576.

[28] Floquet, iii, p. 165; Benedict, *Rouen during the Wars of Religion*, p. 148; ADSM 1B 93, 16 Jul 1576.

[29] ACR A 19, 28 Oct 1576; B 2, 9 Feb 1576; ADSM 1B 93, 14 Mar 1576.

[30] ADSM 1B 93, 11 Aug 1576.

[31] ACR A 19, 10 Nov 1576. The royal will was ignored and Bigot pursued a hawkish line at Blois before his support was eventually bought by the king: Picot, *Histoire des Etats généraux*, ii, p. 365.

More disturbing for the crown was the remarkable consonance between family ties and political conviction among deputies elected for the First and Second Estates of upper Normandy and Picardy. Marion de Martimbosc, a leading counsellor of the cardinal de Bourbon, vicar-general of the diocese of Rouen and chancellor of the cathedral chapter, was returned for the First Estate of the *bailliage* of Rouen.[32] Adrien de Tiercelin, a confidant and longstanding servant of the Guise family, was elected for the Second Estate of the *bailliage* of Amiens.[33] In 1570, the year in which his younger brother Jacques became lieutenant of the duc d'Aumale's company, he was a witness with André de Rubempré to the partition of the Roncherolles lands. His son-in-law Antoine de Bigars, who had historical reasons for his antipathy to the Huguenots, was returned as the representative of the *bailliage* of Rouen. Bigars was later one of the most important League captains in Normandy and his younger brother was ensign of Aumale in 1588.[34] Rubempré was elected for the Second Estate of the comté of Ponthieu and François de Roncherolles was chosen to represent the *bailliage* of Gisors.[35] The result in the *bailliage* of Caux was more contentious: 'le catholique Charles Martel seigneur de Fontaines, élu sans doute grâce aux voix protestantes, est écarté et même injurie par le gouverneur parce qu'il parlait librement et résistoit aux cóntraventions qui se faisoyent en l'assemblée contre la loy ancienne'.[36] An inveterate foe of the protestants of the Caux and the Martel family, Jean de Moy arranged for the election of an officer of his *ordonnance* company.[37] It was among the upper Norman and Picard delegates that the League had its strongest support, consistent with the family connections that Picard leaguers enjoyed in upper Normandy. The upper Norman and Picard nobility was the dominant axis of the League – demonstrated by the fact that when the king wished the Second Estates to vote him money it was Tiercelin, Bigars and Roncherolles who were prevailed upon to use their influence.[38]

The arrival of large numbers of ultra-catholic deputies at Blois coincided with the struggle over the wording of the covenant of the League which all royal subjects would soon be required to swear. As Robert Harding has pointed out, the form of the League covenant as sanctioned by the king in December 1576 was conservative; it sought to bolster support for the pacification in the provinces; and it said nothing about the extirpation of heresy. Indeed it expressly protected protestant worship until a decision had been reached by the Estates.[39] As the events of late 1576 and early 1577 were to prove, the leaguer activists at the Estates and in the provinces differed from the crown and the large number of moderate deputies in their

[32] Frondeville, *Conseillers*, p. 450. He was nephew of a former *bailli* of the duchy of Aumale. For a list of delegates: Lacourcé and Duval, *Recueil*, iii, p. 3.

[33] His career is summarised in Orlea, *La noblesse aux Etats généraux*, pp. 131–7.

[34] Vindry, p. 202; BN Carrés d'Hozier 93, fo. 45.

[35] Farin, *Histoire de la ville de Rouen*, ii, p. 406.

[36] La Popelinière, quoted in Orlea, *La noblesse aux Etats généraux*, p. 92.

[37] Charles de Goutimesnil: Vindry, p. 366.

[38] Picot, *Histoire des Etats généraux*, ii, p. 348.

[39] Harding, *Anatomy of a power elite*, p. 66.

interpretation of the covenant of association. In order to retain authority independent of royal control, the Picard and upper Norman leadership organised clandestinely and surreptitiously changed the wording of the articles of association.

Henri III, assuming he had placed himself in control of the League and effectively drawn its fire, opened the Estates-General on 6 December 1576.[40] The overwhelming preponderance of catholics at the Estates ensured that there was unanimous pressure for action to permit only the exercise of catholicism in the kingdom. Conflict in the Estates arose over the means by which this was to be achieved. Ultra-catholics favoured another war. However, this would entail the imposition of further fiscal burdens, making an inquiry into the royal finances essential. Normandy was one of the seven provinces which voted for the renewal of hostilities.[41] The First and Second Estates were the most vociferous in favour of a new offensive; they had most to gain from a catholic triumph and the nobility could expect military commissions and offices. The Third Estate was troubled by the cost of another campaign, which had no more chance of succeeding than its predecessors. When the disastrous state of the royal finances became clear in January 1577 their scepticism turned to obduracy. They now called for fiscal retrenchment and balked at voting for taxes.

Meanwhile the catholic nobility, strengthened by the local organisation of the League, prepared for a new campaign. As soon as the king gave his blessing provincial officers seized on the opportunity to dispense commissions: 'Sa majestie me dit que elle avoit envoyé en plusieurs endroits, pour continuer l'association que l'on avoit commencée en Picardie, & Monsieur de Carouge lui avoit mandé qu'il l'avoit faite en son Gouvernement, auquel l'on lui bailloit 200 chevaux pour [y estre employé] et 1500 hommes de pied et autant qui demeuroit en Pays pour la garde d'icellui.'[42] The League hierarchy worked closely at Blois. Adrien de Tiercelin and André de Bourbon-Rubempré acted as spokesmen for the three Estates of Picardy and reported back to Humières on 20 December that, following meetings they had attended with the king, Henri was no longer an obstacle to the expansion of the League.[43] Their correspondence demonstrates that, despite the shift in the royal position, the League still remained 'nostre association'.[44] Perceptively, they did not entirely trust Henri's overtures of good faith. In order to maintain local control of the League and ensure that its true purpose was retained, the leaders of the League made sure that the oath sworn to uphold the articles of the League recognised them as leaders in their own right, and did not reduce them to the role of mere royal appointees. The articles presented by Jean de Moy to the inhabitants of his *gouvernement* were altered. He removed the clause which guaranteed the safety of

[40] For this and following: Picot, *Histoire des Etats généraux*, ii, pp. 322–40.

[41] Opposition to the war was strongest in the south where peace had never been established: M. P. Holt, 'Attitudes of the French nobility at the Estates-General of 1576', *Sixteenth Century Journal*, 18 (1987), 489–504. [42] Lacourcé and Duval, *Recueil*, iii, p. 2.

[43] BN MS Fr 3329 fo. 117, Tiercelin to Humières, Blois, 20 Dec 1576. [44] *Ibid.*

law-abiding protestants. On 22 February 1577 the king wrote angrily to Humières, having discovered his adulteration of the articles of association. Humières had effected changes which suggested that forces of the League should be ultimately answerable to the Estates.[45]

The main hindrance to the success of the League now came from the towns who feared the cost, should they swear to uphold the articles of association. On 28 December it was confidently predicted that Amiens 'feront nulle difficulte de se joindre avec les associez et contribuer'.[46] Resistance in Normandy was already demonstrating this to be a delusion. When Carrouges presented the oath of association to the *échevins* of Rouen they refused to comply, and the magistrates of the parlement declared that 'ils ne pouvoient signer sans expres commandement du roy . . . et sur la deliberation . . . il fut aresté que l'on attendroict'.[47] In the event the parlement was not forced to sign as a corporate body, and the choice was left to the conscience of the individual. Even the cathedral chapter was now circumspect. When on 27 December the cardinal de Bourbon ordered the chapter to swear the oath, they deferred a decision until they had consulted their counterparts in Amiens and Beauvais despite pressure from Moy and Carrouges.[48] *Premier président* Bauquemare urged them to choose deputies to attend an assembly of the clergy convened to discuss means of providing money for the war.[49] Here was the crux of the problem for the First Estate. They wanted to defeat the protestants militarily but, along with the towns, it was they who would have to bear the cost. The equivocation of the chapters of Paris, Chartres, Le Mans and Amiens over signing the leaguer covenant bore witness to the doubts the clergy now harboured.[50]

The creeping resentment against the crown's fiscal demands meant that the noble leaders of the League had to cooperate even more closely to achieve their aim of establishing a powerful army. They were also extremely wary of the negotiations between the queen-mother and the Huguenot leadership in the south.[51] The continued failure of the Third Estate to vote money at Blois led the king to abandon plans for a new offensive and place his faith in negotiating a more acceptable peace in early March 1577. This followed the conversion of the hardline catholic duc de Montpensier to religious toleration and the collapse of support for war at the Estates, now supported by only three provinces: Picardy, Champagne and the Orléanais.[52]

As the political atmosphere became more conducive to compromise, so the clandestine intrigues of the hardliners became more elaborate. The solidarity of the

45 Harding, *Anatomy of a power elite*, pp. 96; BN Cinq Cents Colbert 16 fo. 104; *Letters de Henri III*, iii, pp. 85–8.
46 BN MS Fr 3329 fo. 119, Tiercelin to Humières, Blois, 28 Dec 1576.
47 ADSM 1B 92, 13 Feb 1577. 48 ADSM G 2171, 4 and 12 Jan 1577.
49 *Ibid.*, 24 Jan 1577. 50 *Ibid.*, 25 and 26 Jan 1577.
51 Picot, *Histoire des Etats généraux*, ii, p. 325. Rubempré was part of the embassy dispatched to the south and was thus in a good position to keep his fellow leaguers informed.
52 *Ibid.*, ii, pp. 369–71.

League hierarchy in upper Normandy and Picardy was facilitated by close kinship ties, regular and secret meetings and a constant exchange of letters, often in cipher, which betray the sensitivity of the contents and the desire to plan strategy without royal interference. Pierre de Roncherolles acted as an intermediary between Moy and Humières. At the end of January 1577, when the difficulties of financing an army were becoming apparent, a meeting was arranged between the two men at Neufchâtel in upper Normandy.[53] What took place at the meeting is not known and much of the correspondence is vague on details of political strategy because oral communication was much safer. Another council meeting, this time at Abbeville and in the presence of Tiercelin and Rubempré, is alluded to in a letter of 9 April 1577 – Moy writing to Humières apologising for his absence.[54] Roncherolles attended as his representative. Under discussion was the failure of Amiens to pay its contribution. The major problem facing the League in Picardy was the failure of many towns to subscribe to it. Amiens refused to sign anything that undermined its privileges, and the king dispensed it from signing for the sum of 8,000*l*.[55] It seems that the council of the leaguers delegated Tiercelin to meet the mayor of Amiens. He was prepared for this encounter by a memoir drawn up for him by François de Roncherolles, who had emerged as the main link between the League hierarchy and the court.[56] Everyone now feared a re-negotiated peace and it was Maineville's task to follow developments. He wrote with great hope in cipher to Humières after receiving secret assurances from the king, who had: 'luy mesmes baille une particulliere et secret instruction a l'archevesque de Vienne [one of the royal negotiators in talks with the Huguenots] par laquelle il exprimoit sa derniere resolution qu'il n y eust delà Loire aucun presche depuis il luy avoit mande par le sr descars deja les picards et les normans . . . ne l'endureroient pas'.[57] Clearly Henri felt himself specifically under pressure from a section of the Norman and Picard nobility. Maineville provided the link to the king as the emissary of these malcontents.[58] His information was relayed back to Picardy and Normandy and subsequently discussed in council. Thus Moy, Tiercelin and Humières met secretly and corresponded throughout May. On 28 May they agreed to hold a council in order to deliberate over the drafting of a formal letter to the king, presumably on the subject of the peace. The letter of convocation was again written in cipher, but more significantly the three senders also appended their names in cipher, suggesting the danger of their activities.[59]

53 BN MS Fr 3329 fo. 131, Roncherolles to Humières, Pont-Saint-Pierre, 26 Jan 1577.

54 *Ibid.* fo. 154, Moy to Humières, La Meilleraye, 9 Apr 1577.

55 Despite their ambivalence to the League, the Amienois were strongly opposed to the return of protestant worship to Picardy: *Délibérations de l'échevinage*, pp. 55–8.

56 BN MS Fr 3329 fo. 156, Tiercelin to Humières, Amiens, 18 Apr 1577.

57 *Ibid.* fo. 164, Maineville to Humières, Chenonceaux, 7 May 1577.

58 Maineville was aided by Marion de Martimbosc, vicar-general of the cardinal de Bourbon: ibid. fo. 171, Roncherolles to Humières, Pont-Saint-Pierre, 26 May 1577.

59 *Ibid.* fo. 167, Moy, Tiercelin and the sieur de Sainte-Marie to Humières, 14 May 1577. Some of these leaguers had already held preliminary discussions at Blagny.

The dispute with the king over control of the association in Normandy required that close contacts be maintained among Norman and Picard leaguers. Moy kept Humières informed of his efforts to ensure that his relative, Pierre de Roncherolles, was appointed *maître de camp* of all League forces in Normandy. Roncherolles successfully solicited the support of Carrouges, governor of Rouen.[60] But in lower Normandy the loyal governor, Matignon, had already appointed one of his own men. The king declined to honour his promise to Moy to appoint a sole *maître de camp*, provoking the ire of the leaguers. Surviving letters show that much effort was spent maintaining the resolve of the wily Carrouges, and more intriguingly that copies of the royal correspondence to Matignon were circulated among the conspirators.[61]

Little evidence exists to suggest that the Guise were involved in supporting the activities of League sympathisers, beyond the fact that some of these men were familiars or served the family. But it was during this period that Maineville entered Guise service. He had already made his reputation as a deputy at Blois. His call for the non-catholic princes of the blood to be stripped of their accession rights, which earned him the hatred of Condé in particular, was part of the strategy of the cardinal de Bourbon to legitimise his catholic nephews as heirs to the throne with Guise support. When the Peace of Bergerac was signed in September 1577, proscribing all leagues and associations, Maineville was residing at Aumale's château at Anet. He was provided with an early copy of the treaty by the duke and then communicated its contents to his colleagues: 'Il n'est pas question sinon d'aviser a ce coup si Péronne leur [the Huguenots] demeurera et si nous logerons parmi nous nos ennemis deja tout offencés contre nous mais surtout si nous confesserons dieu devant les hommes ou si le renierons, dieu nous face la grace de tenir mieux nos serments.'[62] Maineville thus appealed to religious sentiment in his call for the maintenance of the League. The League was founded on a principle and was not concerned with the details and specifics of a pragmatic religious pacification. Although there was little opposition to the new peace, which was less lenient to the protestants, Maineville's call had wide appeal and the League did not entirely disappear as the king had desired.

One reason for Henri's willingness to keep the channels of communication open with Damville and the Huguenots in 1577 was his growing mistrust of the Guise. At the opening of the Estates-General the king made changes to the traditional order of precedence, in order to diminish Guise's prominence in the ceremony. This was no manner in which to treat the victor of Dormans and it is no surprise

60 *Ibid.* fo. 169, Moy to Humières, La Meilleraye, 24 May 1577; Lettres de Henri III, pp. 174–5, 196, 211.

61 BN MS Fr 3329 fos. 165 and 171, Roncherolles to Humières, Pont-Saint-Pierre, 9 and 26 May 1577. It is not clear whether copies of the royal correspondence to Matignon were sent to Moy by the king as a matter of course. The letters of Henri III to Matignon during this period make no mention of such a policy.

62 *Ibid.* fo. 171, Maineville to unknown, Anet, Oct 1577, in cipher.

that the duke failed to appear.[63] The diary of the duc de Nevers demonstrates that, during the royal sojourn at Blois, Guise was rarely present at the most secret councils of the king. Once Henri had legalised the League and placed himself at its head, Guise asked leave to go and begin its organisation in his *gouvernement*. Henri refused, fearing the dominance of Guise in Champagne and a consequent diminution of royal authority.[64] On 27 December 1576 the king frankly confided his suspicions to his closest advisors.[65] He obviously felt it safer to have the duke at court where he could better observe his activities. Guise found his position at court increasingly untenable as even his brother-in-law, Montpensier, had joined the *politique* faction. Montpensier had much to gain from severing ties with the ultra-catholics. He was elevated in the order of seniority at court ceremonials, having recently triumphed in his precedence battle with Guise, under way since 1575.[66] More serious was the queen-mother's continued hatred for the Guise: 'la Royne courroussa contre Monsieur de Guise, qui'il vouloit la guerre, et qu'il y en avoit beaucoup qui la desiroient, et qu'il ne la falloit faire'.[67] While negotiations sponsored by Catherine continued with the Huguenots and their allies, a desultory campaign was fought in the south, which both sides lacked the necessary resources to prosecute effectively. On returning to Champagne Guise was once again forced to borrow money in order to pay his troops, using his own plate as a guarantee.[68] This only compounded his already serious debt problem which was soon to force him to sell substantial lands. When peace was finally signed Guise made little protest, partly because the terms were favourable to the catholics but also because of his own financial plight. In July 1577 Antoinette de Bourbon complained that his rights were so extensively alienated that he 'ne peut tirer un sol de son revenu'.[69] The pragmatic attitude to the Peace of Bergerac was also prevalent throughout France. The humiliating Peace of Beaulieu had been expunged and once more protestantism north of the Loire remained weak and beleaguered.[70] Guise's own interest now turned to international affairs.

THE SEARCH FOR A CAUSE, 1578–1584

In July 1577 Don John, Philip II's governor-general, seized Namur with the aim of organising a new campaign against the States-General of the Netherlands. In November he sent emissaries to Guise, who was stationed on the frontier, asking for troops and Guise was glad to oblige.[71] Likewise, the States-General appealed for

[63] Bouillé, iii, p. 42; De Thou, vii, p. 448.
[64] Lacourcé and Duval, *Recueil*, iii, p. 32. Guise finally left court on 7 March 1577.
[65] *Ibid.*, p. 31. Nevers was himself not overtly hostile to the Guise as he too favoured a warlike policy.
[66] *Ibid.*, p. 60. [67] *Ibid.*, p. 53. [68] Bouillé, iii, p. 62.
[69] BN MS Fr 3338 fo. 86, Antoinette de Bourbon to the duchesse de Nemours, Joinville, 1 Jul 1577.
[70] Benedict, *Rouen during the Wars of Religion*, pp. 152–3.
[71] P. O. de Törne, 'Philippe II et Henri de Guise. Le début de leurs relations', *Revue Historique*, 167 (1931), p. 324; Constant, Les Guises, p. 103; Bouillé, iii, pp. 63–5. These soldiers may have simply

outside help. Anjou was approached and he promised to do his best to prevent Guise from aiding the Spanish further.[72] By November 1577 Guise had returned to Paris, where he set about reinforcing his links with the city hierarchy. He arranged the huge festivities at the hôtel de Guise for the marriage of his servant, Louis de Hacqueville, sieur de Vicourt, to the daughter of Claude Marcel, *prévot des marchands*.[73]

Spanish attempts to stir up factionalism in France and divert French attention from the revolt in the Netherlands are well documented. The duc de Guise, far from being a traitor to the *patrie*, acted in the same way as other princes – with the good of his own house in the forefront of his mind, and not tied to the interest of either Valois or Habsburg. The Spanish made approaches to Henri de Navarre, and paid pensions to noblemen in Guyenne and to the protestant mercenary captain, John Casimir.[74] Henri de Montmorency-Damville courted both Spain and Savoy in the 1580s out of financial necessity.[75] Indeed the Spanish hoped to create a catholic malcontent alliance between Guise and Montmorency. The Spanish ambassador, Juan de Vargas Mexia, reported to Madrid in March 1578 that Guise would make an ideal ally since he was out of favour at court and heavily in debt. Following the excitement of Don John's crushing victory at Gembloux (January 1578), there was even talk of an invasion of England supported by Guise, discussed when Guise met Vargas again in April. However, these talks had no political consequences. It was Anjou's flight from the French court in February and the danger that he would raise an army to assist the Dutch that made an alliance with Guise even more imperative for Philip.[76]

The duke found the offers of Spanish assistance welcome because his status was under increasing pressure at court. Tensions came to a head on 27 April 1578 when three of the king's *mignons* were slain in a duel with a group defending the honour of the duc de Guise.[77] Henri was mortified by the deaths of his favourites and the entire Guise family, accompanied by the duc de Lorraine, left court on 3 May in

deserted the French army because of arrears of pay and in any case their transfer relieved Guise of the problem of unpaid troops remaining in his own gouvernement.

[72] M. P. Holt, *The duke of Anjou and the politique struggle during the Wars of Religion* (Cambridge, 1986), p. 93.

[73] On the magnificence of this occasion, see Bouillé, iii, p. 65; L'Estoile, *Journal du règne de Henri III*, p. 157. The Hacqueville were an important element of the Parisian League. André was *président* of the League parlement in the 1590s and his daughter was the mistress of the chevalier d'Aumale. Louis, a representative of a cadet line, was in the household of the duc d'Anjou in 1581 and his father had signed the League of Péronne in 1576: BN Pièces Originales 1462 fos. 91, 327; Dossiers Bleus 343 fo. 16. On the Marcel: Carroll, 'The Guise affinity and popular protest', p. 142.

[74] Constant, Les Guises, pp. 105–10.

[75] J. Davies, 'Neither politique nor patriot? Henri de Montmorency and Philip II, 1582–1589', *Historical Journal*, 34 (1991), 539–66.

[76] Törne, 'Philippe II et Henri de Guise', pp. 326–9.

[77] Bouillé, iii, p. 70; L'Estoile, *Journal du règne de Henri III*, p. 186. Strictly speaking these men were neither champions of the duc de Guise nor in his retinue. He was acquainted with them and offered his protection after the duel.

great discord with the king. The violence did not stop there and on 21 July another *mignon*, Saint-Mégrin, was attacked and killed by thirty assailants in the rue du Louvre. The duc de Mayenne was immediately suspected of a revenge attack for improper advances that Saint-Mégrin had made towards the duchesse de Guise.[78]

Guise was *persona non grata* at the court and he did not return until March 1579.[79] Without access to the king's ear his *crédit* fell and his financial affairs became pressing. The whole question of noble finances and indebtedness is complicated and fraught with difficulty. Clearly political and economic fortunes were closely intertwined. As Guise lost favour it is likely that he found it increasingly difficult to satisfy his creditors or raise new loans. In August 1578 the comté of Nanteuil had to be sold to Gaspard de Schomberg for 120,666 *écus* and a further two seigneuries were sold to the duc de Lorraine in November 1581 for 288,000*l*.[80] Moreover the duc de Guise was not the only member of the family forced to alienate land. Charles d'Aumale, who had reached his majority in 1579, was immediately forced to sell the barony of Bec Crespin to Nicholas Romé, a major creditor, since he was 'pressé par les creanciers que feu monsieur son pere luy a laisse'.[81] Aumale's position was especially acute as he was failing to achieve the same status that his father had enjoyed, most significantly lacking his own *gouvernement*. This was within the king's patronage and Henri, a shrewd and subtle manipulator of royal favour, was not foolish enough to allow the Guise to possess too many key posts. In 1579 the duc d'Aumale lost a precedence case against the duc de Nevers in the privy council, which would have been inconceivable ten years before.[82] Henri III also subverted the entrenched Guise position at court by undermining the rights and jurisdiction of the offices they held. Henri de Guise had inherited the office of *grand maître* from his father. The king managed to diminish its jurisdiction and thus the power of the duke by increasing the status and competence of the *prévôté de l'hôtel*, and by creating the new office of *grand maître des cérémonies*. Laurent Bourquin has shown how the king undermined Guise's influence in Champagne by the appointment of Joachim de Dinteville as lieutenant-general.[83] Henri was not intent on an open break with the Guise and he continued to bestow favours upon them, but he did want to restrain their influence.[84] The king seems to have had a more affectionate relationship with the duc de Mayenne than with the duc de Guise. This was due either to genuine affection or to an attempt to undermine family solidarity by fostering fraternal jealousy. Thus it was Mayenne who received major commands

78 L'Estoile, *Journal du règne de Henri III*, pp. 190–1.

79 Constant, *Les Guises*, p. 108.

80 Bouillé, iii, p. 50.

81 BN MS Fr 18246 fo. 161. See also, Lechevalier, *Notice historique sur la baronnie du Bec*, p. 12.

82 BN MS Fr 18246 fos. 116–61.

83 J. Boucher, *Société et mentalités autour de Henri III* (3 vols., Lille, 1981), i, p. 207; Bourquin, *Noblesse seconde et pouvoir en Champagne*, pp. 93–134.

84 The king continued to be generous. Mayenne and Elbeuf received 100,000*l* and 100,000 *écus* respectively on their marriages. Guise received a gift of 500,000 *écus* in 1582 at a time when the king was especially frightened about his dealings with Spain: Boucher, *Société et mentalités autour de Henri III*, i, p. 283.

between 1577 and 1586 against the Huguenots in the south, and Henri was glad to consent to his accession to the office of admiral in 1578.[85]

For Guise, the prospects of attaining honour through royal service were bleak and, like thousands of other noblemen, he looked elsewhere for opportunities to further his career. Service with another prince would raise his stature and demonstrate his power and merits to what he perceived as an ungrateful and poorly counselled monarch. Guise, like Anjou, who felt stifled by his role at court, saw military glory and prestige abroad as a means of raising his status in France and improving his bargaining position with the king. He also began to show greater interest in international affairs after the Peace of Bergerac, while always keeping his political options open. He now, rather belatedly, turned his attention to the plight of his aunt, Mary Stuart. He was encouraged by her emissary, John Leslie, bishop of Ross, who had arrived on the continent in 1574 to secure aid for Mary and her party in Scotland. Leslie was given the office of suffragan and vicar-general of the diocese of Rouen by the cardinal de Bourbon in 1579.[86] Guise was sincerely interested in helping his cousin and her son, James VI, but he never committed himself to projects outside France to the detriment of his status in the kingdom. Similarly, a Spanish pension did not make him a puppet of Spanish policy. The dynastic and historical links of the Guise meant that they favoured intervention in Scotland while Philip II was more concerned with England. The Spanish monarch's relations with England were complicated: he wanted to avoid war while at the same time preventing English intervention in the Netherlands. Similarly he was ambivalent in his motives for giving pensions to French noblemen. He was perfectly happy to have someone like Guise as another 'carte française', capable of diverting Valois attention away from the Low Countries but he would have been horrified at the prospect of a successful Guise invasion of the British Isles, even if it was designed to restore catholicism. Such an attack was under discussion and was fully supported by Don John, who hoped to marry Mary Stuart and thereby acquire a kingdom, until his death in October 1578. This only served to increase Philip's jealousy of his half-brother, fostered by Antonio Peréz.[87]

The proposals for a joint venture against England inevitably drew the duke to Normandy. During the summer of 1578 he paid his first visit to Eu. The town organised a magnificent entry for him and his large retinue, and during his stay he pledged to build a new family residence.[88] Seeing the strategic importance of Eu as a port on the Channel coast, the duke would strive in the coming years to improve

[85] L'Estoile, *Journal du règne de Henri III*, p. 187.

[86] *Dictionary of National Biography*, xi, p. 975.

[87] Constant, *Les Guises*, pp 108–10. Törne, 'Philippe II et Henri de Guise', pp. 333–4, also notes that Philip's attitude to the projected invasion depended heavily on Spanish success in the Low Countries. The pension given to Guise has been estimated at 10,000 *écus* per quarter.

[88] Bouillé, iii, p. 74 n. 2. Building began almost immediately but was interrupted in 1588 and even by 1661 only half of the château was complete: P. Seydoux, *La Normandie des châteaux et des manoirs* (Paris, 1989), p. 108.

its anchorage, enabling it to receive vessels of up to 300 *tonneaux*.[89] At the beginning of 1582 he met the bishop of Ross and a number of Jesuits in the town, where he granted them permission for the establishment of an English Jesuit college and donated £100 towards the cost. Eu served as a training centre for priests destined for England and acted as a magnet for English catholic exiles.[90] In order to finance these diverse projects Guise obtained royal permission to codify the custom and privileges of the comté, enabling him to rationalise and reassert his rights and dues.[91] His growing interest in Normandy was reflected in the appointment of a Norman, Jacques Du Val, seigneur de Mondreville, as his *chef de conseil* in the early 1580s.[92]

The time that Guise spent at Eu fuelled speculation that he was behind the resistance mounted by the Estates of Normandy in 1578 and 1579 against royal attempts to increase the *taille*. The family was always a convenient target for suspicion in time of crisis, especially for their enemies and the crown. Undoubtedly the Guise did play a role in the disputes of 1578–9, but their political goals and the extent of their involvement are ambiguous. Clearly, the governor of Burgundy, the duc de Mayenne, had much to gain from supporting the Estates of Burgundy. His open support of the province against the crown largely compensated for the low credit and status he had enjoyed there.[93]

The conflict with Burgundy in May 1578 provided a warning to the king of the problems he was likely to face when the Norman Estates gathered in the autumn. The Burgundians had dispatched emissaries to urge the Normans to join them in forcing the king to reduce taxation. These entreaties found a receptive audience because taxes levied without the consent of the Estates, undertaken in 1574 and 1576 as an emergency financial measure, threatened to become habitual.[94] Considerable anti-tax unrest in lower Normandy prompted the king to send *surintendant des finances* Pomponne de Bellièvre to placate the assembly.[95] The tax burden and the infringement of provincial rights made the elections for the Estates of 1578 more than usually important. The election of Guise clients and servants to the assembly is an indication of the extent of Guisard influence in the region. It was also an acknowledgement that these men had the protection of powerful malcontents, making them more effective deputies in the face of intense royal pressure.

When the Estates finally met in Rouen on 17 November 1578, the representatives of the upper Norman *bailliages* could claim strong affiliation with the ultra-

89 J. Darsel, 'L'Amirauté en Normandie: I –Amirauté d'Eu-Le Tréport', *Annales de Normandie*, 19 (1969), p. 269.
90 F. Fabre, 'The English College at Eu, 1582–1592', *Catholic Historical Review*, 37 (1951), 257–80.
91 AN KK 1088 fo. 170.
92 Margry, *Pierre Séguin*, p. 10. Jean Péricard was secretary of the council.
93 Drouot, *Mayenne et la Bourgogne*, i, p. 103.
94 On this and following: J. R. Major, *Representative government in early modern France* (New Haven and London, 1980), pp. 213–15.
95 *Lettres de Henri III*, iv, pp. 92, 97.

catholic faction in the province; the dominant axis of this grouping, the Moy–Roncherolles, succeeded in the selection of its men for the Second Estate.[96] A list of the electors of the Second Estate of the *bailliage* of Rouen survives. The three men who convened in Rouen in November were all representatives of the ultra-catholic faction.[97] One of these, Barthélemy de Limoges, sieur de Saint-Just and *maître des eaux et fôrets* of the *bailliage* of Rouen, was of a powerful office-holding family formerly associated with Diane de Poitiers. His father's position as lieutenant of the royal *vénerie* under the duc de Guise in the 1540s and 1550s enabled the family to dominate royal forest office in the *bailliages* of Rouen and Gisors. Barthélemy began his career as an archer in the company of the duc d'Aumale in 1565 and both he and his brother Georges obtained posts in the royal *vénerie*.[98]

The electors returned Nicolas Vipart, baron de Becthomas and younger brother of the most senior Norman in Aumale's military retinue in the 1560s. Claude Vipart, as an officer of Aumale's company, had recruited his neighbours and social contacts, such as Barthélemy de Limoges, to serve as gendarmes. The role of Vipart as both patron and client is confirmed by the fact that when he was unable to represent the *bailliage* of Rouen at the provincial Estates in 1586, it was Limoges who took his place.[99] The presence of his men at the Estates gave the duke influence and access to information. As a great Norman magnate he had an interest in protecting his tenants from royal taxes. The Croismare, Vipart and Limoges were prominent members of the Holy League in Normandy during the 1580s and 1590s, but the events of 1578–9 demonstrate that their long history of political activity and opposition to the policies of Henri III predated the first revolt of the catholic princes in 1585.[100]

More significantly, the crisis of 1578–9 provides further evidence of growing

[96] For a list of deputies: *Cahiers des Etats de Normandie sous le règne de Henri III*, i, pp. 310–13. Charles de Goutimesnil represented the nobility of the Caux, a function he had fulfilled at the Estates-General of Blois on the intercession of Jean de Moy. François de Fumechon, sieur de Guerneville, representing the nobility of the *bailliage* of Gisors, was a member of the Roncherolles affinity and had been present as a tutor to the children of the deceased Philippe de Roncherolles at the *partage* of 1570: ADSM 2E1 341, 20 Jul 1570.

[97] *Cahiers des Etats de Normandie sous le règne de Henri III*, i, p. 297. Marc, sieur de Vaudesart, was *maître d'hôtel* of André de Rubempré and Charles de Croismare held a post in the household of the duc d'Aumale: BN MS Fr 21534 fo. 2129, 16 Jul 1574; Frondeville, *Présidents*, p. 206.

[98] Barthélemy married Jeanne Pétremol in 1565, thus allying himself with one of the most senior families in Guise service. Gabriel II was *capitaine des gardes des eaux et fôrets* in 1584: Catalogue des actes de Henri II, 1550, p. 230; BN MS Fr 32764 fos. 15–16; 32868 fo. 467; 16899 fo. 242; Cinq Cents Colbert 54 fo. 348; AN KK 133B, 10 Mar 1566. Frondeville, *Présidents*, pp. 177–9; Frondeville, *Conseillers*, p. 620. Etienne, sieur de Prunas, an archer of the marquis d'Elbeuf in 1569, was noted in the muster roll as 'demeurant pres d'Ivry'. The youngest brother Jean-Maximilien resigned his office of lieutenant-general of the admiralty in Rouen in 1588 for 3,000 *écus*: AN MC LIX 9, 31 Jan 1588.

[99] Farin, *Histoire de la ville de Rouen*, ii, p. 410.

[100] For example, Barthélemy Limoges's younger brother, Jean-Maximilien, lieutenant-general of the admiralty at Rouen, was a notable ultra-catholic activist in the 1580s and 1590s. In 1589 he was charged by the Catholic League with the seizure of all Huguenot property in Normandy: ADSM 1B 699, 14 Jun 1589.

Guise influence among non-nobles, affording the first clear instances of servants elected as representatives for the Third Estate. Mathieu Dupont, the *greffier* and later *receveur* of Elbeuf, represented the *vicomté* of Pont-Audemer.[101] The *vicomté* of Neufchâtel returned Christophe Cherie who would soon succeed his father as *vicomte* of the duchy of Aumale. A number of documents survive testifying to the important services performed by the Cherie for the duke. Far from being rustic officials with a parochial outlook, they were of Amiens bourgeois stock, landowners in Picardy and were married into the elite of Rouen bourgeois society.[102] Ultra-catholic candidates did exceptionally well in upper Normandy, reflecting the strength of catholicism in the region and reinforcing the impression that those already associated with opposition to royal policy were perceived as more capable of withstanding royal pressure. The Guise were out of favour with the king and Mayenne had already indicated his support for provincial institutions. Candidates from the Guise affinity or opponents of royal religious policy could be relied upon to resist royal pressure.

Despite the presence of Bellièvre at the Estates and the special address he delivered, the *cahier* of remonstrances presented to the king was strongly worded. Deputies were particularly angered by royal violations of the privileges of the province enshrined in the fourteenth-century Norman Charter. They demanded the reduction of taxation to the levels set under Louis XII.[103] Henri made small concessions in his demands for money and ordered the Estates to reconvene in March 1579 for an extraordinary session. On this occasion the king sent the maréchal de Montmorency as a special commissioner to accompany Bellièvre. Meanwhile, Antoine Séguier, a *maître des requêtes*, was dispatched to lower Normandy to explain the royal position to local notables.[104] Here, urgent action was essential because opposition to tax increases was more violent and threatened to develop into armed revolt. Jacques de Matignon, governor of lower Normandy, reported to Bellièvre on 25 November 1578 about:

> les menees et praticques . . . qui se faisoit par nos voisins qui ont monstre le chemin aux autres . . . les deputez des bailliages de Caen et de Cotentin ont este ceulx qui ont donne coeur et persuade les autres de prendre la resolution . . . Je fuz adverty quils estoient avoir beaucoup de bonnes instructions de la coste de la Bretagne.[105]

[101] ADSM 2E1 360, 11 Jun 1580; 362, 5 May 1581.

[102] Nicole Cherie was *vicomte* of Neufchâtel in 1569 and of Aumale from 1574 until 1581. He was a bourgeois of Amiens and married to Marguerite du Four, offspring of an important Rouennais catholic bourgeois family. Pierre, who lived at Aumale, acted as a guarantor in the financial transactions of the duke: ADSM 2E1 329, 19 Feb 1565; 348, 18 Jan 1574; 1B 2152 1 Dec 1588; AN 300 AP I 224 liasse 3, 11 April 1587; *Délibérations de l'échevinage*, p. 69.

[103] Major, *Representative government, p. 214; Cahiers des Etats de Normandie sous le règne de Henri III*, i, pp. 6–8. The destruction caused by Anjou's troops was also mentioned.

[104] M. Foisil, 'Harangue et rapport d'Antoine Séguier, commissaire pour le Roi en Basse-Normandie (1579–1580)', *Annales de Normandie*, 26 (1976), 25–40; *Lettres de Henri III*, iv, pp. 99–100.

[105] BN MS Fr 15905 fo. 199, Matignon to Bellièvre, 25 Nov 1578.

In December Henri wrote to his officers in the strife-torn province ordering them to apprehend all trouble makers. He thanked Matignon for preventing a disturbance at Coutances and wrote to him again concerning more serious trouble:

Je croy que vous avez bien peu entendre ce qui est advenu à Caen d'un nombre de six ou sept cens païsans qui se sont presentez aux esleuz, ausquelz ilz ont remis et rejecté desdaigneusement le mandemans qui leur avoient esté envoiez pour l'assiette des tailles . . . disant qu'ilz n'avoient aucun moien de payer . . . empescher de tout votre pouvoir telles desobeissances en donnant ordre [à] ceulx de ma noblesse qui semblent les favoriser, et donner ceste hardiesse au peuple.[106]

Fearful that Normandy would provide a bad example to other provinces, Henri was determined to avert any large-scale unrest. In order to ensure that royal commands were effectively enforced, trusted lieutenants were dispatched. One of the royal *mignons*, François d'O *surintendant des finances*, was granted the captaincy of Caen and in March 1579 troops were despatched to Le Havre.[107] Henri's concessions at the Norman Estates of March 1579 – a small reduction in the *taille* and a confirmation of the Norman Charter – failed to halt all the disturbances.[108] The king blamed rogue elements in the Norman nobility and his suspicions fell on his brother, several Huguenot and malcontent servants of whom had been elected to the Estates. Like the ultra-catholics they could in no way be accused of being 'king's men'. In lower Normandy protestantism remained strong and Anjou possessed the duchy of Alençon and a large clientele. The Huguenot, Jacques du Pont-Bellanger, was elected for the Second Estate of the *bailliage* of Caen.[109] Jean de La Haye, seigneur de Chantelou, representative of the nobility of the *bailliage* of Evreux was a member of Anjou's household.[110] He and Henri de Silly, seigneur de La Roche-Guyon, were involved in raising troops for Anjou's abortive campaign in the Low Countries. The presence of these ill-disciplined troops further inflamed the anger of the peasantry, and the king saw them as a potential threat to the stability of the province. La Roche-Guyon was raising troops in the vicinity of Rouen in December 1578 and compelling them to swear an oath of loyalty to Anjou, an act which was widely interpreted as the basis of a new league in Normandy rather than as part of the requirements for service in Flanders.[111] La Roche-Guyon was a protestant and suspected of collusion with the representative for the Second Estate of the Cotentin in March 1579, Simon de Piennes, sieur de Grainville, 'qui

106 Lettres de Henri III, iv, p. 140.

107 G. de La Rue, *Essais historiques sur la ville de Caen* (2 vols., Caen, 1820), ii, pp. 262; *Lettres de Henri III*, iv, p. 170. These troops were commanded by a loyal Norman, the seigneur de Larchant.

108 Major, *Representative government*, p. 214.

109 For preliminary information on the Pont-Bellanger: Chenaye-Desbois, xvi, p. 114; ADSM 2E1 334, 11 and 12 Mar 1567.

110 By 1582 he was a *chambellan ordinaire* of the duke: ADSM 2E1 365, 4 Jun 1582. The depredations of the 6,000 troops who marched through Normandy inflamed local discontent: Bouquet, ed., *Documents concernant l'histoire de Neufchâtel-en-Bray*, p. 25.

111 ACR B 4, 11 Dec 1578.

est de la nouvelle religion et recogneu avoir manyé beaucoup de factions en ceste partie là'.[112] Above all, the king feared the controlling hand of his brother who had returned to his Norman lands in January 1579, after the collapse of his expedition to the Low Countries. Bellièvre was immediately dispatched to obtain assurances of Anjou's loyalty and investigate his links with the troubles in Normandy. The English ambassador who, because of the projected marriage of Anjou to Elizabeth I, had a close interest in the affairs of the duke, reported that: 'the Duke of Guise and Maine have no part in these popular emotions . . . Those of the best credit in Normandy resort daily to Monsieur, and the king is informed that they desire his protection.'[113] Anjou had thus acquired an ideal pretext for another revolt. That he did not seize it was due to the fact that much of his princely ambition had been satisfied by the generous provisions of the Peace of Monsieur. Above all he was intent on pursuing a kingdom for himself and he needed the king's blessing to marry Elizabeth. In August 1579 he departed for England but his troublesome Norman servants did not accompany him and rural violence failed to diminish. Henri issued orders for the arrest of La Haye, La Roche-Guyon and Pont-Bellanger: 'pour grandes fautes commises contre depuys la tenue desdictz Estatz, qui n'ont rien en communs avec le faict d'iceulx Estatz combien qu'ilz essaient de le faire croire aultrement affin de couvrir leur faulte particulliere par l'auctorité d'une grande compagnie'.[114] La Roche-Guyon was in great danger, not only being accused of plotting to seize Rouen but also charged with plotting to poison the king.[115]

Declared outlaws and bereft of the protection of their patron these men feared for their lives. Anjou may have disavowed their actions and abandoned them to their fate. La Haye and La Roche-Guyon fled Normandy and headed for the safety of the latter's estates in Lorraine. Along with other protestants they soon became involved in plans to form a malcontent pact with the Guise. It is no surprise to see strict religious divisions once again confounded and we are also provided with clues as to why so many of Anjou's '*politique* party' found it easy to join the Catholic League in 1584. The ability to change patrons did not mean that loyalty was so weak as to have been completely cynical. The flight to Lorraine was logical, both men knowing they would receive refuge and a sympathetic welcome. Efforts by Guise, who remained *persona non grata* at court, to attract Huguenot and *politique* malcontents to his service seemed to be succeeding. With this end in mind he had been in contact with protestant leaders, and was prepared to guarantee their freedom of worship. Senior Huguenot figures like Navarre, La Noue and Duples-

[112] *Lettres de Henri III*, iv, pp. 164–5, 177.

[113] *CSPF*, 1578–9, p. 431. Anjou admitted that an association was formed for the purpose of service in the Netherlands and he was certainly solicited by the local nobility for his protection. However, he complained that the disobedience of the Estates prevented him from receiving his pension, which was assigned on the revenue of the *généralité* of Caen: BN MS Fr 15811 fos. 35–7, Bellièvre to Henri III, Caen, 10 Mar 1579.

[114] *Lettres de Henri III*, iv, p. 268.

[115] ACR A 20, 22 Aug 1579.

sis-Mornay were not inclined to trust their old adversary, and similar moves to interest Anjou in an alliance of malcontents also foundered.[116] The suspicions of the protestant leadership failed to dampen the ardour of their co-religionists. Even Duplessis-Mornay's brother, attracted by the opportunity to serve princes of renown, joined the coalition. Undoubtedly he and his comrades were reassured by the heterodox atmosphere of the ducal court at Nancy, but kinship bonds were largely responsible for forging the alliance. La Roche-Guyon's younger brother, the comte de Rochepot, was a favourite of Charles III duc de Lorraine, and La Haye was closely related to intimates of the duc de Guise.[117] One of Guise's most trusted servants, the comte de Vignory, was particularly active in contacting and recruiting among his protestant friends and kinsmen.[118] According to de Thou, on Vignory's death in 1580 his papers were confiscated lest the duke's machinations be fully exposed. Clearly the duke had an interest in protecting his public persona as an unbending foe of heresy.[119]

This unholy alliance of malcontents, which was joined by the German Calvinist John Casimir, was invited by the duc de Lorraine to spend carnival at Nancy in 1580. A catholic–Calvinist plot to seize strategically important and Lutheran Strasbourg was mooted, for which the conspirators hoped to receive Spanish financial assistance. The futile plotting demonstrates Guise's desperate search for a cause with which to augment his honour and display his prowess, to show that the king could continue to ignore him only at his peril. Guise faced a series of dilemmas which would only be relieved by the constitutional crisis created by Anjou's death in 1584. To help his aunt, to pay off his debts and to maintain his status, he had to regain influence at court by making his absence a source of distress for the crown. To do this he searched for alliances both at home and abroad. His conscience was untroubled by the dialogue with his former enemies, whether catholic moderates or Huguenots. However, he had to be wary of alienating his own ultra-catholic clients who formed the backbone of his following and therefore of his power.

Fearful of his intentions and needing his support in the imminent outbreak of hostilities in the south-west, the king recalled Guise who returned to court on 16 March 1580 accompanied by 1,500 horsemen.[120] In an attempt to satisfy his ambitions the king named him as deputy to the duc d'Anjou, recently created lieutenant-general of the kingdom. The reconciliation was largely cosmetic. Henri

[116] *Mémoires et correspondence de Duplessis-Mornay* (12 vols., Paris, 1824–5), i, pp. 122–3; *CSPF*, 1578–9, p. 414.

[117] La Haye was the nephew of Adrien de Tiercelin, a leading member of the Catholic League in Picardy and brother-in-law of Christophe de Bassompierre, a close friend of the duke. For the background to this affair: L. Davillé, *Les prétensions de Charles III duc de Lorraine à la couronne de France* (Paris, 1909), pp. 24–31; Constant, *Les Guises*, p. 111–12.

[118] His most bizarre recruit was Robert de Heu, seigneur de Malleloy, whose uncle Gaspard had been a key figure in the reform movement in Metz and was summarily executed in 1558 on the orders of the cardinal de Lorraine: 'Mort de Gaspard de Heu, seigneur de Buy', *Bulletin de la Société de l'Histoire du Protestantisme Français*, 25 (1876), 164–8.

[119] De Thou, viii, pp. 557–9. [120] Bouillé, iii, p. 82.

III's ill health and inability to produce an heir exacerbated the political uncertainty and Guise's search for new allies and fresh causes did not cease.

DIVERGING INTERESTS: THE BUILDING OF NEW FAMILY RELATIONSHIPS

The decline in the confessional aspect of politics after the Peace of Bergerac in 1577 diminished the opportunities for noble youth to forge a career in arms and Guise hatred and anger at individual Huguenots had been satisfied by the assassination of Coligny in 1572. The family was now represented by a new generation, many of whom were too young to remember the paranoia and insecurities of the 1560s. Complete solidarity in the pursuit and defence of family interest was no longer so necessary. The creation of distinct but related branches of the same house was inevitable as blood ties weakened and the fluid political situation demanded more independent strategies. While the duc de Guise was out of favour at court it was even more essential for the cadets to pursue their individual careers. Regular family councils and the marriage between cousins allowed a common family strategy to withstand the weakening of blood ties. On 6 August 1576 Charles duc de Mayenne was married to the comtesse de Tende at Meudon. The whole family then repaired to Joinville where a double marriage was celebrated in November: Charles duc d'Aumale married his cousin Marie de Lorraine, daughter of the marquis d'Elbeuf, and Diane de Lorraine, sister of the duc d'Aumale, wedded François de Luxembourg, comte de Roucy.[121] The first marriage was an attempt to reinforce family solidarity. The dowry of 100,000*l* provided by the duc de Guise eased the financial difficulties of Aumale, although this sum was not immediately forthcoming, probably due to Guise's own troubles. The double marriage provided an excellent opportunity to take counsel and formulate a common strategy towards the formation of the Catholic League in Picardy. The dominant presence of the ageing matriarch, Antoinette de Bourbon, was a feature of these unions and councils.[122]

Charles de Lorraine, duc d'Aumale, twenty-three in 1579, had more reason than his older cousin to be dissatisfied with his treatment by the king, who declined to offer him a governorship. His interest in Picardy can be traced to the early 1570s when his *ordonnance* company became increasingly Picard in composition. After 1576 the duke recruited followers among sympathisers of the League of Péronne. In 1579 he visited Amiens for the first time.[123] Granting the governorship to Aumale would have been the height of royal folly. The frontiers of Picardy had been increasingly sensitive since the revolt of the Netherlands, and the interest of the duc d'Anjou in the conflict ensured that the governorship remained one of the most important royal charges. There is some evidence to suggest that Aumale was either more pious than other members of his family or strove more cynically to

[121] Anselme, iii, pp. 491–2.

[122] Guise still owed the sum to his cousin two years later: Bouillé, iii, p. 50, n. 3.

[123] *Délibérations de l'échevinage*, p. 71.

exploit catholic anxieties. His Jesuit education at the University of Pont à Mousson, founded by Charles cardinal de Lorraine, certainly contributed to his rigid orthodoxy. His hopes of advancement must have been high on reaching his majority since his cousin and close friend, Philippe-Emmanuel de Lorraine, duc de Mercoeur, was the brother-in-law and confidant of the king.[124]

In November 1579 the prince de Condé, frustrated by the failure of his peaceable efforts to regain effective control of the governorship of Picardy, seized La Fère. The king did little to force his withdrawal, sending the queen-mother to negotiate his submission.[125] Condé infuriated the local population by ravaging the countryside and attempting to seize Doullens. The prince complained to Henri that Aumale was trying to resurrect the Picard League in contravention of the Peace of Bergerac.[126] On 15 June an army finally left Paris to reduce La Fère after Condé had gone to the Empire to recruit mercenaries. The royal army was commanded by the maréchal de Matignon and contained Henri's favourites: Jean-Louis de La Valette, later duc d'Epernon, and Anne de Joyeuse.[127] This force was joined by a significant number of Picard leaguers, such as Rubempré and Tiercelin led by Aumale:

> Il duca di Aumale ha mandati a chiamare i suoi amici, e massime delle leghe di Normandia e Piccardia, delle quali è capo; credesi per il più non avrà gran seguito, per essere la più parte delle dette leghe di ordinanze degli uomini d'arme, le quali sono comandante di andare a quel campo; e quanto ai volontarii, non sono troppo caldi.[128]

The English ambassador confirms in his dispatches that Aumale was at the head of the League contingent, and further speculated that he was likely to receive the governorship of Picardy in recognition of his contribution at La Fère.[129] The confrontation between the houses of Lorraine and Bourbon at La Fère is symbolic of their struggle for influence in Picardy. The siege went well for the royal army but Matignon, perhaps as a means to prevent the leaguers making political capital out of storming La Fère, offered the beleaguered garrison generous terms. An enraged Aumale left camp without taking his leave of the royal commander, irate that he had been stopped from striking a blow to the pride of a rival.[130]

Aumale must have realised that he had little chance of being offered the governorship of Picardy. Henri showed throughout the La Fère crisis that he

[124] Anselme, iii, pp. 793–5. Aumale's sister, Catherine, was the third wife of Nicholas de Lorraine (d. 1577), comte de Vaudémont and duc de Mercoeur, and therefore step-mother of Philippe-Emmanuel. Philippe-Emmanuel's younger brother, Charles, future cardinal de Vaudémont, had been the valet de chambre of the duc d'Aumale and his companion at university in 1574: BN MS Fr 22441 fo. 82.

[125] De Thou, viii, pp. 394–5. Condé had received other places of surety in lieu of Péronne at the Peace of Bergerac but had not given up hope of retaking Picardy.

[126] *Lettres de Catherine de Médicis*, vii, p. 250, n. 1; De Thou, viii, p. 395.

[127] L'Estoile, *Journal du règne de Henri III*, p. 249, adds that this departure of the *mignons* to war was a cause for mockery in Paris.

[128] *Négociations diplomatiques de la France avec la Toscane*, iv, p. 333.

[129] *CSPF*, 1579–80, pp. 384, 428. [130] De Thou, viii, p. 397.

preferred an accommodation with Condé to augmenting Aumale's reputation with the Picard nobility. The absence of royal favour did not engender a sharp decline in the fortunes of the Aumale. The Guise still enjoyed a great deal of influence over church patronage which enabled them to provide for Aumale's younger brother, Claude chevalier d'Aumale, without dividing the inheritance of their father and financially weakening the ducal house. In 1572 the cardinal de Guise resigned the abbey of Bec to his nephew. This abbey was worth 24,000*l* a year in 1576, twice the revenue of the duchy of Aumale. He was able to acquire smaller abbeys *in commendam* such as Auchy at Aumale itself, and on the death of the cardinal de Guise in 1578 he inherited others.[131] The evidence for the financial stability of the Aumale branch is ambiguous. The barony of Bec Crespin was sold in 1579 but the duke's creditworthiness remained high. In 1583 he borrowed nearly 42,000*l* to equip a galley for his younger brother Claude who, as a knight of the order of Saint John, had been summoned to Malta. Claude's expedition was a success and the profits from ransomed prisoners were reinvested in equipping new ships.[132]

Although still without a *gouvernement*, the duke inherited the office of *grand veneur*, one of the *grands offices* of the realm, from his father. In 1571, the establishment of the *vénerie* employed 340 men, most of them nobles, at a cost of 68,400*l*.[133] Its importance was heightened by Charles IX's obsession with hunting. The *grand veneur* oversaw the appointment and payment of the officers of the *vénerie*, as well as the lucrative captaincies of the guard of the royal forests. The correlation between the Aumale affinity and the officers of the *vénerie* is clear from two surviving account rolls of 1571 and 1584. Employment in the *vénerie* was provided for his household officers and men-at-arms: over twenty families appear both on the rolls of the *vénerie* and as members of either the household or the company of the duke. Representation was strong from Normandy and especially the Vexin, where the Aumale lands were extensive. These families supplemented service in the *vénerie* with the exploitation of royal forest office, often granted at the intercession of the Guise. A number of them fought for the Catholic League in the 1580s and 1590s.[134]

[131] *Lettres de Henri III*, iii, p. 499, iv, p. 70.

[132] AN MC VIII 391 fo. 183; XXIX 83 fo. 249, 26 February 1588. The coherence of the Aumale affinity is evident from the interdependence of the brothers' households: nobles, such as François de La Chaussée and Philippe de L'Isle, and non-nobles, such as *avocat* Regnauld Loyseau and *contrôleur* Nicolas Michel, served both siblings.

[133] BN MS Cinq Cents Colbert 54 fo. 348. This establishment includes the *veneurs des toiles de chasse* and the *garde des fôrets*. Not all of those appearing on the roll were paid.

[134] The biggest Norman recipients of ducal patronage during this period included the Gaillardbois, who held four positions in the *vénerie* and a further three served in the duke's ordonnance company, and the Nollent, who provided three members of the ducal ordonnance company and one officer of the *vénerie*. Both families provided captains for the League. Other noble Norman families which appear both on the rolls of the *vénerie du roi* and in the households and retinues of the Guise include: du Moutier, Crèvecoeur, Silly, Faverolles, Cartula, Ballue, Limoges, Carvoisin, Londel, Bahuet, Caruel. On the Guise as brokers of royal forest office: BN MS Fr 3942, 'Role des expeditions commandes par le roy', 1560–6; AN KK 133B fo. 47v, 23 Feb 1566.

By 1584, when the second surviving account roll was taken, the effectiveness of the office of *grand veneur* as an instrument for the dispensation of patronage had diminished. The accounts show that only 24,552*l* were spent on the wages of the officers of the *vénerie*. The 60 per cent reduction in expenditure since 1571 reflects Henri III's lack of interest in hunting.[135] This provides yet more evidence of Henri's unconventionality; it shows that the king's rejection of traditional noble pursuits in favour of more cerebral and pious contemplation had political as well as cultural consequences. He diminished the status of the duc d'Aumale at court and he undermined the traditional flow of patronage to clients of the Guise: neither patron nor client can have been satisfied at such 'unkingly' behaviour, which reinforced the widely held notion that Henri III lacked traditional martial values. By building up his clientele among the discontented Picard and Norman nobility, Aumale was partially able to offset his political misfortune at court by strengthening his provincial power base.

The career of Charles de Lorraine, marquis d'Elbeuf, took an entirely different direction to that of his cousin and brother-in-law. While Aumale failed to make an impression at court, the fortunes of the marquis improved immensely in the same period. His status and wealth were increased by the inheritance of the Rieux lands in Normandy. Moreover, the options he had for finding allies were greater than his cousin because he was related to families among the protestant elite, the Rieux, the Laval and the Coligny, through his mother Louise de Rieux. His education was very different to that of his cousin. On the death of his parents in 1566, Charles d'Elbeuf's preceptor, Remy Belleau, was appointed governor. By 1574, when his charge was eighteen, Belleau had attained the most senior position in his household as *maître d'hôtel* and *surintendant*. Belleau was a former protestant and his Erasmian humanist influence was different from that of the Jesuits.

Elbeuf's education and kinship ties partially explain how he straddled the religious and political divide, and entered the service of the duc d'Anjou. When the envoys of the States-General of the Netherlands arrived at Tours on 6 September 1580 to discuss once more a treaty with Anjou, Elbeuf was present on the duke's council. When the duke agreed to provide an army to assist the rebels, it was Elbeuf who was chosen as his lieutenant-general.[136] Elbeuf's elevation was not made on military considerations. Anjou had a little military experience but Elbeuf, three years his junior at the age of twenty-four, was a complete novice. It was as a member of the Guise family with protestant connections that he could add viability to the notion of Anjou's army as a 'union sacrée'. He could gather a substantial following from among Guise clients, while fighting alongside the large protestant contingent would create no problems. Paul de Coligny, comte de Laval, who commanded a large force of Bretons, was his relative. The two enjoyed revenues

[135] AN KK 145 fos. 12–180.
[136] Holt, *The duke of Anjou*, p. 134; *Documents concernant les relations entre le duc d'Anjou et les Pays-Bas*, P. Muller and A. Diegerick, eds. (5 vols., Utrecht, 1889–99), iv, pp. 101–2.

from the Rieux lands in Normandy jointly and amicably in anticipation of a *partage*.[137]

Anjou ordered the army, which was coming from all over France, to assemble in June 1581 at Château-Thierry, part of his apanage. The duke and the marquis were both in Normandy in the spring of 1581, agreeing to rendezvous at Evreux in May. Elbeuf was accompanied by a substantial following of 500 gentlemen.[138] Anjou raised his own troops by handing out commissions to his household officers; recruiting was therefore intense in Normandy from where many of these men originated.[139] Unfortunately, nothing is known about the following of the marquis, although concentration of recruitment in Normandy is consistent with the increasingly Norman character of his retinue. He would have handled recruitment in the same way as Anjou – by awarding commissions to trusted clients and household officers. The officers of his company also included men who were later Catholic League captains, and who had probably been involved in the League of Péronne.[140] Elbeuf's army was not a feudal levy and he was compelled to raise considerable funds in order to finance the expedition. Between June 1580 and June 1583 he constituted *rentes* on his Normandy lands to a capital value of 112,200*l*, obligations partly met by the sale of the seigneury of Quatremares for the sum of 80,000*l* in December 1583.[141] The purchaser was Jean de La Haye, seigneur de Chantelou, who had begun his career as *chambellan* in Anjou's household before joining the duc de Guise in 1579, and who would become one of Elbeuf's lieutenants in the Catholic League in Normandy.

The expenses that Elbeuf incurred on the expedition were not rewarded by glory or the bestowal of lucrative offices. After the euphoria over the relief of Cambrai (18 August 1581) evaporated, it became clear that Anjou lacked the resources to keep the army together. Elbeuf left the army soon after the fall of Cambrai, ostensibly because of illness but, if the Tuscan ambassador is to be believed, due to serious disagreements with Anjou:

> il detto marchese ne partì molto sdeganto, e di tal sorte, che, dopo aver preso licenza, uscendo della camera di Sua Altezza [Anjou], disse sì che tutto il mondo presente l'intese, e ella ancora la potè udire: che egli aveva otto mila uomini a sua devozione, i quali menerebbe al servizio del re di Spagna; e che, se avesse saputo, quando partì dal Chatelet per andare a

[137] On the death of Coligny in 1586, Elbeuf became *tuteur* and *curateur* of his son: Broussillon, *La maison de Laval*, iv, pp. 324–6.

[138] *Documents concernant les relations entre le duc d'Anjou et les Pays-Bas*, iv, pp. 65, 74.

[139] Prominent among them were: Guillaume de Hautemer, seigneur de Fervacques, the governor of the duchy of Alençon, *président du conseil* and *premier gentilhomme de la chambre* of the duc d'Anjou; Jacques de Rouxel, seigneur de Médavy and lieutenant-general of the duchy of Alençon. Both men supported the Catholic League: DBF, xiii, p. 1191; V. des Diguères, *Etude historique et généalogique sur les Rouxel de Médavy-Grancey* (Paris, 1870), p. 36.

[140] For example, the Picard Ponthus de Bellefourrière had been an archer in the company of the duc de Guise in 1569, was *guidon* of Elbeuf's company from 1577 and was later governor of Corbie for the League in 1589: Vindry, p. 304.

[141] Appendix B; ADSM 2E1 367, 28 Oct 1586.

Cambrai, quello che aveva saputo dipoi, sarebbe ito a trovare il principe di Parma, dove si assicurava che la metà delle forze di Sua Altezza lo avrebbero seguito. E, oltre di lui, molti altri ne sono partiti con poca volontà di tornarlo a servire di un anno; di sorte che bene gli servirà di avere di quelli che fanno cantare i ciechi.[142]

Relations between the two men never improved thereafter and the French campaign degenerated after the early success of Cambrai. When Elbeuf offered his services again in March 1582, Anjou was 'content to have once made trial of him, without going that way again'.[143]

On the marquis's return to court in late 1581, the supremacy of La Valette and Joyeuse in the affections of the king was apparent. In September the vicomté of Joyeuse had been created a *duché-pairie*, with the added proviso that it superseded all non-princely *pairies* because of Joyeuse's marriage to Marguerite de Vaudémont, sister of the queen.[144] La Valette had been made duc d'Epernon in November 1581, and the following June Joyeuse was presented with the office of admiral.[145] The king, although he esteemed Mayenne 'to be of a more settled nature than his brother', was determined to allocate the major royal offices to men whom he could trust.[146] The Guise were appeased in the form of substantial reimbursement for Mayenne, who gave up the admiralty for 120,000 *écus*, and with the elevation of Elbeuf to a *duché-pairie* 'à la requête et instance de ceux de la maison de Guise, déplaisants de voir les ducs de Retz, de Joyeuse et d'Epernon, précéder en honneur, grade et qualité, le marquis d'Elbeuf'.[147] However, this show of favour was far surpassed by the gift of 100,000 *écus* and the office of *premier gentilhomme de la chambre*, bestowed upon Epernon at the end of February 1582.[148] Guillaume de Saulx-Tavannes even mocked the elevation of the marquis:

poste qu'il n'aurait pas recherché si vite, s'il eut attendu et se fut soucie d'être grand d'être élevé, et que, comme personne incapable et de peu de moyens, il n'aurait jamais obtenus, si on considéré les degrés qui l'y avaient conduit et si on eut voulu, pour lui conférer cette dignité, que l'âge l'en eut rendu quil l'eut meritée par ses services.[149]

Elbeuf lacked high office and credit at court but he was a prince with the landed wealth to support his new dignity. His status was greatly increased by his marriage in February 1583 to Marguerite Chabot, dame de Pagny, daughter of the aged and ailing Léonor, lieutenant-general of Burgundy. The dowry consisted not only of Pagny and its château but also lump-sum payments totalling 12,000*l*, and the rights to 8,000*l* per annum in *rentes*. The contract also stipulated that Chabot would resign his office of *grand écuyer* to his new son-in-law.[150] The marriage thus provided

142 *Négociations diplomatiques de la France avec la Toscane*, iv, p. 396. The real reason for the marquis's withdrawal was more likely illness: AMC A 14 liasse 7, Jul 1581.

143 *CSPF*, 1581–2, p. 583.

144 L'Estoile, *Journal du règne de Henri III*, pp. 273–4.

145 *Ibid.*, pp. 281, 301.

146 Davila, *Historie of the civill warres*, p. 490.

147 L'Estoile, *Journal du règne de Henri III*, p. 297.

148 *Ibid.*, pp. 294–5.

149 Quoted in Maille, *Recherches sur Elbeuf*, p. 85

150 BN Cabinet d'Hozier 216 fo. 101. The final stipulation does not seem to have been carried out.

Elbeuf with the office he coveted and once again reinforced the bonds between the Guise family in Normandy and their ancestral roots in eastern France.[151]

The king did not openly alienate the Guise for he continued to make money gifts to them, even if not on the same scale as to the *mignons*. It is easy to exaggerate the financial and political difficulties of the family in the early 1580s. Even in receipt of his Spanish pension the duke did little to fulfil his obligation to prevent Anjou's incursions into Flanders. He had not become a Spanish pawn: in October 1581 Anjou and the prior of Cato, pretender to the Portuguese throne, were entertained at Eu.[152] Having settled many of his debts, he was able to recommence land purchases and begin building the new ducal seat at Eu. In May 1582 he bought five-sixths of the comté of Courtenay valued at 160,000*l* and the following month he purchased the seigneury of Argillières in exchange for 3,000*l* worth of *rentes*.[153]

After the collapse of the catholic–protestant malcontent alliance in early 1580 the attention of the duc de Guise turned to the British Isles. An opportunity to assist Mary and James VI was created by Philip II's interest in diverting France and England from the Netherlands, and by the weakening of the earl of Morton's anglophile regime, especially after the return to Scotland of Esmé Stuart, earl of Lennox.[154] In January 1581 Guise was commissioned by Mary to form an 'association' in her name.[155] Negotiations to this effect involved the pope and Philip II. Mary remained hopeful of military intervention, telling Guise in September 1582 that he could easily seize Stirling with 500 men.[156] He was undoubtedly more realistic and had different aims from his fellow conspirators. As a letter from John Leslie, bishop of Ross, in October 1580 to the general of the Jesuits demonstrates, Guise was primarily concerned with events in Scotland and ensuring that the catholic party gained control of James VI.[157] He was suspicious of becoming involved in Spanish plans to destabilise the English polity and therefore disrupt aid to the rebels in the Netherlands. Leading an attack on England would be hazardous and not in his own interests since, as Ross commented, the duke believed such an action might well result in Mary Stuart's execution.

The diplomatic intrigue surrounding the invasion projects has been treated in great detail elsewhere.[158] However, the Norman dimension and its political conse-

[151] The Chabot had a long association with the Guise. During the 1580s and 1590s Chabot remained nominally loyal to Henri III and Henri IV. In reality he was simply too decrepit to leave the château of Pagny where he had retired. He was thus a marginal figure in Burgundian politics and was deprived of his office of lieutenant-general by Henri III in 1588: DBF, viii, p. 133; Drouot, *Mayenne et la Bourgogne*, i, pp. 103, 157–8.

[152] D. Le Beuf, *La ville d'Eu* (Paris, 1844), p. 347.

[153] Bouillé, iii, p 312, n 1. Jean de Rambures was a Picard client of the duc d'Aumale and was made governor of the duchy of Guise in 1588.

[154] Davillé, *Prétensions de Charles III duc de Lorraine à la couronne*, pp. 30–54. Donaldson, *Scotland: James V–VII*, pp. 165–80.

[155] *Lettres, instructions et mémoires de Marie Stuart*, A. I. Labanoff, ed. (7 vols., London, 1845), iv, p. 185. [156] *Ibid.*, p. 301. [157] *Ibid.*, vii, pp. 153–4.

[158] J. Kretzchmar, *Die invasions projekte der katholischen mächte gegen England zur zeit Elisabeths* (Leipzig, 1892).

quences require elaboration. Rouen, home to a large number of English and Scottish exiles, was the base for the coordination of missions to the British Isles and for the printing and dissemination of propaganda.[159] Guise showed his commitment to the cause by founding the English Jesuit college at Eu in 1582, but it would take much more than this to help Mary. Military help from France for the Marian party in either England or Scotland would require support from the Norman nobility and officers of the admiralty. Henri III's eagerness to relieve Mayenne of this office is thus explained. Despite the secrecy of negotiations and preparations in Normandy, the reports of the well-informed English spies in the province shed light on the activities of the Guise and their supporters. The duke and the cardinal remained in close contact: Guise spent much of 1581 in Normandy and in May visited the archiepiscopal residence at Gaillon three times. The cardinal resided in Normandy during the summer, presiding over a provincial synod in Rouen. The bishop of Ross, now installed in the diocese of Rouen as vicar-general and suffragan of the cardinal, was responsible for coordinating the conspiracy in Normandy.[160] He strove to interest the Norman nobility in Mary's cause. In December an English agent reported on a number of secret meetings at Rouen and Pont-Saint-Pierre between the bishop and 'those gentlemen being known to be of troublesome dispositions and enterprisers of actions'.[161] These were meetings of the ultra-catholic faction, involving Jean Le Myre, a senior figure in Jean de Moy's household, Moy's younger brother Jacques, seigneur de Pierrecourt, and their cousin Nicolas, sieur de Vereins. As captain of Honfleur and Harfleur, Jacques's support was vital to the commanders of the armada. Nicolas had recently purchased the office of *grand maître des eaux et fôrets* of Normandy, and as nephew of the cardinal de Pellevé was well connected to the ultra-catholic hierarchy.[162] The joint host of the conferences, Pierre de Roncherolles, baron de Pont-Saint-Pierre and kin to the Moy, represented the other pivotal axis of the ultra-catholic faction in upper Normandy. The final link in the conspiracy was Michel de Monchy, *conseiller* in the parlement of Rouen and intimate of the cardinal de Bourbon, who sheltered English émigrés.

Ross wooed these men who were both close to the Guise and veterans of the Catholic League, especially since Jean de Moy was vice-admiral. The preliminary discussions with the local nobility went well and the duc de Guise spent much of 1582 in upper Normandy. In May the Jesuit Robert Parsons reported that at a meeting held in Rouen the duke had pledged his friends and relatives to the

[159] J. Bossy, 'Elizabethan catholicism: the link with France', unpub. Ph.D. thesis (University of Cambridge, 1960), pp. 82–4.

[160] He was an active figure in Rouen in the 1580s: ADSM G 2173, 23 Oct 1580; 2175, 21 Sep 1583, 11 Oct 1583, 8 May 1584.

[161] *CSPF*, 1581–2, p. 399.

[162] Le Myre was man-at-arms in Moy's company in 1581 and was present at important financial transactions on behalf of his master: BN MS Fr 21537 fo. 2261; ADSM 2E1 348, 18 and 19 Feb 1574. He was also lieutenant of Harfleur (1581–9) under Jacques de Moy: Vindry, p. 377. Adrien de Bréauté, who was also present at the councils, was likewise close to the Moy.

invasion scheme.[163] During summer 1582 he was preparing ships, and the duc de Mayenne was lodging with the cardinal de Bourbon at Gaillon. Spies reported that in July all the Guise family assembled in Normandy for special consultations, presumably to take counsel with their local clients.[164] The outcome of these meetings was the decision to send François de Roncherolles, seigneur de Maineville, as an envoy to James VI to urge on him a plan of joint action.[165] These plans were immediately wrecked by the unstable political situation in Scotland. Morton and his faction regained their grip on power in August 1582 when the young king was seized and Lennox forced to flee.[166] Henri III could not ignore the control now exercised by the English and their supporters over the traditional ally of France. In October 1582, therefore, a royal embassy departed to secure the release of James, Maineville being officially attached to this mission.[167] Maineville spent the winter in Scotland using the 4,000*l* he had borrowed on the Rouennais money market to galvanise the anti-Morton forces.[168]

In May 1583 he returned home, having completely failed to form a strong pro-Guise, anti-Morton faction. By the time he landed in France, rumours of the conspiracy in Normandy had become widespread. The king acted swiftly to strengthen his position by appointing the duc de Joyeuse as both governor and admiral of the province.[169] The project was, like all attempts to help Mary, beset by many practical difficulties and perhaps also by the lack of real political conviction. Guise demanded 100,000 *écus* from the Spanish before he would make any move against England. He had received a paltry 10,000 *écus* by September 1582 – enough, as Philip intended, to trouble the English but inadequate and too late in the season to launch a seaborne invasion.[170]

Soon after Maineville returned from Scotland he was interviewed by Guise, probably at Eu.[171] His report confirms that Guise had been planning to help Mary by aiding the catholic faction in Scotland rather through an invasion of England.[172] However, the failure of Maineville's mission and the evident lack of enthusiasm among the Scots nobility for his cause forced the duke to reconsider military intervention in England, as originally favoured by Mary, Philip and the pope. In June 1583, the conspirators held a council in Paris which agreed a joint Guise–

[163] 'Letters and memorials of Robert Parsons SJ', L. Hicks, ed., *Catholic Record Society*, 39 (1942), p. 148. [164] *CSPF*, 1582, p. 141.

[165] *Calendar of State Papers, foreign series, Scotland*, M. J. Thorpe *et al.*, eds. (London, 1858–1969), 1581–3, p. 123.

[166] Donaldson, *Scotland: James V–VII*, p. 178. Plans to aid Morton lacked substance: *CSP, Scotland*, 1580–6, 363, 373, 378.

[167] A. Teulet, ed., *Papiers d'état . . . rélatifs à l'histoire de l'Ecosse au XVIe siècle; tirés des bibliothèques et des archives de France* (3 vols., Paris, 1851–60), ii, p. 531; *Lettres de Catherine de Médicis*, viii, pp. 64, 67. [168] *CSP, Scotland*, 1581–3, p. 301.

[169] The outlines of the conspiracy were known to and embellished by the traitor Nicholas Salcedo, who was executed for the attempted murder of the duc d'Anjou: Cimber and Danjou, x, pp. 139–69.

[170] Croze, *Les Guises, les Valois et Philippe II*, i, p. 266. In May 1583 he received a further 20,000 *écus*: Törne, 'Philippe II et Henri de Guise', p. 333.

[171] *CSPF*, 1583, pp. 358, 373. [172] For this and following: *CSP, Scotland*, 1580–6, pp. 479–86.

Spanish landing in England, though all present had reservations and substantial differences remained between the allies. Guise demanded substantial Spanish aid and Philip, hoping to avoid open warfare with England, wanted responsibility for the invasion to fall on the duke.[173] The problems of organising such an expedition that involved different interests hampered the planning and efficacy of the operation.[174] The English exiles and catholics, supported by Mendoza, the Spanish ambassador in London, were nervous about the designs of the Guise and desired greater Spanish involvement. Despite telling the Spanish otherwise, Guise continued to concentrate his attention on Scotland. His hopes of joining with James were raised when the Scottish king evaded his anglophile captors in June 1583. Soon after the escape, Guise wrote to James proposing a joint expedition.[175] In November Spanish policy was unravelled when catholic plotters were arrested in England and divulged the entire plan. Thereafter Guise continued to place the emphasis on Scotland and cooperation with his kinsman.[176] Mendoza complained to his master that the Guise considered only their own dynastic interests and were apt to put 'the question of religion into second place, as a mere accessory to politics'.[177]

English agents maintained a watch on the movements of the duke during the summer. He spent most of July at Eu surrounded by English exiles who were obviously pleading for his help.[178] Evidence pertaining to the preparations of the invasion force is scant. Elbeuf was reportedly readying three ships at Harfleur and in August 1583 an army was assembling at Honfleur, Le Havre and Fécamp, commanded by Mayenne and the comte de Brissac.[179] The seigneur de Sarlabous, ailing governor of Le Havre, the most important French naval port on the Channel, agreed to sanction its use after a visit from Guise in early summer. Sarlabous's affective ties to the Guise – he had served as a commander in the Scottish campaigns of 1549 and 1559–60 and his brother had taken part in the murder of admiral Coligny in 1572 – may have underlain his decision.[180] The operation also needed the support of the subordinates of vice-admiral Jean de Moy, by now a senior figure on the Guise council controlling the ports of Harfleur and Honfleur. English spies observed the duc de Guise, Mayenne and the cardinal de Bourbon, arriving at Moy's château at 'La Milleraye [*sic*], where they stayed five or six days, holding council every day'.[181]

173 'Letters and memorials of Robert Parsons', p. lix; *CSP, Scotland*, pp. 482–3. The Spanish ambassador in London was also concerned that the attention of the Guise was being diverted by domestic politics.

174 For the plans and the problems involved: *CSP, Scotland*, 1580–6, pp. 492–5, 503–5.

175 Donaldson, *Scotland: James V–VII*, pp. 179–80.

176 *CSP, Scotland*, 1580–6, pp. 502–3, 509, 527, 589, 595.

177 *Ibid.*, p. 492. 178 *CSPF*, 1583–4, pp. 36–7.

179 *Ibid.*, p. 57. This force was to join with Spanish paid mercenaries at Dunkirk, sailing to England to rendezvous with English catholic forces: *CSP, Scotland*, 1580–6, pp. 503–4, 505–6.

180 Forestié, *Corbeyron de Cardaillac-Sarlabous*; Crouzet, *La nuit de la Saint-Barthélemy*, p. 446.

181 *CSPF*, 1583–4, p. 57.

It was during these meetings that the comte de Brissac arrived from Le Havre to inform his fellow conspirators that the sailing had to be postponed, owing to lack of money and doubts about the objectives of the operation. Guise immediately withdrew the money he had advanced.[182] The commitment of the duke to building his new residence at Eu can only have served to divert his own resources and the Spanish subvention away from the expedition. Although the duke was able to lay the foundations of an invasion and attract some support among the Norman elite, he lacked the finances to carry his plans through. The position of 1559–60 was reversed. This time local cooperation had been forthcoming due to the expansion of the Guise power base in Normandy, but without control of royal finances the project was bound to fail, even with Spanish aid. The English realised they had little to fear, and the assessments of their spies are more sober than those of 1559–60. They understood that the duc de Guise did not wield the same authority at the court as his father had done formerly. As the English ambassador reported in May 1584: 'I do not doubt the duke of Guise's good will and promises to help the King of Scots, but see no reason to fear his performing anything, for his means are small and his credit smaller . . . those of that house come but very seldom to the court and when they come there is no good countenance given to them'.[183]

[182] By October all preparations had been halted: *CSPF*, 1583–4, pp. 57–8, 185.
[183] *CSPF*, 1583–4, p. 493.

6

The triumph of the Guise affinity in Normandy

He of Normandy spake further that Kings were as well tied to keep promise to their subjects as their subjects to them, and that one being broken of his part his subjects should be driven (being no more able to bear the burden) either to seek somebody that might succour them or else to go as men in a ship without a stern, that in a storm let all go in a venture, and either be without a care, desperately, what rock they touch on first, or if they find by God's grace any place of succour, they worship it ever after as a God.

This speech was delivered by Guy de Longchamps, governor of Lisieux and representative of the Norman nobility, to the assembly of Saint-Germain in 1583. According to the English ambassador, its barely veiled threat led to the arrest and imprisonment of the speaker.[1] On the eve of the death of the heir to the throne tensions between centre and periphery threatened to paralyse the polity. A contemporary Norman memoir echoed a common patriotic sentiment when it stated that 'Ceux de Paris . . . jamais n'aymèrent le pays de Normandie, ni les habitants dudit pays.'[2] In recent years historians have reassessed and rehabilitated the reign and character of Henri III in the light of his attempts at reform; they stress his success in maintaining peace and reforming the polity before 1584.[3] Henri has been seen as a progressive, almost modern figure. Unusually for a French monarch, Henri was a highly intelligent man, and some of his reforms were well intentioned and politically astute. However, the word 'reform' has to be seen in its contemporary context: the idea of reform and the nature of its implementation were more complicated than historians have admitted. The common language of reform should not make us oblivious to the tensions between the conflicting objectives of the royal council and provincial elites. To the latter, desiring a minimum of interference, 'reform' from the centre often looked like an attempt to erode provincial liberties and raise taxes. In Normandy, suspicion of royal intentions had not been allayed by the king's climbdown in 1579. Taxation was not the only issue which angered local elites. For example, the reform of the royal forests in Normandy, a rational attempt

[1] *CSPF*, 1583–4, pp. 267–8.

[2] A. Pottier, *Revue rétrospective Normande: documents inédits pour servir à l'histoire de Rouen et de la Normandie* (Rouen, 1842), p. 41.

[3] The rehabilitation of Henri continues: Chevallier, *Henri III*; F. Sauzet, ed., *Henri III et son temps* (Paris, 1992). Reforming tendencies are concisely summarised in J. Nagle, *Le droit de marc d'or des offices* (Geneva, 1992).

by the crown to reassert its rights, angered powerful vested interest groups which fulminated against royal agents in the remonstrances of the provincial Estates.[4] The frenzy of reforming activity of the late 1570s and early 1580s culminated in the assembly of Saint-Germain. Its remedies for the perceived disease of the body politic were a response to provincial discontent.

As Robert Harding has shown, the issue of legal and political reform cannot be dissociated from the contemporary moral and religious context. The discourse of political and social malaise was articulated in terms of sin, and royal attempts to encourage piety were part of a wider upsurge in devotional activity. However, Henri's sincere efforts to promote catholic piety did little to placate provincial suspicions about the immorality of the court. Moral corruption was seen as the cause of political, economic and social instability. The rule of the sybaritic *mignons* was the clearest manifestation of a deeper cancer.[5] In early 1581 several French bishops, led by the cardinal de Bourbon, held provincial councils in order to promote the Council of Trent and religious reform, an issue still dividing political society at Saint-Germain.

Although the Guise were proponents of 'reform', they were the beneficiaries of unpopular policies, such as the sale of office. In the summer of 1581 the king made substantial gifts of offices valued at over 200,000*l*, enabling the duke to quit his debts.[6] The king saw the hand of the Guise behind the hostility of many of the provincial representatives at Saint-Germain. He believed that Henri de Guise was largely responsible for the cardinal de Bourbon's confrontational opening address. In addition, a feud between the Aumale and Epernon began with a quarrel between the chevalier d'Aumale and Epernon at Saint-Germain.[7] These simmering provincial discontents and personal rivalries were the background to the dynastic and religious crisis engendered by the death of the heir to the throne, Anjou, in June 1584.

The rise of the Catholic League has been interpreted in terms of a Spanish-controlled aristocratic plot, as an urban bourgeois revolution and most recently as a manifestation of eschatological religious anxiety.[8] There are elements of truth in all these, but to press the claims of one explanation is reductionist and fails to take account of local peculiarities and variations. Much work remains to be done on the interaction between social discontent, religious anxiety and political machinations, especially in the provinces. In particular our understanding of the politics of the

[4] Henri II and Charles IX had been forced to compromise in the face of the hostility of the parlement, Estates and nobility of Normandy. Henri III had tried to curtail the abuse of royal forests in 1579 but had had to back down in the face of local hostility. In 1583 the newly despatched commissioner was denounced as an enemy of the province: M. Devèze, *La vie de la fôret française au XVIe siècle* (2 vols., Paris, 1961), pp. 105–7, 212–15.

[5] R. Harding, 'Revolution and reform in the Holy League: Angers, Rennes, Nantes', *Journal of Modern History*, 53 (1981), 379–416.

[6] J. Boucher, *La cour de Henri III* (Rennes, 1986), p. 60; AN MC VIII 389 fo. 94, 19 Feb 1582.

[7] *CSPF*, 1583–4, pp. 216–17.

[8] The first explanation has been largely discredited. For a review of the literature: B. Diefendorf, 'The Catholic League: social crisis or apocalypse now?', *French Historical Studies*, 15 (1987), 332–44.

1580s has made little advance since the nineteenth century. By studying the development and structure of the Catholic League in Normandy it is possible to achieve a more profound understanding of the dynamics of factional politics and social and religious unrest.

THE REVOLT OF THE CATHOLIC LEAGUE AND THE STRUGGLE FOR NORMANDY, 1583–1588

Guy de Longchamps' harangue at the assembly of Saint-Germain shows how deeply the ideology of a contract between king and subject was embedded in the political culture of sixteenth-century France. During the crisis of 1578–9 the king had attempted to break the contract between the Normans and the crown. Anjou had been chief among those able to 'succour' the province. After his death, those who sought to protect their rights, privileges and identity looked to the Catholic League for support.

Longchamps belonged to the Norman provincial elite. His catholic credentials were impeccable: he was Aumale's captain of Lisieux in 1562, and kin to the des Buaz, themselves longstanding servants of the Guise and stalwarts of the ultra-catholic faction in Normandy.[9] His speech at Saint-Germain should be seen in the context of widespread anxiety among the provincial elite articulated in the remonstrances collated by royal commissioners. Taxation and venality were a source of dissension at the provincial Estates throughout the 1580s.[10]

The relative stability of the kingdom following the Peace of Bergerac in 1577 enabled the king to reduce the debts of the monarchy by increasing taxes and selling offices. The importance of Normandy, in terms of both tax revenue and patronage, made it imperative to reassert royal authority. Since the death of the duc de Bouillon in 1574 the governorship had been divided among three local men. The king may have been concerned about growing Guise interest in the province and was certainly aware that one of the three governors, Jean de Moy, was closely involved with Guise preparations for the invasion of England in 1582 and 1583. Shortly after his humiliation by the Norman Estates, Henri III began to alter the structure of government in the province. In 1580, Jacques de Matignon was promoted to the post of *maréchal*, ensuring that his governorship of lower Normandy fell into abeyance.[11] In February 1583 the king took the bold decision to reunify the province

[9] Guy married Marguerite des Buaz in 1550; his son, Jean, married Nicole des Buaz, and the two families often appear together in the notarial archives: BN Carrés d'Hozier 391 fo. 4; ADSM 2E1 332, 22 Jun 1566. The dowry of Guy's daughter, Renée, was paid by Nicolas des Buaz: ADSM 2E1 348, 26 Jun 1574. Guy may have had a personal antipathy to the king who, as lieutenant-general of the kingdom and heir to the throne, had arranged his temporary dismissal in 1568.

[10] The remonstrances of the duchy of Normandy collated for Saint-Germain are found in BN MS Fr 17870 fo. 120. Among the chief complaints were: the lawlessness of the soldiery; the cost of justice and the proliferation of offices; the high rate of taxation and peasant indebtedness.

[11] *Lettres de Henri III*, iv, p. 203.

into a single governorship under his favourite, Joyeuse. The former governors were compensated with a payment of 6,000*l* and retained as lieutenants-general: Carrouges for the *bailliages* of Rouen, Evreux and Caen, and Moy for those of Caux, Gisors and the Cotentin. In turn their own lieutenants retained their posts, and Carrouges even ensured that his son would inherit his office.[12] Such measures were designed to alleviate the dishonour of demotion, but the installation of a man who was neither a prince nor a Norman was an unprecedented move and fears about the concentration of royal power seemed justified, since Joyeuse was already admiral. This and other attempts to introduce royal favourites upset the Norman political classes. Normally loyal officers, such as Hervé de Longaunay, openly protested at their demotion.[13] Had Joyeuse acted astutely he might have found a base of support. He was identified with uncompromising catholicism, unlike his fellow *mignon* and rival Epernon, and could thus expect few complaints from the ultra-catholic elites. When he made his entrance into Rouen on 25 March 1583 he was accompanied by the elite of the Norman nobility.[14] His tenure of the governorship began auspiciously when he had an unpopular venal municipal office suppressed by the king.[15] He managed to prevent the garrisoning of Rouen by royal troops in 1585, and in July 1587 it was at his behest that town representatives were able to plead for tax reductions before the royal council.[16] But Joyeuse could not conclusively dissociate himself from unpopular royal fiscal measures, and he quickly aggravated local notables by assigning major offices to his entourage. Joyeuse was fortunate that both the governorships of Le Havre and Dieppe fell vacant soon after his arrival. In 1583 command of Dieppe was granted to his relative, Aymard de Clermont, seigneur de Chatte. The following year another relative, André de Villars-Branças, originally from Provence, became governor of Le Havre.[17] On the eve of the League, the structure of power in Normandy had undergone a radical transformation. Joyeuse's control of the admiralty and the two largest ports in the province effectively terminated Guise plans to invade England. The concentration of power and patronage in his hands challenged the authority of the traditional elites and would contribute to the ambivalence of the Le Veneur and Moy in supporting the crown against the League.

The appointment of Claude Groulard as *premier président* of the parlement of Rouen in April 1585 was a more serious blunder. Although a Norman, Groulard was a repentant Calvinist, a protégé of Joyeuse and did not fulfil the age requirement for such a senior office.[18] The obvious fear was that he would represent the

[12] BN MS Fr 3306 fos. 74–7. Among the lieutenants retained were: Jacques de Rouville, seigneur de Grainville-la-Teinturière; Jacques Le Veneur, son of Tanneguy and comte de Tillières; Hervé de Longaunay, a lieutenant in lower Normandy; and finally, Jacques de Moy, younger brother of Jean and seigneur de Pierrecourt. [13] *Ibid.* fo. 65, Henri III to d'O, Paris, 1 Feb 1583.

[14] ACR A 20, 25 Mar 1583. [15] *Ibid.*, 11 Jun 1583.

[16] Benedict, *Rouen during the Wars of Religion*, pp. 171–2; ACR A 20, 1 Jul 1587.

[17] *DBF*, viii, pp. 1495–6; Borély, *Histoire de la ville du Havre*, ii, pp. 178–9.

[18] Floquet, iii, pp. 181–4; Frondeville, *Présidents*, pp. 68–9.

interests of Joyeuse and the king rather than the corporate body he now headed. Such concerns were reinforced by the innovative fiscal measures presented to the parlement for registration between 1585 and 1587.[19] Antipathy to Groulard swelled the malcontents in the parlement. The anti-Groulard faction was headed by the Bauquemare and their kinsmen, relatives of the former *président* and creditors of the Guise family, and included influential men such as the *procureur-général*, Georges de La Porte, whose family benefited from Guise patronage.[20]

Normans were at the heart of the League from its inception. Among those who gathered with the house of Lorraine in council at Nancy, as the heir to the throne lay dying, was François de Roncherolles. After Anjou's death he signed the secret Treaty of Joinville (31 December 1584) on behalf of the cardinal de Bourbon. This demanded the extirpation of protestantism inside and outside France and the exclusion of Henri de Navarre as heir. The association was supported by Spain with a subvention of 50,000 *écus* per month.[21] Although the aims of the Catholic League seem quite straightforward, the strategy of the Guise family is harder to define. Protestant claims that the family was intent on seizing the throne have never been substantiated.[22] Religious orthodoxy and political calculation combined in the rebirth of the Catholic League, and harmonised with family strategy. War against heresy offered the opportunity to crush Henri de Navarre and marginalise moderate catholic enemies at court. Ascendancy at court would secure the family's status and the crusade against heresy complemented the pursuit of its dynastic interests in Scotland and England. The Manifesto of Péronne (30 March 1585), issued by the rebel princes, was an attempt to appeal to the popular imagination; its reforming message attracted those who saw heresy as the root of political and social malaise. It called for fiscal retrenchment, highlighted the dangers facing the catholic faith, demanded the convocation of regular Estates-General, and made barely veiled references to the corrupt rule of Epernon and Joyeuse.[23]

During the meetings at Nancy and Joinville plans were drawn up and support solicited. Local leadership came from two main elements. First, there was the Guise and their *amis*: the duc de Guise was given the task of securing Champagne, Mayenne Burgundy and Mercoeur Brittany, while Elbeuf and Aumale would raise

[19] These edicts were consistently rejected: Floquet, iii, pp. 230–2.

[20] La Porte was an influential member of the Catholic League and his hatred of Groulard continued after its demise: Frondeville, *Présidents*, p. 275. La Porte's mother was a creditor of the duc d'Elbeuf. His nephew, Guillaume de Lyvet, was in the retinue of the duc d'Aumale in 1589: ADSM 1B 3215, 26 Sep 1589. His brother-in-law, Antoine de Colas, was an officer in the *vénerie du roi* under Aumale for twenty-five years: ADSM 2E1 2293, 15 Jun 1592; AN KK 145 fo. 12. In 1560 Colas was granted a royal office in the *vicomté* of Rouen on the intercession of the duc de Guise: BN MS Fr 3942 fo. 11v.

[21] On these events: Bouillé, iii, pp. 125–8.

[22] The arguments are outlined in Constant, *Les Guises*, pp. 193–200. He concludes that the duc de Guise coveted above all the office of *connétable*.

[23] 'Declaration des causes qui ont meu Monseigneur le cardinal de Bourbon et les Pairs, Princes, Seigneurs, villes et communautez Catholiques de ce royaume de France: de s'opposer à ceux qui pour tous moyens s'efforcent de subvertir la religion catholique et l'Estat', Cimber and Danjou, xi, p. 9. The choice of Péronne, cradle of the League, was highly symbolic.

Normandy and Picardy respectively. Charles II de Cossé, comte de Brissac, a longstanding ally of the Guise and a considerable landowner in the province, was Elbeuf's principal lieutenant in Normandy.[24] The second group consisted of disgruntled noblemen who, on the death of Anjou, had lost their patron and who were now denied access to royal patronage by the dominance of Epernon and Joyeuse at court.[25] Anjou had possessed a large following in the province, part of which rallied to Elbeuf's standard.[26] The League army which assembled in Normandy in the early months of 1585 was a microcosm of the wider movement. It represented a noble revolt that, notwithstanding the financial backing of Rouennais bourgeois, enjoyed little active support in the towns.

Little of substance has been written about Elbeuf's revolt in Normandy. The progress of his army demonstrates a high degree of leaguer organisation, the composition of League support in 1585 and the attitude of the Norman elites to the rebellion. The cardinal de Bourbon had not been present at the signing of the Treaty of Joinville and continued to reside in Paris until 15 March 1585, when he left for his official residence at Gaillon. Elbeuf had slipped out of Paris some days before, despite the king's precautions. Preparations for the revolt were already well under way. Elbeuf's wife, Marguerite Chabot, had been in the province since at least December of the previous year and her long sojourn at Le Havre corresponds with attempts to entice the governor into rebellion.[27] Brissac arrived in the vicinity of Rouen in the early days of March. During the next two weeks the cardinal de Bourbon rejected appeals by the king to return to court.

The rebel leaders began to muster their forces and raise funds by selling *rentes* in Rouen.[28] Elbeuf and Brissac raised 30,000*l* this way. The negotiation of these large contracts and transport of the specie involved close cooperation with Rouennais financiers. Transactions were undertaken by the household officers and local seigneurial officials of the rebel leaders. Some of the money came from longstanding Guise creditors, such as the wealthy widow Marie de La Haye.[29] Other

[24] Brissac had been dishonoured by the disastrous expedition to the Azores in 1582, aimed at aiding the Portuguese against Spanish domination. He was especially annoyed that Epernon should have the office of colonel-general of the infantry which had once belonged to his brother. Guise stood by his old friend during his disgrace: Brantôme, vi, pp. 146–7.

[25] For an example of the motives for rebelling against the king: N. Le Roux, 'The catholic nobility and political choice during the League, 1585–1594: the case of Claude de La Châtre', *French History*, 8 (1994), 36–50.

[26] Jean de La Haye, seigneur de Chantelou, and Silly de La Rocheguyon had been implicated in previous Guise conspiracies. Other Norman malcontents included the disgraced former *mignons* François d'Espinay, seigneur de Saint-Luc and son-in-law of the comte de Brissac, and François d'O, governor of Caen: Chevallier, *Henri III*, pp. 424–7.

[27] She was resident for some weeks: Borély, *Histoire du Havre*, ii, p. 165 n 1.

[28] ADSM 2E1 2284, 26 and 27 Mar 1585. The procurations for these transactions show that Brissac was stationed at Montfort-sur-Risle and Elbeuf at Neufbourg.

[29] Her sons were stalwarts of the League. Jean Puchot was a captain of the city militia and served on the Leaguer city council and Pierre was a *conseiller* in the parlement: *Délibérations de la ville de Rouen*, p. 252; Frondeville, *Conseillers*, pp. 532–3.

creditors had political motives for supporting the revolt, such as the opponents of *président* Groulard, Jacques and Charles de Bauquemare, who lent Brissac 1,500*l* in July 1585.[30] No clear correlation of moneylending and future adherence to the League emerges. Political consideration had to be balanced by financial calculation. The latter motivated Pierre du Quesne, *conseiller*, who advanced Brissac 9,000*l*. Although he later married his daughter and heiress to the son of a League captain, he was not a natural rebel and in the wake of the fall of Rouen to the League in 1589 he joined the royalist parlement at Caen.[31] François d'Orléans, bâtard de Rothelin, was the largest single creditor of the rebels in 1585, but this was no guarantee of his continued support and his future loyalties are difficult to discern.[32] The role of Eustache Trevache, Elbeuf's chief agent in these transactions, confounds attempts to draw simplistic conclusions about the motives of League adherents. Trevache was a Rouen bourgeois and protestant and had been a seigneurial official for Elbeuf since the early 1570s. It seems unlikely that he was ignorant of his lord's intentions, since the duke was accompanied by 500 horse. Doubtless Trevache was given assurances of safety for himself and his family, which is credible given Elbeuf's association with the protestant nobility.[33]

Elbeuf was to escort the cardinal de Bourbon to Péronne, where the League manifesto would be issued and the standard of revolt raised on 31 March. Thereafter Elbeuf's plan was to attract support as he crossed Normandy, joining up with Brissac – who had retired to his governorship of Angers – in lower Normandy.[34] Royal officers and the provincial elite made no attempt to obstruct the duke's progress, despite the publishing of the royal edict against taking up arms.[35] Some, like the Moy, were sympathetic to the League; but the inactivity of the majority reflects the predatory and neutralist tendencies of the politically active class. Crucially, with the governor absent from the province, there was no magnate around which potential royalist support could coalesce, and without the local nobility there was little hope of containing the revolt, for the crown lacked the funds for mercenaries. The activities of Jacques de Moy, seigneur de Pierrecourt,

30 ADSM 2E1 2004, 11 Feb 1588. Charles Romé advanced 4,000*l* to Brissac. Marie de Romé, damoiselle de Fresquiennes, lent money for the defence of Rouen in 1592: ADSM C 2314, 30 May 1592. Although the Romé had links to the Guise and played a role in the League, they were by no means all leaguers or activists: Frondeville, *Présidents*, p. 420.

31 *Bulletin de la Société Historique et Archéologique de l'Orne*, 13 (1894), p. 10; Frondeville, *Conseillers*, p. 503.

32 Rothelin was a Norman landowner and half-brother of Léonor d'Orléans, duc de Longueville. He was not a League captain during the civil wars but his presence in the king's retinue which entered Rouen in July 1588 is not an indication of his latent royalism, since many of the Normans present later subscribed to the League: C. de Robillard de Beaurepaire, *Séjour de Henri III à Rouen aux mois de juin et juillet 1588* (Rouen, 1870), p. 37.

33 Trevache had close business links to orthodox catholics: Brunelle, *The New World merchants of Rouen*, p. 77.

34 The duke made an abortive attempt on the château of Arques near Dieppe: *Négociations diplomatiques de la France avec la Toscane*, iv, p. 567.

35 C. Valois, ed., *Histoire de la Ligue, oeuvre inédite d'un contemporain* (Paris, 1914), p. 91.

one of the royal lieutenants in upper Normandy and a Guise sympathiser, illustrate the paralysis of royal government. Ordered by the king to rendezvous with Carrouges to prevent the concentration of League forces, he waited at Gisors, complaining that it was not possible to gather his men in time and bargaining with the king for an increase in the size of his *ordonnance* company and an additional bodyguard of thirty mounted arquebusiers. Not only did he neglect his duty in failing to arrest Brissac's lieutenant at Harfleur but he was also unable to prevent a rendezvous of League troops at La Ferté-en-Bray. When he called on the assistance of the town notables 'Ils m'ont faict response que de sortir hors leur ville quicter leurs femmes et enfans qu'ils ne le pouvoient faire . . . sy [nous] ne sommes promptement secourez qu'ils [the League] se feront maistres de la campagne'.[36]

Lower Normandy was the natural operational base for Elbeuf as the governor of Caen, the disgruntled *mignon* François d'O, had already been won over to the revolt. Bayeux was also vulnerable to the rebels because the *vicomté* was held by the Este, whose French affairs were administered by a Guise-dominated council. On 3 April Elbeuf left Caen and marched on Bayeux. He was met by the governor of the château, captain Clément, who ordered the inhabitants to open their gates, 'leur disant qu'il estoit son serviteur et que ne luy denyoit l'entrer par le chasteau'.[37] Elbeuf remained in Bayeux at least until 9 April, garrisoning the château with fifty men and leaving them six months' pay. Clément's adherence to the League seems to have been organised well in advance, and he now joined the duke's army with four companies of foot. Elbeuf also attempted to augment his forces by attracting royal officers, not neglecting to entice them with 'de belles promesses et beaulx pretexts'.[38] Bayeux became an assembly point for troops arriving from all over Normandy and it was expected that the duke would soon have 6,000 men. The League forces were maintained from royal revenues, at least 17,000 *écus* being confiscated from the coffers of the *généralité* of Caen.[39] Inevitably, troops also levied *subsistances* on the local population, which had become a serious burden since Anjou's musters for the Low Countries campaigns. This situation was exacerbated by harvest failures and the powerlessness of the authorities to halt Clément's depredations in the area.[40] Peasant disturbances such as had occurred in 1578–9 threatened to recur, and whilst Elbeuf was at Bayeux 'trois ou quatre mille personnes des villages se plaignent à luy que l'on les contraignes de paier'.[41]

Elbeuf's forces were officered largely from his own household and from the wider Guise affinity in Normandy. The 1589 deposition of Valentin de Vallée, sieur

36 BN MS Fr 3395 fo. 52, Pierrecourt to Henri III, Gisors, 10 Apr 1585.

37 BN MS Fr 3358 fo. 39, Carrouges to Henri III, 10 Apr 1585. This report was compiled from the eye-witness statement of an *échevin* of Bayeux. 38 *Ibid.*

39 BN MS Fr 3974 fo. 79. The size of the League army is an exaggeration; other sources put the figure at between 1,800 and 3,500 men.

40 Clément's troops kidnapped a bourgeois of Saint Lô and killed his servant: ADSM 1B 3205, 2 Jul 1586, 'Supplication de Michel Rouxelin'.

41 BN MS Fr 3358 fo. 39, Carrouges to Henri III, 10 Apr 1585.

de Blancfossé, provides a unique insight into the troop-raising for the revolt.[42] Vallée was a professional soldier in the household of Adrien des Buaz, sieur des Noyers, whose military career had begun at fifteen in the Metz garrison. He went on to serve under des Buaz in Anjou's ill-starred adventure in Flanders. In 1585 des Buaz was persuaded by his cousin to join the League and advanced the money to raise 800 local men: the result was a mercenary regiment prepared to serve anyone for pay, consisting of separately raised companies. Troops were thus being raised by a system of subcontracting – Brissac commissioning des Buaz who commissioned in turn his contacts and clients.[43] The personal links of this system to the League hierarchy meant that he was more than a mere mercenary and therefore relatively dependable. Brissac had already used his services in the Azores, and his role in the 1585 revolt suggests that his service in Flanders was under Elbeuf.

The des Buaz originated from Falaise, and owned land and offices across lower Normandy. They were well integrated into the provincial elite and had a history of support for orthodoxy. Adrien's father had been captain of Toucques for twenty years before his death in 1582 and his uncle, René, had been vicar-general of the cardinal de Bourbon and a leading member of the ultra-catholic faction in Rouen in the 1550s. The family was at the centre of a nexus of marriage alliances between supporters of the League, including Guy de Longchamps, the outspoken Norman delegate at the assembly of Saint-Germain.[44]

Having mustered his forces, Elbeuf left Normandy in mid-May and marched to join Brissac at Angers.[45] Negotiations between the duc de Guise and the queen-mother delayed a decisive thrust, but by mid-June the League force at Angers was preparing to join the other rebel armies at Montargis. Joyeuse was sent down the Loire valley to parry this threat, which resulted in a skirmish near Beaugency in which the royalists had the advantage.[46] In the peace signed at Nemours on 7 July 1585, Henri swore to uphold the religious clauses of the League covenant and pay for a new war against the Huguenots. The Guise were given command of troops paid for by the crown with towns as surety, but Henri made great efforts to recover control of the crucial provinces of Picardy and Normandy. During the negotiations Aumale had demanded the governorships of Péronne, Ham, Montdidier, Corbie, Roye and Montreuil; in the event he had to be satisfied with Rue. Elbeuf became the first member of his branch of the family to become a governor when he was

[42] His deposition is in the form of a confession for the purpose of gaining remission for murder, an annual liberty accorded under the *privilège* of Saint-Romain and administered by the cathedral chapter of Rouen: ADSM G 2176 fos. 307–11, partially reproduced in Floquet, *Histoire du privilège de Saint-Romain*, i, pp. 378–80, ii, pp. 439–40.

[43] Vallée was a sergeant in 1585, rising to company ensign in 1588.

[44] See footnote 9 above.

[45] Jacques Le Veneur, comte de Tillières and lieutenant of the governor, moved no further into lower Normandy than Bernay, where he complained of his lack of supplies and money: BN MS Fr 3408 fo. 77, Tillières to Henri III, Bernay, 8 Apr 1585. He was probably sympathetic to the League.

[46] *Négociations diplomatiques de la France avec la Toscane*, iv, p. 580; L'Estoile, *Journal du règne de Henri III*, p. 382.

appointed to the Bourbonnais, a move which advantageously kept him away from Normandy.[47]

The king hoped to use the peace to reassert his authority in the provinces and weaken the League. In Normandy, Caen was assured when, in return for his re-entry to the royal council and elevation as a chevalier du Saint-Esprit, François d'O handed over the command of the town to a Languedocian client of the duc de Joyeuse. Henri also conferred on his rehabilitated *mignon* the office of lieutenant-general in an attempt to counterbalance the lukewarm support of the traditional political elite. The policy of advancing royal favourites galvanised normally loyal officers into open defiance of the crown. In February 1586 Henri wrote to Tanneguy Le Veneur, sieur de Carrouges, having been warned that 'vous faictes amas et assembler de voz amis, pour empescher et vous opposer aud. sieur d'O', and Henri had to promise that he would not diminish Carrouges's authority 'sans recompense'.[48] Catherine de Médicis had to inform both him and Jacques de Moy, seigneur de Pierrecourt, that the decision to elevate d'O was not hers and that she would do nothing prejudicial to their honour.[49] Aware that the Moy were more closely tied to the Guise, the king's letter to Pierrecourt on the matter was notably blunt and made no mention of any recompense. In July 1586 Jean de Moy was passed over for the command of a naval task force in favour of the governor of the Dieppe, a Joyeuse protégé.[50]

The history of Henri III's attempts to undermine the Guise is familiar. First, the army sent against the Huguenots in Guyenne under Mayenne was ill supplied and ended in failure. In 1587 a new army was more lavishly equipped under Joyeuse and sent against Navarre, but Guise was left without resources to face Navarre's German mercenary reinforcements.[51] At the end of 1587 Henri's plans for victory over the protestants and the destruction of the Guise were in ruins. Joyeuse was defeated and killed by Navarre at Coutras in October while Guise defeated the German *reiter* army at Vimory and Auneau. The king had supplied Guise with only 12,000 *écus* and ten companies of foot. Just as in 1575, the duke's victories were won largely by his own forces and those of his kinsmen. The Norman contingent was led by Elbeuf. The resounding defeat of the *reiters* raised the credit of the duc de Guise to new heights and the king had lost his only reliable force at Coutras. Despite the relatively rich secondary literature on the Catholic League after its seizure of power on 12 May 1588, little serious research has been done on the motives behind and prelude to Guise's famous entry into Paris on 9 May. In the early months of 1588 the Guise family and the king were sliding into open confrontation, the major issues

[47] Compare the demands made by Guise on 2 June and what he actually received. He, Mayenne and Mercoeur received the best settlement: Bouillé, iii, pp. 151, 155–6.

[48] BN MS Fr 3310 fo. 48, Henri III to Carrouges, Paris, 27 Feb 1586.

[49] *Lettres de Catherine de Médicis*, ix, pp. 6–7.

[50] BN MS Fr 3310 fo. 48, Henri III to Pierrecourt, Paris, 27 Feb 1586; fo. 81, Henri III to Moy, Saint Maur des Fosses, 3 Jul 1586. This despite Moy being vice-admiral and having been offered the command by Joyeuse.

[51] Chevallier, *Henri III*, pp. 602–10.

of contention being Epernon's position and the control of two key provinces: Normandy and Picardy.

The Treaty of Nemours had been a compromise by which the king managed to prevent the Guise gaining control of Picardy and Normandy. The defeat of the *reiters* brought this issue once more to the fore. After Auneau, Guise was furious when the Germans were accorded generous terms by the king, leaving France unharmed. He believed that reward was due him for his services. Joyeuse's death left the offices of admiral and governor of Normandy vacant.[52] The king's decision to grant both posts to Epernon aggravated the antipathy between the Guise and Epernon, which had already led to confrontation in Picardy.

Conflict between the king and the League for control of the provinces intensified in early 1588. Henri was determined to assert his authority in the sensitive province of Picardy, where Aumale continued to conspire with the Spanish and his sympathisers in the towns.[53] Following his failure to obtain the governorship of Picardy at Nemours, Aumale took advantage of the peace to extend his control, taking Le Crotoy, Doullens and Pont-Rémy in March 1587 and unsuccessfully attempting to seize Boulogne. The king was infuriated by this egregious act of rebellion but postponed a showdown, hoping to strengthen his position in the autumn. The victory of the Guise and the destruction of the royal army made it imperative to reassert royal authority. Confrontation in the first months of 1588 was inevitable and inflamed by the bitter enmity that the Guise family felt for Epernon.

Aumale's army was composed of traditional followers of the Guise, such as the Tiercelin and the des Essars, and adherents of the League of Péronne. These men were linked by ties of common service and kinship. A number of them held lands from or lived in the vicinity of the duchy of Aumale.[54] Aumale's unsuccessful attack on Boulogne, of which Epernon was governor, had resulted in the murder of one of Epernon's servants.[55] The *mignon* was even more furious when Aumale defeated an

[52] Constant, *Les Guises*, pp. 163–4. I have been unable to find any specific reference to Guise's demands but this is plausible.

[53] Henri's determination to act is clear as early as January 1588: BN NA Fr 2743 fos. 134–5, Henri III to the marquis de Pisani, Paris, 27 Jan 1588.

[54] The des Essars had served the Guise in a number of capacities since the 1540s. Montreuil-sur-Mer, where François des Essars was governor, was thus assured for the League, but he was also supporting his *amis* as well as following his lord. In the 1570s he had served as ensign in the *ordonnance* company of Adrien de Tiercelin, and he was related by marriage to Aumale's *maître de camp* in Picardy. Aumale's army which besieged Boulogne in 1587–8 can be reconstructed from F. Lefebvre, *Les Huguenots et la Ligue au diocèse de Boulogne* (Boulogne-sur-Mer, 1855). Among the adherents of the Catholic League in the 1570s were: Jean de Rambures, governor of the duchy of Guise in 1588 and Aumale's chief lieutenant in Picardy; Robert de Monchy, seigneur de Caveron, married to the niece of the cardinal de Pellevé and brother of fellow League captain Louis de Monchy, seigneur d'Aussennes; Antoine du Hamel, the former ensign of Aumale's company and his *maître de camp* in Picardy in 1588; Jean de Caron, seigneur d'Amery, Aumale's ensign, who was killed at the siege. Anne de Tiercelin had not signed the League of Péronne but his father, Adrien, had been closely associated with its consolidation in Picardy in 1576–7. Antoine de Mascarel was also not a signatory of the League, but was a major upper Norman lord and former *chambellan* of the duc d'Anjou.

[55] De Thou, x, p. 640.

attempt to relieve Boulogne. These incidents ignited the simmering feud that existed between the two. According to L'Estoile it was the king, who believed that only subtle manoeuvring would defeat the League, that prevented the situation becoming critical.[56] For his part Aumale complained of a plot against him engineered by Epernon's lieutenant, when 'deux des siens trouvé en ma maison desguisez y estoient venus en intention de me tuer ainsi qu'ils ont confesse par leurs propres bouches'.[57] Aumale retaliated: two attempts were made on the life of the *mignon* in the early months of 1588.[58]

In January 1588 the house of Lorraine gathered at Nancy to formulate its strategy.[59] Aumale was to increase his efforts in Picardy, Guise was to seize Sedan and Jametz, Elbeuf and Brissac were to raise Normandy against Epernon. It was probably at this council meeting that it was decided to increase efforts to seize substantial towns, which alone afforded security. Aumale undertook secret negotiations with the pro-Guise faction in Abbeville and seized a suburb to 'empescher que les Gascons que y voulloit mettre monsieur d'Epernon n'y entrassent'. The governor, Roncherolles, and other leaguers prevented the town cannon being fired but opinion was hopelessly divided and the majority was against a garrison, whichever side it represented.[60]

Elbeuf began recruiting in Normandy in March and raised his standard at his château of Harcourt, in the proximity of Rouen. According to Elbeuf's lieutenant, Antoine de Bigars, his forces numbered 5–7,000 men.[61] The duke visited the city on 7 March, ostensibly on private business, but few were fooled by this.[62] Elbeuf was taking counsel in the city and soliciting support, and he borrowed at least 18,000*l* from his Rouennais friends. In April Guise sent agents to Rouen, as well as other large towns in northern France, in preparation for a *putsch*. The governor tightened security.[63] On 26 April 1588 Epernon left Paris with a small army to take possession of his *gouvernement*, entering Rouen on 3 May.

Many royal officers were compromised by the revolt. Epernon ordered Hervé de

[56] L'Estoile, *Journal du règne de Henri III*, pp. 488, 490. Boulogne's strategic significance was amplified by the execution of Mary Stuart and the sailing of the Spanish Armada.

[57] BN Cinq Cents Colbert 10 fo. 197, Aumale to Henri III, Aumale, 21 Aug 1587.

[58] Chevallier, *Henri III*, p. 618; L'Estoile, *Journal du règne de Henri III*, p. 545.

[59] The family renewed its demands for the publication of the decrees of Trent and the prosecution of outright war against heresy supported by an adequately funded army.

[60] Prarond, *La Ligue à Abbeville*, i, pp. 311–40.

[61] 'Mémoires d'Antoine de Bigars, sieur de La Londe', *Société de l'Histoire de Normandie, Mélanges*, 5th ser. (Rouen and Paris, 1898), p. 18. The infantry consisted of the regiments of Guillaume Perdriel, *maître d'hôtel* of the duc de Guise, Jacques Le Conte, baron de Nonant, and Adrien des Buaz, sieur des Noyers. Anne de Tiercelin, seigneur de Possé, and Philippe de Tiercelin, seigneur de la Ferté-Villeneuve, were also present in the army; their father, Jacques, had been Aumale's lieutenant in the 1570s and their cousin was currently serving in Aumale's force in Picardy; their cousin, Louise, was married to Antoine de Bigars: ADSM 2E1 2005, 27 Apr and 9 May 1588.

[62] BN MS Fr 3302 fo. 76, Henri to Carrouges, Paris, 7 Mar 1588.

[63] ADSM 2E1 2005, 9 May 1588; Croze, *Les Guise, les Valois et Philippe II*, ii, p. 332; *CSPF*, 1586–8, p. 590.

Longaunay, his lieutenant-general, to prevent the concentration of League forces and wrote again a few days later to inform him that his son was one of the rebels.[64] Nothing was done to attack the rebel army and letters written by the king ordering the intervention of Carrouges and the Moy went unheeded.[65] Nevertheless, the elite of the Norman nobility did not fail to turn up to the *joyeuse entrée* of the new governor on 3 May. Thus in the first days of May the capital of Normandy was swarming with noblemen and soldiers, including large contingents of leaguers and the retinue of their foe, Epernon.[66]

In Rouen the League commanded sufficient support, but lacked the kind of pretext which had precipitated the Day of the Barricades in Paris on 12 May 1588, when the entry of a large number of royal troops into the city aggravated an already volatile situation. In Normandy the League was dominated by a noble leadership, largely Guisards and malcontents, with financial support from sympathetic sections of the Rouennais urban elite. The crown's support was atrophied by comparison. The paralysis of royal government in Normandy occurred because, without the money to pay for a mercenary army, it relied on provincial officers who often sympathised with the Guise and were not inclined to chance life and fortune when the prospects were so uncertain. The Paris uprising against the introduction of royal troops was a communal revolt supported by a significant number of Guise clients and their followers.[67] The king's flight to Chartres left the city in the hands of the Sixteen (a clandestine organisation of bourgeois leaguers) and Guise, and made the allegiance of towns and royal officers in the provinces of central importance to both sides. Normandy was of particular significance, especially for the royalists. During his sojourn in the province, Epernon made efforts to ensure the loyalty of the former clients of Joyeuse. In February an English agent reported from Dieppe that *premier président* Groulard had been dispatched to ensure the loyalty of Villars, governor of Le Havre.[68]

Rouen itself remained neutral but the king could depend on the support of the *premier président* and he began to make considerable efforts to win over the Rouennais.[69] Taxes were abolished, offices suppressed and the unpopular Epernon replaced by a prince of the blood, the duc de Montpensier. The city Council of

64 *Papiers de Hervé de Longaunay, gouverneur de la Basse-Normandie (1575–1589)* (Saint Lô, 1897), pp. 19–20.

65 BN MS Fr 3394 fo. 54, Henri III to Carrouges, Paris, 28 Mar 1588; fo. 55, Henri III to Moy, Paris, 28 Mar 1588; fo. 63, Henri III to Pierrecourt, Paris, 20 Apr 1588.

66 ACR A 20, 3 May 1588. Mendoza assured Philip II on the 8th that the Rouennais had won over Epernon's troops and that his fate was sealed.

67 R. Descimon, 'La Ligue à Paris: une révision', *Annales ESC*, 37 (1982), 72–128; Descimon, *Qui étaient les Seize?*; Carroll, 'The Guise affinity and popular protest'. The role of the clergy in fostering the League in Paris and the piety of Guisards and leaguer activists should not be underestimated: A. Ramsey, 'Piety in Paris during the League, 1585–90: an urban community in transition', unpub. Ph.D. thesis (University of Columbia, 1991).

68 *CSPF*, 1586–8, p. 515.

69 For this and following: Benedict, *Rouen during the Wars of Religion*, pp. 174–5.

Twenty-Four was eventually convinced by these gestures and the king was invited to the city, making his entry on 13 June 1588. It was reported that La Meilleraye and Pierrecourt 'both hold for the League'. They did not openly join Elbeuf, maintaining a calculated inactivity which incapacitated the royalist cause in upper Normandy. Their cousins Louis de Moy, sieur de Gomméron and François de Moy, sieur de Richebourg, were more actively engaged in the League, taking part in the events of 12 May in Paris.[70] Even the loyalty of the Le Veneur family was not assured. It was common knowledge at court that the governor, Carrouges, and his son 'dépendoient en quelque façon du duc de Guise et de la ligue'.[71] As lieutenant-general of Normandy, Carrouges had done little to obstruct the League in the previous years, but the king now bought his loyalty with the offer of a *brevet* for the office of *maréchal* when a vacancy arose and a pension of 3,333 *écus*.[72] In the meantime his son, the comte de Tillières, *bailli* of Rouen, continued to lean towards the League. In April 1588 an English agent reported that: 'M. la Carewge, captain of Rouen, who serves the King, and his son, on the third of this month are fallen in great discord in the city, and [a] procession [has been] sung throughout the city upon the Guise's side, whose part M. de Carewge's son doth serve'.[73] *Président* Groulard attributed this split to kinship: 'le comte de Tillières ayant espousé la belle-soeur de M. d'Elboeuf, avoit secrettement, encore qu'il n'en fait semblable, faict profession de la ligue; de sorte qu'ayant entendu que le roy venoit à Rouen il se fascha fort'.[74] His reservations as to the king's arrival were eased with a royal gift of 15,000 *écus*.[75] Jacques-Auguste de Thou had been dispatched by Henri from Chartres to gauge the mood of local notables and ensure the loyalty of royal officers.[76] He went first to Evreux where the bishop, Claude de Sainctes, was a leaguer, then to Rouen to address the parlement and *échevins*, and then to Dieppe which, with its strong reformed community, was fiercely against the League. At Le Havre the governor, Villars, had already been won over by the Parisians with 30,000 *écus* and de Thou received a cold welcome. At Lisieux, Jean de Longchamps continued the pro-Guise tradition of his family. De Thou received the support of Caen before consulting the Moy at La Meilleraye, who gave nothing away except their suspicion of Villars.

The king remained in Rouen until 21 July, trying to buy support while negotiating with the League leaders in Paris. Although he had secured Rouen, the Moy and Tillières were uncommitted and Lisieux and Le Havre had defected to the League. The king's sojourn in Normandy did not go unopposed. Elbeuf was absent in Paris

70 De Thou, x, p. 248.

71 Quoted in Beaurepaire, ed., *Séjour de Henri III à Rouen*, p. xxiv.

72 AN M 458, Le Veneur, Jul 1588.

73 *CSPF*, 1586–8, p. 589. The procession probably refers to either a penitential procession or a thanksgiving for the victory at Auneau.

74 Claude Groulard, *Mémoires*, Michaud and Poujoulat, 1st ser., xi, p. 554.

75 Beaurepaire, ed., *Séjour de Henri III à Rouen*, pp. xxxiv, xxxix.

76 For this and following: De Thou, x, pp. 305–10; *Mémoires depuis 1553 jusqu'en 1601*, Michaud and Poujoulat, 1st ser., xi, pp. 326–7.

in talks with Guise, but his wife, Marguerite Chabot, who played an important role in the organisation of the League forces, was left in charge of the army.[77] A series of letters written from Rouen by a royalist nobleman during the king's stay reveal the desperate state of his cause. He was effectively surrounded in the city with League troops at Montivilliers, Pont-Audemer, Neufbourg and Pontoise.[78] The humiliation of the king was complete and he conceded to the demands of the League enshrined in the Edict of Union of 21 July 1588.

CONSTITUENTS OF LEAGUE SUPPORT

Most historians would now agree on the crucial and autonomous role played by popular forces in political society. Historians have long since rejected the idea that the Catholic League was dominated by the Guise and ultimately Philip of Spain. Following Henri Drouot, Robert Descimon has characterised the Sixteen in Paris as a movement of the lesser bourgeoisie defending municipal autonomy and the community against the encroachment of royal power and the divisive effects of venality. Denis Crouzet has explored the religious mentalities behind the League, although he pays insufficient attention to how religious ideology articulated political and social grievances. But, outside Paris, the evidence for the contribution of popular mentalities to and popular participation in the urban revolts of the League is ambiguous. The scale of the Day of the Barricades was unique and due to specific circumstances.[79] League *coups de main* in the provincial cities in 1588–9 may have enjoyed popular support, but were usually executed by factions within the ruling elite. Nevertheless, there is evidence to suggest that League aims reflected religious anxieties and provincial discontents, and enjoyed widespread support in Normandy.

Royalists and leaguers were sensitive to their public image and aware of the importance of propaganda. The image of the duc de Guise as military hero, which became a legend after his murder in 1588, was popularised in pamphlets and iconography.[80] The representation of his image was not confined to Paris. The town of Rouen had a commemorative *jeton* struck in honour of the duke's victory at Auneau in November 1587. The medal had the legend 'Civitas Rothomagensis' and on the reverse an eagle was portrayed ready to tear its prey apart with the device 'Lartifice est detruict par la vertu'.[81] Symbolic reference to Guise's struggle against the *mignons* would have been clear. Epernon retorted by striking a medal on his

77 'Mémoires d'Antoine de Bigars', p. 18.

78 BN NA Fr 238 fo. 23, Thomas Auber to Georges Auber, Rouen, 24 Jun 1588.

79 For critiques of Descimon's model: Benedict, *Rouen during the Wars of Religion*, pp. 182–9; Harding, 'Revolution and reform in the Holy League'; D. Crouzet, *Les guerriers de Dieu: la violence au temps des troubles de religion vers 1525 –vers 1610* (2 vols., Paris, 1990), pp. 287–97.

80 In Paris alone in late 1587 twenty pamphlets were published eulogising his victories: D. Pallier, *Recherches sur l'imprimerie à Paris pendant la Ligue, 1585–1594* (Geneva, 1976).

81 BN MS Clairambault 1204 fo. 123.

elevation to the governorship; its device evokes the duke as the harbinger of peace. The engraving represents Jason and the Argonauts (the king and his people) being rescued by the self-sacrificing dove (Epernon) from their fate on the clashing Cyanean rocks (the League and the protestants).[82] The sophistication of popular political culture in Rouen is manifested by the interpretation and inversion of propaganda. When Elbeuf camped in the vicinity of Rouen during carnival in 1588, the Abbaye de Conards, an infamous ludic confraternity, ridiculed the Guise and the League. The confreres' distribution of mock insignia to the people suggests that Elbeuf had been distributing his badge in the city, further evidence of leaguer attempts to attract popular support.[83] These appeals to opinion beyond the traditional city elites, and the critical representation of political conflict in popular festivity, demonstrates the vitality of the public sphere in provincial cities in the later sixteenth century.

According to a memorandum from Carrouges to the king in April 1585, large sections of the town were suspected of being pro-League. But the document is vague and mentions no names. The Council of Twenty-Four were loyal but the parlement, the clergy, the 'people' and the city's Spanish community were untrustworthy.[84] The widespread popularity of war against the protestants was confirmed by the warm reception of the Edict of Nemours.[85] However, the parlement's rapid registration of the edict did not mean it would support measures designed to pay for war, and fiscal innovations were repeatedly blocked. It was particularly aggrieved by increases in the sales of offices in the parlement. In August 1587 the king complained that the magistrates of the parlement of Rouen were 'jaloux de la conservacion de leurs authorité aux despens et diminution de la mienne'.[86]

The tension between corporate and royal interests manifested itself in factionalism. The appointment of Groulard as *premier président* in 1585 and his subsequent sponsorship of unpopular royal legislation divided the magistrates. For a faction in the parlement he embodied the illegality of royal fiscal legislation and the unhealthy accretion of power in the hands of the non-Norman *mignons*. Had Joyeuse not died in 1587 his regime may have prospered due to the considerable resources of patronage at his disposal. But the task of the governor was hampered by the Guise faction which had been a powerful interest group in the parlement since before the beginning of the Wars of Religion. Guise clients among the magistrates formed the nucleus of the faction favourable to the League in the parlement before 1589. These men were activists who played an important role in the League coup of February and who provided the leadership of the League between 1589 and 1594. A number of prominent leaguers, such as the Bauquemare, were creditors of the Guise. At

[82] F. Feuardent, *Jetons et méraux depuis Louis IX jusqu'à la fin du consulat de Bonaparte* (3 vols., Paris 1904–15), ii, no. 6089.

[83] Corvisier, A. 'Une société ludique au XVIe siècle: l'Abbaye de Conards de Rouen', *Annales de Normandie*, 22 (1977), p. 191.

[84] BN MS Fr 3358 fo. 42, discussed in Benedict, *Rouen during the Wars of Religion*, p. 171.

[85] Floquet, iii, p. 230.

[86] BN MS Fr 3394 fo. 65, Henri III to Carrouges, Aug 1587.

least one parlementaire family, the Péricard, owed its prominence solely to Guise patronage and *conseiller* Michel de Monchy, a relative of the cardinal de Pellevé, had two brothers fighting with the army of the duc d'Aumale in the late 1580s. Other supporters of the League in the parlement could be termed creatures of the Guise. The grandfather of Louis Garin, *conseiller* since 1582, had been *bailli* of Elbeuf and the family continued to benefit from Guise patronage. One of Louis's brothers became a monk at the abbey of Bec and the other two were men-at-arms in the company of the duc d'Elbeuf.[87] Obviously the ties of kinship were important in the decision on which side to take and the examples are numerous. For example, Louis Garin was the son-in-law of *conseiller* Guillaume de Paixdecoeur who ranked among the senior captains of the Rouen militia under the League.[88]

The *cahiers de doléances* of the provincial Estates commonly voiced opposition to royal policy. Representatives favourable to the League were conspicuous in the provincial Estates and at the Estates-General of 1588. The Norman Estates complained about taxation, excessive sales of venal office and the spiralling cost of justice. Appendix E lists those Guise clients and leaguers present at the Estates between 1584 and 1588. Guise influence in the Estates is especially notable after the successful revolt of 1585. The two noble representatives chosen by the Estates that year to present the remonstrances to the king were both League captains. Its first article congratulated the king for the Edict of Nemours and for ensuring the unity of the faith, but also urged him to 'garder, entretenir et inviolablement observer' its clauses.[89] In 1586 the Estates again urged the king to uphold the edict and the following year they admonished him for his indulgence towards protestants who had not complied with its requirement to leave France.[90] In addition to noble clients, representatives of the First Estate, invariably chosen by the cathedral chapters, also pressed for the prosecution of the war against heresy. More remarkable was the presence of Guise servants returned for the Third Estate. During years of crisis, such as 1578–9 and after 1584, Elbeuf's servants ensured their election to the Estates for the *vicomtés* of the *bailliage* of Rouen, suggesting both the level of support for the duke, where he was the major landowner, and a degree of sympathy for the League among the rural elites. Praise of the monarchy for its embrace of the League was tempered by continuing criticism of royal fiscal policy. The king funded his war from forced loans and liberally rewarded the duc de Joyeuse from strained Norman revenues.[91]

By 1588 criticism of the regime had become quite explicit. One of the best-known pamphlets of the civil wars, the *Histoire tragique et memorable, de Pierre de Gaverston*, which intimated that the king and Epernon were sodomites, is not

[87] Frondeville, *Conseillers*, p. 357.

[88] *Ibid.*, p. 341; G. Valdory, 'Relation du siège de Rouen en 1591', *Société Rouennaise de Bibliophiles* (Rouen, 1871), p. 6.

[89] *Cahiers des Etats de Normandie sous le règne de Henri III*, ii, pp. 108, 303.

[90] *Ibid.*, pp. 150, 204.

[91] In December 1586 the king constituted an annual *rente* of 11,000 *écus* on the *recettes-générales* of Normandy in favour of Joyeuse: ADSM 2E1 2294, 11 Aug 1592.

usually associated with events in Normandy, but the pamphlet clearly states that it was composed in Le Havre on 16 May only days after the duke entered Rouen to take up his governorship, and claims that his reception by the parlement had been a farce.[92] It belongs to the local propaganda battle. Epernon's unpopularity is evident from the address delivered on behalf of the cathedral chapter, whose *pénitencier* turned the customary honorific address into an extraordinary attack. The promise made in 1585 to combat heresy was being undermined by 'politiques' and 'machiavellistes' and the onus of the war against heresy was on Epernon: 'C'est à vous d'y remedier, si voulez faire l'office d'un bon Gouverneur. Vous en avez la puissance, pour avoir l'oreille, la faveur, le credit, le coeur et l'auctorité du Roy en main. Il ne reste que la bonne volonté, de laquelle vous ferez paroistre les effects quand vous voudreez.'[93] Epernon's stay in the city was tense. The Spanish ambassador, Mendoza, was in contact with the League faction and a plot to seize the duke was forestalled by the Day of the Barricades in Paris.[94]

The Edict of Union (July 1588) and the Estates-General of Blois were to eradicate protestantism and to exclude Henri de Navarre from the throne. There was intense competition at the elections for the Estates-General, with the king failing to ensure the election of sympathetic delegates. Appendix E shows the disproportionate influence of Guise clients at Blois. The cardinal de Bourbon was himself elected for the First Estate of Rouen, Brissac represented the *bailliage* of Caux and the Roncherolles once more ensured the election of a family member to represent Gisors. Even in lower Normandy, where support was much weaker, the League made headway. Although Caen was generally an area of royalism, the future League captain of Bayeux was elected. The only exception to this tide of success was in the *bailliage* of Alençon where the royalist *bailli*, Jacques de Renty, used illegal methods to overcome his opponent, Gabriel de Vieuxpont, sieur de Chailloué and lieutenant of Brissac's company.[95]

Lists of electors are rare, but one survives for the Second Estate of the *bailliage* of Rouen.[96] Eight of the twelve noblemen present at the election are identifiable, and none seems to have been an active royalist.[97] Three of those present were closely associated with the Guise; another would serve in the armies of the League; one would sit on the leaguer city council; and one man, sometime captain of the Rouennais militia, probably had League sympathies.[98] The 'contest' was a foregone

[92] *Histoire tragique et memorable, de Pierre de Gaverston Gentilhomme Gascon . . . Dedié à Monseigneur le Duc d'Espernon* (n.p. 1588).

[93] *Remonstrance Faicte A Monsieur d'Espernon, Entrant En l'Eglise Cathedrale de Rouen, le 3 de may 1588* (Rouen, 1588), pp. 5–7.

[94] Croze, *Les Guises, les Valois et Philippe II*, ii, pp. 333, 337.

[95] Lacourcé and Duval, *Recueil*, iv, p. 45; Orlea, *La noblesse aux Etats généraux*, p. 98.

[96] ACR A 20, 27 Jul 1588.

[97] The kinship links of Richard Martainville, one of the largest landowners in the *bailliage*, suggest royalist leanings. But he does not seem to have fought for Henri IV's cause, being present in Rouen during the League hegemony: ADSM 2E1 2293, last Jun 1592; 2E1 2295, 17 Nov 1593.

[98] Barthélemy de Limoges was of Aumale's affinity and previously involved in the provincial elections

conclusion. Nicolas Vipart, previously elected to the provincial Estates during the 1578 crisis and a Guise man, was returned.

Analysis of the Third Estate is more problematic. At Gisors and Alençon League sympathisers were returned. Once more information on the representatives of the *bailliage* of Rouen is more replete. One of them, Guillaume Colombel, was a leaguer with close connections to the ultra-catholic hierarchy.[99] Fellow delegate Robert Hannivel also came from the city elite and served as an *échevin* in 1590–1 during the League hegemony. He bought *rentes* from the duc d'Elbeuf in 1586 and his brother-in-law was a creditor of the duc d'Aumale and *intendant* of the cardinal de Guise.[100] But his ambiguous and sometimes bizarre behaviour at the Estates-General demonstrates that there was no simple connection between such ties and leaguer activism. During the opening weeks of the Estates he presided over the Norman delegation, claiming the prerogative as deputy of the city of Rouen. His precedence was disputed by Caen and he was destituted amidst accusations that he was using his position to defend Rouen privileges.[101]

Thereafter, Hannivel pursued an independent line. One eye-witness even inferred that he had been bought by the king. The suspicion increased during mid-November as the chasm between the king and the Third Estate over taxation widened, and Hannivel was nearly defenestrated for divulging the debates of the assembly. When the king complained that the Third Estate was being misled by malcontents: 'le dit sieur de Hannivel print la parole, lui offrant tous les moyens de sa bonne ville et qu'il avoit esté chargé, où il receut quelques coups de pied . . . pour luy faire cesser son discours'.[102] In an age when all men were the king's servants, Hannivel's behaviour exposes the ambiguity of the terms 'royalist' and 'leaguer' before the outbreak of open civil war in 1589. Hannivel, who later held municipal office during the League, refused to countenance the prosecution of corrupt royal financiers who were among the chief targets of the League leadership at the Estates. The staunchly loyal delegates from Caen, who would form part of the backbone of the royalist cause in Normandy after 1589, fulminated at the excessive tax burden. Paradoxically, the isolation of Hannivel ('il feust demeuré a pescher sa mare') was due not to moderation but to his religious radicalism; his support for maintaining

during the 1578 crisis. Various relatives of Héris were in the household and *ordonnance* of Elbeuf. Jean de Gaillardbois had served under the Aumale in the *vénerie du roi* since 1560. Both Robert Deschamps, sieur du Réel and bourgeois, and Martin du Bosc, sieur d'Emendreville, sided with the League: ADSM 1B 3216, 1 Mar 1590; 2E1 2293, 31 May 1592. Etienne Lafonds' position as captain of the largely ultra-catholic city militia implies sympathy for the League.

99 Guillaume served as an *échevin* of Rouen during the League hegemony. Romain Colombel had served on the judicial council of the duc d'Aumale in the 1560s and 1570s; he had been *bailli* of Mauny and a pensioner of the cardinal de Lorraine in 1561: ADSM 1ER 1589; G 6595.

100 Appendix B; ADSM 1B 702, 5 Oct 1590; 2E1 943, 13 Sep 1591. His son-in-law was a *conseiller* in the leaguer parlement.

101 For this and following: Lacourcé and Duval, *Recueil*, iv, pp. 37, 120, 122, 131; v, 33–5, 79, 120, 130.

102 'Minutes des lettres trouvées parmi les papiers d'Adrien Ballue, chanoine de Rouen', *Bulletin de la Société de l'Histoire de Normandie* (1875–80), pp. 281, 284.

current levels of taxation was echoed by the duc de Guise in his efforts to persuade the Third Estate to pay for the war against heresy.[103] Although the Third Estate agreed in principle with the extermination of heresy, they wanted reductions in taxation, the restitution of communal liberties and the abolition of venality. Henri de Guise spent the last weeks of his life trying to convince the Third Estate to support the war against Henri de Navarre without alienating his supporters among the delegates. His attempts to reconcile the antithetical demands of crown and province were terminated by his murder on 23 December. The debates in the Third Estate in November and December 1588 revealed the essential paradox between the religious militancy and the parochial conservatism of the Catholic League. Guise's martyrdom ensured that the disparate factions of the League would, for a time, reunite against a common enemy.

THE GUISE AFFINITY AND THE FALL OF ROUEN

During its hegemony between the seizure of power in 1589 and the triumph of Henri IV in 1594, the League generated an abundance of administrative, financial and political documentation. Historians have exploited these sources to produce a narrative of the main events and a detailed account of the functioning of the League regime in Normandy.[104] In contrast, its origins and development are obscured by its clandestine nature prior to the seizure of Rouen. Benedict's analysis of the League faction in Rouen and its seizure of power in February 1589 is circumscribed, as he admits, by the fragmentary nature of the sources.[105] By employing hitherto unexploited archives it is possible to reconstruct the events of February 1589 with greater certainty and reinterpret the character of the Rouen uprising. An investigation of the League cadres and their role in the events of February 1589 reveals the interplay among 'the people', the city elites and Guise clients, enabling wider conclusions to be drawn about the interaction of elite and popular politics, patterns of urban elite affiliation and links between the Paris Sixteen and the League in Rouen.

Up to the murder of the duc de Guise, opposition to the king had been expressed in the traditional terms of defending liberties against the machinations of misguided and pernicious royal officials. Having cast off the cloak of dissimulation, Henri III was now revealed to the Catholic League as a tyrant; to many he was the anti-Christ. In Rouen there was great anger but Carrouges quickly acted to stifle unrest, stationing troops at strategic points throughout the city.[106] Solicited by both

[103] Hannivel was undoubtedly trying to ingratiate himself with the king and the duke. At one time close to Henri III, he was forced to give up the important office of *grand audiencier* in 1576. Returning to Rouen to recommence his commercial activities, he obtained letters of derogation in 1584: H. Michaud, *La grand chancellerie et les écritures royales au XVIe siècle* (Paris, 1967), pp. 402–3.

[104] R. d'Estaintot, *La ligue en Normandie, 1588–94* (Paris and Rouen, 1862); H. A. Lloyd, *The Rouen campaign, 1590–1592* (Oxford, 1973).

[105] Benedict, *Rouen during the Wars of Religion*, p. 168.

sides Rouen remained neutral, the governor making every effort to maintain stability: religious processions were banned. Carrouges thus followed the same path as in 1588, trying to maintain control of the city while using his position to bargain with the parties. His position was tenuous: his son, the *bailli*, continued to favour the League, while *président* Groulard felt he was paying insufficient attention to the possibility of violent upheaval.[107]

Modern accounts of the League takeover are based on limited archival research which provides only the barest narrative, but the events are well known.[108] On 14 January Carrouges appeared before the town council in order to defend himself against charges that he was conspiring to betray the town to royalist troops. His excuses were accepted and the assembly gave the governor their full backing. During the last week of January the parlement, and probably also the municipal and sovereign institutions, swore to support him in the event of unrest. In the first days of February an appeal from Carrouges to the crown for immediate reinforcement was intercepted. On 3 February a council of League supporters chaired by *conseiller* Regnault du Pont decided to act.[109]

The events of February 1589 may be reconstructed in greater detail than hitherto, and on this a reinterpretation of the character of the rising may be based. At midday on 4 February League supporters began to assemble and build barricades. At the first news of the unrest the royalist eye-witness, *conseiller* Jacques Dyel, left his house accompanied by three arquebusiers and attempted to reach Carrouges at the abbey of Saint-Ouen but was blocked by members of the city militia under a bourgeois captain.[110] Dyel retreated and joined with the royalist captain of the Beauvoisine quarter, *conseiller* Martin Hally, who, though commanding 200 hundred men, was cautious. Rather than storm the barricades he retreated to the Marché de Veaux and despite Dyel's protestations took up defensive positions: 'qu'il y falloit doucement et que si le tambour sonnoit tout seroit au feu et au sang'. This militia company made no further attempt to intervene on behalf of the governor. The logic of such caution only became clear to Dyel during the late afternoon, when his suspicions that many militia officers were unreliable was confirmed; one of them 'luy dit si le chevalier d'aumale eust esté dans la ville il fust à la sappe de st ouen lors ledit Diel connut leurs intentions differentes et se tint le reste du jour au couvert en sa maison'. Thereafter he made another futile attempt to reach the governor, before being forced into hiding. The following morning the

106 For this and following: *ibid.*, pp. 177–81.

107 Floquet, iii, pp. 283–4.

108 Apart from Benedict, see also Lloyd, *The Rouen campaign, 1590–1592*, pp. 127–8; Floquet, iii, pp. 292–3.

109 The best outline of events is in BN MS Fr 10270 fo. 102. The only other leaguer mentioned is a *sécretaire du roi*, which probably refers to Charles Guérould, *receveur-général* of the cardinal de Bourbon.

110 On this and following: ADSM 1 Mi 347, 'Copie des registres secrets du parlement de Caen', fo. 600, 5 July 1590, partially used by Floquet. The bourgeois captain opposing him was Nicholas Carré, whose family lived in the parish of Notre-Dame de la Ronde: ADSM G 7374, 1589 and 1590.

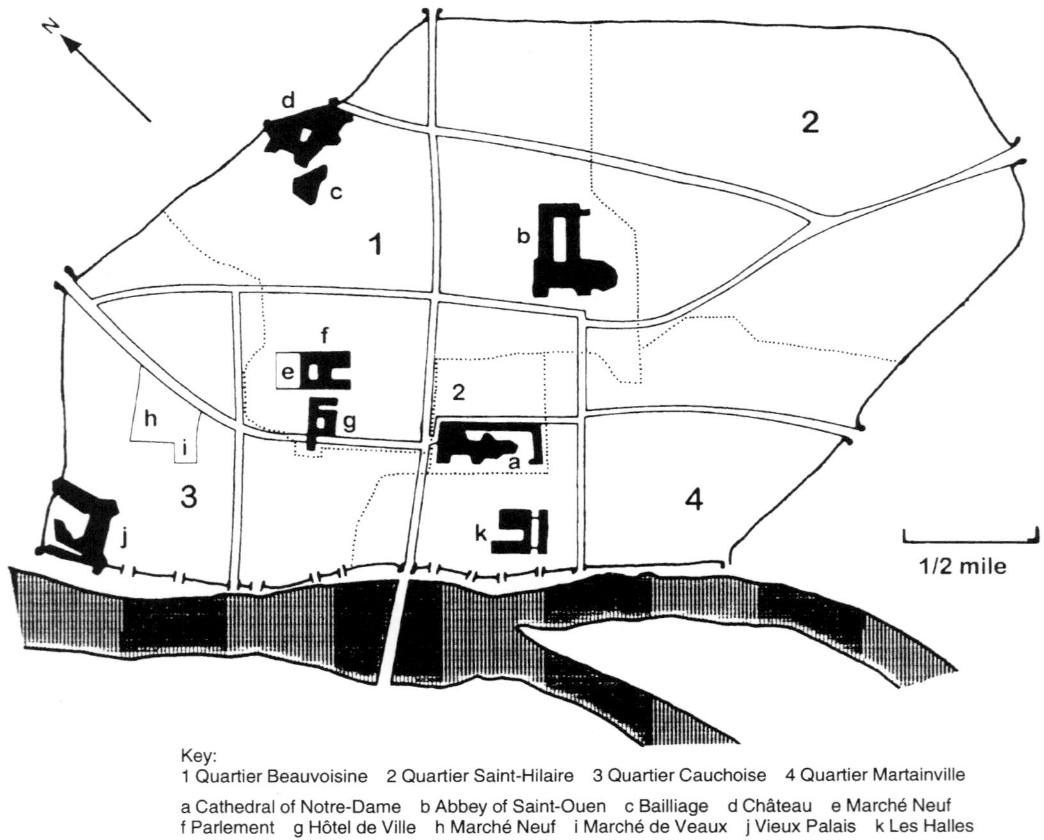

Map 7 Rouen in the sixteenth century

hôtel de ville fell to the insurgents and the League leadership negotiated an agreement with the governor. On 7 February a Council of Twelve was established to direct the affairs of the town and three days later Carrouges swore an oath to work with the League in Paris and ensure the adherence of local administrative bodies; he had already relinquished the city's strong points.

The new regime took immediate steps to strengthen its authority: as early as 7 February royalist sympathisers were being arrested by Guise clients.[111] During these anxious days leaguer noblemen arrived: Nicolas de Moy, sieur de Riberpré, was in the city from at least 9 February; his younger brother, Charles, appears in the notarial records two days later; they were joined on or before the 12th by elements of the Aumale affinity. At least one member of Riberpré's *ordonnance* company was in the city on the eve of the revolt, indicating that elements of his retinue were present during the uprising.[112] The Moy were emissaries of the Guise. Their brothers, Louis and François, had already participated in the Day of the Barricades in Paris in 1588, and their cousin Jean, lieutenant-general of upper Normandy, had been the principal Norman ally of the Guise for twenty-five years. The fragmentary nature of the sources prevents more detailed speculation about the role of the Moy in the Day of the Barricades, and the degree of coordination between urban leaguers and the family remains speculation. A letter written by Jean's brother, Jacques, shortly after the fall of Rouen shows that he was about to secure Pont-Audemer for the League. He justified his actions by invoking the spectre of royalist collaboration with heretics and foreigners: 'c'est pourquoy les Catholiques de ce pais se unissent et banissent de parmy eulx les heretiques suspectz pour essaier de se servir et empescher que les anglois antrent en france et nous vient impietter'.[113]

Clearly the city militia played a crucial role in the uprising. The building of barricades suggests a degree of spontaneous popular action but the participation of some militia units and the neutrality of others were the keys to rapid success. However strong support for the king may have been among the city elite, it was disorganised and ineffective. As Benedict has shown, the city militia had been largely responsible for the anti-protestant disturbances of the 1560s and 1570s, and historians are belatedly recognising the role played by city militias in urban politics. The king recognised its importance and during his sojourn in the city he had ennobled all its captains.[114]

111 Guillaume Péricard's clerical station did not inhibit him from arming himself and searching the lodgings of suspects with his men: *Bulletin de la Société Historique et Archéologique de l'Orne*, 28 (1909), p. 453.

112 ADSM 2E1 938, 9 and 11 Feb 1589; 2010, 3 and 12 Feb 1589. Members of the Nollent and Houetteville families figured prominently in the ducal *ordonnance* company and as officers of the *vénerie du roi*.

113 BN NA Fr 6646 fo. 320, Moy to Hervé de Longaunay, Honfleur, 17 Feb 1589.

114 Lebeurier, *Etat des anoblis en Normandie*, p. xiv. On Paris: R. Descimon, 'La milice bourgeoise et identité citadine à Paris au temps de la Ligue', *Annales ESC*, 48 (1993), 885–906. The militia was largely responsible for the fall of Troyes to the League in 1588: Carroll, 'The Guise affinity and popular protest', p. 149.

6. Claude de Lorraine, abbot of Bec. Second son of Claude duc d'Aumale, the chevalier d'Aumale was the chief hero of the Catholic League before his death in battle in 1591.

The disloyalty of the militia should not be ascribed merely to the unpopularity of royal policies. Dyel only realised that the militia was untrustworthy when one of the captains bemoaned the fact that the chevalier d'Aumale was not in the city to lead them. As in Paris, the Guise were idolised by elements of the Rouennais populace as catholic warrior heroes. Other analogies to the Parisian experience are evident: the strength of the urban League was founded on the ties of vicinage, kinship and common religious belief. Service in the militia was only part of a wider network of neighbourhood solidarity and obligation. The nature of these ties is beyond the scope of this book, although Dyel's account tells as much about the role played by parochial and affinal solidarities within the city. Of the twelve militia captains, at least seven were League sympathisers.[115] For example, captain Pierre d'Eudemare

[115] Most of them are identified by Lebeurier. Activists included Nicholas Carré and Guillaume Colombel, a representative at the Estates-General of 1588. *Conseiller* Guillaume Paixdecoeur had

was reluctant to commit his men against the insurgents. He was probably sympathetic to the League and his actions were circumscribed by his close relations with League activists. The Eudemare had links to the mercantile elite. In September 1588 Pierre's nephew, Jean, had advanced the substantial sum of 2,200 *écus* to the duc d'Elbeuf.[116] Pierre resided in the central parish of Notre-Dame de la Ronde alongside many wealthy merchants and financiers. He enjoyed intimate relations with other Guise creditors resident in the parish. The brothers Jean and Barthélemy Hallé were among the largest creditors of the Guise in Normandy, having advanced Elbeuf 12,000*l* in September 1588. Their father had held all the most important posts in the city hierarchy during the Wars of Religion and Jean had been *trésorier de France* at Rouen since 1579. Support for the League was not confined to moneylending: their cousin, Laurent, *prieur des marchands*, appears on a roll of leaguer captains in 1591. The Hallé, pious catholics, were significant benefactors of their parish church; and Jean acted with Pierre d'Eudemare as treasurer of Notre-Dame de la Ronde during the League hegemony.[117] Although Eudemare cannot be directly associated with the League, his social world – kinsmen, neighbours and business partners – abounded with leaguer activists. Some militia captains were more deeply implicated in the League: Jean Puchot was the son of the largest creditor of the Guise in Normandy, and became a *conseiller* of the city immediately following the League coup; he was the brother-in-law of Jean and Barthélemy Hallé. Kinsmen of the Hallé formed a notable clique in the League hierarchy, underlining the inter-relationship of family, financial, religious and political interests.[118]

The recent explosion of sixteenth-century urban history has transformed our understanding of the internal dynamics of city life. But urban elites were not wholly and sometimes not principally concerned with internal city affairs. The wealthy Rouennais *noblesse bourgeoise* were intimately connected with the upper Norman gentry and the judicial elite were members of provincial and sometimes supra

been a militia captain since 1568 and later commanded the bourgeois militia during the defence of the city in 1591–2. René de Brevedent was of a family with traditional links to the Guise and was resident in the city in March 1594: ADSM 2ème Héritage, 7 March 1594. Pierre Morel appears on the rolls of those lending money to the League: ADSM C 2314, 29 May 1592.

116 ADSM 2ème Héritage, 9 May 1600.

117 On the Hallé: appendices A and B; Frondeville, *Conseillers du parlement, 1594–1640*, p. 142. The Hallé's catholicism was not an obstacle to trade with protestants such as Eustache Trevache: Brunelle, *The New World merchants of Rouen*, pp. 63–77, 153–5. Laurent Hallé was sieur de Mouflaines: ACR A 20, 4 Feb 1591. Eudemare was also related to the financial agent Guy d'Amiens, who had arranged for the payment of sums to the forces of the duc d'Elbeuf in 1585 and who appears on the rolls of those lending money for the defence of the city in 1592: ADSM 2E1 2284, 27 Mar 1585; C 2314, 29 May 1592; Frondeville, *Conseillers*, p. 190.

118 Frondeville, *Conseillers*, p. 532. Jean Puchot's brother, Pierre, was a *conseiller* in the League parlement at Rouen: *Délibérations de la ville de Rouen*, p. 252. Jeanne, sister of Jean and Barthélemy Hallé, was the sister-in-law of Marc-Antoine Bigot, captain of the city militia in 1592 and 1593: Frondeville, *Présidents*, p. 246. Another sister, Madeleine, had married in 1584 Nicholas Rassent, *conseiller* in the League parlement: Frondeville, *Conseillers*, p. 402. The Hallé were also intimately related to Jean Voisin who was elected to the League Council of Twelve following the coup.

provincial kinship networks. Prosoprographical analysis of the leading Rouennais leaguers illuminates both the preponderant role played by Guise clients and the recondite links between the League in Rouen and the Paris Sixteen.

The composition of the Council of Twelve, elected on 7 February and divided equally among representatives of the church, the municipality and the magistracy, gives an indication of the leadership of the League. Benedict has already demonstrated that no social revolution occurred and that League leadership was motivated by a common commitment to catholicism.[119] But another factor united this group: its association with the Guise, the cardinal de Bourbon and their clients. The Council of Twelve was dominated by the Guisard faction.

The four delegates of the First Estate were from the archiepiscopal hierarchy and close to the cardinal de Bourbon: at least two of them owed their elevated position in the hierarchy to the cardinal de Bourbon.[120] The representatives of the magistracy were dominated by the Bauquemare: Jean and Jacques de Bauquemare were both appointed to the council. In the preceding months their presence in the Guise orbit had been consolidated by the development of affective ties. Jean de Bauquemare's sister-in-law, la dame de Sainte-Beuve, had become the mistress of the chevalier d'Aumale, the idol of the Rouennais insurgents, in 1588.[121] Regnault du Pont, the third representative of the magistracy and the only activist to be cited in accounts of the Day of the Barricades, had been a creditor of the duc d'Aumale and was related to the Bauquemare.[122] Servants of the Guise and the cardinal de Bourbon were among the bourgeois representatives. One of them, Michel de Bornes, began his career as secretary to the cardinal de Guise, living in his master's residence in the hôtel de Fécamp in Rouen, and later acting as a tax farmer for local religious foundations. He came from a mercantile family with a presence in municipal office and service and financial links to the cardinals de Guise and de Bourbon.[123] Charles Guérould, also elected to the Council of Twelve, was a cousin of the Bornes and *receveur-général* of the cardinal de Bourbon.[124] The motivation of these men combined sincere religious conviction and dedication to the service of

[119] Benedict, *Rouen during the Wars of Religion*, pp. 180–2.

[120] Pierre and Claude Sécard were nephews of Adam, vicar-general of the cardinal and a prominent figure in the ultra-catholic faction from the 1550s.

[121] By his marriage to Anne de Hacqueville, daughter of André, *maître d'hôtel* of the cardinal de Guise in the 1570s and later *président* of the leaguer parlement of Paris in 1591, Jean de Bauquemare became a nephew of the Hennequin: BN Dossiers Bleus 343 fo. 16v.

[122] AN 300 AP I 223, 21 Jan 1579. Du Pont may have been related to Jean du Pont, *avocat*, and charged with the accounts of Aumale's legal council in 1563: ADSM 1ER 1589, 1563. He was an uncle of the Bauquemare brothers: Frondeville, *Conseillers*, pp. 316.

[123] Michel was *receveur* of the priory of Bonne Nouvelles and *trésorier* of the provincial Estates in the 1580s: ADSM 2E1 930, 3 Sep 1587; 934, 14 Jun 1588; AN MC VIII 383 fo. 1023, Nov 1578. In 1584 Michel's brother, Charles, was *procureur* and *receveur-général* of Fécamp; on his death in 1588 he was owed 8,000 *écus* by the cardinal de Guise. He was also *receveur des deniers communs* of the city: ADSM 2E1 922, 6 Jun 1584; 926, last Oct 1586; 930, 1 Sep 1587.

[124] *Délibérations de la ville de Rouen*, p. 249.

their patrons. The *Conseil de l'Union* appointed Guise clients to key positions in the new regime.[125]

The informal networks of power were as important as formal structures to the functioning of the regime. Some prominent League supporters, such as the Hallé, raised troops for the League and continued to lend money to the Guise, but they remained aloof from a formal role. Real power derived from relationships of service and mutual obligation, and herein lay the influence that the Hallé and other wealthy bourgeois and officers exercised in the new regime. Superficially, the election of the Council of Twelve was undertaken by a 'grand nombre du peuple' in the hôtel de ville on 7 February. In fact, the event was stage-managed. The meeting was presided over by Jean Colombel, *procureur* of the town, a neighbour and former servant of the Hallé, and Jean de Bauquemare acted as *porte parole* of the 'people'.[126]

The limits of popular participation can be seen in the election of a new bourgeois captain: 'et depuys sur la clameur du peuple et signamment de la quartier de Beauvoisine rassemblé, a esté nommé Me Jehan de la Faye, le jeune, avocat, laquelle election a esté faict entendre au peuple qui l'a eue agréable'.[127] The insistence of the Beauvoisine quarter on the election of a lawyer is unsurprising, since it was the location of the parlement and *bailliage* and where the majority of lawyers and magistrates lived. It was home to prominent members of the League leadership, such as the Hallé and the Bauquemare, and League activists proliferated among the ranks of its militia unit. The election of La Faye as captain of the city is emblematic of the central role played by the legal profession in the League in Rouen and elsewhere. His credit undoubtedly reflected his role as an activist, but his status was also derived from his family's services to the Roncherolles. His father, Robert, *bailli* of the barony of Pont-Saint-Pierre, presumably spent much of his time in the Roncherolles residence in Rouen, near the parlement. Like many other Roncherolles clients, the La Faye had strong connections with Aumale.[128] If the 'people' were able to exercise an independent voice, and this is by no means certain, their choice fell on a man intimately associated with the ultra-catholic faction in Normandy.

The League party in Rouen was nourished from its inception by the strong links it established with the Sixteen in Paris. The Guise acted as the main focus of allegiance but were not the only bridge: the Catholic League was fortified by supra-provincial networks below the level of the great aristocracy. The Hennequin were among the most important Guisard families in the Parisian League, although

[125] *Conseiller* Jean-Maximilien Limoges, of a long-established client family, was nominated as commissioner for the seizure of heretics' property: ADSM 1B 699, 15 Jun 1589.

[126] ADSM 1er Meubles 13 Apr 1568.

[127] *Délibérations de la ville de Rouen*, p. 252.

[128] Frondeville, *Conseillers du parlement, 1594–1640*, pp. 53–5. Robert's uterine brother, Nicholas, served in the *vénerie du roi* under the duc d'Aumale. Nicholas's kinsman through his marriage also served in the *vénerie*; his son was *vicomte* of Pont-Saint-Pierre and related by marriage to men in the *ordonnance* company of the duke.

their precise relationship to the radical Sixteen is a matter of debate.[129] With a ramified lineage, their involvement in the League was not confined to Paris; one branch was involved in the League in their native city of Troyes. Less well known are their contacts to the Rouen League leadership. In April 1585, during the first revolt of the League princes, Jérôme Hennequin visited Rouen, ostensibly on business for his abbey of Bernay. However, his *receveur* was Michel de Bornes, who was pursuing the abbey's affairs in conjunction with Regnault du Pont. Thus two members of the Rouennais League council, one of whom was a key figure during the Day of the Barricades, were agents of Hennequin. Since Bornes was also an agent of the cardinal de Guise it seems inconceivable that, at the height of the 1585 princely revolt, the current political and religious troubles were not discussed.[130]

The League leadership in Rouen was thus largely drawn from families with close personal or financial ties to the Guise and the cardinal de Bourbon: the Bornes were servants and financiers, the Hallé creditors. The Bauquemare were motivated by their disillusion with royal policy, but their ties to the Guise went back to the 1540s. The events of February 1589 consisted of a popular uprising instigated and exploited by the Guisard faction. Control of the city militia was crucial, and success was cemented by the arrival of the Moy family and the expulsion of Carrouges. This seizure of power was sanctioned by stage-managed popular acclaim. The ideology of popular sovereignty had been invoked by Guisard insurgents in 1588 to legitimise urban coups, notably in Troyes. The building of barricades in Rouen indicates a greater degree of popular participation than in many Picard and Champenois towns, but Rouen was unlike Paris, which witnessed a spontaneous mass uprising, in that the coup depended on superior organisation and royalist ineffectiveness.[131] The Rouen leaguers were motivated by a desire to defend both the catholic religion and the city against the threat of a royalist *démarche*, but their success was due to a secret organisation, communication system and command structure. Complex networks of kinship and affinal solidarity ensured that religious anxiety was channelled into effective political action.

[129] Descimon, *Qui étaient les Seize?*, pp. 157–8.
[130] ADSM 2E1 2284, last Apr 1585.
[131] For comparisons: Carroll, 'The Guise affinity and popular protest'.

7

The Catholic League in Normandy: hegemony and decline

Traditional interpretations of the League have stressed its internal contradictions, its inherent fragility and the inevitability of its defeat: the parochial and anti-tax basis of the League is juxtaposed with the logistical demands of warfare and centralised military command.[1] Evidence for the essential contradiction of League ideology abounds, but the commonplace interpretation elucidates only partially the history and structure of the League because it concentrates on institutional and formal mechanisms of power and takes no account of the informal power structures of patronage and clientage. The current orthodoxy has deep historical roots; it derives from a tradition of history that views the triumph of 'absolute monarchy' and the rise of bureaucratic centralism as inevitable. In France, this tradition has been reinforced by the nationalist myth surrounding Henri de Navarre.

It is possible to re-interpret the League by inverting traditional assumptions: the League proved to be remarkably resilient in spite of its internal tensions and the weight of forces ranged against it. The death of Henri III in August 1589 was a severe blow to the unity of the royalists. Royalist propaganda and Bourbon hagiography cannot conceal the fact that Henri de Navarre's battlefield victories were hollow, that the royalists too were racked by internal divisions and that Navarre's regime after 1594 was unstable. His victory and continued hold on the throne were achieved by converting to catholicism, by buying off his opponents and by guaranteeing the privileges and rights of League towns. His continued grip on power was assured by sensitivity to the interests of the provincial and urban elites and by deference to his former aristocratic enemies.

A fresh interpretation of the Catholic League demands a sceptical analysis of accounts both contemporary and modern, and the distortions of hindsight must be corrected. As the major theatre of the war, Normandy has been comparatively well served by historical scholarship: the facts have been established and the narrative requires little amendment.[2] It is not intended to recount the familiar story of

[1] This interpretation has become an orthodoxy in English textbooks: Salmon, *Society in crisis*, p. 273; D. Parker, *The making of French absolutism* (London, 1983), pp. 33–4.

[2] The standard narrative, *La ligue en Normandie* by Estaintot, is largely reconstructed from royalist sources. Benedict, *Rouen during the wars of Religion* is excellent on the internal divisions within the city and the great siege of 1591–2. Lloyd, *The Rouen campaign*, is the best account of the military campaign.

royalist victories in 1589 and 1590, the heroic League defence of Rouen in the winter of 1591–2 and the capitulation of Normandy in 1594. However, it is necessary to re-examine the basis of and motivation for League support in light of the preponderant influence of the Guise affinity; to adumbrate the strengths of the League armies despite an apparently continuous tide of royalist success; and finally to account for the eventual atrophy of the League and for the fate of the Guise affinity in Normandy.

THE GUISE AND POPULAR REVOLT IN LOWER NORMANDY

Conventionally interpreted as an urban movement aided by elements of the nobility, historians have displayed little inclination to investigate the evidence of support for the League in rural areas. The history of the peasant revolt of the *gautiers* which, according to most historians, flared sporadically during the 1580s before being crushed by the royalists in April 1589, is no exception. That urban institutions bequeath relatively abundant archival sources is undoubtedly the major reason for the concentration of attention on the towns, and the reconstruction of peasant revolt is only possible where judicial archives survive. The sources exploited by Bercé for the seventeenth century do not survive for sixteenth-century Normandy.[3] However, a careful examination of the Rouennais judicial archives, the official correspondence and the local notarial archives permits an investigation of the rural roots of League support.

The origins of the peasant disturbances in lower Normandy lie in the recruitment of troops by the duc d'Anjou in his duchy of Alençon from the late 1570s, and after his death by the League. The intolerable behaviour of the unpaid soldiery was exacerbated by unprecedented levels of taxation and a series of disastrous harvests: in 1587 there was a subsistence crisis.[4] As early as 1579 Henri III ordered the arrest of peasants around Caen who refused to pay the *taille*.[5] Royal correspondence concerning the state of the lower Norman peasantry during the 1580s survives in abundance. The king was sympathetic to the distress of the peasants and furious at the ineffectiveness of attempts to control the soldiery. But his interest in the plight of his subjects was due less to compassion than to his dependence on Norman taxes to support his ailing regime. He also feared the spread of the revolt to the Beauce and the Chartrain.[6] The motivations and nature of the revolt were clear:

> ung nombre de villaiges et paroisses de Normandie, dont plusieurs sont dedans le destroict du gouvernement de la Basse Normandie, soubz umbre qu'ilz se plaignent d'estre quelques foys travaillez du tenement de champs des gens de guerre, se sont unys ensemble pour avoir

[3] Y.-M. Bercé, *Histoire des Croquants* (2 vols., Geneva, 1974).

[4] Benedict, *Rouen during the Wars of Religion*, pp. 172–4.

[5] *Lettres de Henri III*, iv, pp. 140, 177,

[6] BN MS Fr 3306 fo. 22, Henri to the governors of Normandy, Chenonceaux, 9 Sep 1584; 3302 fo. 73, Henri to Carrouges, Paris, 19 Feb 1588; BN NA Fr 1219 fo. 36, Henri III to Longaunay, Blois, 25 May 1581; fo. 46, Henri III to d'O, Paris, 15 Nov 1582; 6646 fo. 161, Brulart to Longaunay, Rouen, 6 Jul 1588; fo. 164, Epernon to Longaunay, Rouen, 28 Jul 1588.

une commune intelligence et s'entre secourir les ungs les autres, à l'encontre des dictes troupes de gens de guerre . . . et s'opposer a eulx de toutes leurs forces et moiens.[7]

The depredations of troops and the lawlessness of noble retinues was a common feature of sixteenth-century life and the criminal records of the parlement of Rouen provide harrowing evidence of the vulnerability of the rural population. For example, in early 1589 fourteen-year-old Catherine Dupuis was seized by soldiers, dressed in military attire to disguise her and clandestinely abducted from her neighbourhood.[8] The surviving contemporary accounts of the plight of the peasantry were written by members of the elite and refer to instances of organisation and resistance only rarely. Documentary evidence demonstrates the effectiveness of the peasant response. In the summer of 1585 the villagers of Moustier-Hubert and environs, situated between Orbec and Vimoutiers, attacked a company of dragoons; they killed some of the soldiers, stole their horses and plundered their baggage, and they even stripped the captain of his plate, his commission and his ensign.[9]

The strains imposed by soldiers on a single community may be illustrated by the case of the parish of Verneusses in September 1583. The parishioners appointed representatives to collect money demanded by the king for the upkeep of royal troops passing through the locality. That this sum was a form of *étape* or *contribution* levied in addition to the *taille* is confirmed by the tenor of the document, which stated that the cash was being paid in order to prevent soldiers from lodging in the parish.[10] Had the villagers been supporting only royal troops these *contributions* would have proved a temporary inconvenience. The rapacity of the soldiers was part of a wider problem recognised by the provincial Estates. Increasing rates of mortality and impoverishment made it difficult to meet ordinary tax demands.[11] Royal troops were less of a problem than those ill-paid and undisciplined regiments raised by commission of the duc d'Anjou and later the League. The activities of the League soldiery are illuminated by the testimony of Valentine de Vallée: 'Estant aux trouppes du captaine Thomas, voulant passer par Orbec, les habitantz feirent résistance, où il y en eut quelques-ungs des ditz habitans, jusques au nombre de trois ou quatre, de tuéz.'[12] In July 1588 the peasants were better organised, as Vallée, in the regiment of Adrien des Buaz, sieur des Noyers:

passant par un village nommé la petite haye [in the vicinity of Montreuil] il feu poursuivi par plusieurs paisantz estantz du nombre de quatre ou cinq mil qui voudroient deffaire led. sieur des Noyers et ses trouppes lequel, ayant été poursuivy prez de huit ou neuf lieus et que tousjours le nombre desd. paisantz croissoit en taschant à l'encercler pour faire un carnage de lui et des siens, feu contraint par leur importunite de se mect en deffence dont y en eu quelques uns tuez et blessez et n'en ne peut dire le nombre.[13]

7 *Papiers de Hervé de Longaunay*, p. 14.
8 ADSM 1B 3215, 21 Apr 1589.
9 ADSM 1B 3200, 20 Jul 1585.
10 ADE 4E29/3, 25 Sep 1583.
11 *Cahiers des Etats de Normandie sous le règne de Henri III*, ii, pp. 6, 38, 43, 66, 71, 193, 201, 231, 253.
12 Floquet, *Histoire du privilège de Saint-Romain*, ii, p. 439.
13 ADSM G 2176 fos. 307–11.

As peasant insurgency became endemic so royal government began to break down. In the summer of 1585 royal officers of the *vicomté* were unable to hold the Montreuil assizes because of an assembly of up to 2,000 peasants. The assizes were a common and convenient focal point, not least as the venue of publication of royal orders for the arrest of malefactors and the sequestration of the tax defaulters' property.[14]

The epicentre of the revolt was the pays d'Ouche, but there was nothing unique about its distress: other regions of northern France also suffered from the depredations of troops but the Ouche had a tradition of resistance to unwelcome outsiders. In 1548 a number of villages, including La Chappelle-Gauthier from which the *gautiers* took their name, had revolted against the imposition of the *gabelle*, and in 1563 peasants in the region of Bernay attacked the protestant army under admiral Coligny.[15] Historians of peasant revolt in early modern France and England have drawn attention to the role played by the variants of topography and modes of agricultural exploitation in determining rural social structure and thus the character of peasant protest and violence.[16] No comprehensive analysis of these variants is possible here, but in the sixteenth century the Ouche was not a region of productive farmland; it was wooded and hilly *bocage* country characterised by dispersed settlement – a poor and backward region of a rich province. The margin between subsistence and famine was smaller than in the wealthy lowlands of upper Normandy and the Bessin, and the local economy was less able to endure the burdens upon it.[17] The administrative structure of the province disadvantaged the Ouche and the rest of lower Normandy. Influential lords were able to influence the partition of taxes to favour their own peasants, and the majority of the great lordships were in upper Normandy.[18] Only the duchy of Alençon could rival the great upper Norman seigneuries, but its administration under the king's brother was chaotic and it was also used as a staging post and winter quarters for Anjou's campaigns in the Low Countries. The revolt spread over the ducal *vicomtés* of Bernay and Montreuil. A single family, the Duclos, dominated local office and abused its positions. The family was involved in both local royal taxation and levying *contributions* on peasants.[19]

14 ADSM 1B 3201, 9 Aug 1585.

15 *Catalogue des actes de Henri II*, ii, p. 76.

16 The typology was first proposed for France by R. Mousnier, *Fureurs paysannes* (Paris, 1967), pp. 334, and developed in C. S. L. Davies, 'Peasant revolt in France and England: a comparison', *Agricultural History Review*, 21 (1973), 122–34. The literature on England is vast, a starting point being D. Underdown, *Revel, riot and rebellion: popular politics and culture in England, 1603–1660* (Oxford, 1985).

17 A. Frémont, *Atlas et géographie de la Normandie* (Paris, 1977), pp. 184–5, 193.

18 That certain *élections* were better at avoiding taxation than others can be seen in records of the *bureau des finances*: ADSM C 1116 fos. 20, 56–7, 137. There is some evidence to suggest that the *généralité* of Caen, whose jurisdiction covered the Ouche, was overtaxed by the provincial estates compared to Rouen. For the complaint of the *trésorier-général* of Caen in 1579: BN MS Fr 15905 fo. 33, Novince to Bellièvre, Caen, 15 Mar 1579.

19 Jean Duclos was *élu* of Bernay in 1580 before becoming *lieutenant-général* of the *vicomtés* of Montreuil and Bernay. In 1580 he travelled to Rouen in order to sell *rentes* for one of Anjou's followers and his

Local royal officers and nobles were unable or unwilling to confront the peasants. Finally, in October 1586, the king ordered the parlement to investigate the disturbances and during the next two months a handful of magistrates and Carrouges, governor of Rouen, despite resistance, had imprisoned fourteen suspects in the *conciergerie* in Rouen.[20] Although neither the charges against them nor their interrogations survive, the names inscribed in the criminal registers provide a unique insight into the peasant leadership. The status of eight of the men is given: a nobleman, two priests, a blacksmith, a poulterer, a barber-surgeon, a royal sergeant and a lawyer. Most of them came from Montreuil and its surrounding villages. The notarial archives demonstrate that these men were *coqs du village* whose families knew one another through business deals and credit networks; they signed their names fluently on contracts, bought and sold small properties and lent money; and they controlled the local church. Some of them had pretensions to nobility and their business dealings show that they possessed both the wealth and the confidence to challenge the local gentry and protect their interests at law. Tiennot Agis, a poulterer, appears at first glance to be the rebel with the lowest status. In fact, the Agis were among the most significant families of Montreuil.[21] Two members of the Champion family were arrested. Peasant leader and priest Guillaume Champion held the living of two parishes; one of his brothers possessed a *sieurie*; another lent money to the local gentry. They were chief among those empowered by the parish of Verneusses to collect and pay *contributions* to local troops. During 1585 and 1586 the Champion borrowed 200*l* from another peasant leader, Jean Dereville, barber-surgeon of Montreuil. This cash was not used to purchase land; indeed the family had recently sold property. It is likely that such a large sum was borrowed by the Champion as an advance to soldiers on their village's *contribution*.[22] Jean d'Escorches was the only captive of unambiguous noble status. Three years later he was a leaguer captain, but in 1586 his rebellion was determined by parochial ties: he was a local landowner and representative of the comfortable gentry who either sympathised with or who were pressured into supporting the peasants. His family had

village, Saint-Aubin de Thenney, was a participant in the revolt: ADSM 2E1 361, 3 Oct 1580; 1B 3212, last May 1588. In 1588 he was accused of having ambushed and assaulted a lawyer from Bernay. Gilles, a lawyer, was *receveur du domaine* and imprisoned for an unknown offence in 1586; among his brothers, Richard was *lieutenant-général* of the *bailli* and Jacques was *enquêteur*. Gilles's son, Yves, was a qualified *écuyer* and involved in violent acts as a household officer of the most important local lord, the baron d'Echauffour: ADSM 1B 3205, 19 and 22 Aug 1586; ADE 4E29/4, last May 1585; 4E29/9, 6 Jan 1588; 4E29/8, 16 Jan and 13 Feb 1588.

[20] BN NA Fr 6646 fo. 76, Henri III to Longaunay, Saint-Germain, 12 Oct 1586. Jean Duclos, charged with the arrest of the ringleaders, complained of the 'menaces, rebellions et resistances' of various inhabitants of Montreuil. A list of those arrested is provided in ADSM 1B 3207, 21 Jan, 5 Feb, 19 Feb, 9 Mar 1587.

[21] The name Tiennot, for Etienne, implies bastardy. Pierre Agis had been *vicomte* of Montreuil; his sons Marguerin and Marc were sieurs of Saint-Denis and Jacques was *curé* of la Goulafrière: ADE E 684, 1580; 4E29/8, 22 Feb 1588; 4E29/4, 4 Apr and 24 Jun 1585.

[22] ADE 4E29/3, 25 Jul, 11, 23, 25 Oct 1583; 4E29/4, last Jun, 1 Jul 1585; 4E29/9, 16 Jan 1588; 4E29/8, 7 Mar 1588.

traditionally been at the heart of the following of the Carrouges, and his *amitié* with the governor of Rouen probably contributed to his swift release without punishment.[23] In the event, all the rebel leaders were released after interrogation: the crown interest lay in prompt disbursement of tax arrears, which required the cooperation of the local elites.

The campaigns of 1587 and the political turmoil of 1588 ended any hope of peace, and anarchy continued to prevail in lower Normandy. In the first weeks of January 1588 the king was warned of 'la sollicitation qui est faicte d'aucuns paroisses cy devant associes en Normandie pour entree en nouveau parti'.[24] There was as yet no evidence of collusion with the Catholic League, despite the presence of priests among the leadership. Indeed, the peasants had been offered support by protestant refugees, so the peasant leaders were aware of political developments beyond their immediate locality. Though peasants attacked troops under Elbeuf, it is little indication of their devotion to the king: the crown rather than the Catholic League was blamed for the breakdown of order. As secretary of state Brulart recognised, the people would only end their resistance when they stopped suffering: 'L'affaire la plus urgent en Normandie, c'est de rompre les troupes de M. d'Elbeuf, dont si le plus estoit nettoyé, le peuple qui en a souffert infiny dommaige n'en appelleroit pas.'[25] The support of the *gautiers* for the League in 1589 must be seen in this context. The presence of priests in the leadership suggests that the peasants were aware of the religious cleavages among the elites. But the peasants had more worldly anxieties than either aristocrats or bourgeois: the defence of lives and property. The outbreak of civil war in Normandy in spring 1589 raised the spectre of widespread famine and devastation. Caen had declared for the royalists but Falaise held firm for the League and was invested by the duc de Montpensier on 18 April. Lower Normandy was to be the main theatre of the nascent provincial conflict.

Only royalist accounts of the 1589 campaign survive, so it is necessary to treat sceptically the written sources: De Thou even claimed that the *gautiers* drank the blood of their victims.[26] But the outline of events is clear. In his attempt to relieve Falaise the League commander, Brissac, was able to make common cause with the *gautiers* even though his troops had been among the peasants' worst oppressors. He was heavily outnumbered, but the *gautiers*' 5,000 reversed the balance. The League army advanced and camped south of Falaise but its forces were divided among three villages and Montpensier was able to attack units piecemeal and, despite some fierce fighting, had crushed resistance by 22 April, whereupon Brissac retreated.

[23] In 1565 Jean and three members of his close family served in the company of Carrouges and his extended kinship ties confirm his association with the Le Veneur. In 1555 his cousin Jacques had received a dowry of 4,500*l*. Both Jean and his relative Thomas d'Escorches served in the League armies: *Bulletin de la Société Historique de l'Orne*, 32 (1913), p. 343; 36 (1917), p. 369; ADSM 2E1 941, 22 Dec 1590; 942, 10 Feb 1591.

[24] BN MS Fr 3302 fo. 65, Henri III to Carrouges, Paris, 21 Jan 1588.

[25] *Papiers de Hervé de Longaunay*, p. 20.

[26] De Thou, x, p. 601.

According to royalist propaganda, Montpensier then moved east in a mopping-up operation, dispersing the remaining peasant units and seizing Bernay, Vimoutiers and the fortified village of Chapelle-Gauthier. The League had been badly weakened and the *gautiers* crushed.[27]

In fact, the royalist victory was more apparent than real. Montpensier could not complete the reduction of the *gautier* strongholds in the Ouche and after his withdrawal to Caen a League garrison returned to Bernay. Brissac had in fact succeeded in his objective of raising the siege of Falaise.[28] Cooperation between League and peasants continued in May when Mayenne entered Normandy. Following his capture of Alençon thousands of peasants rallied to him – though he haughtily disdained their help.[29] The following year a leaguer captain was leading a peasant force, the *Lipans*, in the region of Domfront, Bellême and Séez, and peasants also supported the League in the Cotentin.[30] Peasant bands continued to pose a threat to royalist dominance in lower Normandy and their continued existence made tax collection difficult. In 1594, 'la recette des tailles de l'Election de Bernay n'a pu se faire à cause de la revolte des gaultiers'.[31]

As the League soldiery had been among the worst violators of the lower Norman peasantry, the motivation of the peasants requires explanation. Recent research in both England and France suggests that rural political culture was not unsophisticated. In his analysis of peasant participation in the redaction of the *cahiers* for the Estates-General of 1576, Constant concluded that high politics had an impact in even the most isolated villages of the Bassin Parisien. Villages contained large numbers of zealous catholic peasants concerned about religious reform, and to a lesser extent the reform of justice and finance.[32] Norman peasants were well aware of the threat posed by royalist troops and they were determined to prevent them from advancing from their stronghold in the region of Caen. Religious conscience and the collective memory of the protestant nobility's depredations in the region combined to motivate the peasants: the royalist army included several notable local

[27] Later histories rely largely on the brief contemporary royalist pamphlet: *Extrait d'une missive . . . contenant le Discours de la défaite des Ligueurs et Gottiers . . . par le Duc de Montpensier, le 22 d'Avril 1589* (n.p. 1589); De Thou, x, pp. 600–3; Palma Cayet, *Chronologie novenaire*, Michaud and Poujoulat, 1st ser., xii, p. 126; Davila, *Historie of the civill warres*, pp. 794–8.

[28] Falaise eventually fell to the main royal army in January 1590: A. Meriel, *Le gouvernement de Falaise de 1574 à 1590* (Alençon, 1883), pp. 8, 16. In mid-June 1589 the League garrison of Bernay captured Broglie, situated in the Ouche: Charpillon, *Dictionnaire historique de l'Eure*, i, p. 606.

[29] Report of 25,000 peasants is surely an exaggeration: BN MS Fr 23296 fo. 22.

[30] M. Odolant-Desnos, *Mémoires historiques sur la ville d'Alençon et sur ses seigneurs* (2 vols., Alençon, 1787), ii, p. 353. In the Cotentin, leaguer nobles were elected as captains of parishes: ADSM 1B 5719, 4 Sep 1589.

[31] *Inventaire-Sommaire des archives départementales de la Seine-Inférieure, antérieures à 1790*, series C and D, C. de Robillard de Beaurepaire, ed. (Paris, 1864), i, p. 197.

[32] J.-M. Constant, 'Le langage politique paysan en 1576: les cahiers de doléances des bailliages de Chartres et de Troyes', in R. Chartier and D. Richet, *Représentation et vouloir politique autour des Etats-Généraux de 1614* (Paris, 1982). On late-medieval England, see S. Justice, *Writing and rebellion: England in 1381* (Berkeley, 1994); I. Harvey, 'Was there popular politics in fifteenth-century England?' in R. Britnell and A. Pollard, eds., *The McFarlane legacy* (Stroud, 1995).

protestants, many of whom had reputations for iconoclasm and violence. The local clergy had played a prominent part in the revolt since its inception, and during the campaign of spring 1589 priests and clerics from the episcopal town of Séez were to be found in the ranks of the peasant army.[33]

More difficult to determine is the precise relationship between the peasants and the nobles commanded by Brissac. The Bessin had already witnessed the mustering of tenants by a noble, who had: 'contraint les gens du pays d'achapter et avoir armes, faisant faire monstre de six sepmaines en six sepmaines, combien qu'il ne soit nécessaire: et soubs couleur . . . fait encourir au pauvre peuple de grands fraiz, peines et travaux'.[34] In contrast, the *gautiers* elected their own commanders. Their forces were organised into bands under 'captains' and led by petty nobles, such as the tenants commanded by their lord, the sieur de Saint-Sulpice. Those noblemen who fulfilled their conventional obligation to protect and lead their peasants commanded widespread support. Following Saint-Sulpice's murder by a royalist noblemen in 1589, 120 peasants from the nearby village of Chandei led by two priests and two 'captains' (a professional soldier and a blacksmith) exacted a bloody revenge, butchering the perpetrator and his servant. According to the remission obtained by the villagers, they had taken up arms 'par la sollicitation de plusieurs seigneurs et capitaines qui leur faisoient croire que c'estoit pour la deffence de la religion catholique'.[35] It is suggestive that Guise clients were locally significant: Chandei was a fief of the Nollent, the most significant servants of the duc d'Aumale in the region, and Laurens d'Escambosc, sieur de Boisroger, one of the captains of the *gautiers*, had been part of a large subgroup of lower Normans in Elbeuf's company in 1579.[36]

The nobles commanded by Brissac can be divided into two distinct groups. The first consisted of men of the provincial *noblesse seconde*, such as Jacques de Moy and Jean de Longchamps, representing the nucleus of Guise men at the heart of the League leadership.[37] To this group may be added the local lord Jacques de Beaulieu, sieur de Guerquesalles, whose receipt of a marriage gift of 10,000*l* in cash suggests a man of provincial significance; his marriage ties to the Vipart indicate

[33] The royal army included among others the comte de Montgommery, a local landowner and the most important Norman protestant. After the defeat of the peasants, the local clergy interceded with Montpensier for mercy: Davila, *Historie of the civill warres*, pp. 748–9; 798.

[34] *Cahiers des Etats de Normandie sous le règne de Henri III*, ii, p. 131.

[35] Floquet, *Histoire du privilège de Saint-Romain*, i, p. 437–8.

[36] Richard Nollent, seigneur de Chandei, was a leaguer. His younger brothers Jacques and Julien had served in Aumale's company in the 1570s and his nephew, Jean, was a League captain and household officer of Aumale: ADSM 2E1 943 11 Jul 1591; 946, 10 Mar 1593; 2010, 12 Feb 1589; 1B 703, 18 Jan 1593. Boisroger was near Montreuil. The Escambosc were close to the Vieuxpont, an important local family and longstanding clients of the Guise. Auffay de Vieuxpont had been a fellow archer of Laurens d'Escambosc, whose father witnessed contracts for the Vieuxpont: A. Le Maréchal, *Documents tirées des minutes du tabellionage de Rugles* (Rouen, 1901), p. 45; Meriel, *Le gouvernement de Falaise*, p. 7.

[37] Isaac de Briqueville, seigneur d'Auzebosc, whose father had headed the ultra-catholic faction in 1562, raised peasants in the Caux: Asseline, *Les antiquitez et chroniques de Dieppe*, ii, pp. 14.

that he was also at the core of Guise affinity.[38] A second group came from the Ouche gentry. These men led elements of the peasants during the 1589 campaign and two of them were captured by Montpensier, but they were not primarily motivated by a desire to protect their tenants: they had histories of violent behaviour in common, often perpetrated against those peasants whom they now led. Their conduct during the 1580s requires closer examination.

Jacques Le Cornu, sieur de Roconval, Tanneguy Le Gris, baron d'Echauffour, and François de La Vigne, baron de Tubeuf, were all involved in the excesses perpetrated in lower Normandy. All three appear in the criminal records of the parlement. At the time of the 1589 revolt Le Cornu was a fugitive from justice. Convicted contumaciously of the capital crime of *rapt* (abduction) in 1587, he had defied the royal authorities from his fortified château situated in the Ouche before joining the League army.[39] Le Gris held the barony of Montreuil and was thus well aware of the plight of his tenants, but a dispute with his mother over his inheritance in 1586 led him and his retinue to perpetrate violent acts on his family's property. In 1589 his arrest was ordered for ravaging the lands of his royalist uncle.[40] Similarly, La Vigne had been accused of acts of violence while serving in the League army in 1585.[41]

Le Cornu's attachment to the League displays all the signs of opportunism and the absence of ideological commitment which characterised many leaguer nobles; his actions demonstrate the egocentric nature of noble mentalities governed by notions of honour and self-esteem. The motives of his two colleagues-in-arms had little more to do with the benevolent protection of local peasants. Perhaps, as so often in peasant revolts, they were forced into action by their own tenants, but this seems unlikely since the world of neither man was restricted to the Ouche: both La Vigne and Le Gris were barons with lands scattered all over lower Normandy. Their family connections and military careers provide an alternative explanation and suggest that religion as well as martial atavism played a part in their calculations. Both men were intimately associated with the catholic affinity of Tanneguy Le Veneur, seigneur de Carrouges, the most influential local lord.[42] Carrouges's attachment to the Guise in the 1550s and 1560s was anomalous in a region where protestantism among the nobility was pervasive and where many catholic families tended to be moderates. As governor of Rouen, Carrouges attempted to preserve his position by remaining on good terms with both moderate and radical catholics.

38 Both Moy and Longchamp held land in the vicinity but their respective power bases were in upper Normandy and the pays d'Auge. The dowry due to Beaulieu on his marriage was paid by Nicholas Vipart in 1585, in the presence of the prior of Bec for the cardinal de Guise: *Inventaire-Sommaire des archives de l'Eure*, ser. E, p. 205.

39 ADSM 1B 3206, 16 Sep 1586; 3209, 23 Jun 1587; 5536, 23 Jul 1587; 3213, 28 Jul 1588.

40 ADSM 1B 3205, 19 Aug 1586; 3206, 2 Dec 1586; Charpillon, *Dictionnaire historique de l'Eure*, ii, p. 553.

41 ADSM 1B 3200, 3 Jun 1585.

42 Le Gris's uncle was lieutenant of the Le Veneur company during the 1580s, and it is likely he was named after Le Veneur. François de La Vigne had served as *guidon* in the Le Veneur company from 1563 to 1567 and three members of the Le Cornu family were serving in the same company in 1581.

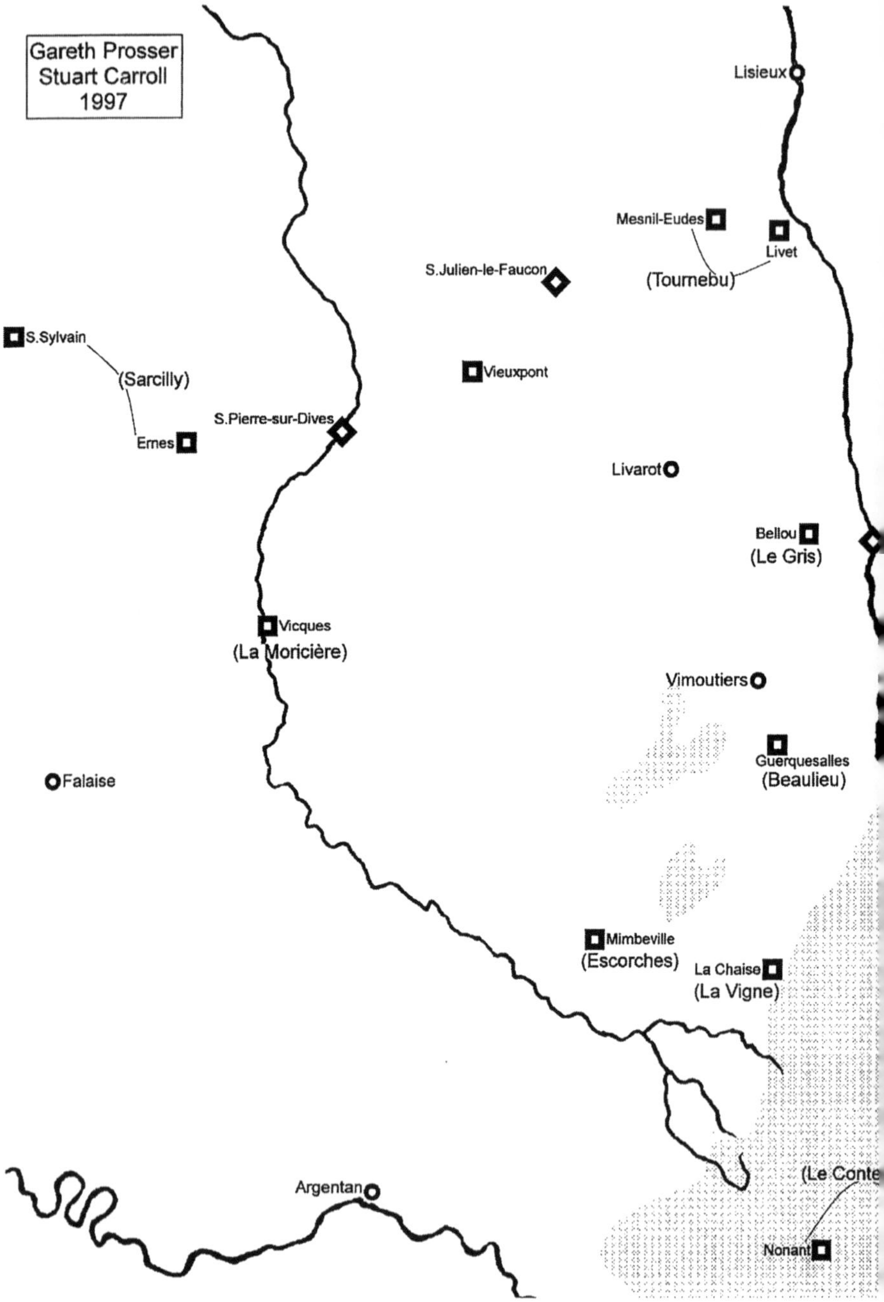
Gareth Prosser
Stuart Carroll
1997
Lisieux
Mesnil-Eudes
Livet
(Tournebu)
S.Julien-le-Faucon
S.Sylvain
(Sarcilly)
Ernes
Vieuxpont
S.Pierre-sur-Dives
Livarot
Bellou
(Le Gris)
Vicques
(La Moricière)
Vimoutiers
Guerquesalles
(Beaulieu)
Falaise
Mimbeville
(Escorches)
La Chaise
(La Vigne)
Argentan
Nonant

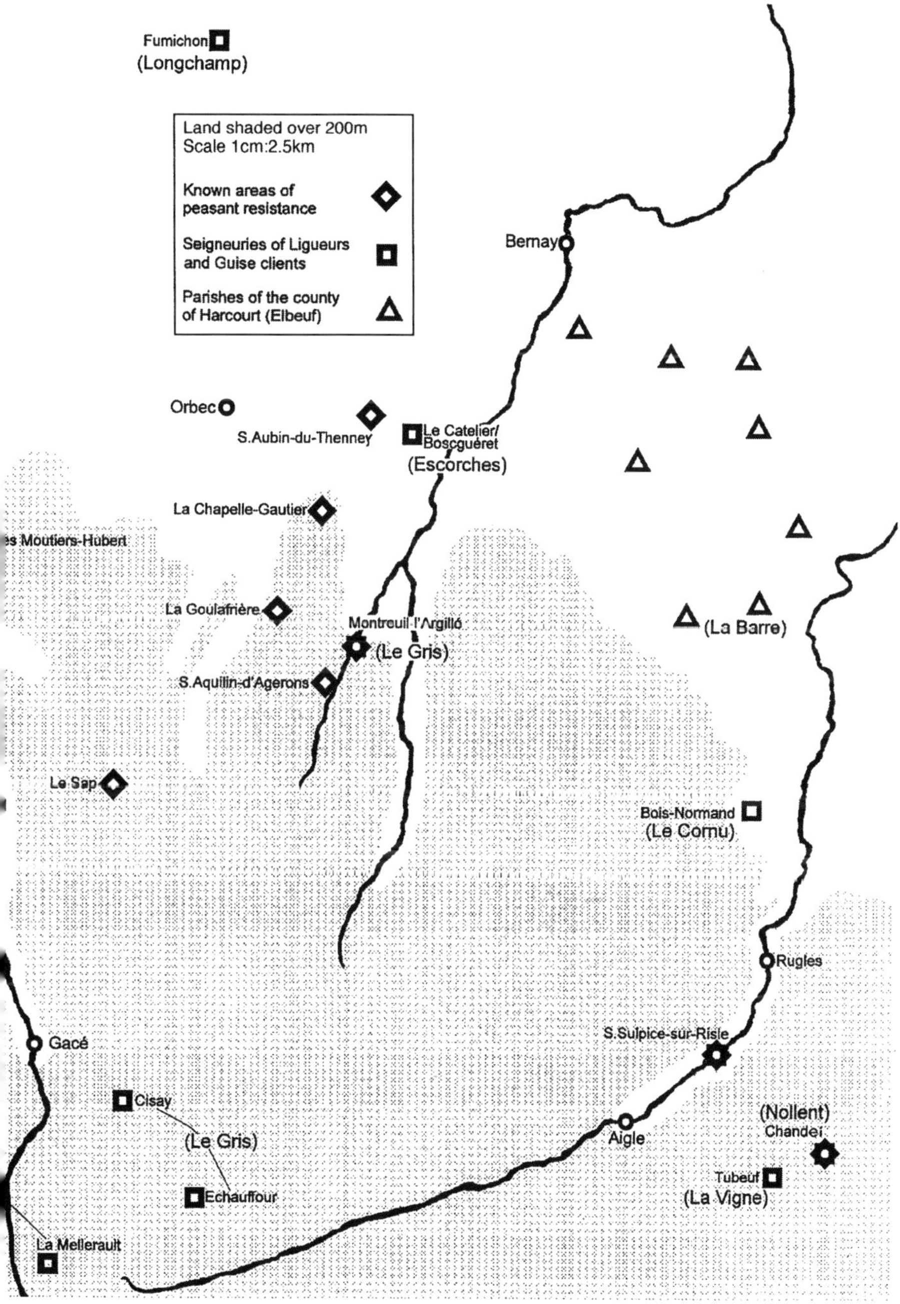

Map 8 The pays d'Ouche in 1589: peasant revolt and the Guise affinity

But his inability to support the League more openly during the 1580s alienated those of his followers, and his son, who had more radical religious opinions. As the cleavage in political society widened in the 1580s, so Carrouges's room for manoeuvre diminished. The atrophy of his traditional lower Norman strength during the 1580s was one consequence of his indecision. During the 1580s men like La Vigne joined the League in defiance of their former patron, and when nobles were forced to choose sides in early 1589 the Le Veneur affinity was torn apart. On the fall of Rouen, the Le Veneur, once at the pinnacle of Norman society, retreated into obscurity. Despite abundant evidence of the predatory nature and the materialist objectives of noble strategy, many noblemen were also inspired to fight for the League for ideological reasons: the lust for honours and plunder did not preclude sincere religious beliefs. In upper Normandy the Moy had capitalised on religious anxieties by supporting the League, and it was they who effectively took power in upper Normandy following the League coup.

SOLIDARITY AND DISSENSION: RELIGIOUS VALUES AND FAMILY STRATEGIES DURING THE CIVIL WAR

The vitality of the infant League derived from its appeal to urban communities and from the strength and size of the Guise affinity in Normandy. Norman nobles were an important component of the League's field armies. At the battle of Senlis in May 1589 they were only surpassed in importance by the Picards, largely drawn into Aumale's service after 1576.[43] The strongholds of the Guise in Normandy, places which were unable to withstand a serious siege but from which the surrounding locality could be controlled, were at the disposal of the League. Lillebonne, Fécamp, Eu, Aumale and Harcourt, commanded by trustworthy servants, ensured the control of large areas of upper Normandy.[44] When Jacques Blondel was ordered to maintain Lillebonne for the League, there was an appeal not to religious sentiment nor to the authority of the *Conseil de l'Union*; instead the language invoked the 'ennemys de la patrye et de Monsieur le duc d'Elbeuf'.[45] Guise clients and leaguer captains were rapidly promoted to or confirmed in local offices by the League and commissioned to raise troops. In upper Normandy the political elite, both urban and rural, was largely pro-League, and only Dieppe held out for the royalists. In lower Normandy, where the Guise landholding interest and clientele were smaller, the former adherents of the duc d'Anjou were important elements of support.[46]

43 A. Bernier, *Monumens inédits de l'histoire de France* (Paris and Senlis, 1835), p. 178.

44 Guillaume de L'Isle, *gentilhomme ordinaire de la chambre* of the duc d'Elbeuf, was captain of the château of Harcourt in 1588. Hellot, *Fécamp au temps de la Ligue*, p. 5; ADSM 6F 11, Recueil des capitaines de Normandie, 12 Sep 1588.

45 ADSM 1E 462, Moy to Blondel, 23 Feb 1589.

46 The examples are numerous: Pierre de Rouxel, seigneur de Médavy, was the son of a major servant of the duke. He was governor of Argentan and Verneuil, and *bailli* of Alençon. His father-in-law, the

Despite the relative strength of the royalists in this region, Caen's security was threatened when the main royalist field army was not campaigning in the province. Until his death besieging Pontorson in September 1590, the League commander in lower Normandy, François de La Moricière, sieur de Vicques, waged a successful campaign against the duc de Montpensier from his base in the Cotentin, supported by the bishop of Avranches who held out against the royalists until February 1591. Royal control of lower Normandy remained tenuous: in 1591 eleven League strongholds remained in the Avranchin and the Mortainais, and it took until the end of 1592 to complete the subjugation of the Cotentin. The mainstay of the League forces in the region was drawn from the Guise clientele: the bishop of Avranches was the brother of the former chief secretary of the duc de Guise, and the Orglandes, who provided a number of captains, had served the house of Lorraine in the late fifteenth and early sixteenth centuries. Even in the distant Cotentin, Mayenne took care to foster the existing ties of *amitié* by writing personally to minor nobles urging them to muster for the cause: 'avecq le plus grand nombre de vos amys que vous pourrez'.[47]

In upper Normandy, the advent of the Catholic League guaranteed the dominance of the Guise, their clients and *amis*. The greatest beneficiaries were the Moy. Jean de Moy, already vice-admiral and lieutenant-general in the province, became *de facto* governor of Rouen on the departure of Carrouges, head of the *Conseil de l'Union* and, in the absence of a suitable princely candidate, effective governor of Normandy for the League. Following his brief flirtation with protestantism in 1562, he had maintained a stance of uncompromising catholicism and close alliance with the ultra-catholic princes. In 1589 only Le Havre, held by Villars, and Dieppe, held by the royalists, lay outside his authority in upper Normandy. His younger brother, Jacques, continued as his lieutenant in upper Normandy and as captain of Honfleur. His cousin, Nicolas de Moy, sieur de Vereins, who had been instrumental in the fall of Rouen, was appointed by Mayenne to the *Conseil de l'Union* in Rouen and rewarded with the *grand maîtrise des eaux et fôrets* of Normandy; in July 1589 he was appointed *bailli* of Gisors.[48] The elevation of the Moy was reward for the exceptional services they had performed for the cause. During the Day of the Barricades in Paris, Nicholas's younger brother, François, sieur de Richebourg,

seigneur de Fervaques, loved by d'Anjou and hated by Henri III, was lieutenant-general for the League in Burgundy. In upper Normandy former household officers of Anjou, such as Jean de La Haye-Chantelou and Antoine de Mascarel, accepted commands for the League.

47 'Lettre écrit par le duc de Mayenne à Jean du Saussay, sieur de Montsurvent, Paris, 8 Dec 1589', *Bulletin de la Société de l'Histoire de Normandie* (1870–1), p. 367. The bishop of Avranches, François Péricard, was aided by his brother Odard; he had brothers sitting on the *Conseil de l'Union* in both Paris and Rouen. The brothers Pierre, Charles and François d'Orglandes were League captains in the Cotentin and contributed to the defence of Avranches. Their brothers-in-law, Jean du Saussay and Jean de Pierrepont-Etienville, were also League captains: Chenaye-Desbois, xv, p. 206; A. Delalande *Histoire des guerres de religion dans la Manche* (Paris and Valognes, 1844), pp. 164, 177.

48 ACR A 20 fo. 410, 4 Mar 1589; ADSM 1B 94, 1 Jul 1589; C 1231, 15 Mar 1589. In addition, Charles de Moy, sieur de Boschion, was captain of Château Gaillard in 1591: ADSM 1B 703, 5 Apr 1591.

had been among the handful of noble insurgents who had battled with the Swiss on the pont Saint-Michel. In 1589 Richebourg was rewarded with the office of lieutenant-general of the League artillery.[49]

The relationship between the Moy and the Guise was mutually beneficial and symbiotic; it was a partnership which defended the catholic faith and elevated both families to new heights. The emotional strength of this 'affinity' was drawn on common religious principles and was fostered by ties of sociability and service. In 1585 the affective ties were strengthened by the marriage of Henri de Lorraine, comte de Chaligny and younger brother of the duc de Mercoeur, to Claude de Moy, heiress of the senior line of the house of Moy. Her dowry included Norman lands, making Henri the fourth member of the house of Lorraine with lands in the province. When Mayenne entered Rouen in February 1589 accompanied by the Moy and Chaligny, his retinue symbolised the Norman associations of the house of Lorraine.[50]

In 1589, the Norman affinity of the Guise turned out in substantial numbers but, in order to galvanise this support and to make sure that it was not ephemeral, the presence of a prince of the house of Lorraine was crucial – his court acting as a focus for the aspirations and the desire of the nobility to serve and be rewarded. The prime candidate for the governorship, the duc d'Elbeuf, was arrested at Blois and held to ransom, not gaining his liberty until 1593. Without an obvious princely candidate, like Aumale in Picardy, positions of authority became the object of factional squabbling. Serious cleavages soon divided the regime's leadership.

The Moy hegemony brought neither stability nor military success: the defeat of the *gautiers* was followed by the victories of Henri de Navarre at Arques (21 September 1589) and Ivry (14 March 1590). These reverses were compounded by royalist plots to seize Rouen. There were internal divisions in Rouen and raising taxes proved contentious – difficulties exacerbated by listless leadership.[51] Jean de Moy was over sixty and decrepit: in November 1589 he was unable to sign documents because of illness. Others had to preside at the *Conseil de l'Union* in Rouen, 'duquel estoit chef le sieur de la mailleraye mais n'y pouvoit le plus souvent vacquer à cause de son indisposition'.[52] Long before his death in October 1591 he had ceased to be the ascendant political and military figure. His family's political and social ascendancy proved to be ephemeral due to the deaths of its senior males: François, sieur de Richebourg, died in 1589 and Jacques, seigneur de Pierrecourt,

[49] BN MS Fr 32369 fo. 270; Pièces Originales 2078 fo. 102.

[50] ACR A 20, 4 Mar 1589; Rodière and Vallée, *La maison de Moy*, p. 61.

[51] The tensions in Rouen are related by both Benedict and Lloyd. Benedict ignores the role of the Moy in the League and Lloyd's account contains many errors. The Roncherolles were closely allied to the Moy, but only one member of the Roncherolles held military office in the province. The family served the League in senior positions outside Normandy: Pierre was governor of Abbeville and François sat on the *Conseil Général de l'Union* in Paris and was lieutenant-general of the Ile de France. Charles de Roncherolles was governor of Vernon until its fall to the royalists in 1590: E. Meyer, *Histoire de la ville de Vernon* (2 vols., Les Andelys, 1874–6), i, pp. 220–1.

[52] ADSM 2E1 2290, 6 Nov 1589; 1B 103, fo. 196.

died the following year. The feud between the Moy and Villars is emblematic of the dissension within the League leadership. Despite Villars's adherence to the League, the Moy had long distrusted him as an interloper in the Caux, where they had traditionally held the lieutenant-generalcy. Villars's growing authority and local credit were confirmed in November 1589 when he killed Nicolas de Moy, possibly in a duel. The reputation of the Moy was further tarnished in February 1590, when the château in Rouen was temporarily seized by royalists.[53]

Following the defeat at Ivry in March, a siege of Rouen became increasingly likely, so Mayenne dispatched his trusted Burgundian lieutenant, Jean de Saulx-Tavannes to Rouen – a move disastrous in the face of Norman suspicion of the outsider. His initial titles of lieutenant-general of Normandy and captain of Rouen were vague and inevitably led to squabbles with Moy and Villars. His attempts to impose his authority in Rouen led to accusations of interference by both the civilian and military institutions, 'disans qu'il est estranger et qu'il ne respecte assez la noblesse'.[54]

It was not Tavannes who benefited from the decline of the Moy family but Villars. Youthful and energetic, he succeeded Jean de Moy's late brother as lieutenant-general of the *bailliage* of the Caux. The power base of the Moy family was reduced to Jean's intermittent appearance as head of the *Conseil de l'Union*, and Tavannes was ousted in the summer of 1591.[55] Villars's rise to power was undoubtedly due to his ability to build a power base in the Caux from his governorship of Le Havre. When Mayenne visited Rouen in the summer of 1591, Villars deployed fifteen ships and 1,500 men outside the city, threatening to defect if Tavannes was not removed as governor. A ruthless man, therefore, who had already killed one of his Moy enemies and was not above threatening his subordinates at Lillebonne: 'je vous asseure que au moindre inconvenience qui adviendra Je le feray tomber sur vos testes'.[56]

Villars's single-mindedness and talent were valuable in preparations for the defence of the city, but did not depend on an individual.[57] Villars had no landed interest in Normandy and his kinship connections, though powerful, were of little significance to most Normans. His household remained largely Provençal in composition.[58] The short passage of time between his appointment as commander and

[53] Bouquet, *Documents concernant l'histoire de Neufchâtel-en-Bray*, p. 70.

[54] ACR A 20, 23 Apr 1591. For the conflicts in Rouen: Lloyd, *The Rouen campaign*, pp. 132–7.

[55] On the death of Carrouges in 1592, Villars was granted the governorship of Rouen, which Moy had exercised only *de facto* since the League coup in the city: ADSM 1B 702, 12 Oct 1590.

[56] ADSM 1E 462, Villars to the inhabitants of Lillebonne, 19 Jun 1589.

[57] He had supported the Rouennais in their conflicts with Tavannes and after his appointment he worked closely with the authorities to prepare for its defence. However, military operations meant that the power of the governor grew in relation to the *Conseil de l'Union* and Villars came to dominate the League as governor and admiral of Normandy after the siege: Benedict, *Rouen during the Wars of Religion*, pp. 209–32.

[58] Villars's household can be reconstructed from the notarial archives. At the siege of Rouen his household contained only one identifiable Norman: Valdory, 'Relation', p. 12.

the royalist investment of the city suggests that much of the strengthening of the defences had already been realised. Villars's remarkable rise to power is to be explained by the composition of the differing groupings that defended Rouen.

Villars had been appointed governor of Le Havre as recently as 1584. His rapid rise to prominence can thus be ascribed to negative factors: to many within the city elite he represented the only alternative to the ageing Moy and the interfering Tavannes. But to the upper Norman nobility Villars was an exemplar of good lordship. His growing local credit was based on martial prowess and the nobility were eager to serve a man of honour. Followers of the Moy began to enter his service at the beginning of the civil war, a response to the inability of the Moy to provide leadership.[59] The series of deaths suffered by the Moy and the vitality displayed by Villars ensured that many clients transferred allegiance to Villars, thus raising his credit throughout the province. Satisfied by the confirmation of offices, it is possible that Jean de Moy himself came to accept Villars's position.[60] In the event, he continued to serve the League and remained in Rouen until his death on the eve of its investment by the royalists. His following continued to form an essential component of the garrison after his death. Villars's incorporation of the Moy affinity was one of the factors which contributed to the successful resistance of Rouen.

The internal divisions and external pressure placed immense burdens on the League. As positions became indefensible so defections occurred, making a royalist victory seem inevitable.[61] The tenacity of the League in spite of its torpid leadership and military defeats has traditionally been ascribed either to Spanish support or to the inability of Navarre to capitalise on his victories. Neither of these factors played a part in the siege of Rouen, and historians have therefore focused on the military and organisational skills of Villars, working in conjunction with the city authorities. Though Villars was overall commander he neither wielded absolute authority nor possessed a sufficient following to defend the city.[62] Certainly the English forces aiding Navarre were supremely confident about the prospects of a quick victory.[63] The motives of the defenders of the city and the solidarities which preserved the League despite its defeats and its fractious structure require further analysis.

[59] For example, his lieutenant in the Caux, Charles de Goutimesnil, sieur de Boisrozé, had formerly been the lieutenant of Moy's company.

[60] The decline of their traditional Cauchois power base was partially offset by the confirmation of other offices *en survivance*. After the killing of his father by Villars, Léonor de Moy was confirmed as the *grand maître des eaux et fôrets*; on his deathbed Jean de Moy was permitted to resign the vice-admiralty to his nephew: ADSM 1B 700, 9 Jan 1590; 2E1 934, 21 Sep 1591. It is possible that an accommodation between the two families was brokered, since Léonor de Moy was serving under Villars's command in February 1591: ADSM 1B 703, 22 Feb 1591.

[61] Charles de Fouilleuse, a longstanding client of the duc d'Elbeuf, was captain of Gisors for the royalists by March 1590.

[62] Though Villars was governor of Rouen, the captaincies of the Vieux Palais, the château and the Fort Sainte-Catherine were not in his gift.

[63] R. B. Wernham ed., *List and analysis of State Papers, foreign series, Elizabeth I* (London, 1964), iii, p. 214.

The defenders of the city numbered 6,000 men composed of indigenous French troops raised and led by the local nobility and supplemented by foreign mercenary units.[64] The presence of so many families associated with the Moy affinity is striking. These men were largely from the Cauchois gentry, some of whom had already transferred their allegiance to Villars as his local credit grew. Even a senior commensal officer of Jean de Moy such as Pierre Sécard was willing to fight for his dead master's most bitter rival. This suggests that nobles were motivated to fight for religious ideals, but were also eager to follow a renowned captain in the hope of augmenting their honour and gaining recognition.[65]

A second group was composed of servants and allies of the Guise, including captains who had led rebel armies under Elbeuf in 1585 and 1588.[66] Household officers of both the duc d'Aumale and the duc d'Elbeuf were prominent in the defence. The latter's council continued to reside in the city during the siege and contributed to the defence. A number of families had followed the Guise since before the Wars of Religion.[67] In addition, magistrates and *noblesse bourgeoise* also took part in the defence. Such wealthy men had close ties to *épée* families; they aspired to aristocratic virtues and often had experience of military affairs. This group did not constitute a distinct entity, for many were linked to their *épée* brothers-in-arms by common ties of service. One example of a *robin* League captain and client of the Guise is Adrien Le Doux, the son of Aumale's *bailli* of Ivry. At the time of the siege he was *président* of the *présidial* of Evreux and he was rewarded by Mayenne with elevation to the office of *conseiller* in the parlement.[68]

The Guise and Moy followings therefore played a crucial role in the defence of

[64] Lloyd, *The Rouen campaign*, p. 141. Valdory, 'Relation', provides a list of noblemen, pp. 2–12.

[65] For a list of muster rolls consulted: appendix C. It should be pointed out that Valdory often gives the family name only, making identification of individuals difficult. This list is certainly an underestimate of the numbers who had served the Moy: Etienne de Rouil, sieur de La Rouillière, man-at-arms (1581); Jacques du Tot, man-at-arms (1574–81); Pierre Calmesnil, man-at arms (1570); Charles Sevestre, archer (1574) and man-at-arms (1581); Jacques d'Argence, man-at-arms (1581); Jean du Corde, man-at-arms of Elbeuf (1579) and Moy (1581); and finally Louis de Braques, sieur de Biennais, a man-at-arms of the seigneur de Pierrecourt in 1569. Other families intimately associated with the Moy and present among the defenders included the Goutimesnil, Coutances and Courcy.

[66] Antoine de Bigars, captain of fifty men-at-arms, Jacques Le Conte, captain of twenty-six light horse, Jean de La Haye-Chantelou, captain of fifty lances, his son, Philippe, captain of 100 light horse, and Guillaume Perdriel captain of foot, had all served with Elbeuf in the 1580s.

[67] Charles de Sarcilly, sieur d'Ernes, was head of Elbeuf's council in Normandy and Henri des Boves was ensign of the duke's company. The close relationship between the des Boves and the Guise goes back to the 1540s. La Chambre, 'ancien serviteur et domestique de Mons. le duc d'Elleboeuf', was also present. Household officers of the duc d'Aumale from the pays de Caux included Robert de Baillieul, sieur de Blangues, and his younger brother Nicholas, sieur de Drumare. Their relative, Jean, had been an agent of the Guise in 1560. Likewise, André de Vieuxpont's presence in the garrison is another example of the loyal services performed for the Guise by his family since 1562: ADSM 2E1 2293, 3 Jan 1592.

[68] Frondeville, *Conseillers*, p. 649. Among others Georges de La Porte, a leading League captain and *procureur-général* of the parlement, was linked by marriage to the families of the Rouennais bourgeois and financial elite, but he was also closely related to Guise clients among the provincial gentry, such as the Collas: Frondeville, *Présidents*, p. 276.

Rouen. The previous siege of the city in 1562 is instructive in this regard. A well-defended early modern city was difficult to reduce by assault. In 1562, the city of Rouen had fallen swiftly because the Huguenots were unable to rely on the support of sufficient numbers of Norman protestant nobles. Although the city contained many protestants, they were not sufficiently committed to the rebellion, but in 1591 the leaguer nobility turned out in numbers with their retinues to save their provincial capital when it seemed that the League in Normandy, which was riddled with internal divisions, was close to collapse. Within the city the defenders could also rely on much larger numbers of committed inhabitants.

Religious conscience and allegiance to one's lord are motivational factors too often neglected in accounts of the League. A number of local minor commanders showed a remarkable degree of loyalty. Jean de Longchamps was forced to yield Lisieux to Navarre in December 1589. He was confined and given a month to decide which side he should join. He refused service with Navarre and joined the garrison of Rouen. Longchamps' actions show that, even as the League appeared to be disintegrating into factional squabbling, the bonds of affinity, conscience and mutual interest were stronger than some historians have acknowledged.[69] Nevertheless, evidence of nobles' opportunism and indifference to religious and political loyalty is too strong to ignore. Valentine de Vallée's deposition for his remission for murder recounts how his captain, Adrien des Buaz, was persuaded to join the League in 1585 by a relative, Jean d'Hémery-Villiers. By 1588 Villiers was a royalist, he was made a *maître des requêtes*, was part of the fugitive court and was a leading figure in the king's negotiations with the Rouennais.[70] In the summer of 1588, after Henri III had made his peace with the League and agreed to abide by the terms of the Edict of Union, des Buaz and Villiers met by chance (at least according to the testimony) at a tavern near Argentan.[71] In the ensuing argument Vallée, while 'protecting' his master, killed Villiers. In a bizarre ending Mayenne and Brissac each wrote to the cathedral chapter of Rouen in support of opposing sides. Both used religion as the central foundation of their argument; Mayenne pleaded against clemency for des Buaz and Vallée, under the *privilège* of Saint-Romain, thus:

> Messieurs Je croy que vous n'ignorez poinct ny la facon de laquelle a esté assassiné le feu sieur de Villiers ny la condition de ceux qui ont commis ceste meschanetté lesquelz encores qu'ilz feussent ses nepveuz sont toutefois recogneuz pour huguenots . . . Vostre privilege est trop sainct et sacré pour estre mis en mains de personnes tant indignes et si contraires a nostre religion . . . empeschez que ses huguenotz jouissent le privilege de l'eglise dont ils ne sont pas.[72]

69 Wernham, ed., *List and analysis of State Papers, foreign series, Elizabeth I*, i, p. 266.

70 Beaurepaire, ed., *Séjour de Henri III à Rouen*, pp. xxiv–v.

71 Villiers was killed between July and October 1588 and therefore the d'Hémery-Villiers still alive in 1589, referred to in *DBF*, xvii, p. 890, must be a relative.

72 ADSM G 3498, 24 May 1589. The inventory of the Archives Départementales wrongly attributes this letter to the duc d'Elbeuf and the date of the letter was 1589 and not 1588: Floquet, *Histoire du privilège de Saint-Romain*, i, pp. 378–9, ii, 439–40.

The favourable letter written by the comte de Brissac is completely different: 'Jay tousjours recommande le sieur des Noyers [des Buaz] tres zelé a nostre religion . . . m'ayant assisté en plusieurs expeditions . . . contre les ennemys de la foi.'[73] These letters were written in a highly stylised way in order to appeal to the religious prejudices of the canons of the cathedral. Mayenne pressed for condemnation because Villiers' brother was one of his servants, but his argument seemed so dubious and ill-considered – there being no evidence that the accused were protestants – that Brissac's was successful. Apart from the complexities of personal relationships in this case it is evident that the future leader of the League was capable of trying to manipulate religious emotions, often in the crudest and most cynical manner. He was not unique in pursuing such a strategy for his own ends. Religious loyalties divided many families, but many lineages exploited confessional divisions. In the 1580s, it had been difficult to arrest Calvinist soldiers when 'une bonne partie d'entreulx se sont refuggiez avec leurs chevaulx et armes en maisons de leurs parens et amys catholliques'.[74] Those men who had previously fought for Anjou in the Low Countries only to transfer their allegiances to the League were not primarily motivated by religious principles.

One factor which historians have largely ignored when considering the strength of the League is the solidarity engendered by horizontal ties of kinship, vicinage, sociability and local patriotism. These factors were relevant to all social groups supporting the League: nobles, peasants, office holders and the urban bourgeoisie. Nobles' actions were shaped largely by a martial and chivalrous ethos, manifested in the desire for recognition and honour through service. Bonds of loyalty and kinship developed through marriage and common service in the Guise affinity in the preceding decades. During the civil war comradeship and kinship were even more important to the survival of a noble house. Some of the most important marriages uniting client families took place between 1585 and 1593. Appendix F lists twelve unions contracted between prominent leaguer families during this period and undoubtedly there were others. In the period of political and religious instability after 1585, marriage reinforced existing solidarities and forged closer relations among Guise clients, many of whom raised and led troops for the League. The most significant alliances, such as that between the des Boves and the Vieuxpont, united families who had served the Guise for generations and whose commitment to the ultra-catholic cause can be traced back to the early 1560s. In

[73] ADSM G 3498, Brissac to the cathedral chapter, Argentan, 1589.

[74] BN MS Fr 3309 fo. 77, Henri III to Carrouges, Paris, 18 Nov 1585. Among the League captains with protestant kinsman was Jacques Le Conte, baron de Nonant. He had previously been an officer in Elbeuf's army. His mother, uncles and aunts were all protestants and, after the death of his father in 1581, his mother erected a chapel in the barony. Huguenots came to worship from all over the *bailliage* of Alençon which caused disturbances and conflict, no chapel having stood there before: C. Vérel, *Le marquisat de Nonant* (Alençon, 1908), p. 46; 'Une paroisse rural du duché d'Alençon: Saint-Germain de Clairfeuille', *Bulletin de la Société Historique et Archéologique de l'Orne*, 12 (1893), pp. 297–8.

addition, at least two unions cemented the ties between Guise supporters in the parlement and in the *noblesse d'épée*.

Marriage contracts and witness lists are the most valuable documents for establishing patterns of sociability and interdependence among the League leadership in Normandy. But the surviving manuscripts elucidate only partially the myriad bonds forged by kinship and sociability which united the League leadership. Evidence of the mundane interaction of members of the Guise family with their Norman clients is fragmentary and has to be inferred by reconstructing households, councils and retinues. Even this evidence pertains only to the senior members of the family and tells us little about the relationship between lord and client beyond the immediate retinue. Documentary evidence for minor members of the Guise family is fragmentary, but it is clear that socialising and interaction among their followers was commonplace. René de Beaumesnil, bastard brother of the duc d'Elbeuf, acted in 1585 as *parrain* of the new bell of the church of Grostheil in conjunction with Anne de Tiercelin, the wife of League captain Antoine de Bigars. Marie de Lorraine, duchesse d'Aumale, though a great Norman aristocrat and sometime lover of Henri III, appears rarely in contemporary narratives of the political events, but the scraps of evidence that survive suggest that she was of immense importance in Norman political society. Unlike her husband who was often in Picardy or in Paris, she was in regular contact with the local elites. She had the leisure to indulge and entertain the Norman nobility in the absence of her husband. In 1578 she took part in the procession of the Puy de Musique in Evreux, an annual religious ceremony, when one of her family's clients, a canon of the cathedral, had been elected as prince of the ceremony. During the League she often resided in Rouen in the absence of her husband, holding court at the abbey of Saint-Ouen.[75]

The marriage between the turncoat Louis de Montgommery and Marie de Bigars in 1593 was the most splendid and the most unusual to take place in Rouen during the League. The lateness of Montgommery's switch to the catholic cause is evidence of the continued vitality of the League. But his wedding is of interest not because of his political conversion – he was not the only member of the Norman provincial elite to join the cause at such a late stage – rather, his conversion from militant protestant to catholic warrior in the space of less than three years further confounds attempts to explain noble motivations purely in terms of confessional solidarity. Most historians have neglected chivalric values as a means of interpreting noble culture during the Wars of Religion and often employ anachronistic nomenclature to describe noble behaviour.[76] All participants in the Wars of the

[75] The prince de Puy, Robert de Quesnel, had been appointed as abbot of Conches in 1560 on the recommendation of Diane de Poitiers: Charpillon, *Dictionnaire historique de l'Eure*, i, pp. 235, 824. Marie, duchesse d'Aumale, was Diane's granddaughter: ADSM 2E1 2290, 3 Feb 1590; 941, 17 Oct 1590, 26 Nov 1590; 942, 11 Feb 1591; 943, 15 Jun 1591 and 11 Jul 1591; 946, 10 and 11 Mar 1593.

[76] 'The nobility developed new codes of honour which allowed them to slaughter each other in senseless bouts of duelling': Parker, *The making of French absolutism*, p. 40.

League shared a common warrior or chivalric culture. The Rouen notarial archives reveal evidence of at least nine ransoms paid between 1589 and 1593, six for royalist prisoners of war. A systematic search of the local archives would reveal more.[77] The capture of a prisoner could be lucrative: Philippe de La Haye-Chantelou was ransomed at 12,000*l* by Sully after his capture at the battle of Ivry. La Haye relied on his Roncherolles kinsmen to meet his obligations and quickly rejoined the ranks of the League. Nobles might also undertake to fight as brothers-in-arms, sharing the profits and the hazards of war. In June 1592 the widow of a League captain challenged the accord reached between her late husband and a comrade 'touchant la donation pretendue avoir este mutuellement faicte entre le feu sieur . . . et luy de leurs bien meubles en quelque chose [qu'ils] peussent concister'.[78] Contemporary commentators often criticised excessive noble behaviour but literary discourse should not be used as evidence for the decadence of chivalric ideals, since the criticism of aristocratic violence and opportunism pre-dates the sixteenth century. Nobles continued to be motivated by such ideals. In 1590 a truce was instituted during the siege of Paris in order that Henri des Boves, baron de Contenan and Robert de Harlay, seigneur de Sancy, distant cousins and 'vrais gentilshommes', could settle their difference honourably using lance, pistol and sword.[79] The ideals of knightly honour and piety were symbolised by the chevalier d'Aumale. In League pamphlets he was portrayed as the virtuous christian warrior and martyr for the holy cause.

Guillaume Valdory's published account of the siege of Rouen should be understood in these terms. He recorded for posterity the deeds, virtues and martial valour of the League nobility, appending an exhaustive list of the valiant defenders of the city. Valdory's oeuvre was not addressed exclusively to the *noblesse d'épée* whose martial aspirations were commonplace in political society, as Valdory's career and status attest. His motives in writing were personal; he was a lawyer turned soldier who, having served as legal counsel to the Guise in Rouen, was eager to ensure that his own martial deeds were recognised. His honour was reflected and augmented by its association with high-status nobles and with the victory of a just cause.[80]

The resistance of the League in the face of the royalist onslaught is also attributable to particularist feeling. The triumph of the League in urban areas in 1588 and 1589 had been partly a reaction against the encroachment of royal power upon local privileges. The principle of local autonomy in League ideology articu-

[77] ADSM 2E1 938, 3 Jan 1589; 941, 12 Nov and 22 Dec 1590; 942, 10 Feb and last May 1591; 943, 19 Sep 1591 and 30 Dec; 945, 30 Dec 1592; 1B 703, 8 Mar 1591. A ransom payment was found in the *tabellionage* of Broglie: ADE 4E/39 7, 1 Apr 1590.

[78] In the accommodation she received only the furniture. Her rival took all the military equipment, jewels and horses, and 1,200 *écus* in arrears of pay: ADSM 2E1 2293, 15 Jun 1592.

[79] Pierre de L'Estoile, *Journal pour le règne de Henri IV*, L.-R. Lefèvre, ed. (2 vols., Paris, 1948, 1958), i, p. 55.

[80] He continued to act as the *procureur* of Elbeuf's standing council in Rouen throughout the League hegemony: ADSM 1B 2153, 5 Aug 1589; 1ER 1940, 6 Mar 1591.

lated an emotional attachment to local identity. Historians have traditionally viewed this particularism as a major weakness of the League, inhibiting strategic coordination. Localities everywhere dreaded the presence of outsiders and foreign troops: the Rouennais feared that the Burgundian, Tavannes, was going to introduce a foreign garrison. Disillusion with the League was increased by reliance on Spanish troops.[81] Paradoxically, provincial patriotism also contributed to the resilience of the League. The army of Henri de Navarre included large contingents of German, English and Gascon heretics. The defence of Rouen was therefore a defence of catholicism and the *patrie* against foreigners. This particularist feeling and Norman separatism are accurately captured by the contemporary memoirs of an ultra-catholic Rouennais cleric who clearly distinguished between 'la Normandie' and the land of the French, the Ile de France:

> Je laisse maintenant à penser lequel c'est de France ou de la Normandie lequel est redevable et le plus tenu l'un à l'autre. Et toutefois, de ce peuple de France, il ne peut sortir une gracieuse parole de sa bouche, qui dise bien des Normands, ni de Normandie. Si est-ce qu'elle est assez grande pour estre mariée à un roi; si elle estoit réduite en royaume; elle croistroit encore.[82]

Particularism was a hindrance to the effectiveness of a supra-provincial military strategy, but regional solidarity was one of the major reasons why Henri de Navarre was unable to follow up his battlefield victories. Unlike Picards, who had little common provincial identity, Normans possessed a strong sense of their own nation and history which was fostered and protected by provincial institutions.[83] The defenders of Rouen were united by affective bonds, by religious conviction and by patriotic sentiment; their crushing defeat of Henri de Navarre forced him to abandon his dreams of victory on the battlefield.

SUBMISSION, DEFEAT AND THE END OF THE GUISE AFFINITY IN NORMANDY?

Rouen was relieved by the duke of Parma on 21 April 1592. Although conditions had become intolerable in the city and Villars had only just been able to hold out, it was a major victory for the League. The new duc de Guise, Charles, and his kinsmen, Mayenne and Aumale, basked in the appreciation of the Rouennais.[84] This, however, proved to be the high point of League fortunes and it was soon faced with a crisis when the inconclusive Estates-General of 1593 failed to find a suitable candidate for the throne. The credibility of the League regime had always

81 Prarond, *La Ligue à Abbeville*, iii, p. 96.

82 'Relation des troubles excités par les calvinistes dans la ville de Rouen', p. 43.

83 In Picardy the *Chambre de conseil des états* had no precedent and it is no surprise that it failed to last more than a few months: F. Pouy, *La chambre du conseil des états de Picardie pendant la Ligue* (Amiens, 1882).

84 Lloyd, *The Rouen campaign*, p. 183. Misgivings about the Spanish forced Parma to camp outside the city.

been undermined by its inability to find a charismatic and viable candidate. The elevation of the ageing cardinal de Bourbon as Charles X had been little more than a stopgap and he perished in royalist captivity in 1590. Economic dislocation and the disintegration of order was compounded by growing mistrust of Spanish influence. Navarre was able to capitalise on this malaise and war-weariness by ceasing the military campaign, attempting to win the support of moderates by abjuring Calvinism (July 1593) and making a virtue of conciliation and negotiation.

It has long been recognised that Navarre's victory was achieved by buying off individual League commanders with both cash and the confirmation of the offices they held. The devastation of the seigneurial economy and the huge debts that captains had run up in order to pay troops meant that, by 1593, only the king could meet the burdensome financial obligations accumulated by the League captains. In Normandy the economy ground to a halt.[85]

By the summer of 1592 Villars had reinforced his position in Normandy when Mayenne made him governor and admiral. Fears about Villars's hegemony were not unfounded as he increasingly undermined the authority of the *Conseil de l'Union*. His ascendancy in Rouen was in contrast to the decentralisation of authority elsewhere. In upper Normandy his subordinates took advantage of the League victory to strengthen their own positions in anticipation of negotiations with Navarre. If Villars was to reach a secret accommodation with Navarre, minor nobles feared being left with nothing but debts and devastated lands. In November 1592, Villars's lieutenant, Charles de Goutimesnil, sieur de Boisrozé, seized Fécamp for himself, beginning a private war with his master for control of the Caux. When Villars signed a truce with the royalists in Dieppe the local League commanders ignored it, intent on building up their own spheres of influence.[86] In December 1592 the disintegration of the League forces into petty baronial armies was such that the parlement had to write to its captains to: 'les inciter de se voyr et avoyr correspondence les ungs avec les autres, quite toutes partialites et divisions qui peuvent estre entre eulx et se joindre de mesme vollonté et affection avec led. seigneur de villars'.[87] Whilst Villars was in Paris with Mayenne, the League captain of Neufchâtel, François de Fontaine-Martel, broke the truce with Dieppe and fighting recommenced. Martel was a good catholic with close links to religious radicals on the *Conseil de l'Union* but his motives for breaking the truce had little to do with his contempt for heresy. A notoriously violent man, he relished the

85 For the economic crisis: Benedict, *Rouen during the Wars of Religion*, p. 226. Upper Normandy suffered heavily for the first time in the Wars of Religion: 'Documents historiques: pillages de gens de guerre, 1589–93', *Bulletin de la Société de l'Histoire de Normandie*, 10 (1909), pp. 242–6. In 1592 François de Fontaine-Martel claimed to have incurred 30,000 *écus* of damage to his land: ADSM 7J 43, 17 Jun 1592.

86 Goutimesnil was not a turncoat: the election for the Estates-General took place and the *Conseil de l'Union* considered him a leaguer: Hellot, *Fécamp au temps de la Ligue*, p. 37; Estainot, *La ligue en Normandie*, pp. 303–5.

87 ADSM 1B 103, 22 Dec 1592. The parlement was also concerned about the pillaging and robberies committed by these troops.

opportunity to promote the interests of his lineage. Having purchased the governorship of Neufchâtel in August 1592 for 8,000*l*, he was determined to secure a good return for his investment by extending the area under his authority. In May 1593 he seized the château of Bacqueville, which belonged to his distant protestant cousins, and in February 1594 he attacked the manor of a fellow League captain. When he finally came to an accommodation with Henri IV in October 1594 he retained the governorship of Neufchâtel and was paid 16,000 *écus*.[88] Even minor League captains were well rewarded by the king. They were granted money from royal revenues in order to meet their debts, usually in the form of arrears to troops under their command, and they were confirmed in their offices.[89] The price that had to be paid to Villars was consequently colossal and it must have been of some relief to Henri when he died in 1595, only months after his submission.[90]

Nevertheless, loyalties were not always easily undermined. Antoine de Bigars, sieur de La Londe, left documents on his death that were collated by his son in 1626, with the help of eye-witnesses who had served under Bigars during the League. This was at a time when the League was viewed as pernicious and families preferred to forget or fabricate the role they had played. Although the memoirs at times exaggerate the role of Bigars in a stylised manner, they glorify and do not try to hide their hero's military prowess in the service of the League, perhaps because they were for private consumption. The narrative dwells on the fact that Bigars felt it dishonourable to sell himself to Henri IV and only submitted when he was totally isolated. He believed: 'Villars qui estoit grandement plein d'ambition, et avoit recogneu que le seigneur de la londe n'avoit faict la guerre que pour la zele de sa religion et qu'au contraire qu'il y avoit dependu une partie de son bien et que tous les autres ne faisoient la guerre que pour leur utilité et profict.'[91] La Londe had thus rejected the overtures of Henri since: 'Je ne traicterez jamais avec mon Roy l'espee à la main' and 'qu'il manqueroit jamais de foy à M. de Mayenne et à sa religion'. He felt loyalty to the Guise and preferred to wait for news of Mayenne's disposition 'de n'estre point acusés de trahison'. In the meantime Villars made his peace and secured the city for the crown. Bigars left Rouen but was contacted by the king and pressed by his relatives at court. Asked to provide troops for service against the Spanish in Flanders he relented and received a commission to raise a company of 100 men-at-arms and twenty-four companies of foot.[92]

[88] Bouquet, ed., *Documents concernant l'histoire de Neufchâtel-en-Bray*, pp. 89, 97. He was accused of a number of assaults and murders before and after the Wars of the League: ADSM 7 J 43, 14 May 1588 and 1612; 1B 3202, 29 Nov 1585; 1B 3215, 13 Apr 1589.

[89] At the reduction of Vernon the seigneur de Rouxel-Médavy was accorded, besides a pension, the offices of *bailli* of Alençon, lieutenant-general of the *bailliage* of Evreux and the governorship of Verneuil, while his father retained the governorship of Argentan. He received 12,000 *écus* to pay the garrison of Vernon, in addition to provision for the payment of arrears to other units under his command from the *aides* of the *élection* of Verneuil: ADSM C 1237 fos. 65–8.

[90] For the benefits accruing to Villars: Benedict, *Rouen during the Wars of Religion*, p. 228.

[91] 'Mémoires d'Antoine de Bigars', p. 34.

[92] *Ibid.*, p. 38.

The disintegration of League forces in Normandy in 1593 and 1594 into competing bands of warlords was indicative of the diffusion of loyalty and the devolution of power. At first glance, the Guise affinity was thus shattered along with the League – the ultra-catholic faction fell into disarray, weakened by the growing cynicism towards religious extremism. The ideological justification for Guise resistance to the monarchy had now been removed and as the League began to collapse the family could no longer satisfy the aspirations of its clients. In fact, the notion of the decline of the Guise is as much a myth as the smooth transition to Bourbon absolutism. The ideological and factional divisions that had contributed to the rise of the League did not disappear following Henri IV's entry into Paris. In Rouen, the parlement continued to be divided by the personal rivalries of the 1580s and it refused to register the Edict of Nantes until 1609. However, Henri's failure to secure the throne by force had been instructive. His successful efforts to undermine the League after the siege of Rouen demonstrate a perceptive assessment of the limits of his military power and the need to be sensitive to the rights of towns and nobles and to the beliefs of catholics.[93] His predecessor had been much more of an innovator and reformer but change generated conflict by impinging on particularist interests. Henri IV displayed the attributes of good lordship. He was a warrior-king unlike his predecessor, whose inability to fight for his crown and whose fanatical personal piety were alien to noble culture. Henri's cautious, conservative and shrewd nature is exhibited in his behaviour towards the house of Lorraine after 1594. His relations with the Aumale and Elbeuf go some way to explaining both his triumph and the fate of Guise power in Normandy.

Charles de Lorraine, duc d'Aumale, was the most unrepentant leaguer in his family. Since 1576 he had built his reputation as head of the League in Picardy and cultivated his affinity accordingly, but the zenith of his authority came after 1589 when he was governor of the province for the League. He spared no expense in pursuit of this important office. As early as April 1588 it was reported that he was running out of money and that all his lands were mortgaged.[94] Whilst he campaigned in Picardy his wife, Marie, looked after the finances as 'sa procuratrice specialle de faire et negocier les faictz et affaires de leur maison'.[95] This included the provision of all offices and the farming and sale of land. At first small parcels of land were sold to placate creditors.[96] By 1594 the financial situation was acute and parts of the seigneury of Boves near Amiens had to be sold.[97] For the duke war meant a serious loss of revenue from his estates, compounded when he sacked Aumale itself as a punishment for submitting too easily to the royalists.[98] His younger brother

[93] The factors which influenced Henri's change of policy are discussed in M. Wolfe, *The conversion of Henri IV* (Cambridge, Mass., 1993), pp. 100–67.

[94] *CSPF*, 1586–8, p. 601.

[95] ADSM 2E1 2003, 13 Nov 1587.

[96] *Ibid.*, 16 Nov 1587. The fief of Guehauville was sold to Christophe Cherie, whose family was closely associated with Guise service, for 1,100 *écus*.

[97] A. Janvier, *Boves et ses seigneurs: étude historique sur la commune de Boves* (Amiens, 1877), p. 172.

[98] Semichon, *Histoire de la ville d'Aumale*, i, p. 308.

found that the revenue from his ecclesiastical benefices was eroded and when he was killed in action in 1591 the abbey of Bec, which was in the hands of the royalists, was granted by Henri IV to one of his supporters.[99] Aumale's losses were partially offset by the fruits of patronage. He was awarded 10,000 *écus* on the sequestrated property of Norman royalists and between June and November 1589 empowered to appoint to five abbeys and one priory.[100] As a provincial governor he promoted the interests of his clients, bestowing on them lands confiscated from protestants in Picardy.[101] The strains of war affected Aumale's affinity. In 1591 Pierre de Roncherolles, governor of Abbeville, was accused by the townsfolk of collaborating with the royalists. Although Roncherolles was acquitted, the duke felt obliged to remove him in order to placate the town.[102] There was a high mortality rate among senior clients of the duke and veterans of the League of 1576. In the space of a few days in 1589 François de Roncherolles and three members of the Tiercelin family were killed. By January 1594 Aumale could still command the support of longstanding clients, but his regime increasingly depended on Spanish troops.[103] Abbeville and Amiens refused to countenance the introduction of foreign troops and when Paris succumbed to Henri IV the Picard towns decided to treat with the king, making Aumale's position untenable. When his Picard power base collapsed, he fled to the Spanish Netherlands, entering Spanish service and dying in Brussels in 1631.

Aumale's exile provides a good example of how Henri IV was able to impose his authority. While the rest of the Guise were handsomely rewarded, Aumale was made an example. There was no *via media* between accommodation and defiance. Charles duc de Guise reached an agreement with the king in November 1594 and Mayenne agreed on a cessation of hostilities on 22 September 1595. Both received generous terms and Guise was granted the governorship of Provence, a province in which he had a landed interest. This was not only a victory against the incumbent and family enemy, Epernon, but also provided a useful base for the pursuit of Guise dynastic interests in Italy. Aumale was offered generous terms by the king but he still refused to submit and was therefore declared guilty of *lèse-majesté* and condemned to death *in absentia*. Aumale soon realised his error and spent the rest of Henri's reign trying to get himself rehabilitated. He and his wife wrote many letters to the king and Montmorency-Damville, the *connétable*.[104]

[99] Porée, *Histoire de l'abbaye du Bec*, ii, p. 355.

[100] ADSM 1B 701, 22 May 1590, letters patent dated August 1589; BN MS Fr 3977 fo. 353, 'Beneffices donnez par le duc de Mayenne despuis le moys de juin 1589 jusques au moys de novembre audict an'.

[101] BN MS Fr 3979 fo. 135, 'Extraict d'un article contenu aux deliberations faictes par M. le duc d'Aumale . . . tenue à Amyens pour pourveoir aux affaires de lad. province . . . Faict à Amyens, le second jour de novembre . . . 1590'.

[102] Prarond, *La Ligue à Abbeville*, ii, pp. 345, 378–86. Roncherolles was paid 3,680 *écus* in compensation by the town but he only resigned when the money was paid in May 1593.

[103] Wernham, ed., *List and analysis of State Papers, foreign series, Elizabeth I*, v, p. 414.

[104] For example, BN MS Fr 2945 fo. 77, Aumale to Henri IV, 1596; 3574 fo. 84, Aumale to Damville,

Henri IV realised the value of such an example to potential malcontents but this does not demonstrate that the Bourbons had 'absolutist' tendencies. In 1595 the parlement of Paris refused to register the royal command calling for the execution of Aumale, and in 1602 the king could still not enforce the condemnation, since the *cour des pairs* failed to meet: 'l'un se disant son allié et ami; les autres alléguaient quelques querelles qui étaient passées entre eux; d'autres mettaient en avant leur indisposition'.[105] In fact, although Henri showed fortitude in withstanding the pressure he was under to grant a pardon, the financial crisis of the Aumale was as important as royal displeasure in ruining the family. When in February 1594 Sully paid a visit to the duchesse d'Aumale, he noted the dilapidated state of the once magnificent château of Anet.[106] Boves was seized in 1606 on behalf of creditors, and in 1609 Ivry was also abandoned to creditors. Financial disaster was compounded by the failure to produce a male heir. In order to accomplish the destruction of the duke, Henri only had to bide his time and undermine him by quartering troops on his lands.[107]

Nevertheless it should not be presumed that Aumale's destruction was inevitable. The duke simply exchanged one master for another, becoming a pensioner of the Spanish king, attending the court of the archdukes in Brussels and leading troops at Amiens against Henri IV in 1597 and at Nieuwpoort against the Dutch in 1600. His new strategy was reflected in the marriages of his daughters: the elder transmitted her father's substantial French inheritance to his kinsman, the duc de Nemours, and the younger wedded Ambrosio Spinola.[108] He remained in contact with his friend and relative the duc de Mercoeur, who expressed the defiant attitude of the house of Lorraine in a letter to Aumale in 1599. Mercoeur alluded to the descent of their family from Charlemagne such that 'personne ne doibt plus doubter ce que vous et les vostres pourrez bien en qualité de ses successeurs remonter sur la mesme throsne' and reconfirmed his commitment to catholicism, demonstrating that his submission to Henri was temporary, and regretting that he had been forced: 'me departir pour quelque temps de l'apparence de mes pretentions sur la Bretagne plustot forcé par le bon sens des envieux de nostre maison que par la justice de leurs armes . . . je me resolus de remettre à une saison plus oportune de reprendre de ce qui m'appartient'.[109] The sentiments expressed in this letter demonstrate the instability of the Bourbon regime. Providentially, the king produced an heir in 1601 and Mercoeur died the following year. And yet the threat

Brussels, 15 Sep 1598; 3832 fo. 83, duchesse d'Aumale to Damville, n.d.; 4766 fo. 240, Aumale to Henri IV, n.d.

105 L'Estoile, *Journal pour le règne de Henri IV*, i, pp. 461–2, ii, p. 71.

106 Sully, *Les oeconomies royales*, D. Buisseret and B. Barbiche, eds. (Paris, 1970–), i, pp. 405–6.

107 Ivry was adjudged to Marie de Luxembourg, widow of the duc de Mercoeur, who had leaned heavily to Aumale. The damage caused by royalist troops at Ivry came to 8,000 *écus*: BN MS Fr 10239 fo. 54, duchesse d'Aumale to Damville, n.d.

108 In 1608 he was governor of Binche and Mariemont: H. Lonchay et al., eds., *Correspondance de la cour d'Espagne sur les affaires des Pays-Bas au XVIIe siècle* (6 vols., Brussels, 1923–37), i, p. 298.

109 BN MS Dupuy 88 fo. 340, Mercoeur to Aumale, La Roquette, 14 Jul 1599.

posed to the king by the Guise had already diminished because the family could never be united as it once had been. In Normandy the decline of the Aumale brought to an end the dominant influence exercised by the house of Lorraine in the province. But influence did not cease altogether as Charles, duc d'Elbeuf, began to establish his branch of the family on an equal footing with that of his cousins. In 1593 he escaped the captivity in which he had been held since the murder of Henri de Guise at Blois. Elbeuf was made League governor of Poitiers but he did not take part in any offensive actions and remained on good terms with the royalist provincial governor of Poitou, even reaching agreement over the division of the *taille*. Negotiators from the town were sent with the consent of the duke to parley with Henri IV, and in June 1594 Poitiers submitted, Elbeuf becoming the first member of his family to yield. He was well rewarded, remaining as governor of Poitiers and receiving a pension of 30,000*l* p.a.[110] The Elbeuf continued to be well treated by the Bourbons. In choosing exile, Aumale forfeited the office of *grand veneur* and the king shrewdly granted it to Elbeuf in addition to the governorship of the Bourbonnais. In 1619 Elbeuf's son married the illegitimate daughter of Henri IV and was made governor of Picardy, demonstrating the confidence placed in the family.[111] Elbeuf's prior links to the protestant leadership were undoubtedly of great benefit in his rehabilitation.

Joseph Bergin has already shown that historians ignore the continuing power and influence of the Guise in the early seventeenth century at their peril.[112] In Normandy, the decline of the Aumale was offset by the resilience of their Elbeuf cousins. In 1605 the duc d'Elbeuf inherited the entire comté of Harcourt on the death of his nephew, Guy-Paul de Coligny, comte de Laval. When the wars of the 1590s came to an end, Elbeuf no longer required the services of a large military retinue and in any case Henri IV was forced to reduce standing companies because of the penury of the crown.[113] The reconstruction of the shattered Norman economy needed local expertise and a standing council to oversee administrative, financial and judicial decisions. This council in Normandy was headed by the duke's wife, Marguerite Chabot, who became the first member of the family to reside continuously at Elbeuf.[114] She was aided in her task by Charles de Sarcilly, *maître d'hôtel* and *intendant* of the duke, who had supervised the duke's affairs and headed his council during his captivity. His prominence as a counsellor reveals the unbroken links between families maintained over generations – he was the son of Jean de Sarcilly and Catherine, *batârde* de Lorraine, who were married before the Wars of Religion began. As the political situation in France became less confrontational so the need for the affinity as an instrument of military power and prestige

110 A. Thibaudeau, *Histoire de Poitou* (3 vols., Niort, 1839–40), iii, p. 121.
111 Anselme, iii, p. 493.
112 Bergin, 'The decline and fall of the House of Guise as an ecclesiastical dynasty'.
113 M. Greengrass, *France in the age of Henri IV* (London, 1984) pp. 182–3.
114 Maille, *Recherches sur Elbeuf*, ii, p. 53.

temporarily declined. Affinities now consisted of smaller military retinues and centred upon the management of the family fortune and the household, as they had before 1562. After the disruption of war, in which documents detailing rights and privileges had been destroyed or their enforcement neglected, seigneurial power had once again to be asserted. Marie ordered her agents to pursue all reliefs owed on noble fiefs 'à toute diligence sans intermission'.[115] The unfortunate Eustache Trevache, the Huguenot *fermier* of Lillebonne, was subject to legal proceedings for having the temerity to flee the Catholic League without having paid the agreed total for the lease, and all his property was confiscated, including a grainhouse he owned at Bolbec.[116] Accords were reached with the *fermiers* about reducing the sums they had to pay, since the war had lowered the expected level of revenue. Eloi Perdrix, the *fermier* of Elbeuf received 900*l* of compensation because of the 'abbeuses desd. terres quil y a esté pillé et robbé par les gens de guerre le nombre de vingt deux chevaux qui sont estimez valoir plus de cinq cents escus'.[117] In 1596 the piece of land called the prairie d'Estelan produced nothing because the 'sieur de boisrozé estant en garnison du chasteau de Lillebonne a toujours jouy de lad. prairie pour l'usage de ses chevaulx sans avoir paye'.[118] The reclaiming and enforcement of rights meant building up and maintaining a judicial clientele in the parlement of Rouen and lesser courts. The duke was soon embroiled in scores of cases. If a vassal did something as simple as to refuse to render an *aveu* for his lands, detailing the dues and obligations he owed, a lengthy court case would ensue.[119]

This reconstruction required the efforts of many servants and the support of clients – a process aided by the duke's position as a provincial governor and *grand veneur*. His social position and prestige under Henri IV was higher than it had been in the 1580s, augmenting his status and increasing the patronage he could dispense. In 1605 he died and was buried at La Saussaye near Elbeuf, a ceremony which placed him beside his ancestor, Jean de Lorraine, comte d'Harcourt, buried there in 1472. Elbeuf thus reinforced the relationship between the house of Lorraine and Normandy. Despite the defeat of the Catholic League, Elbeuf represented both the opportunities for the house of Lorraine under the new regime and the survival of his house as a great Norman lineage.

[115] AN T 199/22 fo. 87.
[116] ADC E 353, 13 Nov 1585; AN T 199/22 fo. 87.
[117] AN T 199/24, Compte, 7 Oct 1597.
[118] ADSM 1E 446, Compte de Lillebonne pour 1596.
[119] ADSM 1E 445, 12 Mar 1604. The defaulters in this case were former leaguer captains, Antoine de Canouville and François de Fontaine-Martel.

Conclusion

The expansion of the Guise affinity in Normandy and elsewhere in northern France was one of the most significant factors determining the course of the Wars of Religion. The rise of Guise power was not a consequence of the political and religious turmoil of the civil wars. Already during the 1550s the family was using its influence at court to extend its power base in Normandy and the Ile de France. Nevertheless, the political and religious instability of the Wars of Religion saw a great expansion of Guise influence in the localities, conforming to the model proposed by historians of a weakened monarchy ceding authority and power to the aristocracy in the provinces. The expansion of the Guise affinity was sustained by two factors. First, the unstable nature of the polity and the fluid nature of factionalism at court engendered insecurity and fear among ruling elites. Magnates desired a strong dynasty which offered opportunities for advancement through service and distributed rewards according to rank and merit.[1] Rarely in favour at court after 1563, the Guise sought to counterbalance declining influence at the centre by bolstering their power in the localities. The cultivation of a provincial power base would have been ineffectual without a second factor which contributed to the unity of the affinity. From the 1560s the Guise became a symbol of the struggle against heresy and a focus for the anxieties of large sections of catholic France. Evidence of Guise popularity among ultra-catholics in Paris in the 1560s suggests that support for the family was confined to a set of shared beliefs, and little attempt was made to exploit popular enthusiasm. Nevertheless, during the period between 1562 and 1577 a profound reordering of political allegiance was occurring in large parts of northern France. Religiously conservative nobles traditionally associated with the Bourbon and the Montmorency followed their consciences and looked towards the Guise for leadership. In some cases, such as the growth of Aumale's influence in Picardy, this was associated with the deliberate distribution of patronage in a specific region. Although the Guise were not directly behind the establishment of the League of Péronne in 1576, the involvement of so many of their clients points to the expansion of Guise influence and support among the provincial ultra-catholic

[1] In contrast to his predecessor's, Henri IV's regime was relatively stable because it was able to assuage the anxieties of its most bitter opponents.

nobility. The 1570s also provide the first tangible evidence of Guise influence among the Third Estate. The martyrdom of François de Guise and the role erroneously attributed to his son in the Saint Bartholomew's Day massacre conjured a seductive image of the Guise as catholic heroes and saviours. The military feats against protestants were fully exploited in pamphlets, especially in the late 1580s. But as early as 1578 the appearance of Guise clients among the Third Estate at the Norman Estates presaged an important but neglected aspect of the appeal of the Guise: their defence of traditional rights and promotion of 'reform'. The popularity of the ultra-catholic cause among the Norman elites was manifested in the caucus of clients elected to the provincial Estates in the 1580s.

This study has widened the horizons of traditional political history by elucidating the relationship between aristocrats, their clients and the wider population. It has attempted to analyse the motives of actors in the political sphere who are usually excluded from the traditional narrative. The current historiographical trend, which distinguishes between the study of aristocratic 'politics' and 'popular' religious mentalities, is misguided. The rise of the Guise affinity can only be understood by studying all groups in political society. The lower orders in towns and in rural areas supported the Catholic League at crucial moments in the period from 1585 to 1589, although they remained beyond the control of the leaguer hierarchy. The duc de Guise was idolised because he conformed to the trope of the virtuous christian warrior, and the ideology of the Catholic League appealed to notions of order and tradition, as well as to the concepts of popular sovereignty and conciliar government by the three Estates.

The existence of a large affinity was not tantamount to the control of a province. The campaigns of the duc d'Aumale in Picardy between 1585 and 1587 are instructive. Though many among both the city elites and the lower orders were sympathetic to the aims of the Catholic League, they were suspicious of any attempt to undermine municipal autonomy and above all feared the entry of soldiers into their communities, whether leaguer or royalist. Only the innovative and provocative policies of Henri III and his tyrannical murder of the duc de Guise finally stirred large numbers of towns into rebellion. Rather than attempting to persuade or negotiate, the king tried to counter leaguer influence in the urban centres of northern France by an aggressive policy of altering municipal constitutions and imposing his own candidates on town councils.[2] His most flagrant breach of municipal autonomy occurred when he introduced troops into Paris in May 1588, precipitating the Day of the Barricades. The Guise and their supporters were able to portray themselves as the defenders of corporate privileges.

The fissuring and atrophy of the Guise affinity in Normandy in the 1590s is at first glance a difficult problem to solve, given the steady accretion of family power and influence in the preceding forty years. It can be partly explained by the strains

[2] For Henri's conflict with Amiens and Troyes in 1586 and 1587: BN MS Fr 3398 fos. 158–69; *Mémoire et livre de famille de Nicolas Dare*, M. Bailly de Barbery, ed. (Troyes, 1886).

imposed by the civil war and the inherent contradictions of the Catholic League, the anti-tax and conciliar ideals of which were rapidly compromised by the need to fund and administer a war. The foundation of the Guise affinity was based on the desire both to serve a prince honourably in the expectation of recognition and to meet the threat of heretics and their 'politique' allies. In the final analysis the power base constructed by the Guise during the Wars of Religion was largely dependent on the commitment and activism of those who followed them, and in the 1590s the diverse constituency of Guise supporters which had united in 1589 against a common enemy dissipated into competing groups. During the War of the League nobles found new avenues for service and material reward and pursued independent strategies. After the war there were new power brokers in Normandy who had risen to positions of authority during the League or who were appointed by Henri IV following the reduction of the province. Religious and patriotic fervour, so crucial to the spread of the League in Normandy, was blunted by the realities of war and the elusiveness of victory.

It is axiomatic to most historians of the period that the religious belief of the Guise is one of the least complicated and elementary issues in an otherwise exasperatingly complex series of factors contributing to the outbreak and intensity of the civil wars. After a brief period in which the cardinal de Lorraine supported limited toleration for political reasons, the family became implacably opposed to protestantism. Garrisson-Estèbe's assertion that the 'Guise dynasty . . . was monolithic in its vigorous defence of catholicism from generation to generation' is emblematic of a wider tendency to reduce the ambiguities and complexities of and fluctuations in family strategy to a clichéd shorthand.[3] As recent research on the massacre of Saint Bartholomew shows, this one-dimensional view conceals a mentality which was dominated not by dogma but a wily defence of family honour and an opportunist and flexible reaction to events. Their enemies recognised this, accusing them now of intolerance and now of hypocrisy, of using their position as heads of the French church for self-aggrandisement and of promoting the Catholic League as a vehicle for the eventual seizure of the throne. As this study has shown, the remorseless desire for recognition and social ascendancy was consistent with sincerely held religious beliefs, which included the desire to reform the church. Not only was the defence of church and furtherance of dynasty not hypocritical and incompatible, family members perceived both interests as synonymous. As the Guise became increasingly identified as the leaders of the ultra-catholic faction, so family honour became associated with the defence of the faith. Thus the preferment of 'politique' enemies at court was both a danger to the wider catholic cause and an affront to the family.

Above all this study has sought to demythologise the Guise by demonstrating the varieties of religious conviction among family members and by showing that the

[3] J. Garrisson-Estèbe, *A history of sixteenth-century France, 1483–1559* (London, 1994; French edn, 1991).

remarkable family unity did not arise from a uniform and rigid obsession with a single strategy or narrow doctrine. Crucially for Norman protestantism the Guise remained on good terms with their Calvinist magnate kinsmen, such as the ducs de Bouillon and de Longueville, who could have provided the credit and leadership so clearly lacking in the province in the early 1560s. During their dispute with the Montmorency, affective ties with Condé were skilfully exploited. The diverging strategies of the branches of Aumale and Elbeuf clearly show the accommodation of differing beliefs and interests within the wider dynastic aims of the house. This was most clearly evident after the peace of Bergerac in 1577 and the temporary abatement of religious passions. Aumale revealed his continuing attachment to militancy by secretly putting himself at the head of the remnants of the outlawed Catholic League. Elbeuf joined his protestant kinsmen and borrowed heavily from protestant investors in his ill-starred adventure with the duc d'Anjou. Guise's military prowess attracted protestant servants, and he opened negotiations with the kings of both Spain and Navarre. Had Henri III produced a male heir during these years and ensured a catholic succession then the weaker blood ties of the second generation may have taken their natural course and undermined family solidarity. In the event, it was the common fear of a protestant heir on the death of Anjou in 1584 that united militants and moderates in the family rather than the altruistic feelings of kinship solidarity or the unyielding commitment to a rigid dogma. The size and power of the affinity in the 1580s was partly due to the fact that service was attractive to a range of catholics with differing sensibilities. The evidence for a correlation between family service and innovative forms of devotion is ambiguous. Guise followers in Paris, such as those who helped to found the Sixteen, were more exposed to the first wave of counter reformation indoctrination than noble and provincial clients. Pierre Séguin, a minor *officier* from Senlis and *contrôleur* of the ducal household, embarked on a life of austerity and contemplation in 1587 because of the 'horreur du chemin qu'il tenoit, voyant qu'il n'estoit pas conforme a celui que Jesus-Christ nous a enseigné et il resolut, estant age d'environ vingt-huit ans d'embrasser une vie suivant laquelle il ne put pas estre surpris en la disgrâce de Dieu.' His Godly piety was probably not typical and more accurately reflects the convictions of clients with a Parisian legal background.[4]

Family solidarity was certainly born of anxiety. After the murder of François de Guise in 1563 family policy was formulated in an atmosphere of bitterness and fear. It was important to present a united front against the combined forces of the protestants and the Montmorency. But fear was not the sole factor in ensuring unity. Without disregarding the pre-eminence of the charismatic and powerful ducal line, the Guise differed from other families in the relative wealth and importance of their cadets. In 1581 the descendants of Claude duc de Guise

[4] Margry, *Pierre Séguin*, p. 23. Many lawyers were both members of the Sixteen and Guise men. Jean de Champhuon, *avocat* and former chancellor of Mary Stuart, undertook a reforming drive at Saint-Séverin in 1589: AN LL 923 fo. 150.

through the male line included four *ducs et pairs*. Serious inheritance disputes, a common cause of dissension, were avoided by judicious and generous provision for cadets. Cadets relied on their higher status kinsmen to broker good marriages, to provide them with substantial marriage gifts and to solicit the king for favours. In short, they depended heavily on the patronage of the elder line. The Guise differed from other families only in that they could draw more heavily on the resources of the church, permitting the equitable division of the temporal inheritance and ensuring that even lay kinsmen had access to church patronage. The importance of the church to the fortunes of the Guise cannot be overstated. But largely overlooked is the complex web of commitments which bound family members in a web of mutual obligation, from the pensions bestowed by the elder line on its kinsmen to the patronage of a common core of client families.

A detailed examination of the beliefs of individual family members is beyond the scope of this study and generalisations about the collective convictions of the family should be undertaken with caution. In Rouen, the family supported and encouraged ultra-catholic militants soon after its fall from power on the death of François II, and in the years following the cardinal de Lorraine's return from Trent it became active in the movement for catholic renewal. Support for the Jesuits, many of whom opposed the Catholic League, was closely associated with dynastic interest, especially the patronage of English catholic exiles. In the 1580s the family promoted diocesan reform initiatives, encouraged penitential processions and pressed for the adoption of the articles of Trent. However, with the exception of the university-educated *dévot* Aumale, the search for the roots of Guise religious belief begins not with the interiorised piety of the counter-reformation but with the matriarch Antoinette de Bourbon.[5] Until her death in 1583 Antoinette exercised an influential role in family affairs and ensured an element of continuity at the heart of the household, raising her children and grandchildren at Joinville. Historians of protestantism have long shown how the predominant role enjoyed by noblewomen in the private sphere helped to shape the religious convictions of their sons and husbands. The austere Antoinette had a profound influence on the attitudes of her offspring and their spouses, and though the intellectual atmosphere at Joinville may have been conservative it was not zealous and fanatical.[6] Only the paucity of the documentation has prevented a closer examination of the role played by the Guise women in the furtherance of dynastic strategy. Like most noblewomen, Antoinette de Bourbon, Anne d'Este and Marguerite Chabot, wife of the duc d'Elbeuf, were closely involved in the running of the estates and household and the management of finances. More remarkable is their prominence in the public sphere. The role played by Henri de Guise's sister, the duchesse de Montpensier, in Paris during the League is well known. Less familiar is the position of his wife, Catherine de Clèves,

[5] Though Aumale's zeal is not in doubt, evidence of a deep inner piety is less forthcoming.

[6] For an overview: G. Viard, 'La religion d'Antoinette de Bourbon, duchesse de Guise', *Les Cahiers Haut-Marnais*, 188–9 (1990), 1–11.

who acted as an intermediary with the Paris Sixteen, or of Marguerite Chabot in supporting her husband's rebellion in Normandy in the 1580s.

In a private interview with Henri de Guise in the early 1570s Montaigne came closer than anyone to understanding the motivations of the Guise and to unravelling the relationship between faith and honour:

> le Duc de Guise . . . avoit fait toutes les avances par ses soins, ses services & par ses assiduités, pour gagner les amitiés du Roi de Navarre; mais qu'ayant reconnu qu'il le jouoit, & qu'après toutes ses démarches, au lieu de son amitié, il n'avoit recontré qu'une haine implacable; il avoit eû recours à la guerre, comme à la dernière ressource, qui pût défendre l'honneur de sa maison contre un ennemi qu'il n'avoit pu gagner; que l'aigreur de ces deux esprits étoit le principe d'une guerre qu'on voyoit aujourd'hui si allumée; que la mort seule de l'un ou de l'autre pouvoit la faire finir; que le Duc ni ceux de sa maison ne se croiroient jamais en sûreté, tant que le Roi de Navarre vivroit; que celui-ci de son côté étoit persuadé qu'il ne pourroit faire valoir son droit à la succession à la couronne pendant la vie du Duc. Pour la Religion, ajoûta-t-il, dont tous les deux font parade, c'este un beau prétexte pour se faire suivre par ceux de leur partie; mais son intérêt ne les touche ni l'un ni l'autre: la crainte d'être abandonné des Protestans empêche seule le Roi de Navarre de rentrer dans la Religion de ses pères, & le Duc ne s'éloigneroit point de la confession d'Ausbourg, que son oncle Charles, Cardinal de Lorraine lui a fait goûter.[7]

The re-examination of political society during the Wars of Religion has only recently begun. Though it has been long recognised that noble followings are fundamental to understanding early modern politics and government, this study is the first to chart the development of an affinity – at its height the most powerful in France – in one region over the span of the entire period of the civil wars. In order to achieve a more profound understanding of sixteenth-century political society its findings need to be supplemented by the investigation of servants, clients and supporters of the Guise in other regions and compared to the structure and composition of rival groupings. A more sophisticated analysis and appraisal of the polity is required. The importance of the interplay between elite conflict and popular confessional anxieties has been established. Further research needs to be undertaken. Many sources still remain unexploited and much work on court faction, provincial affinities and religious discourse remains to be done before the complexities and parameters of sixteenth-century political culture are fully appreciated.

[7] This conversation was reported to de Thou by his friend in 1588: *Mémoires*, Michaud and Poujoulat, 1st ser., xi, pp. 330–1.

Appendix A

Buyers of *rentes* from the ducs dAumale

Buyer	*Status*	*Amount livres*	*Date of purchase*	*Reference*
Gilles Gasquerel	bourgeois merchant	700	11.10.50	ADSM 2E1 304
Jean de Saldaigne	Huguenot merchant	250	17.10.50	ADSM 2E1 304
Robert de La Masure	*conseiller* of the parlement	400	06.11.50	ADSM 2E1 304
Gilles Gasquerel		300	04.09.51	ADSM 2E1 305
Jean Le Febvre d'Escalles	*conseiller* of the parlement	210	07.09.56	ADSM 2E1 313
Chapter of Rouen Cathedral		360	07.09.56	ADSM 2E1 313/323
Simon Baudouin	bourgeois, merchant draper	100	07.09.56	ADSM 2E1 313
Jesse de Bauquemare	*conseiller au Grand Conseil*	100	06.10.56	ADSM 2E1 313/323
Nicholas Romé	bourgeois, *secrétaire du roi*	200	25.11.58	ADSM 2E1 318
Robert de Rouvres	*trésorier* of the abbey of Fécamp	200	31.05.62	AN 300 AP I 223
Jesse de Bauquemare		360	10.01.65	ADSM 2E1 334, 13.01.67
Jacques Declainville	bourgeois	400	10.01.65	ADSM 2E1 334, 11.01.67
Jean Le Febvre d'Escalles		420	10.01.65	ADSM 2E1 334, 12.01.67
George Langlois	bourgeois, *secrétaire du roi*	600	19.02.65	ADSM 2E1 329
Nicholas Romé		400	16.07.65	ADSM 2E1 330
Catherine Le Gras	widow of Nicolas La Vielle	100	17.11.65	ADSM 2E1 331
Vincent Puchot	bourgeois merchant	400	28.11.65	ADSM 2E1 331
Jean du Moucel	Huguenot, *contrôleur de la chancellerie*	900	1565	AN 300 AP I 223, 22.04.70

Children and widow of Vincent Puchot		1,000	17.09.66	ADSM 2E1 332
François de Runes	Huguenot noblemen	1,800	10.03.67	AN 300 AP I 223, 22.04.70
Marie de La Haye	widow of Vincent Puchot	600	14.09.70	ADSM 2E1 341
Guillaume Auber	*écuyer*	600	14.09.70	ADSM 2E1 341
Marc-Antoine Bigot	militia captain for League	300	14.09.70	ADSM 2E1 341
Jean Bethencourt	*docteur*	200	14.09.70	ADSM 2E1 341
Jacques de Bauquemare	*président* of the parlement	3,000	29.07.77	ADSM 2E1 909 (prêt)
Adrien de Croismare	*président* of the *cour des aides*	500	21.01.79 (quitted)	AN 300 AP I 223
Richard Regnault	*conseiller* of the parlement	200	21.01.79 (quitted)	AN 300 AP I 223
Charles Puchot	son of Vincent Puchot	300	25.09.79	ADSM 2E1 359
Charles Puchot		200	1583	ADSM 2ème Héritage, 02.03.84
Marc Warne	*receveur* of Aumale	3,000*	1580s	ADSM 1B 5550 (prêt)
Alonce Quintanadoines	*noble homme*	300	10.11.86	ADSM 2ème Héritage
Jacques Ygou		450	06.08.89	ADSM 2ème Héritage
Procuration:		12,000*	07.10.89	ADSM 2E1 2290
Procuration:		6,000*	03.04.90	ADSM 2ème Héritage

* Principal

Appendix B

Buyers of *rentes* from the ducs d'Elbeuf

Buyer	*Status*	*Amount livres*	*Date of purchase*	*Reference*
Jacques de Bauquemare	*président* of the parlement	360	12.08.80	ADSM 2E1 360
Marguerite Romé	widow of Nicolas, *conseiller de ville*	600	11.06.80	ADSM 2E1 360
Catherine Le Gayant	widow of Jean de La Porte, *lieutenant-général* of the *bailliage* of Gisors	600	13.06.80	ADSM 2E1 360
Barbe Le Mercier	mother of Pierre Le Cornier	600	05.05.81	ADSM 2E1 363
Alonce Quintanadoines	Huguenot merchant	900	05.05.81	ADSM 2E1 363
Jacques Jubert	*président aux requêtes du Palais*	1,200	05.05/27.12.81	ADSM 2E1 363/4
Pierre Le Cornier	*conseiller* of the parlement and a royalist	1,600	05.05.81	ADSM 2E1 363
Anne Le Mercier	widow of Marcial de Lomenie	200	05.05.81	ADSM 2E1 363
Marie de La Haye	widow of Vincent Puchot	1,200	12/15.07.81	ADSM 2E1 363/7
Pierre du Quesne	*conseiller* of the parlement and a royalist	300	08.12.81	ADSM 2E1 364
Jean Hallé	*trésorier-général* en Normandie	600	08.12.81	ADSM 2E1 364
Georges Cabreuil	bourgeois	300	27.05.82	ADSM 2E1 365
Pierre Roque	*conseiller* of the parlement	300	13.02.82	ADSM 2ème Héritage, 05.05.1600
Baptiste Le Chandelier	*conseiller* of the parlement	300	14.02.82	ADSM 2E1 365
François de Civille	Huguenot	120	29.05.82	ADSM 2E1 365
André Bonissent	*conseiller* of the parlement and a royalist	150	29.05.82	ADSM 2E1 365
Marie de Bauquemare	niece of Jacques	500	19.05.82	ADSM 2E1 365

Robert Le Roux	*conseiller* of the parlement	300	23.01.83	ADSM 2ème Héritage, 17.08.85
Antoine Premierami	*receveur-général* of the abbey of Bec	400	16.04.83	ADSM 2ème Héritage, 16.04.1600
Anne du Moucel	wife of Adrien de Croismare	950	29.05.83	ADSM 2ème Héritage, 13.05.1600
Jean de Vey	*noble homme*	300	17.06.83	ADSM 2ème Héritage, 06.05.1600
Claude Le Gendre	bourgeois	2,000	27.06.83	ADSM 2ème Héritage, 12.05.1600
Adrien de Croismare	*président* of the *cour des aides*	600	02.09.83	ADSM 2E1 2295
Marie de La Haye		900	27.03.85	ADSM 2ème Héritage, 27.06.1600
Laurence Meilleric		600	27.03.85	ADSM 2E1 2284
Jacques Fizet	*conseiller* of the parlement and a leaguer	150	30.06.86	ADSM 2ème Héritage, 17.06.1600
Marie Gombault	widow of Jean de Croismare, *président*	300	07.07.86	ADSM 2ème Héritage, 03.05.1600
Marie de La Haye		600	07.07.86	ADSM 2ème Héritage, 27.06.1600
Robert Hannivel	*conseiller de ville*	300	08.07.86	ADSM 2ème Héritage, 05.02.1608
Christophe Eude	vicar-general of the archbishop	300	23.07.86	ADSM 2ème Héritage, 10.05.1600
Jean de Rouen	bourgeois	250	09.05.88	ADSM 2ème Héritage, 09.05.88 (*procuration* = 1,200)
Berthelemy Hallé	*conseiller au Grand Conseil*	1,200	09.09.88	2E1 2007
Jean d'Eudemare	nephew of Pierre, militia captain	660	25.09.88	ADSM 2ème Héritage, 09.05.1600
Guillaume Auber	*noble homme*	500	1580s	ADSM 2ème Héritage, 03.05.1600
Jean Hallé		600	08.03.89	ADSM 2ème Héritage, 16.06.1600

Appendix C

Muster rolls consulted

Captain	*Date*	*Place*	*Men-at-arms/ archers*	*BN Reference*
Charles de Moy, seigneur de La Meilleraye	06.01.59	Pont-Audemer	37–56	MS Fr 25800
Jacques de Moy, seigneur de Pierrecourt	22.04.69	Beningne-sur-Seine	29–43	MS Fr 21529
Jean de Moy, seigneur de La Meilleraye	12.01.70	Auffay-sur-Scie	30–40	*
	12.01.74	Auffay-sur-Scie	30–34	*
	28.02.81	Houdan	54–78	MS Fr 21537
Adrien, seigneur de Bréauté	01.05.68	Grainville-la-Teinture	47–41	MS Clair. 264
Philippe de Roncherolles, baron de Pont-Saint-Pierre	20.11.67	Pontoise	20–29	MS Clair. 264
Pierre de Roncherolles, baron de Pont-Saint-Pierre	01.09.85	Abbeville	30–45	NA Fr 8633
Jean baron de Clères	1564	unknown	23–33	MS Fr 5467
Claude duc d'Aumale	05.06.65	Chalons-sur Saône	50–74	MS Clair. 261
	06.10.72	Dreux	51–75	MS Fr 21533
Charles duc d'Aumale	14.10.75	Beaune-en-Brie	21–28	MS Fr 21535
	28.08.81	Saint Quentin	42–89	MS Fr 21538
René marquis d'Elbeuf	01.06.65	Montereau	40–60	MS Clair. 261

	06.02.69	Chinon	33–39	MS Fr 21529
Charles duc d'Elbeuf	1573	Mery-sur-Seine	21–34	NA Fr 8630
	26.02.79	Pontoise	35–42	MS Clair. 267
Léonor d'Orléans, duc de Longueville	24.07.60	Caen	29–49	MS Fr 21525
	04.11.66	Caen	40–60	MS Fr 21527
	29.05.69	Berry	60–70	MS Fr 21530
	11.03.76	Cosne-sur-Seine	51–76	MS Clair. 276
Tanneguy Le Veneur, seigneur de Carrouges	05.06.65	Lisieux	30–45	MS Clair. 261
	26.04.72	Lisieux	30–45	MS Clair. 271
	29.02.76	Brezolles	29–42	NA Fr 8632
	02.08.81	Noyon	57–86	MS Clair. 278

* Printed in Rodière and Vallée, *La Maison de Moy*, pp. 256–69.

Appendix D

The Guise and affinity in Picardy and the evolution of the Catholic League

This appendix highlights only those signatories of the League directly associated with Guise service: BN Collection de Picardie 53 fos. 9–12; MS Fr 3329 fos. 17–18. Due to the difficulties of tracing toponymics, the list is a conservative estimate. In addition, many signatories were close relatives of Guise servants. For an indication of the complex kinship relations binding these families: S. M. Carroll, 'Ceux de Guise: the Guise family and their affinity in Normandy', unpub. Ph.D. thesis (University of London, 1993), appendix F. The sources on the Guise affinity are too diverse to list systematically. It is possible to reconstruct a list of supporters after 1585 from: Prarond, La ligue à Abbeville; A. de Calonne, *Histoire de la ville d'Amiens* (3 vols., Amiens, 1899–1906); Lefebvre, *Les Huguenots et la Ligue au diocèse de Boulogne*; Pouy, *La chambre du conseil des Etats de Picardie*; Bernier, *Monumens inédits de l'histoire de France*.

PICARD FOLLOWERS OF THE GUISE WHO SIGNED THE LEAGUE IN 1577

Jean d'Amerval, sieur d'Assenvilliers: archer of the duc d'Aumale (1575–81)
Jacques d'Applaincourt: ensign (1575) and lieutenant (1581) of Aumale, and governor of the duchy of Guise (1580–8)
Ponthus de Bellefourrière: archer (1569) and household officer (1575) of the duc de Guise, and *guidon* of the marquis d'Elbeuf (1577–9)
Jacques de Biencourt: of a longstanding client family and *gentilhomme ordinaire* of Aumale (1580–1)
Jean du Biez: archer (1572–81) and *écuyer* (1581) of Aumale
Jean de La Boissière, seigneur de Chailly: *conseiller* (1575) of the duc de Guise
Jean de Caron, sieur d'Ameray: man-at-arms of Aumale (1572–81), *gentilhomme de la vénerie du roi* (1584), and ensign of Aumale (1588)
François des Essars, seigneur de Maigneux: of a longstanding client family and later governor of Montreuil-sur-Mer for the League
Nicolas de Fossez: governor of the marquisate of Nesle for the duc de Guise (1575)
Antoine du Hamel: *guidon* (1575) and ensign (1581) of Aumale
Francois de Paillart, sieur de Choquesne: archer of Aumale (1575) and *maître de camp* of the regiment of Picardy for the League (1589)
E. Tassart: man-at-arms of Aumale (1575–81)

PICARD SIGNATORIES OF THE LEAGUE PATRONISED BY THE GUISE AFTER 1577

Jacques de Calonne: man-at-arms of Aumale (1581)
Charles de Caruel: *guidon* of Aumale (1590)

Antoine Dumesnil: archer of Aumale (1581)
Seigneur de Fricourt: captain of Aumale's company of *arquebusiers à cheval* (1589)
François Hanique: man-at-arms of Elbeuf (1579)
Louis de Hauteville: *gentilhomme de la vénerie du roi* and *lieutenant des toiles de chasse* (1584)
Adrien de Lameth: man-at-arms of Aumale (1581)
Louis de Monchy, seigneur d'Inquesson: captain under the command of Aumale (1587)
Francois de Montguyot: archer of Elbeuf (1579)
Nicholas de Lanzeray: captain of Boves (1588) for the duc d'Aumale
Jean de Rambures: *maître de camp* of Aumale and governor of the duchy of Guise (1588)
De Rouvroy: three members of the family served in the companies of Aumale and Elbeuf (1579–81)

OTHER PICARD SIGNATORIES OF THE LEAGUE IN 1577 WHO REBELLED AGAINST HENRI III IN 1589

Philibert-Emmanuel d'Ailly, seigneur de Picquigny and vidame d'Amiens: leaguer captain and son of a signatory
Jean de Belloy, seigneur d'Amy: leaguer captain
Claude de Buigny, seigneur de Cornehotte: leaguer captain
François de Conty, sieur de Rocquencourt: lieutenant of Montdidier (1580–96)
Antoine d'Estourmel, seigneur de Plainville: leaguer captain
Michel d'Estourmel: lieutenant (1576–9) and later governor of Péronne, Montdidier and Roye (1579–94)
Charles de Forceville, seigneur de Caix: leaguer captain (1589–94)
Thibaut de Mailly, seigneur Darmogies: captain of fifty men-at-arms for the League
Robert de Monchy, seigneur de Caveron: leaguer captain
Louis de Moy, seigneur de Gommćron: governor of Ham (1576–94)
François de Saisseval: leaguer captain
Jean de Warluzel, seigneur de Bethencourt: leaguer captain

Appendix E

Guise clients and supporters at the provincial Estates and the Estates-General, 1583–1588

Name	*Status*	*Estate*	*Bailliage/ town*
1583:			
Jean Dadré[1]	*pénitencier* of the cathedral	First	Rouen
Robert Le Bret, seigneur de Neucourt	leaguer captain	Second	Gisors
1584:			
Claude Sécard, *curé* of Saint-Maclou	member of League council	First	Rouen
Guillaume Vipart, seigneur de Silly	leaguer captain	Second	Rouen
Jean Dehors[2]		Third	Gisors
1585:			
Gilles de Goutimesnil, seigneur de Boisrozé	leaguer captain	Second	Caux
Antoine de Bigars, seigneur de La Londe	leaguer captain	Second	Rouen
Robert de Gourfalleur, seigneur de Bonfossé	leaguer captain	Second	Cotentin
Pierre Rocque	leaguer *échevin*	Third	Rouen
Jean Trencart	leaguer *échevin*	Third	Rouen
Richard Marsollet	*verdier* and agent of duc d'Elbeuf	Third	Rouen
Jean Hellye	*tabellion/procureur* of Elbeuf	Third	Rouen
Jean Dehors		Third	Gisors
1586:			
Jean de Vieuxpont[3]	abbot of Saint-Jean de Falaise	First	Alençon
Barthélemy de Limoges	client of Aumale and the Vipart	Second	Rouen
Etienne de Laval	leaguer *échevin*	Third	Rouen
Imbart Le Peinteur	*receveur* of comté of Harcourt	Third	Evreux
Jean Dehors		Third	Gisors
1587:			
François de Cormeilles, seigneur de Tendos	leaguer captain	Second	Rouen
Antoine de Canouville, seigneur de Raffetot	leaguer captain	Second	Caux
Robert Le Bret, seigneur de Neucourt		Second	Gisors
Thomas Dupont	leaguer *échevin*	Third	Rouen
Pierre Guillotz	creditor of League, 1592	Third	Rouen
Jean Dehors		Third	Gisors
1588:[4]			
Georges Turgot[5]	canon of Coutances	First	Cotentin
Jacques du Bosc, seigneur de Coquéraumont	leaguer captain	Second	Rouen

Louis de La Moricière, seigneur de Vicques	leaguer captain	Second	Cotentin[6]
Robert Le Bret, seigneur de Neucourt		Second	Gisors
Guillaume de Laval, seigneur de Tartigny	leaguer captain	Second	Alençon
Simon Le Pigny	leaguer *échevin*	Third	Rouen
Estates-General, 1588:			
Charles, cardinal de Bourbon		First	Rouen
Claude de Sainctes, bishop of Evreux		First	Rouen
Jean de Vieuxpont	abbot of Saint-Jean de Falaise	First	Alençon
Nicolas Vipart, baron de Becthomas		Second	Rouen
Jean d'Escajeul, seigneur de La Bretonnière	leaguer captain	Second	Caen
Charles de Cossé, comte de Brissac		Second	Caux
Charles Martel, seigneur de Montpinçon	leaguer captain	Second	Cotentin
Jean Le Cesne, seigneur de Menilles	leaguer captain	Second	Evreux
Charles de Roncherolles, seigneur de Heuqueville	leaguer captain	Second	Gisors
Robert Hannivel	leaguer *échevin*	Third	Rouen
Guillaume Colombel	leaguer *échevin*	Third	Rouen
Jean Dehors		Third	Gisors
Nicolas Le Barbier	*lieutenant-général* of *bailli* for the League	Third	Alençon

[1] Elected to the abortive leaguer Estates-General of 1590: *Délibérations de la ville de Rouen*, p. 253.

[2] The Dehors were significant office holders in the *bailliage* and the criminal registers of the *parlement* of Rouen record several instances of their arrogant and violent conduct: ADSM 1B 3199, Apr 1585; 3207, 17 Mar 1587. Jean's son, Jacques 'dit capitaine presley', was granted the office of *contrôleur du grenetier* at Gisors by Mayenne and he took part in the League assault of Bayeux in 1590; Nicolas Dehors was appointed *conseiller* in the *cour des aides* of Rouen in 1592: ADSM 1B 3720, 28 Mar 1590; 3BP 9* fos. 108, 111. Christophe Dehors was a seigneurial official of Henri de Lorraine, comte de Chaligny, and a devout catholic, being a *maître* of the confraternity of the Holy Sacrament in Rouen from 1586: ADSM 2E1 936, 24 Nov 1588; G 9869, fo. 1.

[3] Of a significant client family, his elder brother being *lieutenant* of the comte de Brissac.

[4] No nobles were returned for Caen and Caux.

[5] His cousin and a younger brother were League captains and his elder brother was *aumônier* of the cardinal de Bourbon: Frondeville, *Présidents*, p 339.

[6] The records for every *bailliage* do not exist. Only those for Rouen are complete: Farin, *Histoire de la ville de Rouen*, ii, pp. 407–11; *Cahier des Etats de Normandie sous le règne de Henri III*, ii.

Appendix F

Marriages among the Leager nobility

Male	Female	Witnesses
1581		
Thomas d'Oilliamson, seigneur de Saint-Germain League captain	Louise de Tiercelin Sister of Jacques *lieutenant* of the duc d'Aumale in the 1570s; aunt of four of the League captains; sister-in-law of Antoine de Bigars	
Charles de Carvoisin Son of a man-at-arms and commensal officer of the duc d'Aumale	Marguerite de Nollent Dowry 2,000*l* and a substantial landed inheritance	Richard de Nollent, relative of Marguerite; his family was among the most important elements of Aumale's affinity. His two younger brothers had served for a decade in Aumale's company, and his relative, Hector de Nollent, was the duke's lieutenant of the *vénerie du roi* in 1580
1585		
Henri de Lorraine, comte de Chaligny and younger brother of the duc de Mercoeur	Claude de Moy Heiress of the senior line of the house of Moy and niece of Pierre de Roncherolles	
Jean V baron de Vieuxpont Ensign of the company of the duc d'Elbeuf in 1587 and 1588, and League governor of Dreux, Houdan and Hurepoix in 1592.	Marie de Billy Granddaughter of Louis, former governor of Guise and lieutenant of the company of maréchal de Brissac; niece of Geoffrey, grand prior of the abbey of Saint-Denis for the cardinal de Guise	

Jean du Saussay League captain in the Cotentin during 1589 and 1590	Hortense d'Orglandes Of a family closely associated with the house of Lorraine, her brothers were League captains in the Cotentin	
1588		
Fulcran de Houetteville Relative of Louis, *lieutenant des toiles de chasse du roi* under the duc d'Aumale from 1563 to 1580	Barbe de Montaigu Daughter of Philippe, member of the League parlement in Rouen, and Nicole des Buaz; dowry 10,000*l*	Gabriel de Vieuxpont, lieutenant of the comte de Brissac; Henry des Boves *guidon* of the company of the duc d'Elbeuf; Charlotte de Guiry widow of Charles des Boves, lieutenant of the company of the duc d'Elbeuf
André de Fautereau League captain and representative of the *bailliage* of Rouen at the leaguer Estates, 1593	Marie de Fay Sister of Jean, ensign of the company of Jacques de Moy in 1588; sister-in-law of Robert Deschamps, *conseiller* of the city of Rouen during the League; dowry 11,000*l*	Charles des Boves, lieutenant of the compny of the duc d'Elbeuf
Louis Garin *Conseiller* in the League parlement and nephew of the *bailli* of Elbeuf; his brothers served in Elbeuf's company	Marguerite de Paixdecoeur Sister of the captain of the Rouennais city militia during the League.	
Jean de Boyer Ensign of the company and *maître d'hôtel* of the duc d'Elbeuf	Minerve de Sémur Sister of Claude, ensign of the company and captain of the guard of the duc de Guise; dowry 12,000*l*	Jean-Jacques de Suzanne, comte de Cerny and uncle of Charles marquis de Moy
1591		
Robert de Monchy Captain of 50 gendarmes for the League	Anne de Pellevé Niece of the cardinal de Pellevé; daughter of Charles, member of the *Quarante* – one of the leaguer councils in Paris	

1592		
Achilles Cabot Captain of 100 foot for the League	Marguerite Darandel Daughter of Francois, man-at-arms of the duc d'Aumale; dowry 4,000*l*	
1593		
Louis de Montgommery *Maréchal de camp* for the League after deserting the royalists before January 1593; grandson of the great protestant warlord, Gabriel comte de Montgommery	Marie de Bigars Daughter of Antoine, league captain and member of the *Conseil de l'Union* in Rouen; dowry 34,000*l*	Jean de La Haye, captain of 50 lances for the League; Jean Le Cesne, League captain; Guillaume Péricard, member of the *Conseil de l'Union*; Georges de La Porte, *procureur-général* of the parlement of Rouen
Antoine d'Orglandes Brother of Hortense	Marthe du Saussay Sister of Jean	
Precise date unknown		
Gabriel de Vieuxpont lieutenant of the company of the comte de Brissac in 1588	Françoise des Boves Daughter of Charles, lieutenant of the company of the duc d'Elbeuf from 1566 to 1578	

Appendix G

Career summaries of some Guise clients and allies

This appendix provides a brief summary of the careers of those men who appear frequently in the text, which should be consulted for detailed references.

Annebaut, Claude d'	(d. 1552) lieutenant of Louis de Brézé (1525–30), *maréchal* de France (1537) and governor of Normandy (1547–52)
Annebaut, Jacques d'	(d. 1558) younger brother of Claude; bishop of Lisieux in 1539 on the resignation of his kinsman, Jean Le Veneur, and cardinal in 1544
Annebaut, Jean III d'	(d. 1562) son of Claude, *bailli* of Evreux (1547–56) and served with the Guise in Italy, 1556–7
Applaincourt, Jacques d'	seigneur de Hardencourt; ensign (1575–6) and lieutenant (1581) of Aumale; governor of the duchy of Guise (1580–8); founding member of the League of Péronne
Bailleul, Robert de	sieur d'Anserville and *gentilhomme* (1574–5) of Aumale
Bauquemare, Jacques I de	(1518–84) *premier président* of the parlement of Rouen, 1565–84
Bauquemare, Jacques II de	(d. 1616) son of Jacques I; *conseiller* of the parlement of Rouen (1576–93) and prominent member of the Catholic League in Normandy
Bauquemare, Jean-Pierre de	(d. 1619) eldest son of Jacques I; *conseiller* of the *Grand Conseil* and prominent member of the Catholic League in Normandy
Bigars, Antoine de	seigneur de La Londe and son of Louis; married (1575) Anne Tiercelin, sister of Adrien and Jacques; representative at the Estates-General in 1576 and lieutenant-general of Normandy for the Catholic League
Bigars, Guillaume de	seigneur d'Oissel and son of Louis; ensign of Aumale, 1588–91
Bigars, Louis de	(d. 1575) seigneur de La Londe, man-at-arms (1559–61) of Villebon d'Estouteville and captain of the Vieux Palais, 1562–8
Boves, Antoine des	*maître d'hôtel* of Guise, 1540
Boves, Charles des	(?1530–?1587) baron de Contenan, ensign (1550–60) and lieutenant (1560–78) of Elbeuf

Boves, Charles des	son of François and ensign (1564–70) of Guise
Boves, François des	seigneur de Rancé; *gentilhomme* and *maître d'hôtel* (1542–62) and ensign (1547–50) of Guise
Boves, Henri des	son of Charles baron de Contenan, *guidon* of Elbeuf (1580–8) and leaguer captain
Bréauté, Adrien de	(d. 1597) seigneur de Neville and Bréauté; *guidon* of Moy (1561) and lieutenant of Clères (1563); governor of Gisors (1561–72, 1582–5) and Vernon and Les Andelys (1574–6); colonel of the *ban* in Normandy (1587–8)
Brevedent, Denis	(d. 1573) son of Jacques; abbot of La Trappe and canon of Rouen
Brevedent, Jacques	*conseiller* at the parlement (1537–60), lieutenant-general of the *bailliage* of Rouen (1547–67) and financial agent of the duc d'Aumale in the 1550s
Buaz, Adrian des	seigneur des Noyers and leaguer captain in Normandy in the 1580s
Buaz, René des	*conseiller-clerc* of the parlement of Rouen (1550–60) and vicar-general of the cardinal de Bourbon (1550–61); staunch ultra-catholic
Caron, Jean de	seigneur d'Amery; man-at-arms (1581) and ensign (1588) of Aumale
Caruel, Louis de	seigneur de Merey and brother-in-law of Gabriel de La Vallée; *guidon* of Aumale in 1590
Clères, Jean baron de	(1520–63) son of Georges, lieutenant of Louis de Brézé (1525); captain of 100 *chevaux-légers* (1557); colonel of the *ban* of Normandy in 1562 and promoted captain of 30 lances in 1563
Colombel, Guillaume	represented Rouen at the Estates-General of Blois in 1588; *conseiller-échevin* during the Catholic League
Colombel, Jean	*procureur* of Rouen and leaguer activist in 1589
Colombel, Romain	*avocat* and counsellor of Aumale (1563–74); *bailli* of Mauny and pensioner of the cardinal de Lorraine (1561)
Fossez, Denis des	seigneur d'Esponne; *camérier* (1560–4) of the cardinal de Lorraine and *sous* lieutenant (1567) of Guise; nephew of Gabriel de La Vallée
Fossez, Guy des	(d. 1588) son of Denis and ensign (1587) of Aumale
Fouilleuse, Charles de	seigneur de Flavacourt; *guidon* (1573–5), ensign (1576–9) and captain (1583) of Elbeuf; *bailli* of Gisors for the Catholic League
Gaillardbois, François de	man-at-arms of Aumale (1575–85)
Gaillardbois, Jean de	*veneur des toiles de chasse* (1571–84) and captain of Vernon (1571–84)
Gaillardbois, Jean de	*gentilhomme* of the *vénerie* (1560–84)
Gaillardbois, Michel de	*gentilhomme* of the *vénerie* (1571–84)
Gaillardbois, Philippe de	seigneur de Marcouville; man-at-arms of Aumale (1566),

	gentilhomme of the *vénerie* (1571–84) and leaguer captain under Aumale
Hallé, Barthélemy	younger brother of Jean, wealthy Rouen bourgeois, creditor of the Guise and leaguer
Hallé, Jean	*trésorier de France* from 1579, creditor of the Guise and leaguer
Hamel, Antoine du	seigneur de Belleglise; guidon (1575), ensign (1581) and *maître de camp* (1587–8) of Aumale; governor of Rue for the Catholic League
La Brosse, Jacques de	(d. 1562) tutor and lieutenant of the duc de Longueville (1547–51); *maître d'hôtel* (1552–7) and lieutenant (1556–8) of Guise; governor (1558) and lieutenant (1559) of François the dauphin
La Haye, Jean de	seigneur de Chantelou and brother-in-law of Christophe de Bassompierre; representative at the Norman Estates in 1578, *chambellan* of Anjou (1582) and prominent leaguer captain in Normandy
La Marck, Henri-Robert de	(1529–74) duc de Bouillon and son of Robert; comte de Maulévrier and baron de Mauny and Bec Crespin in Normany; governor of Normandy, 1556–74
La Marck, Robert de	(d. 1556) duc de Bouillon, married Françoise de Brézé in 1538
La Vallée, Gabriel de	(d. ?1596) *gentilhomme* (1540) of Guise and *camérier* (1560–4) of the cardinal de Lorraine
Le Cirier, Antoine	(d. 1575) *conseiller* of the parlement of Paris, dean of Notre-Dame de Paris and bishop (1561–75) of Avranches; senior councillor of the Guise and godfather of Pierre Versoris
Le Cirier, Augustin	brother of Antoine; *conseiller* of the parlement of Paris and bishop (1575–80) of Avranches
Le Roux, Claude	(1494–1536) seigneur de Tilly, *conseiller* of the parlement of Rouen (1521–36) and counsellor of Claude duc de Guise
Le Roux, Guillaume	grandfather of Claude and *vicomte* of Elbeuf
Le Roux, Guillaume II	father of Claude; *vicomte* of Elbeuf and *procureur* of René II duc de Lorraine
Le Veneur, Gabriel	(d. 1574) bishop of Evreux in 1531 on the resignation of Ambrose Le Veneur; *chancelier* of the order of Saint-Michel in 1560 and counsellor of the cardinal de Lorraine
Le Veneur, Jacques	(d. 1596) comte de Tillières and son of Tanneguy; *bailli* of Rouen (1576–89) and *guidon* (1578) of Mayenne
Le Veneur, Tanneguy	(d.1591) seigneur de Carrouges and brother of Gabriel; lieutenant-general (1563–91) and governor (1575–83) of Normandy; *bailli* of Rouen (1576) and *bailli* of Evreux

(1567–85)	
Limoges, Barthélemy de	sieur de Saint-Just and son of Gabriel; archer of Aumale (1550) and *maître des eaux et forêts* of the *bailliage* of Rouen (resigned by Georges de Limoges in 1566)
Limoges, Gabriel de	(d. 1572) lieutenant of the *vénerie du roi* (1550) and *grand maître des eaux et forêts* of Normandy and Picardy
Limoges, Gabriel II de	son of Gabriel and *capitaine des gardes des eaux et fôrets* of Normandy (1584)
Limoges, Georges de	(d. 1587) son of Gabriel and *gentilhomme* of the *vénerie* (1560–71)
Limoges, Jean-Maximilien de	(1550–1605) youngest son of Gabriel, lieutenant-general of the admiralty at Rouen until 1588 and from 1581 *conseiller* of the parlement of Rouen
Longchamps, Guy de	seigneur de Fumechon, married (1550) Marguerite des Buaz, representative at the assembly of Saint-Germain in 1583 and governor of Lisieux (1562–87)
Longchamps, Jean de	son of Guy and governor of Lisieux for the Catholic League
Maromme, Louis	*avocat* and counsellor (1563–74) of Aumale
Morainville, Etienne de	seigneur de La Mésangère; *maître d'hôtel* of Guise, 1540–50
Moy, Charles de	sieur de Boschion, younger brother of Nicolas and captain of Château Gaillard for the League
Moy, François de	(1544–89) sieur de Richebourg, younger brother of Nicolas and lieutenant of François d'Espinay Saint-Luc in 1581; among Guise forces on the Day of the Barricades in Paris, May 1588, and lieutenant-general of the League artillery
Moy, Jacques de	(d. 1590) seigneur de Pierrecourt, governor of Honfleur (1565–89) and lieutenant in Normandy under his elder brother Jean
Moy, Jean de	(1528–91) seigneur de La Meilleraye; lieutenant-general, vice-admiral (1563–91) and governor (1575–83) of Normandy; lynchpin of the Catholic League in upper Normandy
Moy, Louis de	(1543–95) sieur de Gomméron, governor of Ham (1577–84) and younger brother of Nicolas; among Guise forces on the Day of the Barricades in Paris, May 1588
Moy, Nicolas de	(1541–89) sieur de Riberpré and husband of Roberte de Pellevé; *guidon* (1570–4) and lieutenant (1576–81) of Jean de Moy, and *grand maître des eaux et fôrets* of Normandy (1578–82, 1589); member of the *Conseil de l'Union* in Rouen
Orléans, François d'	(1535–51) duc de Longueville and comte de Tancarville

	in Normandy; grandson and ward of Claude duc de Guise
Orléans, Léonor d'	(1540–73) duc de Longueville on the death of his cousin François. He abjured Calvinism prior to marrying Marie de Bourbon, duchesse d'Estouteville; governor of Picardy, 1567–73
Pellevé, Nicolas de	(1518–94) bishop of Amiens (1553–63), archbishop of Sens (1563), cardinal (1570) and archbishop of Reims (1589); senior counsellor of the Guise and member of the *Conseil de l'Union* in Paris
Péricard, François	(d. 1639) fifth son of Jean I; bishop of Avranches (1588–1639) and leaguer
Péricard, Guillaume	third son of Jean I; *conseiller-clerc* of the parlement of Rouen (1571–1609) and key member of the Catholic League
Péricard, Jean I	(d. 1570) *procureur-général* (1559–70) of the parlement of Rouen and stalwart of the ultra-catholic faction
Péricard, Jean II	second son of Jean I; *sécretaire* and councillor of Guise in the 1580s
Pétremol, Louis	(d. 1563) *président* of the parlement of Rouen (1549–63), protégé of Diane de Poitiers, counselled the Guise in the 1550s and member of the ultra-catholic faction in Rouen
Puchot, Jean	eldest son of Vincent; militia captain in 1588–9 and married to Marie Hallé
Puchot, Pierre	(d. 1619) son of Vincent and member of the leaguer parlement of Rouen
Puchot, Vincent	(d. 1575) sieur de La Pommeraye; bourgeois of Rouen and, with his wife Marie de La Haye, significant creditor of the Guise
Raoullin, Robert	(d. 1565) sieur de Longpaon; *conseiller* of the parlement of Rouen, 1529–65; *procureur* of Diane de Poitiers and then Aumale; stalwart of the ultra-catholic faction in Rouen
Rémon, Pierre	(d. 1553) *premier président* of the parlement of Rouen (1543–53) and protégé of Diane de Poitiers
Roncherolles, Charles de	(1566–1635) half-brother of François and Pierre; representative at the Estates-General of 1588 and League captain in the 1590s
Roncherolles, François de	(1551–89) seigneur de Maineville, lieutenant of the comte de Soissons (1578–82) and senior Guise agent; representative at the Estates-General of 1576 and lieutenant-general of Paris and the Ile de France for the League
Roncherolles, Pierre de	(1530–1620) baron de Pont Saint-Pierre and governor (1581–93) of Abbeville, which he commanded for the

League; married Charlotte de Moy in 1572

Runes, Antoine de	seigneur de Baizieux; captain of Amiens (1567–97) and *guidon* (1588) and ensign (1591) of Aumale
Sarcilly, Charles de	sieur d'Ernes and son of Jean and Catherine de Lorraine; *maître d'hôtel* (1582–88) and *intendant* (1590) of Elbeuf
Sarcilly, Philippe de	brother of Charles and *maître d'hôtel* (1588) of Elbeuf
Sécard, Adam	*curé* of Saint-Maclou and vicar-general of the cardinal de Bourbon in the 1550s and early 1560s
Sécard, Claude	brother of Pierre and canon of Rouen cathedral; member of the *Conseil de l'Union* in Rouen
Sécard, Pierre	*curé* of Saint-Maclou on the death of his uncle Adam; member of the *Conseil de l'Union* in Rouen
Tiercelin, Adrien de	(1521–93) seigneur des Brosses and pillar of the Catholic League
Tiercelin, Anne de	(d. 1589) son of Jacques and *guidon* of Aumale in 1581
Tiercelin, Jacques de	(1549–78) seigneur de Possé, lieutenant (1563–8) of his brother Adrien and lieutenant (1570–8) of Aumale
Trevache, Eustache	protestant *receveur* of Lillebonne (1574–88) and financial agent for Elbeuf
Valdory, Guillaume	*avocat* at the parlement of Rouen; *procureur* and *conseiller* of Aumale (1568); *procureur* of the chevalier d'Aumale (1588); procureur of Elbeuf (1580–91)
Versoris, Pierre	(1528–88) Parisian *avocat*, counsellor of the Guise from 1563 and founding member of the Paris Sixteen
Vieuxpont, André de	seigneur d'Auzonville and son of Jean IV; cornet of the marquis de Moy (1588) and leaguer captain
Vieuxpont, Antoine de	seigneur de Saussay and brother of Jean IV; royalist infantry captain in Normandy in the 1560s; representative at the Norman Estates in 1562 and 1568
Vieuxpont, Auffay de	brother of Gabriel and archer of Elbeuf (1579)
Vieuxpont, Gabriel de	married to Françoise des Boves; ensign (1580) and lieutenant (1588) of the comte de Brissac and leaguer captain; heir of Madeleine d'Annebaut
Vieuxpont, Jean de	(1559–1623) brother of Gabriel and abbot of Saint-Jean de Falaise; representative at the Norman Estates of 1586 and at the Estates-General of Blois in 1588
Vieuxpont, Jean IV baron de	(?d. 1565) man-at-arms of Annebaut (1552), lieutenant of André de Bourbon-Rubempré (1565) and stalwart of the catholic cause
Vieuxpont, Jean V baron de	(d. 1617) son of Jean IV; archer (1579) and ensign of Elbeuf (1587–8) and leaguer captain
Vipart, Claude	(d. 1570) baron de Becthomas, ensign (1563–5) and lieutenant (1569) of Aumale
Vipart, Guillaume	(1549–96) seigneur de Silly and son of Robert and Françoise de Pellevé; page of Guise (1565), lieutenant of

	Jacques de Moy (1588) and leaguer captain.
Vipart, Nicolas	(1534–?1600) baron de Becthomas and younger brother of Claude; representative at the Norman Estates in 1573, 1575 and 1578, and at the Estates-General of 1588

Bibliography

MANUSCRIPT SOURCES

Archives de la Musée Condé, Chantilly

A: 14
CB: 2
D: 3
GE 20, 32 (tour), 114

Archives Départementales de Calvados, Caen

Série E: 3, 237–9, 353; 2E 882

Archives Départementales de la Seine-Maritime, Rouen

Série B: 1B 91-103, 590–3, 699–706, 2152–3, 3199–207, 3209, 3212, 3215–6, 3720, 3857, 5536, 5550, 5719; 3BP 9*
Série C: 1116, 1228, 1231, 1237, 2314, 8182
Série E: 1E 445–6, 462, 481–2, 486/2; 1ER 1563, 1589, 1764, 1940
Tabellionage de Rouen, 2E1: Registres sur parchemin 304–74; 2ème Héritage 877, 904, 909, 919–46, 2003–15, Mar 1584, Nov 1586, 1589, Mar–Apr 1594, 1600, Feb 1608; Héritages et meubles mêlées 2283–4, 2290–5; 1er Meubles, April 1568, 1586
Série F: 6F 11
Série G: 2161–76, 3498, 5668, 5670, 6595, 6884, 6887–8, 7374, 7525, 7755, 7758, 7759, 9536, 9869
Série J: 138; 7J 3, 8, 43
Série Mi: 1 Mi 345–7

Archives Départementales de l'Eure, Evreux

Série E: 684; 4E29/ 3, 4, 8, 9; 4E39/7

Archives Nationales, Paris

Archives Privées: 300 AP I 102, 215, 219, 223–4, 552; 300 AP II 224
Dom Le Noir: AB xix 3117
Minutier Central: étude VIII, 361–409; LIX 9; XXIX 83

Série K: 92[B]; KK 133[B], 145, 1088
Série L: LL 923
Série M: 458
Série Q: Q[1] 1374
Série T: 199/ 22, 24
Série Y: 124

Bibliothèque Muncipale de Rouen

Archives Communales: A 17–22; B 2–4; M
Collection Leber: 5176
Série Y: 102

Bibliothèque Nationale, Paris

Cabinet d'Hozier: 97, 216, 252
Carrés d'Hozier: 93, 391
Cinq Cents Colbert: 7, 10, 16, 24, 30, 53–4
Collection Clairambault: 261–71, 276, 278, 341–53, 726, 816, 1087, 1204
Collection de Picardie: 53
Collection du Vexin: 17.
Dossiers Bleus: 1, 127, 188, 277–8, 343, 361, 426, 442, 661, 674
Dupuy: 88
Manuscrits Français: 2945, 3118, 3121, 3188, 3209, 3231, 3237, 3302, 3306, 3309–10, 3329, 3338, 3358–9, 3394–5, 3398, 3408, 3413, 3574, 3832, 3942, 3974, 3977, 3979, 4638, 4640, 4766, 5467, 8181–2, 10239, 10270, 15546–52, 15608, 15811, 15876, 15905, 16621, 16899, 17302, 17870, 18246, 20176, 20467–70, 20513, 20515, 20517, 20519, 20529, 20532–4, 20536, 20538, 20541–4, 20545, 20548–9, 20551–4, 20646, 20649, 21525–38, 21543, 22441, 22429, 23193, 23295–6, 25800, 25808–9, 26170, 26291, 26414, 32369, 32764, 32866–8
Nouvelles Acquisitions Françaises: 238, 1219, 2743, 6646, 8625, 8630–3, 21165
Pièces Originales: 486, 496, 781, 1207, 1462, 1749–50, 2041, 2078, 2165, 2958, 3029

Public Record Office, London

SP Elizabeth 70/41

PRIMARY SOURCES

Anselme, Le P. *Histoire généalogique et chronologique de la maison royale de France, des pairs, grands officiers de la couronne & de la maison du roy* (9 vols., Paris, 1726–33).

Articles de la ligue & association de quelques Catholiques ennemis de la paix establie en France (n.p., 1576).

Aubigné, Agrippa d'. *Histoire universelle*, A. de Ruble, ed. (9 vols., Paris, 1886–97).

Belleau, R. *Larmes sur le trespas de Monseigneur René de Lorraine, et de Madame Louyse de*

Rieux Marquis & Marquise d'Elbeuf. Ensemble le tombeau de Monseigneur François de Lorraine Duc de Guyse (n.p., 1566).

Bernier, A. *Monumens inédits de l'histoire de France* (Paris and Senlis, 1835).

Boullay, P. du. *Le tres excellent enterrement du Claude de Lorraine* (n.p., 1551).

Bouquet, F., ed. *Documents concernant l'histoire de Neufchâtel-en-Bray* (Rouen, 1884).

Bourgeville, Charles de, sieur de Bras. *Les recherches et antiquitez de la province de Neustrie à présent duché de Normandie* (Caen, 1588).

Boyvin, François de, sieur de Villars. *Mémoires*, Michaud and Poujoulat, 1st ser., x.

Brantôme, Pierre de Bourdeille, sieur de. *Oeuvres*, L. Lalanne, ed. (11 vols., Paris, 1864–62).

Bulletin de la Société Historique et Archéologique de l'Orne

Cahiers des Etats de Normandie sous le règne de Charles IX, C. de Robillard de Beaurepaire, ed. (Rouen, 1891).

Cahiers des Etats de Normandie sous le règne de Henri III, C. de Robillard de Beaurepaire, ed. (2 vols., Rouen, 1887–8).

Caillières, J. de. *Histoire du mareschal de Matignon* (Paris, 1666).

Calendar of State Papers, foreign series, of the reign of Elizabeth. J. Stevenson *et al.*, eds. (London, 1863–1950).

Calendar of State Papers, foreign series, Scotland, M. J. Thorpe *et al.*, eds. (London, 1858–1969)

Calendar of State Papers, foreign series, Venetian, R. Brown *et al.*, eds. (9 vols., London, 1867–97).

Castelnau, Michel de. *Mémoires, Collection universelle des mémoires relatifs à l'histoire de France*, xli.

Mémoires, Michaud and Poujoulat, 1st ser., ix.

Catalogue analytique des chartes, documents historiques composant les archives du collège héraldrique (2 vols., Paris, 1866).

Catalogue des actes de François II, M.-T. de Martel, ed. (2 vols., Paris, 1991).

Catalogue des actes de Henri II, M.-N. Baudoin-Matuszek and A. Merlin-Chazelas, eds. (Paris, 1979–).

Cayet, Palma. *Chronologie novenaire*, Michaud and Poujoulat, 1st ser., xii.

Chandon, Jean de. *Vie et testament*, P. Chandon de Briailles, ed. (Epernay, 1857).

Chevalier, C., ed. *Comptes des receptes et despences faites en la chastellenie de Chenonceau par Diane de Poitiers* (Paris, 1864).

Cimber L. and Danjou F., eds. *Archives curieuses de l'histoire de France*, 1st ser. (15 vols., Paris, 1834–7).

Collection universelle des mémoires relatifs à l'histoire de France (67 vols., Paris, 1786–91).

Conspiration faicte en Picardie sous fausses & meshcantes calomnies contre l'edict de pacification (n.p., 1576).

Correspondence de Joachim de Matignon, L.-H. Labande, ed. (Monaco and Paris, 1914).

Correspondence des nonces en France: Lenzi et Gualtiero, légation du cardinal Trivultio, 1557–1561, J. Lestocquoy, ed. (Rome, 1977).

Correspondence de Theodore de Bèze, H. Meylan *et al.*, eds. (Geneva, 1960–).

Cuisiat, D. 'Lettres du Charles cardinal de Lorraine, 1525–74', thèse de IIIe cycle (2 vols., University of Nancy, 1970).

Davila, E. C. *Historie of the civill warres of France* (London, 1647–8).

Deux ligueurs de Picardie. Documents historiques sur un maieur d'Amiens et un gouverneur de Gerberoy (Paris, 1874).

Dickinson, G., ed. 'Two missions of Jacques de la Brosse', *Scottish Historical Society*, 3rd ser., 36 (Edinburgh, 1942).

Discours au vray et en abrege de ce qui est dernierement à Vassi, y passant Monseigneur le Duc de Guise (Paris, 1562).

Documents concernant les relations entre le duc d'Anjou et les Pays-Bas, P. Muller and A. Diegerick, eds. (5 vols., Utrecht, 1889–99).

'Documents historiques: pillages de gens de guerre, 1589–93', *Bulletin de la Société de l'Histoire de Normandie*, 10 (1909).

Du grand & loyal devoir fidelite et obeissance de Messieurs de Paris envers le Roy (Paris, 1565).

Extrait d'une missive contenant le Discours de la défaite des Ligueurs et Gottiers par le Duc de Montpensier, le 22 d'Avril 1589 (n.p., 1589).

Farin, F. *Histoire de la ville de Rouen* (6 vols., Rouen, 1738).

Feuardent, F. *Jetons et méraux depuis Louis IX jusqu'à la fin du consulat de Bonaparte* (3 vols., Paris, 1904–15).

Frondeville, H. de. *Les présidents du parlement de Normandie, 1499–1790* (Paris and Rouen, 1953).

Les conseillers du parlement de Normandie au seizième siècle, 1499–1594 (Paris and Rouen, 1960).

Les conseillers du parlement de Normandie sous Henri IV et sous Louis XIII, 1594–1640 (Paris and Rouen, 1964).

Groulard, Claude. *Mémoires*, Michaud and Poujoulat, 1st ser., xi.

Haton, Claude. *Mémoires*, F. Bourquelot, ed. (2 vols., Paris, 1857).

Héron, A., ed. *Deux chroniques de Rouen* (Rouen and Paris, 1900).

Histoire ecclésiastique des églises réformées au royaume de France, G. Baum and E. Caunitz, eds. (3 vols., Nieuwkoop, 1974).

Histoire tragique et memorable, de Pierre de Gaverston Gentilhomme Gascon Dedié à Monseigneur le Duc d'Espernon (n.p., 1588)

Inventaire-Sommaire des archives communales antérieures à 1790. Délibérations de la ville de Rouen, C. de Robillard de Beaurepaire, ed. (Rouen, 1887).

Inventaire-Sommaire des archives de la ville d'Amiens antérieures à 1790, ser. BB, *Délibérations de l'échevinage*, P. Durand, ed. (Amiens, 1894).

Inventaire-Sommaire des archives départementales de l'Eure, antérieures à 1790, ser. E, E. Lebeurier *et al.*, eds. (Evreux, 1899).

Inventaire-Sommaire des archives départementales de la Seine-Inférieure, antérieures à 1790, ser. C and D, C. de Robillard de Beaurepaire, ed. (Paris, 1864).

'Journal d'un bourgeois de Rouen depuis l'an 1545 jusqu' à l'an 1564', *Revue de Rouen et de la Normandie* (Rouen, 1837)

La Chenaye-Desbois and Badier, F. de. *Dictionnaire de la noblesse* (19 vols., Paris, 1863–76).

Lacourcé and Duval, eds. *Recueil des pièces originales et authentiques concernant la tenue des états-généraux* (11 vols., Paris, 1789).

La légende de Charles cardinal de Lorraine et de ses frères, descrite par François de L'Isle (Reims, 1576).

La Roque, G.-A. de. *Histoire généalogique de la maison d'Harcourt* (4 vols., n.p., 1662).

Lebeurier, P.-F. *Etat des anoblis en Normandie de 1398 à 1687* (Evreux, 1866).

Le Maréchal, A. *Documents tirées des minutes du tabellionage de Rugles* (Rouen, 1901).

Le Reveille-Matin des François et leurs voisins (Edinburgh, 1574).

Le Roux de Lincy, A. *Recueil de chants historiques français depuis le XII*[e] *jusqu' au XVIII*[e] *siècle* (2 vols., Paris, 1841–2).

Les recusations envoyees en la cour de Parlement de Paris, contre aucuns des Presidans & Conseillers d'icelle, Par Monseigneur le Prince de Condé & ses associés (n.p., 1562).

L'Estoile, Pierre de. *Journal du règne de Henri III*, L.-R. Lefèvre, ed. (Paris, 1943).

Journal pour le règne de Henri IV, L.-R. Lefèvre, ed. (2 vols., Paris, 1948, 1958).

Lettre d'un gentilhomme champenois escrivant a un sien ami Parisien, pour responce à certains libelles fameux nouvellement publiez (Orleans, 1565).

Lettre d'un seigneur du pays de Haynault envoyée à un sien voisin et amy suyvant la cour d'Espaigne (Antwerp, 1565).

'Lettre écrit par le duc de Mayenne à Jean du Saussay, sieur de Montsurvent, Paris, 8 Dec 1589', *Bulletin de la Société de l'Histoire de Normandie* (1870–1).

'Letters and memorials of Robert Parsons SJ', L. Hicks, ed., *Catholic Record Society*, 39 (1942).

Letters and papers, foreign and domestic, of the reign of Henry VIII, J. S. Brewer *et al.*, eds. (21 vols., London, 1864–1932).

Lettres de Catherine de Médicis, H. de La Ferrière and Comte Baguenault de Puchesse, eds. (9 vols., Paris, 1880–99).

Lettres de Henri III, M. François, ed. (4 vols. to date, Paris, 1959–).

Lettres, instructions et mémoires de Marie Stuart, A. I. Labanoff, ed. (7 vols., London, 1845).

L'Histoire de l'Estat de France, tant de la republique que de la religion sous le règne de François II (n.p., 1576).

Lonchay, H. *et al.*, eds. *Correspondance de la cour d'Espagne sur les affaires des Pays-Bas au XVII*[e] *siècle* (6 vols., Brussels, 1923–37).

Mémoire et livre de famille de Nicolas Dare, M. Bailly de Barbery, ed. (Troyes, 1886).

'Mémoires d'Antoine de Bigars, sieur de La Londe', *Société de l'Histoire de Normandie, Mélanges*, 5th ser. (Rouen and Paris, 1898).

Mémoires et correspondence de Duplessis-Mornay (12 vols., Paris, 1824–5).

Mémoires-journaux de François de Lorraine duc d'Aumale et de Guise, 1547 à 1563, Michaud and Poujoulat, 1st ser., vi.

Michaud, J.-F. and Poujoulat, J.-J.-F. eds. *Nouvelle collection des mémoires sur l'histoire de France* (Paris, 1836–54).

'Minutes des lettres trouvées parmi les papiers d'Adrien Ballue, chanoine de Rouen', *Bulletin de la Société de l'Histoire de Normandie* (1875–80).

'Mort de Gaspard de Heu, seigneur de Buy', *Bulletin de la Société de l'Histoire du Protestantisme Français*, 25 (1876), 164–8.

Négociations diplomatiques de la France avec la Toscane, G. Canestri and A. Desjardins, eds. (5 vols., Paris, 1859–75).

Papiers de Hervé de Longaunay, gouverneur de la Basse-Normandie (1575–1589) (Saint-Lô, 1897).

Paschal, P. de. *Journal de ce qui s'est passé en France durant l'année 1562*, M. François, ed. (Paris, 1950).

Pottier, A. *Revue rétrospective Normande: documents inédits pour servir à l'histoire de Rouen et de la Normandie* (Rouen, 1842).

Prévost, G. A., ed. *Recueil des presidents, conseillers et autres officiers de l'échiquier et du parlement de Normandie par Bigot de Monville, 1499 à 1550* (Rouen and Paris, 1905).

Notes du premier président Pellot sur la Normandie, 1670–83 (Rouen and Paris, 1915).

Registre des délibérations du bureau de la ville de Paris, F. Bonnardot *et al.*, eds. (10 vols., Paris, 1883–1903).

'Relation des troubles excités par les calvinistes dans la ville de Rouen depuis l'an 1537 jusqu'en l'an 1582', *La revue de Rouen et de la Normandie* (Rouen, 1837).

Remonstrance Faicte A Monsieur d'Espernon, Entrant En l'Eglise Cathedrale de Rouen, le 3 de may 1588 (Rouen, 1588).

Ruble, A. de, ed. *Commentaires et lettres de Blaise de Monluc maréchal de France* (5 vols., Paris, 1864–72).

Sainte-Marthe, D. de. *Gallia Christiana* (13 vols., Paris, 1715).

Serres, J. de. *Recueil des choses memorables avenues en France sous les regnes de Henri II, François II, Charles IX, Henri III et Henri IV, contenant infinies merveilles de nostre siècle* (n.p., 1599).

Sully, Maximilien de Béthune, baron de Rosny, duc de. *Les oeconomies royales*, D. Buisseret and B. Barbiche, eds. (Paris, 1970–).

Tavannes, Gaspard de Saulx, seigneur de. *Mémoires*, Michaud and Poujoulat, 1st ser., viii.

Teulet, A., ed. *Papiers d'état rélatifs à l'histoire de l'Ecosse au XVIe siècle; tirés des bibliothèques et des archives de France* (3 vols., Paris, 1851–60).

Relations politiques de la France et de l'Espagne avec l'Ecosse au XVIe siècle (5 vols., Paris, 1862).

Thou, J.-A. de. *Histoire universelle de 1543 jusqu'en 1607* (16 vols., London, 1734).

Mémoires depuis 1553 jusqu'en 1601, Michaud and Poujoulat, 1st ser., xi.

Tommaseo, M. N. *Relations des ambassadeurs vénitiens sur les affaires de France au XVIe siècle* (2 vols., Paris, 1838).

Travers, E., ed. *Rôle du ban et de l'arrière-ban du bailliage de Caen en 1552* (Rouen and Paris, 1901).

Valdory, G. 'Relation du siège de Rouen en 1591', *Société Rouennaise de Bibliophiles* (Rouen, 1871).

Valois, C., ed. *Histoire de la Ligue, oeuvre inédite d'un contemporain* (Paris, 1914).

Vieilleville, François de Scépeaux, seigneur de. *Mémoires*, *Collection universelle des mémoires particuliers rélatifs à l'histoire de France*, xxxii.

Vindry, F. *Dictionnaire de l'état major au seizième siècle*, pt 1: *La gendarmerie* (Paris, 1901).

Vipart, F.-A. de. *Généalogie de la maison de Vipart* (n.p., 1751).

Voisin, Lancelot du, seigneur de La Popelinière. *L'Histoire de France depuis l'an 1550 iusques à ces temps* (2 vols., n.p., 1581).

Voysin de La Noiraye, *Mémoire sur la généralité de Rouen, 1665*, E. Esmonin, ed. (Paris, 1913).

Wernham, R. B., ed. *List and analysis of State Papers, foreign series, Elizabeth I* (London, 1964).

Wood, M., ed. 'Foreign correspondence with Marie de Lorraine, queen of Scotland, 1548–57', *Scottish Historical Society*, 3rd ser., 7 (Edinburgh, 1925).

Bibliography

SECONDARY SOURCES

Amphoux, H. *Essai sur l'histoire du protestantisme au Havre et dans ses environs* (Le Havre, 1894).

Ascoli, P. 'The Sixteen and the Paris league, 1585–1591', unpub. Ph.D. thesis (University of California, Berkeley, 1971).

Asseline, D. *Les antiquitez et chroniques de la ville de Dieppe* (2 vols., Dieppe, 1874).

Ayzac, F. *Histoire de Saint-Denis en France* (2 vols., Paris, 1861).

Baker, J. 'The House of Guise and the church *c.* 1550–1588', unpub. D.Phil. thesis (University of Oxford, 1995).

Baudouin-Matuszek, M.-N. 'Henri II et les expéditions françaises en Ecosse', *Bibliothèque de l'Ecole des Chartes*, 145 (1987), 339–82.

Baumgartner, F. *Henry II king of France, 1547–1559* (Durham and London, 1988).

Beaurepaire, C. de Robillard de. *Séjour de Henri III à Rouen aux mois de juin et juillet 1588* (Rouen, 1870).

Beik, W. *Absolutism and society in seventeenth-century France: state power and provincial aristocracy in Languedoc* (Cambridge, 1985).

Benedict, P. *Rouen during the Wars of Religion* (Cambridge, 1980).

Bercé, Y.-M. *Histoire des Croquants* (2 vols., Geneva, 1974).

Bergin, J. 'The decline and fall of the House of the Guise as an ecclesiastical dynasty', *Historical Journal*, 25 (1982), 781–803.

Billaçois, F. *Le duel dans la société française des XVIe–XVIIe siècles: essai de psychosociologie historique* (Paris, 1986).

Biographie universelle ancienne et moderne (83 vols., Paris, 1811–53).

Biver, P. *Histoire du château de Meudon* (Paris, 1923).

Black-Michaud, J. *Cohesive force: feud in the Mediterranean and the Middle East* (Oxford, 1975).

Boissevain, J. *Friends of friends: networks, manipulators and coalitions* (Oxford, 1974).

Bonnenfant, G. *Histoire générale du diocèse d'Evreux* (2 vols., Paris, 1933).

Borély, A. *Histoire de la ville du Havre et de son ancien gouvernement* (3 vols., Le Havre, 1880–1).

Bossy, J. 'Elizabethan catholicism: the link with France', unpub. Ph.D. thesis (University of Cambridge, 1960).

'The counter-reformation and the people of catholic Europe', *Past and Present*, 46 (1970), 51–70.

'Some elementary forms of Durkheim', *Past and Present*, 95 (1982), 3–18.

Bost, C.-M. *Les seigneurs de Lillebonne* (Luneray, 1987).

Boucher, J. *Société et mentalités autour de Henri III* (3 vols., Lille, 1981).

La cour de Henri III (Rennes, 1986).

Bouillé du Chariol, R. de. *Histoire des ducs de Guise* (4 vols., Paris, 1849–50).

Bourgeon, J.-L. 'Les légendes ont la vie dure: à propos de la Saint-Barthélemy et de quelques livres récents', *Revue d'Histoire Moderne et Contemporaine*, 34 (1987), 102–16.

L'assassinat de Coligny (Paris, 1993)

'Quand la foi était révolutionnaire: les sermons d'un curé parisien, Simon Vigor, en 1570–1572', *La vie, la mort, la foi, le temps. Mélanges offerts à Pierre Chaunu*, J.-P. Bardet and M. Foisil, eds. (Paris, 1993).

Bourquin, L. *Noblesse seconde et pouvoir en Champagne aux XVIe et XVIIe siècles* (Paris, 1994).
Broussillon, B. de. *La maison de Laval, 1020–1605. Etude historique accompagné du cartulaire de Laval et de Vitré* (5 vols., 1895–1903).
Brown, K. *Bloodfeud in Scotland, 1573–1625: violence, justice and politics in early modern society* (Edinburgh, 1986).
Brunelle, G. K. 'Immigration, assimilation and success: three families of Spanish origin in sixteenth-century Rouen', *Sixteenth Century Journal* 20 (1989), 205–19.
The New World merchants of Rouen, 1559–1630 (Ann Arbor, 1991).
Burke, P. *The French historical revolution* (Oxford, 1990).
Buvignier, C. *Jametz et ses seigneurs* (Verdun, 1861).
Calonne, A. de. *Histoire de la ville d'Amiens* (3 vols., Amiens, 1899–1906).
Carrard, P. *Poetics of the new history: French historical discourse from Braudel to Chartier* (Baltimore, 1992).
Carroll, S. M. 'Ceux de Guise: the Guise family and their affinity in Normandy', unpub. Ph.D. thesis (University of London, 1993).
'The Guise affinity and popular protest during the Wars of Religion', *French History*, 9 (1995), 125–52.
Charpillon, M. *Dictionnaire historique de toutes les communes du département de l'Eure* (2 vols., Les Andelys, 1868).
Chestret de Hanneffe, J. de. *Histoire de la maison de La Marck* (Liège, 1898).
Chevallier, P. *Henri III: roi shakespearien* (Paris, 1985).
Constant, J.-M. 'Le langage politique paysan en 1576: les cahiers de doléances des bailliages de Chartres et de Troyes', in R. Chartier and D. Richet, *Représentation et vouloir politique autour des Etats-Généraux de 1614* (Paris, 1982).
Les Guises (Paris, 1984).
Corvisier, A. 'Une société ludique au XVIe siècle: l'Abbaye de Conards de Rouen', *Annales de Normandie*, 22 (1977), 179–93.
Courtaux, T. and the marquis de Touchet. *Histoire générale de la maison de Touchet* (Paris, 1911).
Crouzet, D. 'Recherches sur la crise de l'aristocratie en France: les dettes de la maison de Nevers', *Histoire, Economie et Société*, 1 (1982), 7–50.
Les guerriers de Dieu: la violence au temps des troubles de religion vers 1525 –vers 1610 (2 vols., Paris, 1990).
La nuit de la Saint-Barthélemy: un rêve perdu de la renaissance (Paris, 1994).
Croze, J. de. *Les Guises, les Valois et Philippe II* (2 vols., Paris, 1866).
Darsel, J. 'L'Amirauté en Normandie: I –Amirauté d'Eu-Le Tréport', *Annales de Normandie*, 19 (1969), 291–306.
Daval, G. and J. *Histoire de la réformation à Dieppe* (2 vols., Rouen, 1878).
Davies, C. S. L. 'Peasant revolt in France and England: a comparison', *Agricultural History Review*, 21 (1973), 122–34.
Davies, J. 'Neither politique nor patriot? Henri de Montmorency and Philip II, 1582–1589', *Historical Journal*, 34 (1991), 539–66.
Davillé, L. *Les prétensions de Charles III duc de Lorraine à la couronne de France* (Paris, 1909).
Davis, N. Z. *Society and culture in early modern France* (Stanford, 1975).

Delalande, A. *Histoire des guerres de religion dans la Manche* (Paris and Valognes, 1844).
Descimon, R. 'La Ligue à Paris: une révision', *Annales ESC*, 37 (1982), 72–128.
Qui étaient les Seize? Mythes et réalités de la ligue parisienne (Paris, 1984).
'La milice bourgeoise et identité citadine à Paris au temps de la Ligue', *Annales ESC*, 48 (1993), 885–906.
Devèze, M. *La vie de la fôret française au XVIe siècle* (2 vols., Paris, 1961).
Deville, A. *Histoire du château et des sires de Tancarville* (Rouen, 1834).
Dewald, J. *The formation of a provincial nobility: the magistrates of the parlement of Rouen, 1499–1610* (Princeton, 1980).
Pont St-Pierre, 1389–1789 (Berkeley, 1987).
Diefendorf, B. 'The Catholic League: social crisis or apocalypse now?', *French Historical Studies*, 15 (1987), 332–44.
'Simon Vigor: a radical preacher in sixteenth-century Paris', *Sixteenth Century Journal*, 18 (1987), 399–410.
Beneath the cross: Catholics and Huguenots in sixteenth-century Paris (Oxford, 1991).
Diguères, V. des. *Etude historique et généalogique sur les Rouxel de Médavy-Grancey* (Paris, 1870).
Donaldson, G. *Scotland: James V–VII* (Edinburgh, 1978).
Dournel, J. *Histoire de la ville de Péronne* (Péronne, 1879).
Drouot, H. *Mayenne et la Bourgogne: étude sur la Ligue, 1587–1596* (2 vols., Paris, 1937).
Echkhardt, A. *Remy Belleau: sa vie –sa bergerie* (Budapest, 1917).
Estaintot, R. d'. *La ligue en Normandie, 1588–94* (Paris and Rouen, 1862).
Eurich, S. *The economics of power: the private finances of the House of Foix-Navarre-Albret during the Religious Wars* (Ann Arbor, 1994).
Evennett, H. O. *The cardinal of Lorraine and the council of Trent* (Cambridge, 1930).
Fabre, A. *Etudes historiques sur les clercs de la basoche* (Paris, 1875).
Fabre, F. 'The English College at Eu, 1582–1592', *Catholic Historical Review*, 37 (1951), 257–80.
Fierville, C. 'Le cahier des doléances des trois ordres du duché et bailliage d'Alençon en 1560', *Mémoires lus à la Sorbonne dans la séance du comité imperial* (1876).
Floquet, A. *Histoire du privilège de Saint-Romain* (2 vols., Rouen, 1833).
Histoire du parlement de Normandie (7 vols., Rouen, 1840–2).
Foisil, M. 'Harangue et rapport d'Antoine Séguier, commissaire pour le Roi en Basse-Normandie (1579–1580)', *Annales de Normandie*, 26 (1976), 25–40.
Forestié, E. *Un capitaine gascon au XVIe: Corbeyran de Cardaillac-Sarlabous* (Paris, 1897).
Forts, P. des. *Le château de Villebon, Eure-et-Loire: étude historique et archéologique* (Paris, 1914).
Frémont, A. *Atlas et géographie de la Normandie* (Paris, 1977).
Garrisson-Estèbe, J. *A history of sixteenth-century France, 1483–1559* (London, 1994).
Giesey, R. 'The monarchomach triumvirs: Hotman, Beza and Mornay', *Bibliothèque d'Humanisme et Renaissance*, 32 (1970), 41–56.
Graham, V. and McAllister Johnson, W., eds. *The royal tour of France by Charles IX and Catherine de' Medici: festivals and entries, 1564–6* (Toronto, 1979).
Greengrass, M. 'The anatomy of a religious riot in Toulouse in May 1562', *Journal of Ecclesiastical History*, 34 (1983), 367–91.

France in the age of Henri IV (London, 1984).

'Property and politics in sixteenth-century France: the landed fortune of the Constable Anne de Montmorency', *French History*, 2 (1988), 371-98.

Greenshields, M. *An economy of violence in early modern France: crime and justice in the Haute Auvergne, 1587–1664* (Philadelphia, 1995).

Hamon, P. *L'argent du roi: les finances sous François Ier* (Paris, 1994).

Harding, R. *Anatomy of a power elite: the provincial governors of early modern France* (New Haven and London. 1978).

'Revolution and reform in the Holy League: Angers, Rennes, Nantes', *Journal of Modern History*, 53 (1981), 379–416.

Harvey, I. 'Was there popular politics in fifteenth-century England?' in R. Britnell and A. Pollard, eds., *The McFarlane legacy* (Stroud, 1995).

Hauser, H. *Les sources de l'histoire de France: Le XVIe siècle, 1494–1610* (4 vols., Paris, 1912).

Heller, H. 'A reply to Mack P. Holt', *French Historical Studies*, 19 (1996).

Hellot, A. *Essai historique sur les Martels de Basqueville et Basqueville-en-Caux* (Rouen, 1879).

Fécamp au temps de la Ligue. La légende de Boisrozé (Yvetot, 1897).

Heulhard, A. *Villegagnon: roi d'Amérique. Un homme de mer au XVIe siècle, 1510–72* (Paris, 1897).

Hicks, M. *Bastard feudalism* (London, 1995).

Holt, M. P. *The duke of Anjou and the politique struggle during the Wars of Religion* (Cambridge, 1986).

'Attitudes of the French nobility at the Estates-General of 1576', *Sixteenth Century Journal*, 18 (1987), 489–504.

'Putting religion back into the Wars of Religion', *French Historical Studies*, 18 (1993), 524–51.

Jackson, R. 'Elective kingship and *consensus populi* in sixteenth-century France', *Journal of Modern History*, 44 (1972), 155-71.

Janvier, A. *Boves et ses seigneurs: étude historique sur la commune de Boves* (Amiens, 1877).

Jouanna, A. *Le devoir de révolte: la noblesse française et la gestation de l'Etat moderne, 1559–1661* (Paris, 1989).

Jouen, L. *Jumièges* (Rouen, 1925).

Justice, S. *Writing and rebellion: England in 1381* (Berkeley, 1994).

Kaiser, W. *Marseille im Bürgerkrieg, Sozialgefüge, Religionskonflikt und Faktionskämpfe* (Göttingen, 1991).

Kent, D. and Kent, F. W. *Neighbours and neighbourhood in Renaissance Florence: the district of the Red Lion in the fifteenth century* (New York, 1982).

Kettering, S. 'Patronage in early modern France', *French Historical Studies*, 17 (1992), 872–81.

Knecht, R. *The French wars of religion, 1559–1598* (London, 1989).

Kretzchmar, J. *Die invasions projekte der katholischen mächte gegen England zur zeit Elisabeths* (Lepzig, 1892).

Labande, L.-H. *Le château et la baronnie de Marchais* (Paris, 1927).

La Brosse, J. de. *Histoire d'un capitaine bourbonnais au XVIe siecle: Jacques de La Brosse 1485–1562* (Paris, 1929).

La Ferrière-Percy, H. de. *Histoire du canton d'Athis* (Paris, 1858).

Laheudrie, E. *Recherches sur le Bessin: histoire du Bessin des origines à la revolution* (2 vols., Caen and Bayeux, 1930).
Lamet, M.-S. 'Reformation, war and society in Caen, lower Normandy, 1558–1610', unpub. Ph.D. thesis (University of Massachusetts, 1978).
La Morandière, G. de. *Histoire de la maison d'Estouteville* (Paris, 1903).
La Roncière, C. de. *Histoire de la marine française* (6 vols., Paris, 1899–1932).
La Rue, G. de. *Essais historiques sur la ville de Caen* (2 vols., Caen, 1820).
Lavisse, E. *Histoire de France*, vi, pt 1, *La Réforme et la Ligue*, by J. H. Mariéjol (Paris, 1904).
Le Beuf, D. *La ville d'Eu* (Paris, 1844).
Le Canu, A. *Histoire du diocèse de Coutances et Avranches* (2 vols., Coutances, 1877–8).
Lechevalier, A. *Notice historique sur les barons et la baronnie du Bec* (Paris, 1898).
Lecoy de La Marche, A. *Le roi René* (2 vols., Paris, 1875).
Lefebvre, F. *Les Huguenots et la Ligue au diocèse de Boulogne* (Boulogne-sur-Mer, 1855).
Lefèvre, E. *Recherches historiques sur la principauté d'Anet* (Chartres, 1862).
Le Hardy, G. *Histoire du protestantisme en Normandie depuis son origine jusqu'à la publication de l'édit de Nantes* (Caen, 1869).
Lemarchand, G. 'Le temporel et les revenus de l'abbaye de Fécamp pendant le XVIIe et le XVIIIe siècle', *Annales de Normandie*, 15 (1965), 525–49.
Le Roux, N. 'The catholic nobility and political choice during the League, 1585–1594: the case of Claude de La Châtre', *French History*, 8 (1994), 36–50.
Le Roy Ladurie, E. *Les paysans de Languedoc* (2 vols., Paris, 1966).
Le territoire de l'historien (Paris, 1973).
Carnaval de Romans (Paris, 1979).
L'état royal, 1460–1610 (Paris, 1987).
Lloyd, H. A. *The Rouen campaign, 1590–1592* (Oxford, 1973).
Loth, J. *Saint-Maclou de Rouen: l'église – la paroisse* (Rouen, 1913).
Maillard, E. *Histoire d'Ancenis et de ses barons* (Nantes, 1860).
Maille, P. *Recherches sur Elbeuf: esquisses ou silhouettes de ses seigneurs de la maison de Lorraine* (3 vols., Elbeuf, 1859–63).
Major, J. R. *Representative government in early modern France* (New Haven and London, 1980).
From renaissance monarchy to absolute monarchy (Baltimore, 1994).
Mannier, E. *Les commanderies du grand-prieuré de France d'après les documents inédits conservés aux Archives Nationales* (Paris, 1872).
Marchand, C. *Charles Ier de Cossé, comte de Brissac et maréchal de France, 1507–1563* (Paris, 1889).
Margry, A. *Pierre Séguin: ligueur, reclus et écrivain, 1558–1636* (Senlis, 1896).
Maudit, F.-J. *Histoire d'Ivry-la-Bataille et de l'abbaye de Notre Dame d'Ivry* (Evreux, 1899).
Meriel, A. *Le gouvernement de Falaise de 1574 à 1590* (Alençon, 1883).
Mettam, R. *Power and faction in Louis XIV's France* (Oxford, 1988).
Meyer, E. *Histoire de la ville de Vernon* (2 vols., Les Andelys, 1874-6).
Michaud, H. *La grand chancellerie et les écritures royales au XVIe siècle* (Paris, 1967).
Morel, E. *Houdencourt: seigneurie et paroisse* (2 vols., Compiègne, 1878–82).
Moulierac-Lamoureux, R.-L. *Le roi René, ou les hasards du destin, 1409–1480* (Avignon, 1980).

Mours, S. *Les églises réformées en France* (Paris and Strasbourg, 1958).
Mousnier, R. *Fureurs paysannes* (Paris, 1967).
Moutié, A. *Chevreuse. Recherches historiques, archéologiques et généalogiques* (2 vols., Rambouillet, 1874–6).
Muir, E. *Mad blood stirring: vendetta and factions in Friuli during the Renaissance* (Baltimore, 1993).
Nagle, J. *Le droit de marc d'or des offices* (Geneva, 1992).
Neuschel, K. *Word of Honor: interpreting noble culture in sixteenth-century France* (Ithaca, N.Y., 1989).
Nicholls, D. 'Inertia and reform in the pre-Tridentine French church: the response to protestantism in the diocese of Rouen, 1520–62', *Journal of Ecclesiastical History*, 32 (1981), 185–97.
Nugent, D. *Ecumenism in the age of reformation: the colloquy of Poissy* (Cambridge, Mass., 1974).
Odolant-Desnos, *Mémoires historiques sur la ville d'Alençon et sur ses seigneurs* (2 vols., Alençon, 1787).
Orlea, M. *La noblesse aux Etats généraux de 1576 et de 1588: étude politique et sociale* (Paris, 1980).
Pallier, D. *Recherches sur l'imprimerie à Paris pendant la Ligue, 1585–1594* (Geneva, 1976).
Parker, D. *The making of French absolutism* (London, 1983).
Pastor, L. von. *The history of the popes from the close of the middle ages* (40 vols., London, 1891–).
Picot, G. *Histoire des Etats généraux considérés au point de vue de leur influence sur le gouvernement de France de 1355 à 1614* (4 vols., Paris, 1872).
Pimodan, G. de. *La mère des Guises: Antoinette de Bourbon, 1494–1583* (Paris, 1889).
Porée, A.-A. *Histoire de l'abbaye de Bec* (2 vols., Evreux, 1901).
Potin de La Mairie, N. *Recherches historiques et biographiques sur les possessions des sires Normands de Gournay, Le Bray Normand et Le Bray Picard* (2 vols, Gournay, 1852).
Potter, D. 'The duc de Guise and the fall of Calais, 1557–8', *English Historical Review*, 118 (1983), 481–512.
'A treason trial in sixteenth-century France: the fall of marshal du Biez, 1549–1551', *English Historical Review*, 105 (1990), 595–623.
War and government in the French provinces: Picardy, 1470–1560 (Cambridge, 1993).
A history of France, 1460–1560 (London, 1995)
Pouy, F. *La chambre du conseil des états de Picardie pendant la Ligue* (Amiens, 1882).
Prarond, E. *Histoire de la Ligue à Abbeville, 1576–1594* (3 vols., Paris, 1873).
Prentout, H. 'Les Etats provinciaux de Normandie', *Mémoires de l'Academie Nationale des Arts et Belles Lettres de Caen* (3 vols., Caen, 1925–7).
Prosser, G. 'After the reduction: restructuring Norman political society and the *Bien Public*, 1450–65', unpub. Ph.D. thesis (University of London, 1996).
Ramsey, A. 'Piety in Paris during the League, 1585–90: an urban community in transition', unpub. Ph.D. thesis (University of Columbia, 1991).
Réaux, E. *Histoire des barons de Maule* (Paris, n.d.).
Richmond, C. 'After Macfarlane', *History*, 68 (1983).

Robbins, K. 'The social mechanisms of urban rebellion: a case study of leadership of the 1614 revolt at La Rochelle', *French Historical Studies*, 19 (1995).
Rodière, R. and Vallée, E. *La maison de Moy* (Le Mans, 1928).
Romier, L. *Les origines politiques des guerres de religion* (2 vols., Paris, 1913).
Le royaume de Catherine de Médicis (2 vols., Paris, 1922).
La conjuration d'Amboise (Paris, 1923).
Catholiques et Huguenots à la cour de Charles IX (Paris, 1924).
Saint-Denis, H.-M. *Notices historiques sur les communes des environs d'Elbeuf* (8 vols., Elbeuf, 1885–90).
Salmon, J. H. M. *Society in crisis: France in the sixteenth century* (New York, 1975).
Saulnier, E. *Le rôle politique du cardinal de Bourbon (Charles X), 1523–1590* (Paris, 1912).
Sauvage, M. 'Les troubles de 1562', *Etudes Lexoviennes*, 1 (1915).
Sauzet, F., ed. *Henri III et son temps* (Paris, 1992).
Schnerb, B. *Bulgnéville: l'état bourguignon prend pied en Lorraine* (Paris, 1994).
Semichon, E. *Histoire de la ville d'Aumale* (2 vols., Paris, 1862).
Seydoux, P. *La Normandie des châteaux et des manoirs* (Paris, 1989).
Shannon, S. C. 'The political activity of François de Lorraine, duc de Guise (1559–1563): from military hero to catholic leader', unpub. Ph.D. thesis (University of Boston, 1988).
Sutherland, N. M. *The French secretaries of state in the age of Catherine de Medici* (London, 1962).
The massacre of Saint Bartholomew and the European conflict, 1559–1572 (London, 1972).
Princes, politics and religion (London, 1984).
Taylor, L. *Soldiers of Christ: preaching in late medieval and renaissance France* (Oxford, 1992).
Thibaudeau, A. *Histoire de Poitou* (3 vols, Niort, 1839–40).
Törne, P. O. de. 'Philippe II et Henri de Guise. Le début de leurs relations', *Revue Historique*, 167 (1931), 323–35.
Underdown, D. *Revel, riot and rebellion: popular politics and culture in England, 1603–1660* (Oxford, 1985).
Valois, N. *Le conseil du roi au XIVe, XVe, et XVIe siècles. Nouvelles recherches suivies d'arrêts et de procès-verbaux du conseil* (Paris, 1888).
'Les états de Pontoise, août 1561', *Revue Historique de l'Eglise de France*, 29 (1943), 237–56.
Venard, M. 'Arrêtez le massacre!' *Revue d'Histoire Moderne et Contemporaine*, 39 (1992), 645–61.
Vérel, C. 'Une paroisse rural du duché d'Alençon: Saint-Germain de Clairfeuille', *Bulletin de la Société Historique et Archéologique de l'Orne*, 12 (1893).
Le marquisat de Nonant (Alençon, 1908).
Viard, G. 'La religion d'Antoinette de Bourbon, duchesse de Guise', *Les Cahiers Haut-Marnais*, 188–9 (1990), 1–11.
Vincent, C. *Des charités bien ordonnées: les confréries normandes de la fin du XIIIe au début du XVIe siècle* (Paris, 1988).
Wanegffelen, T. 'Le plat pays de la croyance: frontière confessionnelle et sensibilité religieuse en France au XVIe siècle', *Revue d'Histoire de l'Eglise de France*, 81 (1995), 391–411.

Wolfe, M. *The conversion of Henri IV* (Cambridge, Mass., 1993).

Wood, J. *The nobility of the élection of Bayeux, 1463–1666: continuity through change* (Princeton, 1980).

The king's army: warfare, soldiers and society during the French Wars of Religion, 1562–76 (Cambridge, 1996).

Index

Index

Index

Index

CAMBRIDGE STUDIES IN EARLY MODERN HISTORY

*The Old World and the New**
J. H. ELLIOTT

*The Army of Flanders and the Spanish Road, 1567–1659: The Logistics of Spanish Victory and Defeat in the Low Countries Wars**
GEOFFREY PARKER

*Richelieu and Olivares**
J. H. ELLIOTT

*Absolutism and Society in Seventeenth-Century France: State Power and Provincial Aristocracy in Languedoc**
WILLIAM BEIK

*The Princes of Orange: The Stadholders in the Dutch Republic**
HERBERT H. ROWEN

Lille and the Dutch Revolt: Urban Stability in an Era of Revolution
ROBERT S. DUPLESSIS

The Nobility of Holland: From Knights to Regents, 1500–1650
H. F. K. VAN NIEROP

Classes, Estates and Order in Early Modern Brittany
JAMES B. COLLINS

Early Modern Democracy in the Grisons: Social Order and Political Language in a Swiss Mountain Canton, 1470–1620
RANDOLPH C. HEAD

War, State and Society in Württemberg, 1677–1793
PETER H. WILSON

From Madrid to Purgatory: The Art and Craft of Dying in Sixteenth-Century Spain
CARLOS M. N. EIRE

The Reformation and Rural Society: The Parishes of Brandenburg-Ansbach-Kulmbach, 1528–1603
C. SCOTT DIXON

Labour, Science and Technology in France, 1500–1620
HENRY HELLER

The King's Army: Warfare, Soldiers, and Society during the Wars of Religion in France, 1562–1576
JAMES B. WOOD

Spanish Naval Power, 1589–1665: Reconstruction and Defeat
DAVID GOODMAN

State and Nobility in Early Modern Germany: The Knightly Feud in Franconia, 1440–1567
HILLAY ZMORA

The Quest for Compromise: Peace-Makers in Counter-Reformation Vienna
HOWARD LOUTHAN

Charles XI and Swedish Absolutism, 1660–1697
A. F. UPTON

Noble Power during the French Wars of Religion: The Guise Affinity and the Catholic Cause in Normandy
STUART CARROLL

Titles available in paperback marked with an asterisk*

The following titles are now out of print:

French Finances, 1770–1795: From Business to Bureaucracy
J. F. BOSHER

Chronicle into History: An Essay in the Interpretation of History in Florentine Fourteenth-Century Chronicles
LOUIS GREEN

France and the Estates General of 1614
J. MICHAEL HAYDEN

Reform and Revolution in Mainz, 1743–1803
T. C. W. BLANNING

Altopascio: A Study in Tuscan Society 1587–1784
FRANK MCARDLE

Gunpowder and Galleys: Changing Technology and Mediterranean Warfare at Sea in the Sixteenth Century
JOHN FRANCIS GUILMARTIN JR

The State, War and Peace: Spanish Political Thought in the Renaissance 1516–1559
J. A. FERNÁNDEZ-SANTAMARIA

Calvinist Preaching and Iconoclasm in the Netherlands, 1544–1569
PHYLLIS MACK CREW

The Kingdom of Valencia in the Seventeenth Century
JAMES CASEY

Filippo Strozzi and the Medici: Favor and Finance in Sixteenth-Century Florence and Rome
MELISSA MERIAM BULLARD

Rouen during the Wars of Religion
PHILIP BENEDICT

The Emperor and his Chancellor: A Study of the Imperial Chancellery under Gattinara
JOHN M. HEADLEY

The Military Organisation of a Renaissance State: Venice c. 1400–1617
M. E. MALLETT AND J. R. HALE

Neostoicism and the Early Modern State
GERHARD OESTREICH

Prussian Society and the German Order: An Aristocratic Corporation in Crisis c. 1410–1466
MICHAEL BURLEIGH

The Changing Face of Empire: Charles V, Philip II and Habsburg Authority, 1552–1559
M. J. RODRÍGUEZ-SALGADO

Turning Swiss: Cities and Empire 1450–1550
THOMAS A. BRADY JR

2360549R00170

Printed in Great Britain
by Amazon.co.uk, Ltd.,
Marston Gate.